Astellas Pharma US, Inc., formerly Fujisawa Healthcare,
is proud to play a critical part in helping
Chris Klug
achieve long-term health following his
liver transplant.

Through his amazing journey from transplantation
to bronze medal glory and beyond, Chris has never been
afraid to
Seize the Day

Astellas is pleased to present his inspirational story.

Learn more about Chris at
www.TransplantExperience.com
and discover health tips, education, and advice
for each phase of transplantation—
pre-transplant, the first year, and beyond year one.

astellas
Leading Light for Life

TO THE EDGE AND BACK

My Story from Organ Transplant Survivor to Olympic Snowboarder

by Chris Klug with Steve Jackson

Carroll & Graf Publishers
New York

TO THE EDGE AND BACK
My Story from Organ Transplant Survivor to Olympic Snowboarder

Carroll & Graf Publishers
An Imprint of Avalon Publishing Group Inc.
245 West 17th Street
11th Floor
New York, NY 10011

AVALON
publishing group incorporated

First Carroll & Graf edition 2004
3rd printing December 2004

Library of Congress Cataloging-in-Publication Data is available.

ISBN: 0-7867-1422-0

Printed in the United States of America
Interior design by Susan Canavan
Distributed by Publishers Group West

To my mom and dad, the best parents in the world.
To my family, Jim, Jason, and Hillary—I love you!
To Missy, my best friend and the love of my life.
To my donor family and all donors—you are my heroes.

Contents

A Foreword from Steve Jackson

first met Chris Klug in the spring of 2000, shortly after he'd been told that he needed a new liver, and soon, or he would die. He was a professional snowboarder who had a rare, life-threatening liver disease; I was a journalist in search of a medical story.

The funny thing is that while we are nearly twenty years apart in age—and I am an "old school" skier, the natural enemy of the snowboarder (or so I thought)—we became friends. It is an easy thing to do with Chris; he is one of the most approachable, genuine, and outgoing people I have ever met, a remarkable trait considering his status as an athlete and Olympian.

As such I was present through a number of dramatic moments in his life. We began our conversation that summer as he grew weaker and doubts started to creep in. I was waiting for him at the hospital after he got "the call." I remember how excited he was to be getting a second chance at life, but how troubled he was about the circumstances by which he was going to be saved. I leaned over a surgeon in the operating room to witness one of the most incredible performances of skill I have even seen. I was there when he woke and let us all know that he was back. I was lucky enough to rally around Europe and North America to catch some of his races. And I was standing in the snow at the 2002 Winter Olympics when he achieved his dream (although that has now evolved into another dream and another Olympics).

I'm glad that I met Chris before the operation, because the experience changed him, and it's unusual to get to witness such a transformation in another human being. It doesn't sound right to say that it changed him for the better—though he will tell you exactly that—because Chris was already a pretty good guy. Like most great athletes, he could be self-centered or so focused that it would come off that way. But he was also incredibly loyal and giving to his family and friends, as well as kind and gracious to everyone else he met—traits that his friends will tell you he gets from his parents. And if he was proud of his accomplishments as an elite-level athlete, he was also the first to laugh at his foibles—well, if not the first, then close on the heels of his band of friends.

This transformation was evident immediately after the operation and has only grown in the years that have followed. You could call it a maturity, especially when it comes to shouldering the responsibility of sharing the life-saving message of organ donation. I can imagine other athletes and celebrities who in similar situations would pay lip service and a nominal amount of personal involvement before going on about their lives. But Chris has continually increased his dedication to the cause.

Still, it's more than that. Coming so close to death changed him to where, as he says, "it's like seeing the world through a new set of eyes." He's still a big goofy kid in many ways, but there is also a quieter appreciation for life. If we could all live with such dedication to making every moment count, our lives would be richer and fuller. It is my hope that this book will inspire its readers to see the world as Chris sees it—a place of joy and beauty, where the truly important things are laughter, friendship, and the pursuit of dreams—as well as to further the cause of organ donation.

Writing this book with Chris in the first person—through his eyes, in his voice—was a challenge. It had to stay true to how he views his experiences and the world as a whole, and yet to get to know him, you have to see him as his friends and family do. This was difficult to include in the narrative without embarrassing Chris, who doesn't want to appear as if he's boasting. So it was my decision to occasionally break from his point of view and introduce these other voices speaking in the present so that you, the reader, will see that aspect of him. As such, I leave you to begin reading this book with a quote from one of his friends that I think sums up how many people regard him.

> *"I had never seen anyone so determined to win, and win he did not only in snowboarding but in life. His ability to bounce back from an organ transplant and become the Olympic athlete that he is today should not surprise anyone who knows him. We all hope to leave our mark in some way on this world, and Chris is doing so as a spokesman and hero for organ donation worldwide."*
>
> —Tad Dobson, October 2003

The Starting Gate

"Three minutes!"

My already jacked-up heart jumped like a panicked rabbit when the race referee bellowed out how much time I had to get positioned in the starting gate. I'd only just arrived at the top of the chairlift. All I wanted to do was catch my breath, get a drink, and focus on my upcoming race against Nicolas Huet of France. Then in a few minutes, Nicolas and I burst from the starting gate, riding side by side, tilting our boards on edge to carve as fast as we dared around twenty-six gates—red course rider on the right, blue on the left. And when we had crossed the finish line, the world would know who won the bronze medal in snowboard racing at the 2002 Winter Olympics in Park City, Utah.

That's what I wanted, but that's not the way it was going. Instead, the most important moment of my eighteen-year career was now less than three minutes away, and I was freakin' because of a broken fifty-cent piece of metal on one of my boots.

Six hours earlier, I'd arrived on the Olympic hill stoked and looking forward to the possibilities the day represented. The weather was perfect. A chilly morning with scattered clouds and snow flurries had gradually warmed into a mild afternoon with the sun reflecting off the snow beneath clear blue skies. Course conditions at the start were perfect for racing—what I call "Colorado Super-Grip"—not ice but smooth, hard-packed snow that would hold my edge no matter how I railed it.

Looking down the hill now as U.S. team technicians Jay "Coop" Cooper and Thanos Karydas worked frantically on my boot, I tried to focus on the side-by-side parallel giant slalom course that snaked down to the finish line. *Blue is you, red ahead.* But it was such a beautiful day, and I found myself looking out beyond the slope and over the crowd below at the white-blanketed Wasatch Mountains that rose all around me. A sprinkling of leftover snowflakes, sparkling like tiny slivers of glass, drifted and danced on a slight breeze.

A magical moment, for sure.

I could almost feel, as well as hear, the roar from the twenty-five thousand spectators in the finish area, who'd been cheering and waving the flags of their countries since morning. I'd never seen so many people at a snowboard event—not even in Europe, where they follow winter sports like Americans do football teams and where winter athletes are national heroes. The crowd included a hundred or so of my family members and friends, many of them dancing around like idiots as they held up big blue foam fingers proclaiming "Chris Klug" Number One.

Well, I wasn't going to be Number One. We knew that already. I'd been riding too inconsistently—losing an edge and sketching on a run, falling behind, then scratching and clawing my way back to kill it on the next run so that I could move on to the next round. Nothing had come easy all morning, but I'd made it through four runs—five, including yesterday's qualifier—and had stayed in the hunt.

Then a big mistake, a fall, in the semifinals had cost me a shot at the gold and silver medals. I was disappointed but had to put it out of my head and concentrate on beating Nicolas for the bronze.

In a way, I'd seemed almost destined to be in the bronze medal race. A couple of months earlier, Jan Wengelin, the U.S. Alpine Snowboard Team head coach, noted that the race for the bronze medal was the toughest mentally for an athlete. "You need to prepare for it," he warned, as if he already knew something I didn't.

What he meant was that when a rider makes it into the "Big Final" at the Olympics, he or she knows they are going to win either the gold or silver medal. You can let it all hang out and take chances to win the gold; if it doesn't work, you're still the Olympic silver medalist. However in the "Small Final," only the winner gets a medal; the loser gets nothing except the experience.

Now, don't get me wrong—as experiences go, being in the Olympics is about as good as it gets for an athlete. Competing against the best in the world while representing your country in front of twenty-five thousand spectators and a couple billion television viewers is a pretty sick—sick meaning good—feeling. I'd first started dreaming about it when I was a twelve-year-old grom ripping it up on Mount Bachelor in Oregon and snowboarding wasn't even allowed on most U.S. ski slopes. Back then, even other boarders laughed at me whenever I put snowboarding and Olympics in the same sentence.

So it was great just to be part of the whole Olympic scene. But as a competitor, the games are about winning medals, and I'd already had the experience at the 1998 Olympics in Japan of coming up just short. I'd set a goal right then and there at the base of Mount Yakebitai, and now I was one run from achieving it . . . or from losing again.

Anybody who knows me will tell you how much I hate losing. It doesn't matter if it's football or snowboarding or a rousing game of chess with my dad, I get ticked off and always want another chance to get even. I guess my saving grace for being that competitive on the fields, slopes, or at the coffee table is this: give me a few minutes to grind my teeth, and I'll be back laughing and smiling with my friends and family. They know I'd do anything in the world for them . . . especially if they'll promise me a rematch.

Looking down at the Olympic snowboard course, I didn't want to disappoint them or for that matter let down my friends, as well as other Americans watching the Olympics on television. Not on our home turf, not after what happened that past September when terrorists crashed into the World Trade Center. I'd also been in the air that morning with my girlfriend, Missy, certain that we too were about to crash. Like most other Americans, it had changed me, but not as much as a related event had just a week before this race.

I'd been proud to represent my country at the games in Nagano,

Japan, the first Olympics to include snowboarding. But it didn't compare to what I felt at the opening ceremony of the 2002 Winter Olympics in Salt Lake City, when I helped carry into the stadium the torn and charred American flag that was found in the rubble of the twin towers on September 11, 2001. For the rest of my life I'll remember that quiet, powerful moment like it was yesterday.

Yet, an Olympic medal represented more to me than a sports achievement or a chance to wave the flag. I also hoped to use that podium to champion a cause without which I never would have lived long enough to be on that hill, looking at those mountains and listening to that crowd.

Just eighteen months earlier, with my liver failing due to a rare disease, I needed a transplant or I wasn't going to see my twenty-eighth birthday. Now here I was, twenty-nine years old and racing in the Olympics, thanks to the skill of doctors and nurses, the support of my family and friends, lots of prayers, and a heartrending decision made by strangers. I felt that I had an obligation to spread the life-saving message of organ donation, and the best way to do it was from an Olympic podium.

Still, no one was going to just hand me a medal. Even in the best of circumstances winning the second run against Nicolas wouldn't have been easy. We were great friends and surfing buddies, but also fierce competitors.

We'd all but tied in the first run, so it was going to come down to who won the second. Only now it was going to be a lot harder for me, because a vital buckle on my front boot had snapped, and no matter what Coop and Thanos tried, it seemed there wasn't going to be enough time to remove and replace it.

Nicolas was already in the starting gate when the start referee yelled again. "Two minutes, Klug!"

"Take off the boot!" Coop yelled.

I groaned and shut my eyes. This wasn't fair, not after everything I'd been through. Why did it seem that time was always running out on me?

Chapter 1

Sketchy Beginnings

A s I look back over the years leading to that gut-twisting Olympic moment, two opposing themes stand out. One is how much I love being alive. I am reminded of it every time I float atop twenty inches of fresh Colorado backcountry pow. Or sit on my surfboard as the sun sets and casts a golden glow over the water and the Oregon shoreline. Or share a laugh, even at my own expense, with my friends and family. And, of course, each time I enter the starting gate at the beginning of a race.

The other theme dominating my now thirty-one years of life has been how close I've come to losing it, more than once.

The first time was shortly after my birth on November 18, 1972, at Rose Medical Center at the University of Colorado Hospital in Denver. Mom knew that something was not quite right when she noticed that her beautiful baby boy's fingernails and eyebrows hadn't grown in. But the nurses whisked me off to intensive care, and nobody told her that anything was seriously wrong—not until the next morning when a young doctor entered the room as she was happily writing birth announcements.

Apparently, this guy had missed the medical school class on bedside manner. When he saw what she was doing he warned her, "Uh, I'd hold off on that."

I was not okay, he said. I had something called hyaline membrane disease. It meant that the lining of my lungs was not fully developed, and as a result I had pneumonia. I might not survive even as long as it took those birth announcements to reach the people she was sending them to.

Mom panicked. Dad had been there for my birth the day before and then come by in the morning to see her. But he'd since left for Vail, the ski resort town more than a hundred miles to the west where he managed the Lion's Square Lodge. He'd planned to come back that night after work, but Mom called him now in tears. "They're saying our baby might not make it."

My parents had met in 1967 while at college in suburban Chicago— Warren, who was twenty-two, at Lake Forest College and Kathy, just eighteen, at Barat College. In the spring of 1968 my dad moved to Colorado to attend the University of Denver's hotel and restaurant management program and asked Mom to come and live with him. He had in mind a housemate; she had in mind marriage. As with most things she sets her mind to, Mom won.

It was tough financially in those early days. Dad came from a split family and never had a lot of money; Mom was from a conservative, well-off East Coast family who weren't keen on her getting married at that moment. So she and Dad had decided they'd go it alone. Mom worked a variety of jobs and attended school part-time; a full-time student, Dad waited tables at an upper-crust Denver restaurant to pay his college expenses and support his new family. They drove an old Chevy convertible with an odometer that had rolled over two hundred thousand miles, and lived in a tiny, two-bedroom house near campus.

Money got even tighter when Mom got pregnant with my brother, Jim, and had to quit work and drop out of college to prepare for the baby. My parents had agreed that she would stay home while their children were young. Whatever it took, they were determined that their kids would have safe, stable and, most of all, fun childhoods.

They had no medical insurance to cover the pregnancy, and going to their families for help was not an option. Then Father Edward Gray, the priest who'd married them, and the congregation of St. Mark's Episcopal Church in downtown Denver rallied to help them out. They hooked Mom up with a family physician, and the church covered all the costs.

Most of the congregation was older, and it had been some time since an infant had been born among the church's members. So everyone was nearly as thrilled as my parents when Jim was born on June 24, 1969, and a few days later my parents brought him to the sanctuary to be baptized. (My dad notes that many years later, the church was turned into a nightclub called The Church, and the small side chapel where he and Mom got married was made into a sushi bar.)

Overwhelmed by the generosity, my parents asked Father Gray how they could repay the debt. He told them not to worry about it just then—that there would come a time when they would be called upon to help someone else in need. "You'll know," he said.

Dad graduated in 1970 and the little Klug family moved up to Vail, where he'd landed the job managing a new ski lodge. Two years later, Mom was pregnant again—with me—but the local clinic didn't deliver babies, so she was sent to Rose Medical Center off Colorado Avenue in Denver as my supposed delivery date came and went. The doctors thought that I was overdue and induced my mom into labor, but they had the original dates wrong and I was born prematurely. My family and friends would later say it was the first and last time I ever showed up anywhere on time, much less early.

When Mom called Dad and told him that I might die, he told her not to worry—that God would watch over me—and that no matter what happened, I would not be alone and neither would she. He was on his way.

Dad was going to need a little watching himself. He'd already made the trip once that day but immediately got back in the car to drive what in those days took three to four hours. In November the weather in the mountains could turn bad and the road treacherous in a matter of minutes.

Mom wasn't alone, even before he completed the difficult drive. After hanging up with Dad, she was still crying in the nursery when a nurse came in and walked over to where I was lying in one of those clear plastic box incubators. The nurse passed her hands over me and then said something mysterious, at least to my buttoned-down mom.

"Ooooh, I detect a strong aura," the nurse cooed. "This baby has a strong aura."

Oh, great, Mom thought, *my baby has hyaline membrane AND an aura.* Having led a somewhat sheltered life—and therefore missed the beginnings of New Age philosophy—she had no idea what the nurse meant by an aura. But she noticed that the woman seemed pleased, so she dared to ask, "Is that good?"

"Oh, yeah," the nurse assured her. "Don't you worry, honey, he's going to make it."

At that point, Mom would have taken anything positive. *My baby has an aura; he's going to make it!* But aura or not, I was still in trouble. In fact, things were pretty sketchy for me in those first weeks, but my parents say I let them know that I wasn't going to give up my life without a fight. Mom says I made her laugh one day when she looked at me in the incubator. Maybe it was just indigestion and gas (my friends would lay odds on the latter as the stronger possibility), but she claims that I had such a determined look on my face that it appeared as though I was willing myself to get better.

At last, nearly a month after my birth, the doctors said I could leave. Appropriately enough, they chose to release me on the day of a major snowstorm.

Night had fallen by the time we reached the summit of twelve-thousand-foot Loveland Pass with the snow still dumping. The wind whipped the big flakes around, hampering visibility on the slick road as the Chevy lugged over the top.

We were on our way down the west side, following the taillights of the car ahead of us as it negotiated the hairpin turns, when suddenly the other vehicle plunged off the road. Horrified but helpless, my parents stopped and watched. It looked like a tragedy in the making. The slope was steep, but somehow the car kept going straight down and didn't turn sideways, which would have caused it to roll over. In fact, it looked like it was surfing on a crest of new snow. The car came to rest a couple of hundred yards below; then the interior light of the car went on, and my parents saw the occupants get out, sinking deep into the fresh snow, apparently unharmed.

Other cars and highway department snowplows had pulled over to assist the now-stranded motorists, so my parents went on. But for my mom, it was just one more frightening moment to heap on top of what she and Dad had already been through. She still remembers wondering if there was ever going to be a safe place in the world for me.

However, I didn't let such a rough beginning slow me down. My parents had grown up in families that placed a strong emphasis on sports, including skiing, and they were no different—not that they had to do much persuading. My brother and I launched ourselves into every outdoor activity that we could find and certainly grew up in the right places for it.

It was in Vail I first learned to ski when I was about two by riding between my mom's legs, or attached to a "Racer Chaser," a sort of kid on a leash. Then in 1976, when Jim was seven and I was four, the family packed a U-Haul and moved to Bend, Oregon, on the east side of the Cascade Mountains. There my dad took over as president of the management company that ran the Inn of the Seventh Mountain resort on the road leading to the Mount Bachelor ski area.

I have traveled all over the globe, and I still believe that Central Oregon is one of the most beautiful places in the world. It is a perfect blend of high desert and dense conifer forests from which jagged volcanic peaks—Three Sisters, Mount Washington, and Mount Jefferson—jut like stone fingers.

The Inn of the Seventh Mountain was seven miles west of Bend, the last development on the road to Mount Bachelor, which was another seventeen miles. When Dad arrived, he developed the inn from a winter-only destination into a year-round resort that included a full recreation department with a swimming pool and ice-skating rink. The inn was also surrounded by national forest lands, so I essentially lived in a giant playground, where I could ride my bike on forest trails or, if there was an opening, hitch a ride on whitewater raft trips on the Deschutes River arranged for hotel guests.

Wintertime in Bend centered on the Mount Bachelor ski area. My brother and I were soon racing with the Skyliners Ski Team, as was every other kid in town. It was just the way it was—in Hawaii kids learn to surf; in Bend they learn to ski.

I was certainly living a healthy lifestyle, but fate was not done kicking me in the ass. The early bout with pneumonia left me with a severe case of asthma, which was compounded by allergic reactions to what seemed to be just about everything. It got particularly bad when I was around dogs, horses, or dust. Not that it prevented us from owning dogs, or me going to play with friends who had horses, or Jim and I jumping off the loft in our house World Wrestling Federation–style into piles of cushions on the living room floor below, which would raise a cloud of dog hair and God knows what else into the air and my lungs. A few hours after any of these events, there was a good chance I'd end up in the emergency room at St. Charles Medical Center.

The asthma was tough on me and my family. My poor brother, Jim, who was as healthy as a horse, suffered through a family life in which at any time—middle of the night or at the dinner table—his parents would have to rush his wheezing, frightened kid brother off to the ER. I know it scared my mom, but I think it particularly affected my dad, who could remember his own battles with asthma as a kid and knew the horrible feeling of not being able to breathe no matter how hard you tried.

Sometimes all it took to get past the trouble was to get hooked up to an inhalator, or an oral Albuterol treatment. But there were several times when I didn't respond to the machine or the drugs and was in real danger.

I was lucky to have as my pediatrician Dr. Peter Boehm, a young internist who'd opened his practice about the same time we moved to Bend. Boehm was particularly good with kids and explained things so that a grade school kid could understand. Yet even Dr. Boehm couldn't stop me from having attacks.

The worst was on my tenth birthday. It was more disappointing than the others, because I was supposed to play Captain Hook in our school production of *Peter Pan*. These weren't just any school plays—they were the extravaganza productions of a wonderful teacher, Jack Ensworth. Everything Mr. Ensworth did as a teacher was big, especially his annual stage production, and Captain Hook was a juicy role. I mean, who wanted to be that tights-wearing sissy, Peter Pan, anyway?

Who knows, if things had gone differently, maybe I would have wound up in another profession (watch out Orlando Bloom). I'm still angry about it. But back then I was just scared to death when a few days before the play was set to open, I felt the tightening in my chest and throat that signaled the start of another asthma attack. A bad one.

Instead of play fighting with Peter Pan, I battled for my life. I didn't respond to the inhalator or any of the drugs. My blood wouldn't oxygenate—in other words, my body wasn't producing enough red blood cells, which carry oxygen to the various organs and muscles. I was suffocating from the inside out.

With my life hanging by a thread, my folks never left me alone. They took shifts—one sitting or sleeping at my side at all times, while the other went home to care for my brother and new baby sister, Hillary, who'd been born a month earlier.

During one of her shifts, my mom found herself standing by my bed, holding my hand as I slept, like she had when I was an infant at Rose Medical. Watching me struggle, she inhaled deeply and then exhaled, willing my lungs to follow her example. *Breathe in,* she thought, *breathe out. Breathe in, breathe out.* She would have stood there breathing for me all night, but my dad showed up and relieved her. The other kids needed her at home too.

Dr. Boehm brought his partner in to consult, and they decided to use an arterial line. It involved making a small cut into the artery of my wrist and inserting what looked like a glass eyedropper, which was then hooked up to a machine that pumped oxygen directly into my blood stream. It hurt like hell, and I started bawling like a baby. But it worked . . . at last the feeling of slowly suffocating faded and then was gone.

When I fell asleep that night, my dad was on watch. He remembers looking at me lying there in that hospital bed with all sorts of tubes and wires attached to my body and thinking, *How can this be what God has in mind for this wonderful kid?*

"When he was awake, you could see that he was afraid and in pain," Dad says now. "But he was so good about it and trying to put on a brave face so that we wouldn't worry."

Whatever God had planned for me, it wasn't to die in that hospital bed or, as I wrote in a poem about the experience, "at the end of that long white hall." But seventeen years later, Mom would recall my struggles to survive as a child and see them as a training ground for the most important race of my life.

Chapter 2

Skatin'

My road to the Olympics, for all of the potholes and hairpin turns I had to navigate, got a great start in my parents' home. As thoroughly as I try to prepare myself to compete, Mom and Dad prepared me for life.

They emphasized to all of their kids that we were to set goals for ourselves—whether it was in academics or sports. Aim high, they said, risk falling short, because it was more important that we try than that we succeed.

They also made sure we understood that no life is without challenges. And once we made our decisions, we also were expected to accept responsibility for the results. No excuses. We were participants, not bystanders, in our destinies, and no matter how things went, we weren't to think of ourselves as helpless or as victims.

We lived in a house with rules. My parents wanted to know where we were and who we were with. At home we were expected to help with chores, earn the "extras" we wanted, and keep up with our schoolwork.

I'll admit that even though I worked hard at school and got good grades, academics were never my greatest priority. That spot was taken by an overwhelming desire to be with my friends and play as long and hard as I could. I must have driven my teachers crazy—in the classroom and at Sunday school—the way I bounced off the walls until they set me free.

I had a tough time learning to read. But my mom sat patiently with me, and we read and reread basic books like *Green Eggs and Ham* until she must have known them by heart and been bored to tears. But she wasn't going to give up on me, nor was she going to let me get frustrated and give up on myself. It still takes me a long time to get through a book, but I enjoy reading, thanks to her. And only once would I consider giving up something important to me, and then my dad was there to keep me fighting on.

My parents didn't just talk about what they expected of us. They provided role models by being involved in the community and their church, Trinity Episcopal, where Dad served as a lay minister and helped found a men's prayer group, and Mom ran the Sunday school.

A lot of people are uncomfortable discussing their religious beliefs or spirituality. But talking about God in our house was as natural and part of the routine as talking about sports, which we also often did.

God wasn't some supernatural dictator to be feared if you "broke the rules." He was more like a friendly—if powerful—uncle who wanted you to do what was right but still watched over you when you didn't. And most importantly, God would be there if things got gnarly.

God also had a sense of humor, and my parents' outlook on life reflected that attitude. Ever since I can remember, my dad has ended grace by yelling—"Yea, God!"—like he's cheering at a football game and God just scored a touchdown. To some people that might sound hokey, but it's a genuine expression from a man who feels a personal, friendly relationship with his God.

Sometimes my own church involvement was a bit too enthusiastic. I was an altar boy on Sunday mornings, and at one special Christmas Eve Midnight Mass, I had the job of carrying the incense burner on a chain. I was supposed to walk solemnly down the aisle, swinging it slowly back and forth. As we were waiting to go into the sanctuary, my competitive juices kicked in. I was sure that no other altar boy had ever even attempted the "around-the-world loopty-loop," swinging the incense burner a full 360 degrees over his head, especially not when already lit.

I know now that I should have swung it faster, because it stalled at the top of the swing and some of the burning coals fell out onto the carpet. A moment later I was stomping out all these little fires that sprang up on the carpet, while the director of the altar boys nearly had a heart attack.

They left that carpet there—with all its little burn marks—for years. They probably figured it was a good way of pointing out to future altar boys that there was a right way to swing the burner and a wrong way. (And I bet I'm still the only kid who attempted the full 360!)

What I think I've always respected about my parents and their beliefs is that they walked the walk. It was never enough just to go to church or participate in church activities, like food drives or prayer meetings. Religion wasn't a once a week obligation but a road map on how to live your life with integrity every day of the week. They emphasized to us that when someone reached out to help you—like the congregation at St. Mark's had helped them when Mom was pregnant with Jim—you repaid that kindness by helping someone else. I saw what genuinely good people my parents were and wanted to grow up to be the same sort of person, and someday the same type of parent, so it was easy for me to accept their spiritual beliefs.

My parents also emphasized that being Christian didn't equate to "no fun." In fact, their mission in life seemed to be making sure we were dead tired at the end of every day from an active life.

We got into the usual sorts of trouble for kids with active imaginations. When I was about six, we moved to a new house on the outskirts of Bend. The landscapers had prepared the yard so they could lay sod the next day. Boy, all that dirt and a hose, and our parents were away at a church retreat for the weekend, and there was only the babysitter to get past. It wasn't long before we'd established a whole network of rivers and tributaries crisscrossing the yard and eventually leading to a huge hole we'd dug with the idea of creating our own Jacuzzi. We'd lined the bottom of the hole with a tarp but it didn't stay in place, and the result was a mud pit that any pig, or bunch of boys, would call heaven on a hot day. You should have seen Mom hit the roof on that one when they got home. It's a good thing we were agile and good at ducking thrown objects or Jim and I might not be here today.

When I was in grade school Bend was a small town with a population of about seventeen thousand. Everybody knew everybody else—and their kids—so it was hard to get away with anything without someone calling your parents. But for the most part, I didn't do anything much worse than throwing snowballs at cars after communion on Sundays. Even that seemed to be living on the edge considering what day it was; after all, God might not have had *that* good a sense of humor.

The first house we lived in was pretty isolated from any neighborhoods, so Jim and I mostly had each other for playmates, which is part of why we were and are so close. But when I was in third grade, we moved into a new house in the middle of town and right on Mirror Pond, which was part of the Deschutes River. Jim and I were thrilled to find ourselves surrounded by an entire army of new friends.

There were summer days when we spent every hour of sunlight, and as many after sunset as our parents would allow, riding our BMX bikes and jumping out of the willow tree across from our new house in downtown Bend and into the Deschutes River. Sometimes we did both by building huge ramps, strapping a life jacket to our bikes, and airing into Mirror Pond.

I also had this thing for machines that went fast. Whenever I got the chance at the inn, I'd hop into one of the Cushman workman's carts and drive it around as fast as possible. I never had much trouble rallying around the inn. But it was a different matter on a family trip to Puget Sound, Washington, where I commandeered a golf cart and ran it full-speed into a small outhouse. It knocked over the building and totaled the golf cart. It was Dad's buddy who ran the resort and he snapped on me on the golf course!

"That same side of Chris can be blamed for the fact that he 'owns' several snowmobiles in Canada and the western United States," Jim says. "It's a direct result of Chris being too cheap to purchase the optional rental insurance on day rides with his buddies, and then totaling the machines by being too fast and too reckless."

My favorite thing to do, though, was skateboard. Any money I made mowing lawns in the summer went for new skateboards, and I was a frequent pest at Century Cycles in Bend, or on special occasions, Mrs. A's Skateboard Shop or Skates on Couch Street in Portland. I was so obsessed with the sport that when the town banned riding our boards on city sidewalks and parking lots, I talked my dad into building a twelve-foot-tall plywood quarter-pipe ramp in our driveway.

The only sport I enjoyed as much as skateboarding was playing football. I had a list of maybe fifty kids I'd call to meet at nearby Harmon Park. Some weekends there were so many kids that we'd divide into four teams and have playoffs. We also played at lunchtime, we played at recess, and we played after school until it got so dark you couldn't see the ball unless it hit you in the face.

I dreamed of a career in college and then the NFL as a quarterback, but my early football hero was star running back Walter Payton of the Chicago Bears. That was in part because Dad was from Chicago and still a loyal Bears fan. He called Payton by his nickname, "Sweetness." (Mom, who also liked the running back "because he was an articulate gentleman of the gridiron"—huh?—picked it up and, to our horror, started calling me and Jim "Sweetness" when our friends were around.)

Mom and Dad didn't have to worry much about where we were, as Jim and I transformed our house into command central for every boy in the neighborhood. Poor Hillary had to get used to a house filled with boys, which she did by competing just as hard as everyone else for a spot at the table or in our games. My parents were sure to keep the pantry stocked with the important food groups for growing kids, such as Pop Tarts (they do have fruit in them) and Lucky Charms cereal (plenty of fiber and carbs for energy, plus they're "magically delicious"). The crowning glory was that my mom owned Flanagan's ice cream shop in downtown Bend. After a tough day on the gridiron, or to ease the pain of removing a layer of skin while crashing on our skateboards, the Klug boys would lead the troops on an ice cream raid. It's a wonder Mom stayed in business.

During the winter, Jim and I continued to race with the Skyliners. It was fun, and like everything else I ever competed at, I entered each race expecting to win and could be a little sulky if I didn't. Still, I wasn't great at ski racing, nor did I have much passion for it. I was more interested in skiing from jump to jump to jump, catching air, than I was in racing gates. To be honest, I was mostly on the ski team because that's where I could find my buddies, and my brother was there, so I thought it was the cool thing to do.

However, my outlook on winter sports was forever altered when I was eleven years old and in the fifth grade. On winter mornings when there was no school, I liked to go with my dad to the inn. We'd have breakfast together, then he'd go to work while I caught the bus to the Mount Bachelor ski area. One day, a kid about my age got on the bus with what looked like an oversized skateboard platform with a leash attached to the nose. I'd seen a few people riding the contraption on the mountain, and while the skiers made fun of the "ski boarders," I thought it looked like fun.

This, however, was the first time I'd had the chance to study one up close. It was a Burton Backhill, which are to modern snowboards what dinosaurs are to the family parakeet. They were made of laminated wood and had three metal rudders—called "skags," like on a surfboard—for steering, but there were no metal edges as on skis. The bindings were still just elastic bungie cords mounted a few inches from the back of the board (rather than closer to the center, as on a modern board).

The Burton Backhill was produced by a thirty-year-old entrepreneur named Jake Burton Carpenter, who had started hand-making his boards in a garage in 1977. He was one of the early pioneers of manufacturing snowboards—along with guys like Tom Sims, Chuck Barfoot, Dimitrije Milovich, and Bob Webber—but it's impossible to say who actually made the first one. I suppose whoever first got the idea of standing up on a sledlike piece of wood with a sideways stance and "surfing" downhill could say it was their idea.

In 1929, M. J. "Jack" Burchett cut a plank out of plywood, attached his feet to it with some clothesline, and went for a ride on a snowy hill in Vermont. Ten years later, Vern Wicklund made a board with foot straps and a nose leash and was filmed riding it down a hill in Chicago. He even got a patent for his invention.

There doesn't seem to have been a lot of progress for another thirty years. But in 1965 a chemical engineer named Sherman Poppen bound two skis together and attached a rope to the nose as a toy for his daughter, Wendy. Soon all of Wendy's friends wanted what his wife named "The Snurfer." The prototype evolved into a single plastic platform—like a skateboard without wheels—with a leash attached to the nose for steering with the leading hand. A year later, Poppen licensed his invention to Brunswick, a toy manufacturer that sold more than a half million the first season at fifteen dollars a pop.

In the years that followed the invention of the Snurfer and leading up to today's mass-produced, state-of-the-art snowboards, many of the concepts and innovations were developed simultaneously, and not everyone agrees with who came up with what first.

When that other kid got on the ski bus with his Backhill, I knew nothing of the history of snowboarding or the ongoing struggle to gain access to ski slopes. All I knew was that I was one envious little dude as I looked at that kid and his board. I didn't know that I was standing at one of those forks in the road, one that would lead me to the Olympics.

In December 1983 Mark Bowerman, the owner of Century Cycles, called. His shop was only a mile from my house, and I'd been down there nearly every day pestering him about Burton boards. He was letting me know that he'd just received a shipment of what he called "snowboards."

I was down there practically before he hung up the phone. I walked in, and stacked against a wall—their wood tops polished like expensive violins, so shiny I could see my drooling face—were the Burtons.

Bowerman rented boards to me and two of my friends, Josh Eddy and Eric Tuft, whom I'd alerted about the exciting news. We took off immediately for Skyliner Snow Park, where we hiked up the sledding hill and then rode down through the powder. I couldn't believe it. It was like floating on snow. I was so stoked. Even numerous "face plants" couldn't wipe the smile off my face.

The next time I went out boarding, I was with my friend Brandon Harrington, who was on skis. We went to Mount Bachelor and headed straight for the orange chair. I was sure that I was ready to rip it up. I'd been skiing almost since I could walk, and I'd had no real problems on the little sledding hill with the snowboard. All of which meant I was about to get a quick humility lesson.

Without metal edges, the board wouldn't hold crossing the hard-packed snow of a groomed slope; I couldn't turn without sliding out and landing on my face or my back, depending on whether it was a toe-side or heel-side attempt. I realized that I had to stay in the pow on the sides of the slopes. Fortunately at Mount Bachelor, they groomed only the middle of the runs, so there was plenty of the loose stuff over on the edges, next to the trees . . . where I learned to ride.

I began begging my parents for a Burton snowboard for Christmas, only to meet unexpected resistance from my mother. She'd been skiing since she was a child and came from a long line of skiers. Because of my competitive nature, she thought that ski racing was one avenue that would fulfill my need for speed, thrills, and competition that no other sport could match. She figured that snowboarding just wasn't going to do it for me.

Besides, she said, it looked dangerous. And Santa Claus did not approve of dangerous toys.

I wasn't listening. Right up to Christmas, I rented a board every chance I got and prayed that Santa would have mercy on me. I wasn't going to put my eye out with it or anything.

Santa Claus lives. I know it because on Christmas morning, a brand-new, gleaming Burton Performer, the next step up the evolutionary ladder from a Backhill, was waiting under the tree for me.

I think Mom was a little miffed at Santa and glared at him most of the day whenever the subject of the board came up. But he just ducked and kept saying what a wonderful day it was. I agreed . . . maybe the best ever.

So that was how I joined the small ranks of snowboarders on Mount Bachelor. At the time there were maybe a couple of older guys and the occasional snowboarding tourist, but it was mostly me and about a half dozen of my friends ripping it up, learning how as we went. We figured out pretty quickly that the leash was lame and didn't help much with steering; instead, we leaned forward or back to apply pressure to the toe-side or heel-side edges to turn. We also discovered the joy of riding in the deep powder beneath the trees, or in backcountry bowls that we hiked into, or off some high mountain road where we got somebody's dad to drop us off at the top and then meet us at the bottom.

We were lucky that Mount Bachelor was so open-minded, and we thought that other ski resorts would be just as welcoming of snowboarders. Never did it cross our minds that Bachi might be one of the few resorts that was accepting of the new sport.

I learned the cold, hard truth in February 1984 when I went with my family on a ski vacation to Sun Valley, Idaho. We reached our destination only after a ten-hour, white-knuckled (at least for my dad, who was driving) trip through a blizzard. But at last we reached the Sun Valley Lodge.

The Sun Valley ski resort was the first in the United States, and the lodge featured a "wall of fame" that was lined with signed photos of famous skiers and visiting celebs dating back to the beginning of the resort, like Friedl Piffer, Dick Durrance, and Stien Erickson. I dreamed that someday my photograph would be up there, only I'd be holding my *snowboard* up for the camera, not skis.

Our reward for the intense drive was a record snowfall of nearly three feet. Waking up in the morning and seeing all that untracked powder, I could hardly wait to get out the door of the lodge. However, first I had to argue with my mother, who wanted me to take my skis—which she'd insisted on packing—instead of my board. I won that round probably because she was as anxious to hit the new pow as I was, but I ran into another snag after we got to Mount Baldy, the main ski mountain at Sun Valley.

We bought our lift tickets and no one said a thing. I had scooted my way up in the lift line until I was just about to load when the lift operator looked at my board and said, "No way."

Despite being miffed at the lift operator for harassing her son, my mom told me to take the ski bus back to the lodge across from the resort and get my skis. Ever since Santa answered my prayers, she'd hoped I'd grow out of it, and getting turned away at the lift line was another reason why I should. "Go get your skis and forget this snowboard thing for now," she said.

I refused. "I'll go find a hill."

"Yeah?" she replied sarcastically. "And where are you going to do that? They won't let you on the slopes."

I looked around. The new snow shimmered so bright in the sun that it hurt my eyes. Mount Baldy was the tallest mountain around, but it was surrounded by a lot of beautiful, snow-covered hills, most of them untracked. "They don't own all the mountains, Mom."

Before she could reply, my dad sided with me. "Let him go find a hill," he said. "What could it hurt?" I knew not to hang around long enough for Mom to figure out a comeback and took off, leaving Dad to his fate.

Mom still talks about how she was fuming when she and the rest of the family got on the lift. Near the top of the lift, she happened to look across the valley to Dollar Mountain, which was next to the Sun Valley Lodge. What caught her attention was a tiny figure just starting to climb the slope of Dollar. Then it was time to unload, and Mom forgot about the climber and skied down with my dad and Jim.

Riding back to the top, she remembered and looked across the valley again. Now the climber was halfway up the hill, laboring through waist-deep snow. She thought she caught the flash of red pants as the climber paused. She looked harder then nudged Dad.

"Is that Chris?" she asked, already knowing the answer.

Yeah, I'd taken the bus back to the lodge and decided to ride Dollar. However, the climb was pretty hairy. With every step I took up the slope, the snow made ominous groaning sounds as it settled and shifted, and I was beginning to wonder if it was such a good idea.

Over on Mount Baldy, my parents worried as well. They knew more about avalanches, yet as Mom watched me struggle up the hill, she had a change of heart about my snowboarding.

"I knew he was a kid who thought he could do anything, overcome any obstacle," Mom says, looking back. "He didn't let something even as frightening as that asthma attack stop him from doing whatever he set his heart and mind on. But watching him laboring up that slope, I felt a whole new appreciation for his determination. I realized how much he loved snowboarding and how wrong I'd been to try to stop him."

Climbing Dollar Mountain took a lot of work. I kept "post holing," sinking up to my hip with each step. I just wanted to get to the top of that hill and ride my board back down as my way of saying to hell with the Sun Valley ski resort.

At last I reached the top and stood there for a moment, exhausted and drenched with sweat. The slope below me was pristine. There were no tracks in the snow other than those I had made climbing up.

Taking a deep breath, I pointed my board downhill and took off, gathering speed before leaning into that first arcing turn. The snow hissed as I sank nearly to my waist and rose again as if I were soaring through a cloud. I banked into another turn. Reaching out with my uphill hand, I touched the snow as I passed, like a surfer dipping his hand into a wave.

All too soon, I reached the bottom of the hill and looked up. I'd left my mark on the world in a graceful cursive line like an author signing his name to a book. I'd proved my point. *They* didn't own all the hills. *They* couldn't stop me from snowboarding. As for my mom, she never again said anything to discourage me from snowboarding.

Chapter 3

Shred Culture

We were driving up the road to Mount Bachelor, loaded up in my buddy Jeff's GMC Jimmy beater, when one of the guys pulled out a water bong to smoke weed. It was pretty much part of the ritual to get high before a day of riding our asses off in the powder. Hell, some of my friends smoked their breakfasts. . . . *Breakfast of champions, dude.*

As soon as we passed the inn, the car would be filled with blue smoke, a band like Guns N' Roses, or maybe something mellower such as Bob Marley and the Wailers, would be cranked on the stereo, and somebody would pass the bong and the latest issue of *International Snowboard* magazine. Sometime during the day, I could also expect that someone would light up a joint or a pipe on the chairlift, maybe stop off in the woods out of sight of the tourists and ski patrol, for a quick toke. Skiers did it too, but it was practically a religion for snowboarders, or at least that was the perception.

However, I wasn't into pot and didn't smoke. I was more interested in studying the snowboarding tricks and backcountry riding photographs in the magazine. . . . Plus my friends wouldn't let me.

There were a lot of stereotypes and myths about snowboarders in those early days—some of them deserved and some not—that kept us on the outside looking in, struggling for acceptance by one of the world's oldest and most tradition-bound sports. Archeologists have found five-thousand-year-old pictographs of skiers on cave walls, but the times were a-changing (as that old-school singer Bob Dylan used to say).

In the years since I got my first Burton Performer and then started jumping into cars with a bunch of pothead shredders on the way to the mountain to ride, the sport had taken off. Not that acceptance had necessarily followed popularity.

The early years of snowboarding had been passed in the back-country away from the ski slopes. Sun Valley wasn't alone; the vast majority of ski areas in the United States refused to allow snowboards. Skier participation—defined as people who were seven years old or older and skied at least once that year—had reached an all-time high of twelve million. That was a jump of nearly two million from the year before. Why worry about a few snowboarders?

In 1985 only 39 of about 600 ski resorts in the United States allowed snowboarding, less than 7 percent. Three years later, there were still only about 50 resorts that would. Snowboard participation numbers were a little over a million riders who boarded at least one day each season.

Unfortunately, the more snowboarders, the greater the animosity from skiers, who envisioned their playground being overrun by skate-or-die anarchist hordes of teen-aged shredders. Even the resorts that allowed snowboards didn't always treat us as equals with skiers. Some of the resorts permitted snowboarding only on a few select slopes, and snowboarders had to ride certain chairlifts. Some resorts required snowboarders to take a test with a ski instructor and demonstrate that they were able to ride in control—something not even the rankest beginning skier ever had to do.

Snowboarders were perceived as nonconformists, to put it politely— or less kindly, as *punk-rocking, beer-swilling, pothead party animals with body piercings and ridiculously baggy clothing*. Skiers even came up with endearments to refer to us, such as *knuckle-draggers*. Or they mocked the lingo, shouting down from the chairlifts, *"Hey duuuude! Are you shredding, duuuude?"* From the reaction of some skiers and resort managers, you'd have thought the Bloods street gang had invaded the slopes and was doing drive-by shootings while riding snowboards.

I concede that there were those who cultivated the image of rebels-without-a-cause on snow, and at times we were our own worst enemies. It didn't help that snowboarding originally was—and to a certain extent, still is—marketed to adolescent boys, who act like . . . adolescent boys. Those who did not grow up as traditional skiers did not know lift-line etiquette; they swore, engaged in loud horseplay, trampled on people's skis, smoked cigarettes in line (and pot in the woods).

Snowboarders developed a free-spirited culture that I both love and feel is a big part of its allure. But it also fed those prejudices and misperceptions that many of us had to combat in order to get snowboards on the slopes and to legitimize competitive snowboarding as a sport and competitive snowboarders as serious athletes.

To understand the evolution of the snowboarding culture, you have to look at who it originally appealed to. Yeah, skiers certainly played a large role in the development of the technology and drive to gain access to the slopes, but no sociology study of snowboarding is complete without acknowledging the role of the surfing and skateboarding scenes too.

There was a lot of cross-pollination of the populations participating in the sports. On the East Coast many of the big names in snowboarding came out of ski racing, like Jake Carpenter, Chris Karol, and Betsy Shaw. Some were also surfers and skateboarders, but for sure most of the early snowboard legends on the West Coast emerged from the skate and surf crowds. Guys like Tom Sims, Rob Morrow, Bert LaMar, Damian Sanders, and Don Szabo.

The guys I was riding with on Mount Bachelor had also been my skateboarding buddies since we were little kids. By high school, most of us were also surfing the cold waters off the Oregon coast.

Whether drawing lines on secret Northwest point breaks, or riding metro viaducts, or shredding freshies in the Cascades, many of those drawn to surfing, skating, and snowboarding were what sociologists might call "fringe kids." They weren't considered athletes, mostly because they couldn't have cared less about playing organized sports, like football, basketball, or baseball.

Or even ski racing. In ski towns like Bend and Aspen, where everyone who was anyone was on the ski team, many committed the ultimate sin of getting bored with their dads' sport and leaving the slopes. But some were discovering snowboards and coming back, or trying to when the resorts would let them.

Snowboarders tended to be free spirits—which in part meant free of "the rules" and free of having to conform to "normal." Even the baggy, casual way of dressing that caught hold in the mid to late 1980s and replaced designer ski parkas and stretch pants suggested both freedom of movement and freedom from their parents and the editors of teen fashion magazines (until they, too, caught on and suddenly it was fashionable for middle-class white kids to look like they had grown up in the 'hood.)

Partly by choice, partly due to the attitudes of skiers, snowboarders lived in their own little world. We even had our own language, which had also evolved from the lingo of the surfing and skateboarding cultures. "Gnarly" could mean extreme or dangerous, or it could also mean cool. A "grom" was a good young rider who followed older riders around. "Sick" (pronounced siiiick) actually meant really great. "Epic" described the best ever.

Yes, I am ashamed to admit that we sometimes fell into the stereotype and called each other "dude" and a line from a conversation might consist of: *Dude, you should have seen us shredding the blower, face shots galore.*

Of course, these were cultures that liked to party after a hard day of paddling, skating, or shredding. Rebels in everything else, they were often also the kids who just said yes to marijuana and sometimes harder drugs.

I grew up in the middle of it, as Mount Bachelor was one of the early magnets for snowboarders due to its annual average snowfall of more than 350 inches. I loved the attitude as well as the sport, but I wasn't into smoking weed.

When it came to sports, I was sort of a freak. On one hand, I thought of myself as a so-called serious traditional athlete, especially when it came to football. I had dreams of being a star college quarterback followed by a fabulous NFL career. I mean I was obsessed.

One night when I was in junior high, my mom came home and found our front yard lit up like a stadium. I had dragged every lamp and extension cord I could find out of the house and set them up to illuminate the Klug Bowl. Then I insisted that my maternal grandmother, Nanny, run wide-receiver patterns so that I could practice throwing the ball.

As Nanny gasped for air and told me to "put more zip on it next time," Mom demanded to know what in the hell I was thinking using her good living room and bedroom lamps. I told her I needed more practice—then threw a little curveball by claiming that I'd spent so much time on homework that I'd run out of daylight to practice. She looked at me through narrowed eyes—she knew damn well that the homework was an excuse and really I was just trying to create what it would be like to play "under the lights." She had a hard time to keep from laughing, but she also ordered me to dismantle my stadium and get it all back in the house . . . *now.*

I was a freak, however, because I also fit in with the skateboard and snowboard crowd. I didn't have any spikes in my clothing, nor was my eyebrow or nose pierced. In fact, I looked like a pretty straight All-American kid with an Ivy League haircut who wore polo shirts to school almost every day. But away from school, I wore the uniform— baggy Gotcha clam digger shorts, a loose Maui & Sons sweatshirt, with a hood or baseball cap turned backwards—and I loved the creative anarchy of snowboarding every bit as much the structure and tradition of football.

It's a credit to my parents that they let me find my own way. They knew that at times I was running with a pretty shady group of characters in the snowboarding and skateboarding circles—some of my friends were always getting into trouble of some sort—but they handled it with a mixture of trust and rules. They expected me to consider the choices and make the right decisions, then, right or wrong, to live with the consequences.

One of the decisions I'd made was that I wasn't going to smoke pot. I admit that there were times—maybe listening to Bob Marley singing about the benefits of smoking "ganja"—when the idea of getting high and cruising through the trees sounded intriguing. But I really wasn't interested, and even if I had been, my friends who *were* smoking wouldn't let me.

I remember one incident in particular in junior high when a few of us were on an adventure looking for skateboarding terrain—abandoned cement dikes or unused culverts. These prime spots tended to be remote, and therefore my buddies could light up with impunity. This particular time the joint got passed to me, but one of my friends intercepted it.

"No way, Klug," he said.

He wasn't being stingy, but we'd grown up together and these guys had been at my home or at school when I suffered asthma attacks. They'd seen the fear in my eyes and the worried looks on my family's faces as I gasped for air and was rushed off to the hospital. I still carried an inhaler everywhere I went. It was rarely necessary anymore, but they weren't taking any chances.

On days like that ride to Mount Bachelor, when the bong came around to me, I just passed it on to the next guy and turned back to the magazine photographs showing some of my snowboarding heroes ruling it, pulling the latest tricks or burying lines in bottomless blower. That was enough to get me high.

When I look back on those times, the memories are bittersweet. Some of my friends eventually paid the price for the choices they made—one was shot and killed at a party, others had run-ins with the police over drugs and other crimes and went to prison or otherwise screwed up their lives. But they were true friends in those early days, guys who looked out for me. It seems that throughout my life when I've needed friends to get me through the rough spots, I've been really blessed (just don't tell them I said that or they'll whup my ass!).

In those days, most snowboarders didn't specialize. There wasn't the schism that would emerge later between the competitive snowboarders and the free-riders, who feel that competing, especially professionally or at the ultimate sports venue of the Olympics, is a sellout to snowboarding's laid-back heritage. But that's because they don't know the history of their sport or have forgotten the days when the best of the backcountry "pow dawgs" were also tossing their boards into retro VW buses or old, indestructible, rusted-out Subarus and heading for competitions and struggling to find sponsors so that they could afford the lifestyle.

Some of the sport's historians say that the first national snowboarding race was held in April 1981 at Ski Cooper near Leadville, Colorado. However, most generally recognize the 1982 National Snowsurfing Championships held at the Suicide Six ski area in Woodstock, Vermont, as the first big event to bring in the best riders from all over the country to compete. It was certainly the first to bring in the major media, including reporters, photographers, and crews from *Today, Good Morning America,* and *Sports Illustrated.*

The snowsurfing championship featured a slalom race and a downhill race on a steep, icy slope that lived up to the area's name as out-of-control boarders moving at sixty miles an hour blew out of the course and got carnaged at an alarming rate—those who made it to the bottom stopped by crashing into hay bales.

The spring of the next year, Jake Carpenter sponsored the National Snowboarding Championship at Snow Valley, Vermont. Not to be outdone, Tom Sims announced he would be sponsoring the World Snowboarding Championships at the Soda Springs ski area near Lake Tahoe, Nevada. Not only that, Tom said he was introducing a new event: the half-pipe.

When Sims announced the half-pipe addition to his competition, he said that riders would have to enter all three events to win the overall title. Carpenter and his Burton team threatened to boycott the event. The guys from the East Coast felt that the half-pipe had nothing to do with snowboarding and everything to do with skateboarding. But the show went on, the half-pipe event was a success, and when Jake started up the U.S. Open in Vermont, the biggest snowboarding event in the country, his pipe became a legend.

The first year on my board, I was super psyched to explore Mount Bachelor and work on my riding. I loved the sense of freedom that riding trees, bowls, and ungroomed slopes gave me, but the next season I also wanted to race. I started experimenting by popping quarters into the automatic starting gates at the Marlboro Ski Challenge, a slalom course set up under the yellow lift at Mount Bachelor, and racing my buddy Jim Patterson, who was on skis. Then I started competing at little local events on Mount Bachelor sponsored by Bowerman's Century Cycles, but I wasn't on the Performer anymore. After that first season, I'd gone into Hutch's bicycle shop in Bend and ordered a cherry red Swallowtail Pure Juice 1400 FE made by Sims. That little metal-edged beauty arrived just in time for the season.

The metal edges opened up a whole new snowboarding experience. When I first saw boards with the edges, I didn't understand the point. Why would you want to ride anything but powder? But after I got the Swallowtail, I was riding with Jim Patterson when he said, "Dude, that's got metal edges, you can carve."

What he meant was that instead of being confined to the chopped-up powder on the sides of a run, I could tip 'er up on edge and the board would hold on hard-pack. From that point on, I was free to float turns in pow—fresh snow, so light it feels more like floating—or rail arcs on the groomed parts of the mountain. The advantage in racing was quickly apparent too. Instead of sliding around turns, which actually brakes and slows the board, I could carve for better control, without losing speed.

Not that I was always in control. Once after getting carnaged beneath a Mount Bachelor lift, I was lying on my back trying to figure out if I was still in one piece when I heard my mom's worried voice.

"Christopher, are you all right?" She was on the chairlift above me looking down.

I realized what the scene must have looked like. I'd exploded on impact—one glove was lying off to the right, another somewhere on the left, my hat was ten feet up the hill, and my goggles were twenty feet below me. I laughed. "Looks like I'm having a yard sale out here."

In the fall of 1986 I joined the rest of the first group to compete in the Northwest Series held throughout the season at ski areas in Idaho, Washington, and Oregon, including a couple at Mount Bachelor. The series attracted the top riders in the Pacific Northwest, like Craig Kelly, John Caulkins, Dan Donnely, Kris Jamieson, and Rob Morrow, as well as a few Canadians.

There were three divisions for each gender. Little *menehunes,* aka groms, like me were in the junior division; the others were in either adult amateur or pro divisions. Many of the pros—and I use that term loosely, as they were usually competing for purses of maybe a few hundred dollars—rode for the different manufacturers like Team Gnu or Team Sims, which covered their expenses and, if they were lucky, paid them a little too.

I relied on Team Mom and Dad for my financial support, as well as to get me to the events. They'd load me and whatever friend needed a ride into their old Mercury Marquis station wagon or Dad's equally old woody Jeep Wagoneer and drive hundreds of miles while "the boys" slept or chatted comfortably with the occasional loud demand for a restroom or food stop.

I thought I was pretty hot stuff on my Pure Juice Swallowtail. My footgear had also changed thanks to perhaps the most important invention since the wheel: that silver-gray miracle of adhesion—duct tape. My friends and I had discovered early on that wrapping a few feet of the tape around the top few inches of our moon boots stiffened them up and gave us better stability and more control over the board.

After the first season, I switched to Sorrels, which look like lace-up, rubber hiking boots with thick felt liners. They were stiffer than moon boots, but we still improved on them, too, with three or four wraps of duct tape. That stuff was so important that I never went anywhere without an industrial-sized roll in my gear bag.

The Northwest Series, like most of the competitions that were popping up around the country, consisted of multiple events: alpine, meaning a slalom or giant slalom (which usually turned into a banked slalom with all the snow we received in the Northwest back then) and sometimes both; the half-pipe; and moguls. In the future, the alpine snowboarders and half-pipe snowboarders would be on completely separate teams and compete in separate events, but in those days you competed in all three.

In December 1986 I was reading *TransWorld Snowboarding* magazine, one of the first slick-papered, full-color publications devoted to snowboarding, when an advertisement caught my eye. It was an announcement for the annual North American Snowboard Championships in Banff, Canada, in March sponsored by the Achenbach brothers' Snowboard Shop and Chuck Barfoot of Barfoot Snowboards, the Canadian equivalents of Tom Sims and Jake Burton Carpenter.

All the big names in snowboarding were going to be there, even Europeans! I begged my dad to take me, and he agreed. I could hardly wait to show the big boys what I could do on my new board, a black Terry Kidwell Pro-Model. It was one of the first "twin tips," or a board with the rounded, upturned tips on both ends that was ideal for freestylin', instead of the usual rounded on one end and square on the other.

Just the memory of how I got my hands on the board is a classic tale from the early days of snowboarding. Not many more years would pass before snowboard company representatives would be making money by the basketful and at least trying to come off as respectable businessmen. But things were a little different in the second half of the 1980s. Back then, reps might get a few boards and head off to resorts, stay in the cheapest motels they could find, ride their asses off, convert a few new riders to their company's product, then sell the boards to pay for their expenses and enough gas to get home.

Occasionally, they were known for supplementing their incomes in other ways. In this case, I met a Sims representative named Richard on Mount Bachelor who said he was stoked on my riding after seeing me bust a method grab off a small mogul. I told him I was fired up about his Terry Kidwell and wanted to know where I could get one. Looking around conspiratorially, as if the trees might have ears, he said he had a second board he could sell me for three hundred dollars. If I wanted it, I had to meet him that evening in the parking lot of the Poplar Motel in Bend.

Having persuaded my mom that I really *"neeeeeeded"* the board to win, and wheedling her into driving, we arrived in the parking lot, where the rep was conducting *other* business out of the trunk of his car. Thank God my Mom was a little naive about such things and didn't know what was going on, or I might never have gotten my Terry Kidwell.

As it turned out, I didn't exactly have the most auspicious start to racing in the big leagues in spite of my sleek new ride. I'd expected to clean up in the junior boys division in Banff, which started with a giant slalom race. I was killing it, too, until I got confused at the bottom and missed the finish line. I couldn't believe it. I didn't miss a gate, or crash and burn, to get disqualified in my first international race in front of all the big names in the sport. I was winning but couldn't find the finish line . . . how humiliating.

Chapter 4

Pigskin and Pow

The single-track trail up Pilot Butte climbed for a mile through scrub juniper, crisscrossed by an obstacle course of logs laid across the trail to combat erosion, and seemed to go straight up. Rust-red volcanic cinder dust filled the path, the finer particles hovering in the air, coating my mouth, choking off my breath. Near the top, the path grew so steep and the footing so loose that I had to scramble the last few yards using my hands as well as my feet, about ready to cough up a lung. But I kept driving my legs, willing myself to the top.

The view was worth the effort. I could see the volcanic peaks of the Oregon Cascade range: glacier-coated Mount Hood; jagged, independent Mounts Washington and Jefferson; the Three Sisters jutting up next to each other like a Boy Scout salute; Broken Top; Three-Fingered Jack; Black Butte; and Mount Bachelor.

I thought I lived in heaven, but there wasn't time to admire my surroundings just then. Coming up the trail behind me was the rest of the Mountain View High School varsity football team. Most of them I'd been playing ball with since those childhood games in Harmon Park: Jim Patterson, Justin Petersen, Mark Roberts, and my "adopted" brother, Jason Gillam. I had to get going. The race wasn't over until I got to the bottom, and as the starting quarterback entering my senior year, it was important to me that I win.

While I was pursuing snowboarding in the winter and spring, every summer and fall was dedicated to football. My sophomore year I'd been the JV starter but didn't see a lot of time with the varsity. Maybe it was because I loved throwing the ball downfield so much that I had to be reminded by the coaches that the long bomb/Hail Mary wasn't the only play in the book.

As a junior, I wasn't the designated starting quarterback, but I'd worked hard and partway into the year I'd become the starter. My rise to the top had begun that year with the traditional run up Pilot Butte.

Every August, Coach Clyde Powell closed summer training camp—a grueling two-week ordeal of twice-a-day practices in ninety degrees and full pads—with the "Watermelon Challenge." The *challenge* was for the team to race up and down the butte, which rose more than five hundred feet from the middle of Bend; the *watermelon* was supplied at the picnic afterward.

I'd won the challenge in my junior year. In part, it was my competitive nature. I couldn't play a game or enter a race without thinking I should win it. Because my asthma had set me back as a child, I had always made it a point of out-working everybody around me to prove that I belonged, especially on the football field. Plus, I had a legacy to live up to at Mountain View. Bigger and stockier than me, my brother, Jim, played defensive and offensive line and had been named all-state in his senior year and was off playing football at Dartmouth.

Entering my senior year of high school, I knew that I would soon be faced with a choice between football and snowboarding. I loved both sports equally, but there were times when I felt torn between the two, neither of which was very accepting of the other.

My snowboarding friends would have never gone to watch me play a football game. Even those who were competing had been drawn to snowboarding in part because it was the antithesis of organized sports like football. No coaches. No formal training regimen.

A lot of the guys I had raced against in the early years had stopped competing. They were burned out on it and headed off for the trees and backcountry. I understood where they were coming from—I loved deep, untracked powder as much as any of them.

Some of my best memories of snowboarding were those early years before it was "mainstreamed." Mount Bachelor could be a pretty inhospitable place; storms from the Pacific howled in on gale-force winds and regularly dropped a few feet of powder in a matter of hours. Fair-weather skiers would pack it up and head indoors to play video games and drink hot cocoa, but we'd be out there ripping it up with the mountain to ourselves. We were the few, the proud, the frost-bitten, in our element and having fun.

Yet there was nothing like a bright, sunny morning after the storm had cleared. A favorite expression of ours was "NO FRIENDS ON A POWDER DAY," which would set off a wild scramble to be the first to lay fresh tracks in a pristine snowfield. I mean there were some things you'd do for a friend, but no one in their right mind gave up the first tracks.

However, I also loved working hour after hour on my half-pipe routine or carving giant slalom courses set up for skiers until my legs were hammered. In the starting gate I was all business, a competitive, hard-nosed athlete who absolutely hated to lose. Still, it never took me more than a few minutes to realize that while I may have lost, I was doing something I loved, and then my ridiculous laugh (my friends alternately call it my Scooby-Doo, after the dog cartoon character, or my hyena giggle) would be turning heads in alarm or amusement all over the slope.

On the other side, my football teammates gave me a hard time about "being *a snowboarder*" (said with a sneer). They thought that all boarders were stoners and went around saying "Dude" to each other fifty times an hour; in other words, we were not "real athletes." Most figured we snowboarded because we couldn't make it skiing.

I was under pressure from some teammates to focus on football and forget the weekend snowboard training. There were always little comments, and not all of them were said in jest. I remember once as I was walking to Coach Powell's conditioning class and a friend, Wade McCone, one of the most hard-core football players and a general Mountain View badass, appeared. He looked at me and made a face like he'd eaten something bad. "Klug, why are you always wearing all that snowboarder crap?"

Now, if you competed in snowboard events, or rode for sponsors, you tended to pick up a lot of "product," otherwise known as "swag," like T-shirts, jackets, and gloves. As an amateur, it's what you got instead of cash, along with the occasional new snowboard deck. I don't even remember exactly what I was wearing, probably a Team Sims jacket, maybe a "Get Bakerized" T-shirt.

"It's free," I shrugged. "And I'm a snowboarder. It's what I do."

"Whatever," he muttered, then adopted the Waimea big wave stance and surfed the sidewalk all the way to class.

Even my brother, Jim, had given me a hard time when I first started competing. He'd continued ski racing into high school and kept asking when I was going to "forget about this snowboarding . . . it's a passing fad." But he finally realized that I loved it as much as he enjoyed his favorite pastime, fly-fishing. After that, he joined the rest of my family as one of my greatest supporters.

Sometimes I got support where I didn't expect it. A snowboarding friend of mine, Steve Shipsey, an older rider who'd moved to Bend in 1987 with Craig Kelly and Kelly Jo Legaz, helped me put it into perspective. He'd also played football in high school and during several chairlift conversations told me the two sports were not incompatible. "As long as you enjoy doing both, then do both." The main thing, he said, was that I had to follow what my heart was telling me, not what other people said.

In the meantime, I was enjoying both and had found success on the gridiron and on the slopes. After missing the finish line that first day in Banff three years earlier, I did better the next day in the half-pipe by placing second.

The half-pipe back then wasn't like the super pipes you see today at the Olympics or X-Games that have walls twenty feet high from trough to edge and are built using heavy machinery. Early pipes were essentially large ditches that had been dug out with shovels and the snow thrown to the sides to create ramps. I was pretty proud of my hand plants, methods, and mute grabs back then. At least until I saw

Jose Fernandez, a pro rider from Switzerland, win the men's pro half-pipe by finishing his run with a full layout backflip. He didn't even land in the pipe but (fortunately) in between shocked spectators, who scrambled to get out of his way.

My favorite part of that competition was getting to meet and even hang out a little with a few legends of our growing sport—guys I'd mostly only read about in magazines, like Bert LaMar, who had just won the World Championship crown, and Fernandez, as well as some of the best in the Northwest, such as Shannon Melhuse, Keith Wallace, Michele Taggart, and Robbie Morrow.

These riders were proof that the sport was growing up. They were sponsored by the snowboard manufacturers, and some even had their own "pro-model" boards (like my Terry Kidwell) named after them. On the podium, they had quickly adopted the professional ski racer's habit of holding their boards up so that the cameras and spectators could see the company logo.

Some were better at marketing themselves than others, which occasionally created a sort of resentment from those who were either not very good at it or saw it as "selling out." Of course, some of the latter were the guys who were still into trashing motel rooms and brawling at the local bars because that was the way snowboarders were "supposed to act." But they weren't the majority, and there was a new generation of boarders coming up who liked to have fun and appreciated the backcountry heritage but were also serious about snowboarding as a sport and a possible career.

The North American Overall Junior Boys Champion that year at Banff was Tad Dobson, from Lake Oswego, Oregon. Although he'd raced in the Northwest Series, I didn't know him. But at Banff I was left to wonder "who in the hell is this kid?" He was the same age as I was and had just cleaned up by winning all of the events in our division. When I got home to Bend, I knew two things—I loved to compete against the best, but to do so, I was going to have to get better.

Getting better in those days for most snowboarders was a do-it-yourself project. There weren't many coaches, even for the pros. There wasn't even an agreement on what techniques or equipment worked best, and even the best riders were making it up as they went along.

Competitive snowboard racing, called alpine racing, continued along as a poor cousin to alpine ski racing. Our competitions looked like we were just doing what skiers did, only slower. Even the gates were the same tall poles used in ski racing and not exactly ideal for snowboarders. In fact, they hurt.

In a slalom turn, a snowboard racer leans much farther over the snow than a skier does to get on the edge. So we had a choice of playing it safe and swinging wide of the poles, or getting whacked if we stayed aggressive and ran a tight line. Plenty of us finished our day of competition with cuts on our faces, bruises on our chests, and broken fingers from trying to fend off the poles with our hands.

Seeking to improve, I got on the mountain every chance I could— jumping on the first bus at the inn in the morning and not getting back until dark. In between, I spent every moment free riding and popping coins into the Marlboro Ski Challenge and racing the clock.

The next year Tad and I got to be friends racing in the Northwest Series. We seemed to alternate who would take first and who would take second in the boys division at every event. Soon our parents were taking turns carpooling us. We'd hop in with Team Jude (named for Tad's mom, Judy Dobson) or Team Klug, who'd drive sometimes hundreds of miles while we slept or chatted in the back of the car. Then they'd stand for hours in the snow alongside the race course— blue skies or blizzards—cheering, ringing cowbells, and videotaping "the boys." For all their efforts, we barely tolerated the pleas to get us to face the cameras and smile at the end of the day—smiles that usually came off as a pained expression to let them know the great sacrifice we were making in the spirit of cooperation.

One of Team Klug's early epic trips was in 1988 to the Mount Baker ski area in Washington for the Third Annual Legendary Banked Slalom. This time, Team Klug took Tom Routh, another friend from

Bend, and me, with Mom driving eight hours straight through the night while we slept.

Located in the northwest corner of the state, just ten miles from the Canadian border, Mount Baker was one of the first resorts to open its slopes to snowboarders. With annual snowfalls hovering around four hundred inches, there was little wonder why it was popular with shredders.

As with skiing, most snowboard alpine courses were set up on a wide slope with gates zigzagging their way down. There were three main types of races: the slalom, with the tightest radius turn and shortest distance between gates; the faster giant slalom, a more open and longer course with more distance between gates, which were also set wider apart, requiring smoother, arcing turns; and the Super-G, the fastest of them all with wide-open balls-to-the-wall speeds and leg-burner length.

However, the Mount Baker race course dove and twisted down a natural, narrow, steep-sided gully. You could really fly, using the sides of the natural pipe to bank around the curves like a bobsled in a chute or a racecar going around the banked turns at the Indianapolis Speedway. In fact, you could go so fast that the Gs from centrifugal force would throw you so far up the side of a bank that your body would be almost horizontal to the ground. If you didn't hold your edge, you might get "ejected" and suddenly find yourself flying off into space, then landing in ten feet of powder from which you had to crawl out looking like the Abominable Snowman.

There weren't a whole lot of spectators at the event, but a hundred or more competitors gathered in the race area that morning. The scene was typical for a snowboarding competition. Reggae and punk rock music blared from tinny speakers. The aroma of pot wafted over our heads. Racers were getting high in the starting area, which was located under the chairlift, and some were even smoking in the starting gates, taking a last puff or two before hurtling down the course. At one point during the race, a run was delayed—as someone finally announced—because the starter needed to help finish a joint before he could get back on the job. Even the official race slogan was "Get Bak-erized," a play on the pot-smoker's term *getting baked*. The slogan was even on the trophy they handed me that year for winning the boys junior division.

In March, Tad and I flew to Stratton Mountain, Vermont, with my dad for the U.S. Open. Sponsored by Burton, the open was the granddaddy of the competitions; everybody who was anybody, or wanted to someday be somebody, showed up to take on the alpine course and the notoriously big half-pipe. All the best riders in North America, as well as the Euros, and the occasional rider from Japan (where snowboarding was catching on big time) were there.

Considering this was the best-known snowboarding event in the world, Tad and I were amazed that we had to pass a riding test with the Stratton Mountain ski patrol before they would let us go on the hill to practice. I wonder how many ski racers ever had to demonstrate their ability.

The event went well for me. I placed second in the slalom behind Jeff Brushie, who schooled me by two seconds. But I beat him the next day when I placed second in the moguls to J. J. Collier, who wowed the judges by completing a 360 (degree) spin off a jump. The irony is that in the near future, when riders began to specialize, Brushie would become one of the best freestyle/half-pipe riders in the world, while I would concentrate on racing.

My two strong finishes gave me the U.S. Open Junior Overall Championship. I finished off the season by going back to the Banff event (this time flying with Team Jude, accompanied by Easter baskets my mom had made for Tad and me), where I kicked Tad's butt (sorry, buddy, but it was fun). I placed first in the half-pipe, first in moguls, third in the giant slalom, and was crowned the North American Overall Junior Champion.

"The thing I remember most about traveling and competing with Chris is how determined he was to win every competition," Tad recalls. "He was a hundred and ten percent business when it came to competing, but he was also a hundred and ten percent fun when it was time to wind down. Other competitors only saw the competitive side of him while we were on the slopes, but I was fortunate enough to see the goofy/fun side of Chris away from competitive pressures."

I thought I was the best thing to hit snowboarding since metal edges, especially when I landed a sponsorship deal with Sims. My contract entitled me to two new snowboards per season and a "reasonable amount of clothing product to be determined solely by the company." They also agreed to pay my entry fees, lift tickets, and lodging ("lodging not to exceed $25 per person per night"), so long as I used Sims products and placed in the top three at the contests. Team Mom and Dad were still picking up most of the bill, but it was a start.

TransWorld Snowboarding editor Kevin Kinnear and his photo editor, Guy Motil, showed up at the Inn of the Seventh Mountain to shoot part of a photo spread for their spring 1988 edition at Mount Bachelor. I was invited to participate along with some of the legends who had moved to Mount Bachelor, including Craig Kelly, Mike Ranquet, Kelly Jo Legaz, Chris Karol, Todd Van Belkum, Kris Jamieson, and local boys Tom Routh and Sean Dillard.

My "big moment" in the spotlight was at hand. I was going to be in the premier snowboarding magazine with some of the best riders in the world. But when I got to the slopes I realized I'd forgotten my snowboard pants. All I had was an old pair of baggy turquoise sweats from gym class. I looked like I was wearing my pajamas and was thoroughly humiliated.

Motil still got a pretty cool shot of me boosting a backside air off a wind lip against the blue Oregon sky. The caption that ran with the photo said: "Chris Klug has it made. His parents own a beautiful resort called the Inn of the Seventh Mountain outside of Bend that is the closest place to stay to Mt. Bachelor. He's already been snowboarding for four years and is red hot. Judging by his contest results, you'll be hearing a lot more about Chris in the future."

The magazine came out when I was in Breckenridge at my first World Cup event, the World Championships. Kinnear was at the registration desk with a stack of the mags when I walked up. Jeff Brushie was there and picked one up too. "Rad photo, Klug," he said and gave me the thumbs up. I gave him my best "no big deal . . . happens to me all the time" look, but felt my hat get tighter as my head started to swell to roughly the size of a basketball. I was in a magazine, which to a young snowboarder was like being a "made man" in the mob and along with swag was about the only compensation a junior division rider got.

I basically sucked at the event and was moping around when one of the top pro riders, Chris Pappas, patted me on the shoulder. "You were really ripping it up out there, Klug," he said and went on his way. It's amazing I could get my head in the car for the ride home.

The magazine photo and compliments made me more determined than ever to get better. I was dreaming big. In fact, Tad and I shared a dream on those long rides that wasn't even on the map of reality yet.

Every four years in February, my family and hundreds of millions of other people around the world sat glued to the television set watching the Winter Olympics. The images from those times are still stuck in my mind: in 1980 it was watching speed skater Eric Heiden win five gold medals and the U.S. Hockey Team beating the evil Russians at Lake Placid; in 1984 we were jumping up and down yelling as Oregonian Bill Johnson won the downhill skiing gold medal at Sarajevo. Those guys were as much my sports heroes as John Elway and Walter Payton.

Tad and I talked about the day when snowboarding would be an event and we would be there to compete for medals. In those years, only amateurs were supposed to compete in the Olympics. We vowed not to turn pro until we'd been in the Olympics.

"He knew that someday he would be there and that he would represent his country in the sport of snowboarding," Tad says.

However, without public acceptance of snowboarding as a sport, we would never make it into the Olympics, and we were sometimes our own worst enemy. As Kinnear pointed out in an editorial in that same issue of *TransWorld* as my photograph, some snowboarders were "burning bridges."

It wasn't just breaking the rules or being obnoxious at ski resorts, either, Kinnear wrote. Motels and restaurants in ski areas were getting tired of the "look at me, I'm a rock star" behavior. Motel managers complained about boarders placing brand-name stickers on walls and mirrors and furniture, waxing their boards in their rooms and ruining carpets with the shavings, drinking in public areas (especially when it involved minors), and "packing rooms with as many people as possible without paying for the extra guests."

Kinnear noted that restaurant and motel management near contest areas were contemplating banning snowboarders. But worse than that, ski resort managers were pointing to the behavior as reason enough to maybe rethink their welcome, or an excuse to keep their slopes closed to snowboarders. "If you make their primary customers unhappy, the ski areas will be sure to return the favor," he warned.

I didn't know much about all of that; I was fifteen years old, wasn't old enough to trash motel rooms or grope waitresses, which in any case would have brought down the wrath of Team Klug or Team Jude. I did think I was the bomb on the slope, but I wasn't stupid and knew I needed coaching to get better.

Most of the coaching I got in those early years came from my dad. He didn't know much about the technical aspects of snowboard racing, but he gave me other insights that I use to this day. The most important of these was before each alpine event he'd send me to the starting area with the advice, "Plan your race, race your plan."

It sounds pretty simple, but I've never heard anything better. If I could first visualize nailing my run—by studying the gates and choosing what line to take through them, as well as noting changes in the terrain and thinking through how I would adjust to them—I could then carry it out in reality. This was the beginning of my mental game plan training and the development of my competitive mental toughness.

Dad had eventually taken over most of the shuttling me around to the Northwest Series and accompanying me to farther destinations like the U.S. Open in Vermont and Banff. Mom stayed home to take care of my sister, Hillary, and to run Flanagan's. To be honest, she'd get so nervous it would make me nervous. I could count on Dad to stay cool and positive, but left to her own devices, Mom would have eventually bought herself a bullhorn so she could shout instructions to me as I was going down the slope. Looking back, she might have made a better football coach than Dad, but she was smart enough to leave the racing to him.

I eventually got more coaching, but not all of it was centered on running gates on a snow-covered hill. I did get some of that from Jenny Sheldon, the coach of the Mountain View High School ski team, who let me work out with them. She helped me learn how to train for racing and made suggestions on choosing my line through gates. It was also the first time I was able to train on more demanding courses than those set up on the Marlboro Ski Challenge. But she couldn't offer much snowboarding advice. So it was up to me to experiment with my technique as I followed her skiers through the gates.

I went back to Stratton Mountain for the 1989 U.S. Open and won the slalom, beating my nearest competitor by a whopping four seconds. I still loved to ride pipe for fun, but I was focusing more on racing in competitions. The subjectivity of the judged events pissed me off, especially in the early years of snowboarding when there wasn't exactly a strict standard for judging. The clock didn't lie.

I probably learned as much about how to be a competitor from my high school tennis coach, Ana Jamieson. Originally from Germany, Ana was the mother of Kris Jamieson, one of the top riders in the Northwest. She taught me how to be mentally strong and not get too up or down for any one game or tournament. "Relax and trust your preparation," she'd say. "Be consistent and let the other player make mistakes." She was talking about tennis, but the same ideas applied to racing.

Of course, one of the great things about tennis is there are a lot of cute chicks running around in short white skirts. One of them was Missy April. I had just gotten my ass kicked at the district tournament in Pendleton, Oregon, near the end of my sophomore year when I spotted her sitting on a blanket. She had curly bronze hair, beautiful blue eyes, and she never stopped smiling. She was hot, but I wasn't sure how to approach her. For one thing, she was a junior and played for our arch rival, Redmond High School, which was "out in the sticks" about fifteen miles north of Bend.

I saw my chance when I noticed she was sitting with a German exchange student whom I'd met while snowboarding. He saw me and called me over to talk about snowboarding, and I was in there like swimwear.

We talked for a while, and then I asked her if she'd like to maybe hang out after the annual Pole, Pedal, Paddle Race I was entering in Bend that next weekend. The race is a crazy pentathlon that starts with a manic downhill ski run with a few hundred of your closest friends; then as quick as you can you're off your downhill skis and into cross-country gear for ten kilometers, followed by a twenty-five-mile bike ride from Bachelor to Bend, then a 10K run followed by a two-and-a-half-mile canoe or kayak course on the Deschutes River through the middle of Bend to the finish line.

Missy was a ripping skier on the Redmond High team and she didn't think much of snowboarders. In fact, she says now that she thought it was a joke, a fad.

"I NEVER considered trying it, did not cross my mind," Missy says. "When you are a ski racer in particular, you are quite critical of everyone else on the slopes, especially a snowboarder. About this time my little brother, Hub, dabbled in snowboarding, but quickly went back to skiing. That was proof enough that it sucked and was not really a sport."

Of course, that was until she saw me fore-run the course before a ski race. (A fore-runner checks the course for the timing between gates and makes sure there are no obvious problems, like a gate out of place or a malfunction with the timing system.) When she finally saw me tilt a board up on edge and carve a turn riding a single rail, she was very impressed (and after all, this is MY book).

However, that day at the tennis match, Missy was noncommittal, so I was happy to see her in a sea of spectators at the finish line that next weekend. I didn't learn until later that during that entire week she went back and forth as to whether to meet me or not. Then the night before the race she'd gone to her prom with a guy who ended up leaving the dance with a case of mononucleosis and bronchitis, so she figured she "had nothing to lose" (I'm not sure I like the way she puts that). We hung out all afternoon, and that evening she came over to my house and met my parents, which she recalls as something like being a canary in a house full of cats.

For our second "date," I asked if she wanted to go mountain biking. I guess she thought I meant a nice little cruise in the woods, but it turned into the "Bataan Death March" of bike rides. Six hours into the "date" and halfway across a knee-deep stream with her mountain bike on her shoulder, Missy was wondering what she had gotten herself into. When I dropped her off at her home that night in Sisters, Oregon, a little town about twenty miles from Bend, I thought it would be the last time I saw her, but she was a good sport about it.

Missy thinks I was lost the whole time and just acted like I knew where I was going.

"I do remember that we began that journey looking for a waterfall, and I never got to see one," Missy says. "But I had a soft spot for the athletic type, being one myself. Chris was always different than everyone else . . . sincere, not like the average high school boy. I was mesmerized by his kindness—he let me borrow his sweatshirt that day because I was cold, took me to meet his parents, and treated me to an ice cream cone. . . . Of course, all that nice guy got sort of old . . . and after a while, I thought he was kind of a nerd, even though we were great friends."

Of course in the weird way that the female mind works, "nice" and "polite" mean you're dead meat as boyfriend material. She was perfectly happy being "just friends" with me and dating a bunch of losers. Don't tell her, but my continued interest in her had a lot to do with her parents, Ray and Pat, owning Papandrea's, an Italian restaurant in Sisters. They made the best pizza I have ever tasted, so I put up with their daughter's flakiness.

My parents claim they knew that I was, as my mom says, "smitten," the day I turned sixteen and got my driver's license. I immediately disappeared in the gold Isuzu Trooper—an underpowered four-banger soon nicknamed "the Pooper"—my dad bought for me so that I could get around to all my activities and events, and drove the twenty miles to Sisters to see Missy.

I was invited to stay for dinner and was grilled by her ski-fanatic brothers, Rocco and Hubbell, who, like Missy, were racers and thought snowboarders were fair game for a variety of snide comments. Rocco, who was four years older than me, was especially skeptical, saying he thought I was awful uppity for a snowboarder and wondered aloud if someone could actually "race" a snowboard. Of course, most of the once-over had more to do with the fact that I was interested in their sister than with me being a snowboarder. Somehow I survived dinner (Missy's parents called off the dogs), and Missy and I remained friends.

As I was the quarterback of the rival high school, Missy took a lot of (mostly) good-natured ribbing from her guy friends at Redmond about her "boyfriend from Mountain View." The Redmond football team delighted in telling her all the details of how they crushed me, or what they were going to do to me the next time we played. She says it was my own fault because I was so full of myself (untrue!) and strutted around like a barnyard rooster (well, maybe a little).

Being my friend didn't stop Missy from heckling me from the stands during a football game whenever I got sacked or hit. On the other hand, I loved giving her a hard time whenever our high school girls' volleyball teams met (even though she was lookin' good in her volleyball uniform too).

Being Missy's friend wasn't easy—in fact, it nearly got me killed. Once, I went to a basketball game between Redmond and Mountain View and, of course, spent some time after the game talking to Missy. I might have been interested in more than friendship, but she was a senior and going away to college that next fall, plus she had a boyfriend.

Missy had started dating Charley Patterson that fall, and when he saw me talking to her after the basketball game—having already heard that we were close—he decided to beat the crap out of me. It wouldn't have been hard. I was a six-foot-three bone rack with rubber-band muscles and garter-snake pipes; he was the rock-solid star running back at Redmond and an all-state wrestling champ who could have twisted me into a human pretzel and broken every bone in my body.

However, in a moment of insanity, after flirting with his girl I flipped him off and left the building. We got into our cars, and he chased me all the way home and was going to crush me, except my best friend and adopted brother, Jason Gillam, got out of the "Pooper" and invited him to leave—or else. Jason was a lot bigger and a lot meaner and would have whupped him. Jason wasn't really looking to fight—he was just making sure I didn't get a beat down. Charley left and I lived to talk to Missy another day. (Charley went on to a great pro career as one of the pioneers in wakeboarding, and we became great buddies, but for a while I avoided all places where he might find me alone.)

Jason and I had rarely been apart since fourth grade. Growing up, the Klug house had continued to be the prime gathering place for all the boys in the neighborhood. My friends would come over after playing at Harmon Field, then we'd pull a commando raid on the ice cream shop, go back to my house and, often as not, several would end up staying for dinner. Some kids were encouraged to stay more than others, in part because my parents were good at spotting those who might be having trouble at home or in school, and they'd reach out to help.

One of the most frequent guests was Jason. We'd met in Mr. Ensworth's class but bonded on the football field at Kenwood

Elementary during recess. He was the kid with the messy, unkempt hair, who wore the same torn flannel shirt every day and never invited me over to his house. But he loved football as much as I did, and together we organized the mega-games in the park.

I knew early on that Jason did not have as good a family life as I did. But it wasn't for some time that I learned he'd never met his real father, and that his mother and stepfather were unemployed drug addicts. His family was constantly on the move as one landlord after another evicted them for failing to pay rent. When they did have a place to stay, their living conditions were filthy, the floors littered with trash and liquor containers.

An evening at home with Jason's family consisted of watching his parents smoke pot or snort speed. His childhood memories were filled with such Norman Rockwell moments as the Christmas Eve when his mom threw a fit and ripped all the branches off the decorated Christmas tree that had been given to them by a church group, her children too shocked to even cry. Another time, someone drove by and shot at the house, leaving three bullet holes in the walls and three frightened kids cowering on the floor.

The other kids at school picked on them. In return, Jason lashed out, getting into fights and landing in hot water with the school authorities. But his parents didn't give a damn what their kids did in school, nor what they did afterward. If the kids didn't come home at night, nobody noticed. Or cared.

I started bringing him home in junior high to get a good meal. It wasn't long before my mom and dad insisted that he eat dinner with us every night. Then he was doing his laundry and staying after dinner for help from my parents with his homework, just like the rest of the Klug kids. Soon after, my parents began inviting him to go on family outings, such as joining us for church events and potlucks, or family brunch at the Poppyseed, Dad's new restaurant at the inn.

They would have just let him move in with us, but Jason worried about his siblings and went home every night to make sure they were okay. Usually he walked, but on the couple of occasions he accepted a ride from my dad, he'd ask to be dropped off at a corner—ashamed of having anyone see how his family lived.

When Jason was about thirteen, the Oregon Department of Social Services finally intervened and had the police remove him and his siblings from their mother's home. His sister was sent to a foster home, but Jason persuaded the police to call my parents and ask if they'd take him and his younger brother in on a temporary basis.

"Of course," they said, "bring them over." The next day, Mom and Dad took the Gillam boys shopping for new clothes, got them haircuts, and cleaned them up.

The brothers were treated just like the Klug kids. They were expected to follow the rules of the house: do your homework and ask for help when needed; treat each member of the family with respect; be polite (Mom was always on Jason for his table manners. She told us all, "What are you going to do when you're invited to the White House for dinner?"); keep your room clean; help around the house when asked; let my parents know where you're going; and be home when expected.

We all studied together, seated around the family dinner table with Mom and Dad available for questions and to "keep us focused" (in other words, to prevent the boys from harassing Hillary, or simply leaving). That wooden tabletop was grooved from thousands of pens and pencils pressing through paper, creating road maps of algebraic formulas and long-forgotten English essays. In later years my parents could have replaced the table with something new and unmarred, but they kept it in its place of honor as the centerpiece of our family gatherings because of the good memories those grooves represented.

Jason was used to the Klug way and already doing well at school. His little brother, however, had hated school and was failing all of his classes when my parents took him in. Six months later, Josh was a solid B student—a witty, likable kid whose popularity with his school chums blossomed with his self-image. But it wouldn't last.

Eight months after the Gillams moved in with us, Social Services called and gave Jason and Josh a choice. They could stay where they were or go back to their mother, who had supposedly cleaned up her act. Jason saw this as his opportunity to break away from "that hell" permanently and said he was staying. He then tried to persuade his brother to do the same, but Josh ignored the warning and moved back in with his mother. Jason was right, she hadn't changed and his little brother grew up in turmoil and got in trouble with the law himself. I can still remember Mom crying when she heard, saying, "If only we'd had more time."

Mom and Dad "officially" became Jason's foster parents; however, they always referred to him as "our adopted son," so much that other people thought they really had adopted him. Way back when Jim was born and their church helped them out, Father Gray had told my parents that someday they would find ways to help other people. I suppose they were living their faith when they took in Jason, but I don't think they ever saw it as repaying a debt. Not unless loving him as they did their biological sons was part of an installment plan.

"The Klugs are my family," Jason says. "I will never be able to say thank-you enough. And Chris is one of my biggest heroes, not because he became one of the best snowboarders in the world or went to the Olympics, but for saving me from sheer disaster. A life of abuse and neglect is what I faced until I met Chris. . . . He never made me feel 'lucky' to be a part of his family, and didn't judge me by where I came from or the clothes I wore. He was a friend."

I should be honest and explain that I had ulterior motives for wanting Jason in the house. A big, strong lineman on the football team, he was my bodyguard on and off the field. This was important because though I might not have been the biggest guy around, I was probably the cockiest and therefore likely to open my mouth and get my butt kicked (see Patterson, Charley).

So I gained another brother and a bodyguard. More importantly, I learned a lesson from my parents about being a better human being. As I said earlier, what I respect about their faith is that they walk the walk, and I can't think of a better way to illustrate that than to recall Jason's story.

Mostly, I was thrilled to have someone to toss the football around with all day and night. Jason was as obsessed with football, and the possibility of a college and maybe a pro career, as I was.

I was still nuts about the sport and insisted that my entire family strap on the cleats—sometimes literally—to help me get there. If I couldn't find a friend, I'd drag my dad or mom or, if she was visiting, Nanny, my sports-nut grandmother, outside to run post patterns and buttonhooks.

On bad-weather days when I couldn't find any willing participants, I'd set up targets—strategically placed pillows—all over the house and then run around drilling my "receivers." That worked great until I missed the wide-open "tight end" on the living room couch and put a ball through the big bay window. But even that fiasco turned into a good practice session, because when Mom came home and saw what I'd done, I had to scramble for my life as she chased me around with a shoe in hand, yelling, "What in the hell were you thinking?"

Thinking?

I just wanted to be like John Elway and Walter Payton. I wore the same jersey number as Elway, number 7, and admired his toughness as much as his great athletic ability. The game was never over for Elway, no matter how far behind his team was, until the last second had ticked off the clock.

However, the player I emulated the most was still Walter Payton. I kept a poster of Payton on the wall of my bedroom. It showed him busting through would-be tacklers, driving his legs, refusing to be brought down. I'd seen a television special from his playing days that showed how hard he worked out. I was particularly impressed by a segment that showed him running up a steep hill in suburban Chicago to build his legs for both power and endurance. So I started running up Pilot Butte as part of my regular workout, not just for the Watermelon Classic, usually with Jason.

This brings me back to coaches. Of all the coaching I got in those high school years, nothing was more important or lasting than what I learned from Clyde Powell, the head coach of the Mountain View "Cougars" High School varsity football team. He taught me a lot about competing that went beyond football, like learning to work as part of a team. "You can't do it alone," he preached. Powell reinforced lessons my parents had instilled in us kids, like to set goals and to not be afraid to aim high

Football taught me to get back up every time I got knocked down. Then when the other guys think they have your number, throw a bomb for a touchdown . . . or fight back from being behind in a snowboard race. The game taught me to never, ever quit.

It also taught me about leadership. I won the Watermelon Classic again in my senior year, determined to set the tone for myself and the team for the rest of the year.

We weren't supposed to do much. According to the press and the polls our team was too slow and too small; we didn't have any big stars being heavily recruited by major university football programs. But I thought that if we outworked everyone else and pulled together as a team, we could make the state high school playoffs, and from there who knew what might happen.

These days, Coach Powell remembers that I wasn't the greatest quarterback as far as skills and arm strength.

"But he was the guy the rest of the team rallied around," Coach Powell says. "He seemed to recognize that as an individual he might not get too far, but as part of a team, he thought he could do anything. And he worked hard as a student of the game. He wanted to understand, not just play."

We played our hearts out that year, and the thing that stands out about that team was that we never gave up trying. Sometimes it paid off, and sometimes it didn't, except that we often learned more from our losses than our wins. And we surprised the critics by making it to the second round of the state playoffs.

Unfortunately, we lost the game. I was disappointed, but what really hurt was the realization that I would never play another high school football game, and certainly never again play with the guys I'd grown up with. But I was looking at it all wrong. When I got in the locker room there was dejection—no one wanted to lose short of our goal—but there was also a lot of pride in what we'd accomplished together. We were a team, start to finish.

I would have gladly traded the region's co-offensive Player of the Year award I received to have played in just one more game with those guys. But I also knew that I needed to capture that memory, surrounded by Jason and our childhood friends, some of them probably for the last time. We'd all be off to college or to work by that time the next year, and who knew when or if we'd all be together again.

A dozen years later, my memories of playing in high school are as good and as important to me as being in the Olympics. The camaraderie, the friendships . . . that feeling of being part of something bigger than myself and working toward a common goal. I also learned something that would matter a whole lot more later than it did right then, and that was to enjoy the moment, because you never know when you've played your last game together.

Chapter 5

Olympic Dreams

"Why don't you turn pro?" The reporter from *Snowboarder* magazine smiled when he asked the question, noting that my winning times the previous season were often better than the men's division racers.

"Because I want to keep my amateur status for college football . . . and so I can race in the Olympics," I replied.

The reporter gave me an amused look and pointed out, "But, Chris, snowboarding isn't an Olympic sport."

"No," I conceded. "But it will be, and I'm going to be there."

I don't know why I said it. I was just starting my junior year of high school in the fall of 1989; still ahead for me were my junior and senior years of high school football. The 1988 Winter Olympics in Calgary had come and gone with no mention of snowboarding. Nor did there appear to be anything in the works for the 1992 games in Albertville, France.

Riding in the Olympics was still just as much a fantasy as it was when Tad and I talked about it in the back of the Team Klug wagon. But I still believed it would happen and that I was going to be there.

Looking back at that comment, I think I already knew that I had reached a fork in the road that turned away from one dream and toward another. I had taken the first step in that direction the year before when two of the top "older" (as in five years or so) riders at Bachelor, Chris Karol and Kris Jamieson, came to me with an offer that, as they say in *The Godfather,* I couldn't refuse.

I'd seen Chris and Kris at competitions, and as a little grom wannabe, I followed them and other top riders around whenever I spotted them ripping it up at Mount Bachelor. They'd been at it from the early days, and I wanted to be just like them when I grew up . . . well, almost.

Chris Karol had taken up the sport and raced for the first time in that infamous 1982 skirmish at Suicide Six where he took second in the slalom and then survived the downhill with minimal bloodshed when he crashed trying to stop after crossing the finish line at sixty-plus miles an hour. The funny thing was that as soon as the competition was over, the Suicide Six ski resort kicked all the snowboarders off the mountain. They still weren't welcome!

Those early days of experimenting with the sport were like a blank sketchbook waiting to be filled in, Chris Karol remembers. "We were having a blast and didn't really care what anybody else thought. The feeling of skateboarding on snow was totally new; improvisation ruled, but things were still a little sketchy at ski areas."

Jake Carpenter knew that in order for snowboarding—and his business—to expand, snowboarders were going to have to gain acceptance in the world of skiing. That meant getting access to the ski slopes. The big resorts were out west, so in 1983 when Tom Sims announced his competition at Soda Springs, California, Jake got an idea. He handed the keys to a white, bare-bones cargo van, and a credit card for gas, to Karol and two other legendary Burton riders, Andy "Dog" Coghlan and Mark Heingartner. Their orders were to drive west and try to ride at as many resorts as they could on the way to Soda Springs.

"We needed mercenaries out there to spread the word," Jake says, looking back on those early years. "It was all about exposure. Basically, we were dealing with a form of discrimination and having a difficult time gaining acceptance. Chris and Andy were great riders, so I thought it would be good for people to see someone who could perform at their level."

Chris, Andy, and Mark "customized" the van by sticking an old mattress in the back and took off. They took turns driving and sleeping until they reached a Denny's restaurant in Denver. According to the map on the placemats at the restaurant, the Lake Eldora ski area near Boulder was closest, so they decided to make that the first stop on their tour.

Arriving at Eldora, they bought their tickets and quickly got on the lift with their boards before the lift operator could decide what to do. But they got to the top and found the ski patrol waiting for them like INS agents intercepting illegal immigrants at the Mexican border. The patrol said they didn't think "ski boards" were allowed.

"Just follow us down," Chris pleaded their case. "See what we can do."

The ski patrol shrugged and told them to go ahead; they were going to have to get to the bottom one way or the other anyway. When the patrol saw that the three could really rip and were in control, their skepticism turned to curiosity. *You know,* some of the patrol members admitted, *it kind of looks like fun.* Chris and Andy were allowed to stay.

The next day, the fearsome threesome was off to the Breckenridge ski resort, where they pulled the same stunt. And so on across the West. Some places refused to let them ride, but with most they went through a similar routine of jumping onto the lift before anyone could stop them, and then talking their way into staying.

Chris Karol had gone back to New Hampshire but eventually returned to the West. He made his way to Mount Hood, Oregon, where ski racers traditionally trained year-round on the glacier, and started the Karol Snowboarding Camp, the first established camp for snowboarders on the snowfields of the volcano. He'd moved to Bend in 1988 with Sanders Nye and added to the Mount Bachelor posse of some of the best snowboarders in the world.

Like me, Jamieson was an Oregon boy, having been raised in Corvallis on the other side of the Cascades. A die-hard skateboarder and surfer, Kris was an outsider in high school; it was only a matter of time before he and his buddies became snowboarders too. In 1985 they saw an article on snowboarding in *Powder* magazine and all went out and bought Sims 1600s. From then on, they were hitting the Hoodoo Ski Bowl or Mount Bachelor every weekend and soon participating in the competitions.

In 1987, Kris's senior year in high school, he booked a trip to the Swatch World Snowboarding Championships in Breckenridge. "It was a huge event," he recalls, "and everyone in the world showed up. All fifty of us."

It was shortly after that I met Chris and Kris. One day I'd finally worked up the nerve to introduce myself, which, having nothing else to contribute, I concluded by pointing and saying, "I'm going to go do a backflip off that kicker." I nailed it and rode away without looking back, feeling like a complete fool. Fortunately, they didn't hold being an obnoxious, know-it-all *menehune* against me. In fact, we became good friends.

My parents thought Kris was a great guy, which was true. After he and his family moved to Bend following his high school graduation in 1987, my parents even let him borrow the station wagon to drive us to events. They also thought he was a good influence, which um, well, uh . . . let's just say I was able to resist.

"He never gave in to the bad habits we had . . . parties, dirt bikes, contraband, in a band, more than one girl at a time . . . the name Karol equals fast-cars-driven-way-too-fast," Jamieson says. "However, when the powder was deep, and the free-riding insane, Klug was always there ready to rip."

Actually, I think Chris and Kris behaved themselves around my parents because they were afraid of my mom.

"Kathy was the original soccer mom. In fact, she was the ultimate and gnarliest soccer mom ever. Dangerously gnarly soccer mom. You never got in her way, or you were in trouble," Jamieson says. "Kathy would have been the world's most famous vigilante if anyone ever laid a finger on her kids. The criminal would have never made it to jail. She would have strapped a bomb to her chest and bear-hugged the man who harmed her kids. That is why Klug may come off as a momma's boy, but truth is, Kathy let him do whatever he wanted. No curfew, and the mountain was always open. We would ride every day, and she never gave us any grief . . . and she always had healthy snacks waiting for us when we got back."

Whatever their "dirty habits," my friends also had positive influences on my life, especially my snowboarding career. For instance, early on I saw Jamieson really railing—carving powerful, clean turns—on his board, wearing what looked like hard-shell ski boots and plate bindings. It was obvious he could hold an edge like I couldn't even fathom with my soft boots and stock bindings. I asked him about the setup. But he didn't just talk about them, he showed up at my house that evening and gave me his extra pair of the fluorescent green Alpina mountaineering boots plus plate bindings.

The Alpinas were a lot softer laterally than ski boots but much stiffer than my regular snowboard boots, which meant my foot wouldn't move around in the boot as much, giving me more control. The plate bindings also held me more firmly on the board, which made for a faster, more precise response. The setup up was kind of deadly at first, almost too responsive. It was easy to catch an edge and get planted into the slope hard—the worst being the "Scorpion," which is when you're body-slammed face forward onto your stomach and the board's momentum continues until it smacks you in the back of the head (looks like a scorpion's tail). But it wasn't too long before I got the hang of it.

As Jamieson says, the new setup allowed us to "GO OFF" at the competitions. The Bachelor shred crew was winning everything. Even in free-riding, he says, "we were going faster, bigger, and sicker than anyone in the country."

However, the most important contribution Karol and Jamieson made to my growth as a snowboarder was not equipment. The summer before my sophomore year, Karol had picked up the telephone and called the coach of the Mount Bachelor Ski Education Foundation ski team, a colorful Canadian named Rob Roy, and asked if he could dry-land train with the ski team.

Rob was looking for more full-time athletes to support the program and said yes. A little later, Jamieson joined him and that's when they asked me. I didn't really understand why they invited me to participate; I mean, I was starting to rip and maybe they just wanted a token grom.

Rob had the credentials. He'd been a member of the Canadian National Ski Team Development Program and raced in some of the North American World Cups. After getting smoked by the great French skier Jean-Claude Killy, who was already a legend on the World Cup circuit and at the Olympics, he saw the writing on the wall and hung 'em up to find his true calling, which was coaching.

We soon had him hooked on coaching snowboarding. One reason was the challenge. Essentially, there was no "base of knowledge" regarding alpine snowboarding; he and whomever he trained would be starting at the beginning of a brand-new sport discipline. But he'd also seen some of the Mount Bachelor shred crew at play and thought that snowboarding was beautiful to watch, graceful and powerful, and he wanted to be part of its coming of age.

In that first year, my sophomore year in high school, I could participate only on weekends. However, as soon as football season was over in my junior year, I jumped in full-bore with Roy and the others, which now also included Peter Foley and Sanders Nye, who both came from ski racing backgrounds and knew the benefits of that sort of training environment, and Bill Harris and Scott Downey. During football season I carried a heavy load of seven classes, but during the winter quarters I could drop that to four. I would be done with my classes by noon and on the slope forty-five minutes later.

Rob saw coaching us as a personal challenge, but also recognized that it was a team effort. Together, our little group was literally inventing the techniques of alpine snowboard racing in North America from the ground up.

"I am a firm believer in the 'first you imitate, then you innovate' approach to technique, so whenever possible I paid attention to what the best in the world were doing," Rob says. "It didn't take too long for us to become among the best in the speed events, so we innovated from there."

With his coaching and my hard work, the 1989–1990 snowboarding season was my most successful yet. I managed three first place finishes in the Northwest Series races. Then in February 1990, I won the slalom and the Super-G at the U.S. Snowboarding Association Amateur National Championship at Snow Valley, California. I might have won the overall championship, but I launched right out of the half-pipe partway through my run and finished second to Mike Basich. In March I wrapped up the season by placing third in the slalom and third in the giant slalom at the U.S. Open at Stratton Mountain. They were the last races I would compete in as an amateur, in part due to the advice I got from the best snowboarder who (I think) ever lived.

As much as I respected Jamieson and Karol, I worshiped the snow Craig Kelly rode across. He was almost universally considered the best all-around rider at the time. Whenever he'd tolerate it, I'd follow him around the mountain, emulating his every move. I'd show up out of nowhere (actually lurking in the trees) to help him set race courses and train with him—not that my help was always so great, like the time I dropped the snow drill bit off the chairlift into several feet of powder. He just shook his head as I tried to shrink inside my parka.

After the 1989–1990 season ended, Kelly came to my house to talk with me and my parents about my future in the sport. My parents knew that he was making a living snowboarding and wanted his opinion of where the sport was going and what my possibilities might be.

Craig pretty much let them bounce sponsorship and other snowboarding business questions off him. I chimed in when I could, trying to steer the conversation toward letting me turn pro. I thought I was ready, but Dad had his reservations about how turning pro might jeopardize my college football plans. Craig was smart, articulate, and I think he helped win my 'rents over to at least the possibility of pursuing snowboarding as a career, if I chose it over college.

The time to make that decision was getting close. When my senior year of football was over, I threw myself into snowboarding harder than ever with the idea of testing the waters as a pro (though I was putting what money I didn't use for expenses into a trust account to preserve my amateur status). I was growing as a snowboarder, and evolving, and there with me was Rob Roy.

Once he agreed to start coaching snowboarders, Rob had thrown himself into the project, spending long hours studying film and watching us run gates to break down what worked and what did not. It helped that he was working with many of the best riders in North America at that time, all with different styles. Along with Karol, Jamieson, and me, we had Peter Foley, Taggart, Melhuse, Harris, plus new additions Kevin Delaney, Dave Dowd, Betsy Shaw, and Victoria Jealouse. We learned from each other as much as from Rob, but he was able to dissect what was working, and we all learned from it and adopted that particular skill in our own riding.

Rob invented new exercises to improve upon what we were doing. He'd have us ride with a long bamboo pole across our shoulders to emphasize keeping them level and the board underneath our bodies in the turn. Or he'd have us ride with only one foot in our bindings to improve our balance. Or we'd board with our hands on our hips to take our upper bodies out of the equation and eliminate counter-rotation to force us to use our hips, knees, and ankles to initiate the turns. He'd break out a whistle and have us switch to the new edge on command to quicken the crossover move from edge to edge.

I quickly learned that training with Rob was more than running gates or working on correct body position. He hadn't spent the last twenty-plus years as an elite athlete and then a coach without learning that it took more than natural athleticism or technical ability to reach the top. He knew that what separated the very good athlete from the great was physical preparation, including nutrition, and mental toughness.

Riding one hundred and fifty days a year with the inevitable crashes can take a toll on your body. Many times I've walked away from bad spills and said to myself, "That's why I work out. I would have broken my neck on that one if I weren't strong and flexible."

It also takes psychological strength. For starters, there's the fear factor. Crashing at fifty-plus miles per hour, especially on an icy race course, hurts—sometimes only bruises, but there was always the risk of concussions, torn ligaments, and broken bones as well. Beyond the fear, it requires focus to race on a slick surface where the tiniest mistake can be the difference between first and last place.

Rob worked us as hard as any football coach I ever had. A favorite method of his, but not ours, was weekly interval training on our slalom boards. He'd break a long run into two sections, and we were supposed to do as many tight slalom turns as we could in each section. He'd position an assistant coach—often his wife, Muffy, in the early years—at the middle and himself at the bottom to take our heartbeats and test our anaerobic capacity and lactate levels. I'd make a hundred-plus turns in between each coach. Think of each turn as squat-pressing twice your body weight from the G-force while moving your feet as quickly as possible from edge to edge.

By the time I'd get to the bottom, it was all I could do to stand long enough to get my pulse taken before collapsing. A normal resting heart rate is about sixty beats a minute; there were times in this interval training when mine exceeded two hundred—more than three per second. It felt like my heart was going to jump out of my chest, and I can remember an occasion or two when my breakfast actually did leave my stomach.

Our off-slope physical training during the summer was just as tough. We did a lot of core single-track mountain biking to build up our legs and improve our "vision"—the ability to process changing terrain and negotiate obstacles at high speeds, which really carried over into snowboarding. It was also good for developing balance and overcoming any fear of going downhill at crazy high rates of speed.

Rob was into road biking as well. It took me a while to get the idea that riding in the lead was a lot more exhausting. He'd encourage me to ride in front for a few minutes and then drop left and allow him to lead for a short time; this would conserve our energy and let us cover a lot of ground fast. Of course, I didn't like being in the back even if it was for a few minutes, so I'd stay too long at the front and toast myself. It might have taken a few dustings, but it taught me the importance of teamwork.

A lot of Rob's lessons and training ideas were unconventional. He had us attend yoga and ballet classes to keep us limber and gymnastic classes to help with our balance and muscle control. Sometimes after a day on the slopes, we'd convene at Blue Lodge on the slope of Mount Bachelor in our riding clothes and go to work with an aerobics instructor. It was a classic scene, a bunch of sweaty snowboarders dancing around in long underwear, pop music bouncing off the walls, while a buff little woman in Lycra yelled things like, *"And one, and two . . . that's right . . . and four. Hooo . . . hooo."* I'd get laughing, and once I start I can't stop. With this crazy hyena giggle of mine, pretty soon the entire team would be rolling on the floor, holding our sides, while the now-pissed-off aerobics instructor tried to make us shape up and get back with the program.

Rob even encouraged my surfing during the summer. It seemed like such a natural extension of snowboarding and was good cross-training for balance, core strength, and agility. Plus, I loved sitting off the Oregon coastline, watching dark green-blue waves crashing into the gray rocks or rolling up the long narrow beaches of ivory-colored sand. I felt at peace out there—for once not competing at something, just enjoying being healthy and strong and alive.

For all the rigorous physical training, Rob considered mental preparation the most important aspect of competing. He used to say there was nothing wrong with losing, it was *how* you lost that could be a problem. If you had prepared yourself to the best of your ability and it simply wasn't your day, then hold your head up, there would be another starting gate. "Losing is a key component of the evolution of great athletes," he'd say.

He taught us to deal with adverse situations on the race course through a variety of offbeat exercises, saying, "Athletes who want consistent training and competing conditions should take up bowling or ping-pong." One day it might be making us ride backward on our slalom boards as fast as we could, which usually resulted in a few good bell ringings. On another day, he'd have us go free-riding in a snowstorm or launching off some huge cornice—essentially a cliff of snow—where you might not even be able to see the landing below you until you were in the air. The idea was that no matter what the weather or slope conditions, we'd be ready for anything and wouldn't let things we couldn't control cause us to lose our focus.

We had plenty of spectacular crashes and yard sales with Rob pushing us. He loved speed events, which he'd excelled at during his racing career, so we trained a lot of Super-G and really fast, open giant slalom courses. But sometimes he got a little carried away there too. I can remember a couple of times I was so haired by the speed and air, I'd call it off after one run. Other times we just sat him down and said, "Dude, this is too gnarly."

Sometimes he backed off, but he knew that for ski racers to get to the top level they had to be aggressive, and he wanted us to develop the same attitude. You couldn't hold back because of fear and expect to beat the best.

Rob could be a lot of fun. He had a lot of great stories about his racing days, especially when he lived in Whistler, Canada, at a place he called "the house of the rising sun" because the parties would go on so long that they often saw the sunrise. But even for someone with his background, it took him some time to get used to all of us.

Peter Foley remembers one morning at a place they were staying at in Breckenridge when Delaney arrived with Dave Dowd for a training camp. "Dowd had been drinking on the ride up from Boulder, and in fact had been up all night partying," Peter says. "He absolutely reeked of booze and weed, and I'm pretty sure that was Rob's first contact with Dowd, or for that matter Rob's first contact with that kind of behavior from someone in sports. Rob kept an amazingly open mind in those days, as these were not the types of scenarios he was used to, coming from the more conservative established ski racing world."

Rob could also be real hard-core when it suited his purposes. He didn't like to waste time or effort once we got to the slope; it was all business. If for some reason my focus or performance wasn't up to his standards, he might call it a day after only two or three runs.

I hated stopping at times like that and wouldn't want to leave. "Let me do one more," I'd beg. I came from the school of more is always better and wanted to keep banging my head against the wall.

"No, you're done," he'd reply, and that would be the end of the argument. *Quality over quantity* was Rob's mantra. It was all about re-creating the race environment, where you couldn't afford mistakes, or if you made them, you had better scratch and claw your way back.

Often he would do or say something that would tick me off to the point where I would have liked to run him over on my board. But I also knew I was getting better, and faster, and I was soon rewarded for "our" efforts.

In my senior year Rob was taking the older members of the team off to Europe to race in World Cup events. I was jealous but knew from my experience as a backup quarterback that if I kept working, kept pushing myself, my time would come, and then I'd better make the most of it.

I was mostly racing Pro Snowboard Tour of America (PSTA) events. Sponsored by car manufacturer Nissan and Bodyglove, the maker of wetsuits, it was the premier race series in North America at the time. The events were scattered around the country and made for exciting TV with pro jumps off ten-foot ledges, usually to flat landings. Lots of riders were hitting hard and blowing out of their bindings for plenty of visual entertainment.

The PSTAs were hotly contested by great riders, including many up-and-coming racers who would be making names for themselves in the years to come. I thought they'd be a perfect transition for me to the international World Cup. Plus the television coverage pleased my sponsors, and big cash purses for expenses pleased Team Mom and Dad, as well as my wallet.

I also liked the PSTA events because they were parallel giant slaloms. Instead of racing against just the clock, as in a regular slalom or giant slalom, a PGS featured head-to-head races, rider against rider. The clock was used to narrow the field to sixteen riders in two qualifying rounds. The top sixteen then went head-to-head for two runs, winner advances, loser has to wait for the next event.

To win a PGS, the eventual victor, as well as the runner-up, would have to make nine total runs—one run to qualify for the final sixteen, eight runs up through the finals. Those of you who ski or snowboard recreationally can try to imagine making ten runs down steep slopes turning as fast and hard as you can. Or for you runners out there, try sprinting the length of a football field ten times against an opponent who's your equal while also maintaining your balance on an object moving across snow at high speeds and over big jumps. Now add the stress and adrenaline of competing when the difference between moving on and leaving disappointed may be a few hundredths of a second.

The PGS was an event that gave the advantage to the stronger athlete with the best endurance, and to the rider who could hold it together physically and mentally for ten runs while pushing the envelope. I felt the PGS races were a perfect fit for me. As a competitor, I loved racing with my opponent right next to me, someone tangible to beat. What I also liked about PGS was that a poor first run wouldn't necessarily knock you out of the hunt; you could make it up in the next run. The important thing was to never quit, no matter how far behind you were.

I'd left the Sims team after the previous season, or rather the Sims team fell apart. All of my teammates were on the Rossignol team, but Rossi sponsorships were limited and they didn't need me at that time.

However, I thought I had a good thing going when I signed with Apocalypse snowboards, a new company out of New York, which had hired French board builder Regis Rolland. He was a top French rider who had starred in the first big European snowboarding film, *Apocalypse Snow.*

My supposed sponsorship with Apocalypse didn't last long. First, they kept promising boards that didn't show. Then when they finally did show, I didn't like them. Finally, in my qualification run at the PSTA event on Mount Bachelor, I flew off a large jump and landed flat. The board cracked in two under my feet, but I somehow managed to cross the finish line with a good enough time to make it into the head-to-head competition.

My teammate, Peter Foley, who was already out of the race, helped me out by loaning me one of his custom-made Rossi boards. I ended up placing in the top ten at Bachelor and was in love with the board. I was supposed to give the board right back to Peter, but I kept it and went to the PSTA race in June Mountain, California, where I placed third.

I admit it. I was lame. Peter was always helping me out. When I was a grom, he was the one who taught me how to "tune" my board for competition by filing my edges to razor sharp and structuring the bottom of my board for speed, as well as how to apply wax for maximum speed on whatever snow conditions I faced, having learned the tricks as a ski racer. He also taught me to judge the condition and temperature of the snow, which affected the wax I chose for the race.

Now I compounded my snaking his board by running over a bunch of rocks with it. Then I made it even worse when I stopped into a shop and, in an attempt to fix the damage, let a guy use his belt sander on it, which completely ruined the bottom. When I finally returned the board and told Peter what I'd done, he was super bummed.

Needless to say, the incident strained our relationship. But it didn't stop me from calling the Rossignol team manager and telling her how much I liked their boards and pointing out how well I had done on Peter's. I had a couple of new boards in time for the next

PSTA event at Hunter Mountain, New York. They weren't the custom boards like the one Peter loaned me—it was a stock Rossi 173—but they were a hell of a lot better than the Apocalypse.

The next PSTA event at Hunter Mountain race course was gnarly; the pro jumps were ridiculously big and the landings even flatter than normal. Guys were going off, catching big air and blowing up on impact left and right, sometimes taking out the guy they were riding next to. But the jumps were nothing compared to what Rob had us going off of in training. I charged off all of them and nearly lost it partway through the finals when I did a full 360-degree turn coming around a gate, but I recovered, and at the end of the day, I was the last man standing. Finally! I'd made it to the top of a pro podium, and with an oversized check for forty-seven hundred dollars in my hands.

In February Rob spoke with my parents about my going to Europe for the Grundig ISF (International Snowboarding Federation) World Cup finals. He thought it would be a good idea for me to gain some racing experience in Europe and had in mind Garmisch-Partenkirchen, the famous Bavarian resort a couple of hours outside of Munich, Germany. My parents agreed, and Mom took me down to the post office in Bend to get my first passport.

Racing in Europe was really well supported by the fans and the sponsors, but we could hold our own in some events. We were as good as it got in the speed events—the Super-G and high-speed giant slalom—because of Rob's "death run" training. But the Euros worked us over in the slalom and more technical GS events.

Most of the European riders had been racing on snow since they were children. In the United States, kids join Little League baseball, or Pop Warner football, or club soccer teams. Traditionally, in the Alp regions of countries like Germany, Austria, Switzerland, Italy, and France, kids were on skis and belonged to the local racing teams, with professional coaches, practically from the time they could stand up.

Winter athletes, especially ski racers, are national heroes in Europe. They can't walk down the street of a town in their home countries, and often in neighboring nations, without being recognized and mobbed.

Snowboarding in Europe didn't have quite the same following as its older cousin, but the sport had caught on and spread like wildfire after the release of *Apocalypse Snow* in 1986. It wasn't long after that the Europeans began organizing their own competitions.

For the most part, European snowboarders didn't run into the same resentment from skiers and resort managers that we had faced in the United States. Euros were all about going fast and sliding across snow—didn't matter if it was skis, snowboards, sleds . . . whatever they could find. Their resorts tended to be less stuffy—and probably less safety-minded—than ours, and skiers were used to seeing just about anything on the slopes. And Europeans loved racing, so when snowboarders decided to try gates, they were welcomed.

The skiers who came over to snowboarding brought with them that technical expertise and coaching they'd received since childhood. They didn't race in perfect snow conditions every day, like we often did in the United States. They were used to training in inconsistent snow in a blizzard on top of European glaciers. They were versatile riders who'd been taught how to compete on snow from childhood.

We all traveled together: Rob, Karol, Foley, Bill Harris, Shannon Melhuse, and Sanders Nye. Being the youngest and this being my first time outside of the United States except for Canada, I immediately began redlining all of them with my endless questions and wide-eyed wonder. They were pretty patient, but I'm sure I drove them nuts.

It was just all so new to me, including the driving. Rob was at the wheel of our rented VW van; the rest of us were in back, checking the scenery. Even going as fast as the van would travel, maybe 75 miles an hour, if he dared get in the left lane to pass someone, a Porsche, Beamer, or Benz would be up on his tail and flashing its lights within a couple of seconds. Then they'd flip us off as they went by at 200-plus klicks (about 120 miles an hour). They loved to haul ass! I thought it was so rad—I was used to slow piece-of-junk pickups in Central Oregon and the Pooper.

I was also surprised, when we arrived in Garmisch, to see what a big deal a snowboard race in Europe could be. They love their winter sports. Snowboarding didn't have quite the same following as ski racing, but it was still a lot bigger deal than I was used to seeing. There were thousands of people there, most of them sauced and eating Wuerstels (hot dogs on steroids), and they swarmed the slope armed with cowbells and air horns, ready to cheer their favorites.

I couldn't speak a lick of German. None of us could. I remember on one of our first dinners together out on the town, the waiter brought menus to us. Everything was in German and we were like, *"Now what are we supposed to do?"* So we closed our eyes and played pin the tail on the dinner by just pointing to places on the menu. A few of us lucked out and nailed a good meal, but others ended up with some sauerkraut/cow's udder mystery dish. After that we ate quite a few times at the only American restaurant in town—Pizza Hut.

Another fond memory was visiting the Hallenbad (the aqua center) to swim and jump off the ten-meter platforms. I kept sneaking into the sauna to see the naked chicks. I couldn't believe it—what a crazy place, you could drive a hundred-plus miles an hour and get sweaty next to some nude babe.

The mountain, however, was intimidating. The Super-G was held up on the Zugspitze, the highest part of Garmisch. There were only two ways to get to the top. You either took the gnarliest tram, suspended on a cable between only two towers, hundreds of feet off the ground, or you had to take a train that actually went inside the mountain and came out on top. I was sketched out by both.

There wasn't much training space, so Rob had to get imaginative. He set our Super-G training course right across the track of the Poma lift (a series of poles with seats on the end that hang from a cable; you're supposed to put it between your legs and let it pull you up the hill). We had to judge our run just right to rip through the people being towed up the hill.

The first day of the event was the giant slalom. I sucked. But Shannon Melhuse took third, which was great except that he'd taken first at a World Cup event a couple weeks earlier in Breckenridge, Colorado, and this finish cost him the overall giant slalom/Super-G title, which went instead to Austrian Dieter Happ.

The next day was the slalom event, fortunately held adjacent to the landing of the Nordic jump at the bottom of the mountain, so I didn't have to take the tram or train. It was practically in the town and people loved that; they could drink, eat sausages, and watch the action without having to go anywhere.

The race course was super steep and, being at a lower elevation, there was no snow. It seemed like we were riding on a mixture of slush, gravel, and grass. To get to the top of the course, we were supposed to ride another Poma, but there wasn't enough snow to cover the track, because they'd pushed every bit they could find onto the race course. We had to carry our boards under one arm while holding the pole with the other and sort of bound along (moonwalk-like) over patches of mud and rocks. You had to be careful not to veer off the course too, or you'd end up face-down in the mud.

I was absolutely in awe of the riders I was up against, all the best in the world. It was my first Euro World Cup; I was out of my element and nervous as hell. As if that weren't core enough, they'd salted the slope, which caused what snow there was to melt and then refreeze into a rock-hard ice rink.

I took my Rossi and filed the edges as sharp as I could get them to hold me on the ice. I was a rookie and so had a starting number at the back of the pack. Nobody outside of my team even knew who I was. Finally, my name was called and I entered the start gate, grabbing the bars on either side, using my arms to propel my board back and forth, and finally busted out onto the snow. The world went silent— no Rob, no famous Euros, no crowd—just me and the course. Time to attack the fall line, tipping my board from edge to edge, toe-side to heel-side, as I carved around the gates.

I didn't make the podium that day—in fact, I was eighth. But that was eighth "attacking from the back" against the very best riders in the world, and in my very first European World Cup race.

What's more, I was the top American finisher and had proved to them as well as myself that I could compete at that level. That night I tried my first experience at après racing Euro-style when Rob escorted me to the discotheque, but it was so smoky, we left after five minutes. Instead I went back to my hotel room and fell asleep dreaming about racing in Europe.

Chapter 6

Leap of Faith

"This snowboarding isn't going anywhere." The headmaster of Deerfield Academy spread his hands as if he was only trying to be reasonable and looked at my parents with a tight smile.

We were sitting in his office, a formal place with a high ceiling and heavy oak trim. The walls were covered with framed Ivy League documents and other prestigious accolades, as well as the photographs of former headmasters—who also seemed to be frowning down at me in disapproval. Maybe that was my imagination, but it was clear that the current version thought snowboard racing was a frivolous pursuit and expected my parents to agree with him.

When I graduated from Mountain View High School in the spring of 1991 with a grade point average of 3.9, I'd been faced with some tough choices. My GPA would have allowed me to attend pretty much any large university, and I could have tried to make their football teams as a walk-on. But at 6' 3" and 175 pounds, I was still considered too scrawny for Division I, so while there'd been some interest from the University of Oregon, Oregon State, and Stanford, in the end there were no scholarship offers.

Several smaller colleges offered scholarships. Two of them were in Oregon—Linnfield College, in McMinnville, which had the longest winning record in college football, and Willamette University in Salem—and another, Trinity College, in Hartford, Connecticut. But I decided to delay my transition into college ball.

I didn't have anything against the smaller programs, but I still dreamed of playing for a larger school, which I thought would give me a better chance of going to the big show, the NFL. If I was going to do that I needed to get bigger and stronger. So I decided to attend Deerfield, a classic New England prep school with an Ivy League curriculum, which would give me another year of high school football as a postgraduate student and time to add muscle. The academics would be good for me too, but waiting to get into a Division I football program wasn't my only reason for putting off college.

I knew that the higher I climbed in either football or competitive snowboarding, the harder it was going to be to do both because of the time demands. I would have to make a choice, but I wanted to delay the decision for as long as possible and thought Deerfield would give me another year to see if time would help me decide which way to go.

I was given a partial scholarship to attend Deerfield, which was as expensive as it was prestigious. Along with an excellent academic reputation, the Massachusetts school boasted one of the top prep football programs on the East Coast. The highlight of the year was when Nanny showed up for a game. She sat me down afterward and let me know where I'd done well and what needed "a little improvement," then started in on the coach and my teammates.

I enjoyed playing for Coach Jim Smith, who was a legend in the prep school ranks. However, I was homesick a lot; plenty of nights, I called the 'rents from the basement pay phone of my dormitory, crying. Yet, it wasn't just family I missed. I wanted mountains. The rolling hills around Deerfield were pretty enough, but they couldn't compare to the Cascades. At home I would stare at the peaks for hours, daydreaming about screaming down some of those narrow couloirs and untracked snowfields.

So I was looking forward to the upcoming snowboarding season, when I would be back in mountains, surrounded by the laid-back, fun-seeking camaraderie that is unique to snowboarders.

That past summer Rob Roy and Chris Karol had put together a snowboard camp at Mount Hood. They hired me for five hundred bucks a month, plus all I could eat and all the gates I could run. I coached, drove the camp bus, and lived with the campers, including some great young riders like Jeff Archibald, a long-haired hacky sack king from Ogden, Utah, whose parents sent him to the camp as his high school graduation present. (He impressed Rob enough to be invited to join our team.) But I mostly worked my ass off training with Chris and getting a lot of individual attention from Rob.

I was motivated by my eighth-place finish in my first World Cup at Garmisch-Partenkirchen and determined to take my riding to the next level. I ran so many gates that I'd see myself running them in my sleep and probably tossed and turned as I carved toe-side, then heel-side, then toe-side.

When the World Pro Snowboarding Team, as we were now called, left for Europe at the end of the summer to continue training, I was envious as hell. I was off to prep school back East, but I thought that when football was over, I could catch up to them and jump right into snowboarding with a schedule like I had in high school.

I planned to concentrate on the ISF World Cup circuit, most of which was held in Europe, as well as a few major events in North America. I made an appointment to see the Deerfield headmaster a few weeks before Thanksgiving break to go over my competition schedule and my racing aspirations for the winter. I was used to training, including free-riding days, 100 to 150 days, and competing in no fewer than 20 events over the course of a season. When I explained this, the headmaster laughed. There was no way, he said. "We can probably excuse you for a few days but no more."

Well, no way was I going for that, either. I had busted my butt in school and managed all As and Bs for the fall trimester, despite the rigors of football practice, games, and travel. With a little cooperation, I didn't see why I couldn't pull the same grades and still snowboard.

Even if what he suggested allowed me to make some of the events, I wouldn't be competitive. Winning at Hunter Mountain and placing eighth among the world's best at Garmisch-Partenkirchen had proved that I could compete at the highest level, and I'd improved a lot after my summer on snow at Mount Hood. But I knew I was going to have to work still harder if I wanted to be one of the best riders in the world.

It wasn't just about time to train, either. I couldn't just show up the day of a race and expect to win. It was important to arrive a few days before a major event. The sport was totally at the mercy of Mother Nature, who on a moment's notice could change the snow and weather conditions. You had to be there to adjust—maybe file the edges a little sharper and figure out which wax would run fastest on that particular snow. I also liked to ride the terrain for a day to get a feel for it.

The headmaster didn't see it that way. I left his office and got on the telephone to my parents, who were coming out for my final football game anyway, and set up another meeting with the headmaster to see if something could be worked out.

The meeting with my parents a few weeks later was friendly at first, but he was adamant. Deerfield wasn't set up to design a school schedule around snowboard racing, like the Stratton Mountain School in Vermont, or Carrabasset Valley Academy at Sugarloaf in Maine. That's when he said, "This snowboarding isn't going anywhere."

Whatever the headmaster thought he would accomplish when he made his comment, it crystallized my decision to go in the opposite direction. I was going to give up football, at least for the time being. If snowboarding didn't work out, well, there were always the small college football programs. I got up and left the room with my parents right behind me. When I talked to them afterward, they told me to think carefully about my choices but in the end to follow my heart.

When I got home for Thanksgiving, I wrote to the headmaster telling him of my decision. I was glad I'd gone to Deerfield and learned a lot, but the best part about the experience was that it helped me see clearly what I really wanted to do with my life.

No matter what the headmaster said, I was sure that snowboarding was going somewhere, and I was going along for the ride. I still believed in what my friend Tad Dobson and I had talked about as

Team Klug or Team Jude drove us through the night to some event that now seemed so long ago.

Tad no longer had the same dream. In our senior year of high school I had stepped it up to another level—training every day, focusing on the PSTA pro events and then the trip to Garmisch-Partenkirchen. Tad chose another road. He didn't do any of the pro events, and that fall after graduation he chose to go to the University of Washington on a golf scholarship. But I still believed. I still wanted to go to the Olympics, stand on the podium with the "Star-Spangled Banner" playing, a medal around my neck, and my family and friends in the crowd celebrating with me.

The Olympic rules had changed to allow professionals to compete (at least legally—it could be argued that ski racers, skaters, and hockey teams had been circumventing the rules for years). Snowboarding still wasn't going to be an event at the upcoming games in Albertville, France, but at least I didn't have to worry any more about putting any winnings into a trust account for the day when it was allowed.

Still, deciding to become a professional snowboarder was a huge leap of faith, because there wasn't much money in it. If you were lucky and really good, you picked up some sponsors and maybe won a few purses; usually there was money for the top eight or ten places but not much if you weren't on the podium. Only a few alpine snowboarders made more than a subsistence living, and most of them were Euro-pean, where support for racing was much stronger than in the United States. I had a partial sponsorship from Rossignol, which essentially got me several racing boards and covered my entry fees and some expenses. However, I would still be relying on Team Mom and Dad for most of what it took to get by, including coaching fees, food, travel, and accommodations.

After Thanksgiving I was off to Europe to join up with Rob Roy. He'd also taken a leap of faith and left the Mount Bachelor Ski Educa-tion Foundation ski team to devote himself entirely to snowboard coaching. There were now more full-time snowboarders than skiers in the program, and he believed snowboarding also had more potential for growth. He'd witnessed firsthand the explosion of snowboarding in Europe and Japan and decided to form the World Pro Snowboard Team (WPST), or as I told a reporter, "Rob Roy's Fly Boys and Freaks."

I'd adopted the name from teammate Kevin Delaney, but it was a good description of that crew. Some like me didn't drink much or smoke pot, but the others more than made up for what we didn't do. Sober or not, we all played as hard as we rode, and it was a fun crew to be rallying around Europe with.

For all of our quirks, the people on that team comprised a big chunk of the core of alpine snowboarding in North America and were instrumental in its development. The roster that fall included Roy, Karol, Foley, Nye, Taggart, Melhuse, Harris, Dowd, Delaney, Shaw, and Jealouse, plus Canadian newcomers Nelson Jenson and Ross Rebagliati. We even had a top Austrian rider join the team, Gerry Ring. We'd met him at the World Cup in Garmisch-Partenkirchen the previous season, and Rob convinced him to come to Oregon for spring training camp. He was a great friend and taught us a lot about our sport as well. He brought a different riding technique along with an international racing perspective, and was the best prepared and most intense competitor I'd ever met in racing.

The WPST was one of only four major alpine snowboard training programs in the world. The others were the International Snowboard Team (IST) out of France, the Burton Europe Factory Team out of Innsbruck, and our chief rivals in North America—"Jerry's Kids," otherwise known as the "Cross-M cult," from Truckee, California.

The Cross-M cult members were led by their dark lord, coach Jerry Masterpool, who looked a little like a crazed cowboy poet with his long wild hair, goatee, and the full-length duster coat he favored. In fact, he was a rancher when he wasn't coaching snowboarding and claimed to have ski raced on the World Cup circuit under another name. It was all very mysterious. You'd see his disciples at the races, their clothes and equipment covered with the Cross-M logo. Jerry had a reputation for being a hard-ass and pushing his racers to the edge. If we cursed Rob for setting such gnarly courses that we almost ended up in the rocks on the side, Jerry's kids lived in terror because sometimes they actually did. I swear they all had a sort of glazed look on their faces, as if they'd been brainwashed.

Or so the legend (from his own racers) goes. I liked Jerry a lot. He was a good coach and motivator, producing some of the best racers from North America, including Canadians Jasey-Jay Anderson and Mark Fawcett, and American Mike "Joker" Jacoby.

I got along well with everyone on the team, except for one, and that was my own damn fault. Peter Foley had never quite forgiven me for "borrowing" his board for so long at the end of the previous season, so there was already some tension between us. Then it got worse, and it was sort of, kind of . . . hell, it *was* my fault again.

In early December, we were in Ischgl, Austria, preparing for a World Cup event when Rob decided we needed to get out and train harder for the slalom. Unfortunately, it was six in the morning and still dark outside. The European snowboard racers, who were just getting up, looked outside and saw us leaving for the slope and thought we were crazy. By the time we arrived at the course, there was barely enough light to see from one gate to the next, plus the snow conditions were terrible. I was amazed I didn't get wrecked. Peter wasn't so lucky—he caught an edge in a rut and snapped his ankle.

I was officially sponsored now by Rossignol, although not for much—entry fees, some expense money, and stock Rossi 173 racing boards. So I started drooling when three new custom race boards— one for Karol, one for Melhuse, and one for Foley—showed up a couple of weeks later at a World Cup race in Val d'Isere, France.

I coveted Peter's board, which has to be against another snow-board commandment. But I was riding fast, fast enough to impress Melhuse, who was the top guy for Rossignol because of his wins the previous year. We'd become good friends too, and sometimes roomed together, which gave me the opportunity to sort of, kind of, talk him into mentioning to Rossignol's team manager, Rob McCutcheon, that maybe, I should get Peter's board, which is what happened.

I was a snake, but I was also young, immature, and looking out for Number One. Peter was angry. "That's my board," he told me once, but then didn't mention it again, though I could tell he wasn't going to forgive me for a while. We didn't have much to say to each other for the rest of the year, and I was sad about that. I knew it was my fault, and I missed his friendship and guidance.

All these years later, Peter, who would soon drop out of racing only to become the head coach of the U.S. Snowboard Team, says he believes that selfishness is a common trait among really successful athletes.

"I completely understand the motivation for Chris's actions," he says. "The results he was able to obtain on those boards came at a critical time in his career (no money, trying to decide what to do with his life, etc.). So for his sake it is probably significant that he was a squeaky enough wheel to get those boards."

Peter notes that the other side of the equation is interesting as well, "because not having those boards also came at a critical point in *my* career (no money, trying to decide what to do with my life, etc.).

"We can't know for sure if having those boards would have been enough for me to get the kind of results I needed to keep competing or not, most likely it just accelerated the inevitable: he would have a career as an athlete, and I would have a career as a coach."

As a coach, he says, it's interesting to examine the outcome. "Was Chris successful as an athlete more because of talent or temperament? Was I destined to be more successful as a coach than an athlete due to talent or temperament? Because we all know I have incredible talent. Hehehe."

Peter and I have since mended fences, but back then I guess I was pretty self-centered. I was focused on what I needed to succeed; it was a tough, competitive world for a nineteen-year-old kid to negotiate. "When Chris was young it was almost unbearable at times for his teammates and coaches," Peter said in March 2004. "But I have seen him become more aware of his behavior and make what I consider huge improvements in his character every year of his life."

I was lucky to grow up with a good group of people as role models, both competitors and friends. We were different than other athletes, probably because of our shared backgrounds as outcasts or rebels.

On the race course, snowboarders competed as hard as any other athletes. Everybody wanted to win. Yet when the day was over, it was time to party with our friends, the same guys we'd been battling a few hours before. There were rivalries and personality clashes, but for the most part, snowboarders were a laid-back, easygoing group—the type of personalities who had been attracted to the sport in the first place. We came from a dozen countries and spoke a half-dozen different languages, but we had two things in common that made us a tight-knit community: our love of snowboarding and our love of competition.

Some things had not changed. Reggae, punk, or Euro-techno—some kind of music was blaring from the speakers at the events to entertain the younger crowds that snowboarding attracted (though my teammates sometimes teased me because I also liked country-western). There were still racers on the tour who got high between every run, racers in spiked hair and dog collars, and guys whose idea of working out was getting up before noon. The after-race parties were legendary and, for the competitors who were already out of the running, often got started before the race was over.

I've never been much of a drinker—one or two beers is about all. As my friends are far too willing to point out, I can't "hold my liquor," at least not in the place it was intended to be held. On the handful of occasions when I have overindulged, it usually wasn't a pretty sight.

Of course, the older riders on the circuit tried their best to get "the kid" plastered on a couple of occasions. And I can remember one party during the 1992 season that I did have a hand in sending myself over the top.

We were at a World Cup race in Gsiesertal, Italy (pronounced

SEES-ser-tall, or as Kevin Delaney called it, "Seize up and fall," after blowing a nearly two-second lead after the first run and winding up in fourteenth). This particular event was sponsored by the local Mafia, at least that's what we were told, and nobody was going to ask a lot of questions, if you know what I mean.

Let's say conditions were not optimum. The race piste was pretty much a slightly tilted cow pasture with a T-bar to drag us up the "hill." There wasn't really even any snow; the locals had just sprayed the field with water and let it freeze until it was like racing on an enormous ice skating rink.

I finished seventh that day—which, having not even sniffed a podium since Hunter Mountain, was a hell of an accomplishment for me. In other words, I was primed for a disaster that night.

This being Italy (in the Sud Tirol region, where most of the locals still spoke German because it used to be a part of Austria), the party after the race was as important as the event itself. Everybody—locals, spectators, racers, team sponsors, the Mob—headed for the huge party tent the locals had constructed at the finish line and started drinking like there was no tomorrow.

However, the racing wasn't finished. They'd decided that after everybody was good and lubricated, the top eight men and women finishers would reenact the finals under the lights.

The race organizers passed a hat among the several hundred people in the tent to raise the prize money. This was in the days before the Eurodollar, and there was probably a thousand dollars in a mishmash of every European currency by the time the crowd and the sixteen riders, including me, headed outside for the race.

Norwegian Ashild Loftus won the women's race, and I won the men's. Then we put our heads together. The standard was for 10 percent to go back toward the bar tab to help keep the party rolling, but we decided to donate the entire proceeds to that night's sauce fest. Next thing I knew, I was behind the bar in my speed suit and race boots, having replaced the bartender, who was dancing on one of the tables. The drinks weren't good—I had no idea what I was doing and furthermore couldn't understand German or Italian—but they were strong, as I knew from sampling a few.

It wasn't long before the tent was rocking. The music was cranked and everybody was Euro-dancing on the floor, the tables, the chairs, and even the bar, bouncing up and down and into each other, the racers still in their suits and boots.

Après can go all night in Europe, and this one didn't disappoint anybody by ending early. I woke up the next morning in our Italian pension, the *Gasthof Hoffman,* with a mean dwarf pounding on the inside of my skull with a hammer. When I could open my eyes without the light jabbing a white-hot poker into my brain, I looked down and saw that I was still wearing my liquor-stained speed suit. My feet seemed unusually heavy, which was because I was also wearing my now-cracked-and-ruined racing boots. I remembered something about jumping off the bar, but the rest was a blur of pain. What the hell, I didn't like those boots anyway—they were too stiff. That morning seemed like the right time to change.

Actually, it could have been worse. One of the riders who'd taken his boots off to dance discovered when he was packing the next morning that one of the Burton Europe team managers had peed in them.

Such was the après race lifestyle of Euro snowboarding. I was lucky that I didn't like to drink, or I might have lost a lot more brain cells than I did. However, I soberly partied with the best of them, and I can remember many a night—or should I say dawn—walking home in my snowboard gear after dancing until my legs were putty (and please don't believe my friends who say I dance like Elaine from the television show *Seinfeld,* like someone stuck my finger in a light socket, arms flailing, absolutely no rhythm).

I didn't make the podium that year, but I did place fifth in the giant slalom and sixth in the slalom in February 1992 at the World Cup race in Rusutsu, Japan. The interesting thing about that race is I had broken my hand in training a few weeks earlier and had a cast on my arm. I didn't know it, of course, but I had just started a trend of doing well after a medical setback.

After being kept off the podium for so long, it felt good to at least be knocking on the door. It was a memorable trip for other reasons as well. The Japanese were enthusiastic about the sport, which had come on big-time in the late 1980s. They just weren't sure what to make of North American/Euro snowboarders, and there was the inevitable clash of cultures.

Or maybe it was our lack of culture. For instance, the event organizers in Rusutsu were livid after Shaun Palmer, known to all as "Mini-Shred," rode his board down the hotel's waterslide. I didn't think we would be invited back. Rob, however, says we did get invited to return, but the organizers attempted to put all of us in the employee housing part of the resort—away from the tourists.

"That lasted one night," Rob recalls. "The riders threatened to pack up and go home unless things improved. Things improved, but after that we were never invited back again. . . . This was my first introduction to the dark side or 'bad boy' side of the snowboard culture. I believe that Chris Karol referred to it as the 'seek and destroy' mentality. I didn't like what I saw. I wondered to myself, and to some of the WPST team members, if I had made a bad decision to embrace snowboarding as a sport and as a culture. I didn't want 'my' athletes to be 'bad boys' and I made that clear. Chris Klug was never a problem as a 'bad boy' . . . In fact he was the epitome of our 'work hard–play hard–be welcomed back' philosophy. I had learned over the years the importance of our on-the-road support network; supportive hoteliers and mountain managers were very important to our success."

I should point out that my life on the road was more than just racing, traveling, and partying. It was also my education, and it was a good one. Instead of attending college, I was learning about other cultures and studying languages firsthand. Whenever we got to someplace new, I tried to take in the sights, visiting museums and hiking up to castles.

I was also learning how to be a professional athlete from Gerry

Ring, who was about five years older than me and had been one of the best racers in Europe for years. He taught me the business side of the sport while driving a hundred-plus miles an hour from race to race all over Europe.

As the season began to wind down, I was convinced that I had chosen the right road when I left Deerfield. However, the road very nearly reached an early dead end.

I was in Mariazell, Austria, and called home to check in. It was always good to talk to my family when I was far away, but this time when I talked to my dad, I could tell something was wrong. His voice sounded troubled, and he was not his usual positive, enthusiastic self. He told me he was having problems with his businesses, and it meant big changes financially for the family. He hated to say it, but it was clear: Team Mom and Dad could no longer afford to fully sponsor a snowboarder in Europe.

I knew it was killing him to tell me that. They'd always sacrificed for us kids, and especially me—not just financially, but also with those long days and nights driving hundreds of miles to spend hours cheering for me in the snow as I pursued a sport that might never pan out as a career.

I assured my parents that I would be okay. I bravely volunteered that it was time for me to make this snowboarding pay for itself or go on to something else. Then, as soon as we got off the telephone, I panicked.

The perhaps unrealistic high expectations I'd had after the win at Hunter Mountain had not materialized. I wasn't automatically winning every race, nor did I have a major sponsor. I was getting some expenses and support from Rossignol, but it wasn't enough to pay Rob's coaching fees—about six thousand dollars a season—plus travel, food, and lodging. All the things that my parents had helped to cover but now could not.

Now my winnings went to getting to the next event, and if I didn't perform well there, I couldn't go to the next one after that. I wasn't going to make it, and finally broke down in tears to Rob. He told me to hold on, everything would be okay and he would help. He had some contacts with Burton Snowboards—in fact, he was good buddies with Joe Zangerl, a former coach of the Austrian National Ski Team, the father of alpine snowboard racing in Europe, and current head coach of Burton Europe. Joe knew of me and said he'd see if he could get the company to sponsor me. One of my newer teammates, Betsy Shaw, rode for Burton, and she also introduced Rob to Dennis Jensen, the marketing manager for Team Burton at that time.

Rob, Joe, and Betsy saved my career. Near the end of that 1991–1992 season, we were at a World Cup race in Aspen, Colorado, when I was invited to dinner at the Mezzaluna restaurant with Burton Europe team riders Peter Bauer, Jean Nerva, Dieter Happ, Cla Mosca, and Martin Freinademetz, who were also some of the best racers in the world. What I didn't realize at the time was that the dinner was really an interview. If they thought I was the right guy, I'd get their endorsement at Burton; if not, I was going to be out in the cold.

A couple of weeks later, I got a call from Jensen, who offered me a one-year contract that would cover my expenses. Talk about a load lifted. My path had appeared headed for the precipice, but then I veered back onto the course at the last moment and was picking up speed.

Chapter 7

On the Road

I nervously waited my turn in the starting area above the giant slalom course on *La Face de Belvarde* and just about jumped out of my boots when Rob Roy patted snow on the back of my neck. "What the hell did you do that for?" I sputtered.

"Focus," he said.

Focus. It was December 1993, still early in the season, but it was important to me that I focused and got off to a great start.

The previous season of 1992–1993 hadn't gone as well as I'd hoped, though I had managed to finish on a high note. I thought I'd done everything right going into the year, including moving back to Bend to train. My parents had moved to Pinehurst, North Carolina, where my dad took over the management of a thirty-six-hole golf club and resort called Foxfire, but I still loved Central Oregon. When my old football buddy Jim Patterson and his family offered to let me stay with them, I made Bend my base camp and went to North Carolina only to visit.

There were several advantages to this plan. One was that it gave me the opportunity to see Missy. We'd stayed in touch, writing letters and sometimes talking on the telephone. However, the relationship didn't seem to be going anywhere. I was hoping for more—after all, I was now a sophisticated man of the world, a sponsored rider who'd raced on the most famous slopes of Europe—but she still just wanted to be friends.

"My mom loves to remind me of the time I came home from seeing Chris and she asked me why he wasn't my 'boyfriend,'" Missy recalls. "I said, 'Are you kidding? He's so hyper, he'd drive me crazy.' . . . He was also kind of a geek. . . . By the way, I never told Chris this."

Whatever. I was *never* a geek. She just liked losers and jerks (I don't mean, you Charley, honest!). But I had to be happy with being her buddy. We were both competitive and brought that edge to our activities, including hundreds of games of tennis.

"He didn't want to lose to a girl," Missy says. "Imagine that! He broke two rackets playing against me, because he slammed them into the cement surface when he got beat. We both talked smack the whole time. One of us would fall apart and the other would win.

"We bet dinner sometimes—even then he was notoriously cheap, so you KNOW he hated to lose, and preferred to bet ice cream because he could get it for free at his mom's shop."

As I was saying, the *main* advantage of living in Bend was that I could train with Rob Roy. We ran gates on Mount Bachelor in the late spring until the snow was gone. Then in the summer months, we got in a lot of off-snow training or headed to Mount Hood's glacier to get back on it.

Life was good. I was in peak physical condition with a sweet new contract, so I didn't have to stress over finances. I was especially excited when fall rolled around and Rob had decided that the team needed to move to Europe to train, race, and learn from their snow racing culture.

We invaded Laengenfeld, Austria, a small village in the Oetztal Valley fifteen minutes from the town of Soelden and twenty from the Rettenbach glacier, where we would train. Laengenfeld was a quiet little farming community of maybe a thousand people nestled in the Oetztal, or Oetz Valley. The valley was typically beautiful Tyrolean—accented by the glacier-fed Oetztaler Ache river and hemmed in by spectacularly abrupt gray peaks like the Nederkogel and the Wildspitze, which at 3,774 meters is the highest in the Tyrolean Alps.

We were constantly hiking in the area or riding single-track bike trails that seemed to go straight up the mountains as though they'd been made by the local wild goats. You never knew what you might find over the next hill, such as the pretty *kapellen* (chapels) that dotted the valley, or even an entire village tucked away between the arms of some peak, like the one where I discovered my favorite lunch of *keiserschmarren* (a pancake-like Austrian dish served with applesauce and plum sauce).

Soelden has hosted ski and snowboard World Cups since 1985 and could draw as many as twenty-five thousand spectators for a ski event and maybe half that for snowboarding. They'd gather to watch while blowing air horns, jangling cowbells, and getting fueled up on schnapps. Then, inspired by the racers, they'd hop in their Mercedes, Audis, or Porsches and speed back down the fifteen-kilometer, one-lane alpine road with a dozen hairpin switchbacks, to return to the valley. Not always in one piece.

Of course, every morning I had to travel the same road with the team to train. It was a nutso drive when the pilot was French-Polish rally driver and top snowboarder Andre Machevski, who liked to blast Pink Floyd as he tore around the corners, or Chris Karol, who was usually playing punk rock at cranium-rattling decibels.

The Rettenbach glacier was a popular area to train because of the year-round snow—or more accurately, ice. Ten to fifteen training lanes for laying out courses were set aside for too many teams vying for the best spots. Coaches would line up an hour before the lift opened, their arms loaded with training gates and snow drills, then stampede for the front of the line when the lift started up. I swear Rob would get more fired up for each morning's mad dash than he did for our races.

(European lift lines are insane anyway. Instead of waiting in neat lines like in the United States and for the most part giving each other enough space, Europeans sort of form a herd and push toward the front of the line and don't really care whose new board or skis they trample. Rob told us about a female ski racer he once coached from the States who kept asking the man behind her to get off her skis. When he ignored several requests, she turned around and decked him.)

The views from the glacier were incredible, a huge panorama of the Alps stretching off to the horizon in every direction, most of it above timberline. However, down in the valley it was often hard to see more than a hundred yards because of the fog, so much so that we renamed our home away from home Laengen-fog.

In Laengen-fog our team mushroomed into a snowboarding United Nations. Rob was becoming one of the best snowboard trainers in the world, and even established European racers were joining. Living under the same roof and training with us were Canadian, Swiss, French, Dutch, Polish, Italian, Austrian, German, and Japanese riders.

In November we Americans decided to treat the others to a traditional Thanksgiving dinner with all the fixings. I was really fired up about the whole event. The holiday had always been a big deal at my parents' house. Football games on the television and outside in the yard. Stuffing ourselves until we couldn't eat any more, then stuffing ourselves again. Most of all, just being near my family and thankful for all we had, especially each other. I was really homesick and threw myself into our preparations for a Thanksgiving feast (minus the cranberry sauce, which we couldn't find anywhere). But later I found a quiet corner and called my family.

Food and eating did seem to take up a lot of my time and energy in Europe. Whenever we drove, the highlights of the trip for me weren't the ancient castles, or panoramic views of the sunlit Alps, or the quaint villages with their thin-steepled churches . . . or even the girls. Those were all nice, but the best part was stopping at the *Rosenbergers,* or their equivalent in Switzerland, the *Movenpicks,* which were enormous Euro truck stops. Inside, piled up in great mounds were salads and fruits and all kinds of breads; metal trays yielded all the great European staples from brats a foot long covered with gelatinous brown gravy to breaded Wiener schnitzel, spätzle, and apfelstrudel. And, of course, that great continental favorite pommes frites, otherwise known as french fries. You could have everything loaded up on your plate within minutes of walking through the door and sit down to feast.

Betsy remembers me drooling with anticipation when we were still fifty kilometers from one of those roadside eating palaces. I'd be whining, "I'm so hungry, my body is eating itself."

"No one doubted that this was probably true in his case," Betsy says. "He would heap his plate high, and then sit down and take a full half hour to eat it. While we were busy devouring our food, Klug was worshipping every single bite."

I ate so slowly, the team complained that I should get a job at *Rosenbergers* when I retired from snowboarding so that I could gorge all day. Kevin Delaney even talked the staff at one of the truck stops into giving me a *Rosenberger* employee name tag. (In the spirit of full disclosure, I should point out that Nick Smith, who later became one of my coaches on the U.S. Snowboard Team, thinks that Betsy grossly underestimates the amount of time it takes me to eat at a *Rosenberger*. He swears that when we stop, he knows it's going to be a two-hour layover, most of it watching me slowly consume my food.)

In my defense, I couldn't seem to eat any faster. I didn't understand it yet, and neither did my teammates—who should, however, now feel bad about how much they harassed me—but there was a physical reason why I ate in slow motion. All I knew at the time was that one moment I would be famished, then after a couple of quick bites, I would feel full. But only for a minute, then I'd want to devour everything in sight again.

I was always hungry, except when I was actually eating. Some of it I figured was because of my diet and training. I'd been convinced that athletes needed to avoid all fat and load up on carbohydrates, fruits, and vegetables. And I couldn't cook to save my life, so I juiced everything in the fridge—anyone for a garlic-ginger-carrot-broccoli-fruit smoothie? It makes me sick just to think about some of the concoctions I came up with.

"You'd see him desperately digging into a bowl of pasta without any butter or sauce, or a salad without any dressing," Betsy says. "The poor kid had to eat every hour just to keep standing. I used to tell him to lighten up, eat a burger and some fries once in a while. . . . But even having a beer was getting wild for Chris. I woke up every morning at this house to the sound of his juicer grinding away."

There wasn't much to do in Laengen-fog, except explore, watch cows grazing, or get in pickup games of soccer with the locals. If we wanted a little nightlife, we had to drive into Soelden to visit the ever-popular discos, like the *Bierhimmel*. I spent a lot of my time working out.

"Klug identifies with being an athlete more than anyone I know," Betsy says. "In a sport full of mavericks, like snowboarding, where admitting to actually working out was almost as bad as admitting that you love country music (yeah, that would be Klug), his unapologetic embrace of fitness was admirable. The guy found a way to stay in shape in the grimmest of conditions.

"While the rest of the team sat in their hotel rooms making excuses, Klug was out finding the hole-in-the-wall gym, or jumping rope in the hallways, or scoping out a pool somewhere. He refused to give in to the inevitable on-the-road atrophy, and it paid off for him."

Unfortunately, it wasn't the breakout year of racing I had hoped it would be. I had a hard time adjusting to the new race boards; they were European editions, a lot softer in the flex than I liked, and asymmetrical—meaning one side actually had a longer edge than the other. I was consistently one of the top American finishers— along with Melhuse from my team and Joker Jacoby from the Cross-M cult—but December, January, and February passed without a top-three podium finish.

To be honest, I wasn't enjoying it any more, because my feet were killing me. It sounds like an old joke, but it nearly derailed my career.

The problem started from riding in boots that were a half-size too small because that's all the rep had available. The poor fit led to bone spurs the size of golf balls developing on my heels, a process accelerated by racing. The G-forces generated at high speed in a toe-side turn are tremendous, with most of the pressure focused back into the heel where the Achilles tendon attaches to the bone. The body recognizes the need for more strength in the area and builds more bone.

The slightest pressure on my heels would send waves of pain up my legs. I didn't want anything to touch my heels. I ran around on tour in flip-flops—which are a challenge in snow—and cut the backs out of my running shoes so I could still train and play hoops. After a race, I couldn't get my boots off fast enough; the backs of them felt like they'd been filled with hot coals.

It definitely affected my ability to focus on my races. However, I hoped to put the pain out of my mind to do well at the last race of the season, the U.S. Open at Stratton Mountain. I felt that if I were going to finish the season with a bang, it might come at the scene of one of my earlier successes. I was also aware that I would be performing in front of my "bosses." Burton Snowboards sponsored the U.S. Open, and it was traditional for Jake Carpenter to hand out the awards.

Maybe it was the extra pressure of wondering if they would renew my contract after a so-so year, but I placed third and finally broke the drought of podium finishes. I even managed to look confident (I think) when Jake handed me a check and that year's "trophy," a sheriff's badge inscribed "U.S. Open." I soon had a contract for another year.

I figured Jake had to feel pretty good about the growth of our sport since the days of turning out boards in his barn and sending Karol and Coghlan on their "marketing tour." Since a high of twelve and a half million in 1988, skier participation had fallen five years later by nearly two million participants who had skied at least once in that past year. Meanwhile, snowboarding, which was still not accepted at all resorts, had climbed to nearly two million. What's more, snowboarders tended to hit the slopes more often than skiers, and in less than favorable conditions, so they were buying an increasingly larger percentage of lift tickets. Most resort managers, if not all skiers, were seeing snowboarders in a different light.

"The resorts had been building video arcades for the kids to keep them occupied while their parents went skiing," Jake recalls. "Now we were getting kids back on the mountain. . . . And resorts saw how passionate snowboarders were about using their product. Rainy, crappy days and snowboarders were still out there, but not the skiers. . . . We went from not even a fly on the windshield, to a nuisance, to a threat, to all of a sudden, we were the saviors of the ski industry."

With the new contract my finances were set for the 1993–1994 season, but I was wondering how I was going to get through it with my feet. I told Rob I needed to take some time off and didn't start training with him on Mount Hood until September. Even then, my feet started hurting again as soon as I started riding, and the pain grew worse at the training camp Rob set up in Breckenridge, Colorado, in November.

On Thanksgiving I drove to Aspen, Colorado, to join my dad, who was now managing the Aspen Square Hotel, an upscale condominium/hotel just across the street from the Aspen Mountain gondola.

My parents had never really been happy in North Carolina. They missed the mountains, so moving back to Colorado appealed to them for all kinds of reasons, including sentimental ones. After all, they'd married and started our family there. With several offers on the table, they'd decided on Aspen, in large part because of Christ Church, the small Episcopal parish in the west end of town and its priest, "Father Bob" Babb, who bonded with my dad like a brother.

With the ski season looming, Dad had to start right away and was living on his own while Mom returned to North Carolina so that Hillary could finish the semester. So it was just the two of us for Thanksgiving, with me complaining the whole time about my feet. We went to a few different foot specialists, but no one seemed to have a solution, except maybe to stop snowboarding.

When Thanksgiving was over I headed off to Europe with Rob and the rest of the team. Except for my feet, I was physically in great shape and finally riding well on my Burtons. Paul Maravetz, my custom board builder at Burton, had come out to Oregon that summer and spent time with me at Hood going over the length, design, and stiffness to get my boards dialed in. I hoped that I would just be able to grit my teeth and put up with the pain during the season.

Burton had been supportive so far, but I needed a better showing this year if I wanted another contract. I also needed to prove to myself that hard work would pay off. I hoped to start by doing well at Val d'Isere. However, as I stood looking down *La Face de Belvarde,* the site of the 1992 Olympic downhill and one of the steepest courses I'd ever seen, I wasn't all there mentally.

Normally, I would have been happy with the fresh snow. Coming from the Pacific Northwest, I was more used to riding in pow than were the Europeans, who like their courses icy. My stiff new Burtons would be a solid platform in the banked turns that would develop in the course as more riders went down. But the pain in my heels had been getting worse as the day progressed. It had been agony just to put on my race boots that morning, and now it was tough to concentrate on all the little things it would take to ride well. My mind was as much on my feet as the race . . . until Rob put a handful of snow on the back of my neck.

"Focus," he said as I scraped away the snow. "Remember to keep the board under your body, high-percentage turns, and move your feet."

The pain in my feet wasn't gone. But my head was clear, and I knew what I had to do. Big ruts in the course had already made for some spectacular ejections of some of the top riders by the time I got into the starting gate for my first run.

I looked down the course, planning the line I would take. Our gates were different now, especially designed for snowboarding. International Snowboard Team coach Luc Faye of France had created a new triangular-shaped gate—still tall on one end, but tapering on the other side, where it was held into the snow by a short "stubbie" pole. We turned around the short sides, which allowed us to pick a much tighter line, as we could now lean over the gate without getting whacked in the face, arms, or chest. It had taken some adjustments—you had to remember to hold the inside arm up and away or you might catch it on the panel as you went over it—but it was much better than the old ski gates.

Despite starting back in the pack after the course had been trashed, I won the first run by a good margin. I'd focused on what Rob had said about keeping the board under me, and allowed it and my strength to carve around the turns like I was cutting freshies in the pow on Bachelor. I don't remember if I won the second run, but I did well enough that my combined time gave me my first World Cup win.

I'll never forget standing on top of a World Cup podium for the first time and raising my board above my head as friends and competitors cheered. The seven-thousand-dollar check was pretty cool too. But I think the moment that stands out to me the most was when Peter Bauer, one of the great riders from the Burton Euro team, came up and congratulated me.

A couple of weeks later I flew back to the United States for the Christmas holidays, where my family soon gathered for dinner around the old wood table with the homework indentations. As soon as Hillary got out of school, Mom and Nanny had loaded up a U-Haul truck, and the three of them then drove it cross-country trailing the same old Marquis station wagon that had gotten me to races all over the Northwest. They showed up in a major snowstorm just before Christmas 1993.

I arrived a few days later carrying my first-place trophy for the race at Val d'Isere. Ten years earlier, Santa had brought me the best Christmas present ever, my Burton Performer. Now, Santa and the Grinch who tried to steal Christmas that year (sorry, Mom) got to see the result.

The World Cup win at Val d'Isere moved me up into the top seed, or top fifteen, in the WC standings. This was very important. When you make it into the top seed, you're in the draw to be among the fifteen top riders to get to race first, when the course is in better shape. The top seed riders draw bib numbers 1 through 15 for their starting positions; the rest of the riders start in order of the number of points they've garnered through the season. It is a huge advantage to be in the top seed, and only rarely does a rider come from beyond it to challenge for the podium.

One other thing came out of the Val d'Isere race, a sort of ritual I began to follow both for luck and because it helped me focus before my race. When I get in the starting gate, I reach down and grab a handful of snow and place it on the back of my neck.

The best memories I have of those early years in Europe are of the people I met. Sadly to me, however, some of the early big names in North American alpine snowboarding were no longer racing. In the mid to late eighties, when snowboarding was defining itself and its equipment, riders did everything from backcountry trips into the mountains, slope-style, free-riding, banked slalom, half-pipe, slalom, and Super-G races. Every pro was at every contest doing every event. Riders got together to share equipment innovations and riding styles; it didn't matter if they preferred gates or the pipe.

By the beginning of the nineties, however, the industry was splintering. Racers went one way, freestyle and half-pipe competitors another. In addition, backcountry "Big Mountain" free-riding was inventing itself as a future profession with films and "extreme" competitions, such as Alaska's King of the Mountain—riding incredibly steep and deep conditions after being dropped off by helicopters. Some former competitors, as well as new riders who didn't know the sport's history, even started knocking organized events at resorts as somehow being a violation of snowboarding's antiestablishment heritage. Others were simply tired of competing.

The biggest name in North American snowboarding, Craig Kelly, had pretty much left racing and was in the last days of competing in the pipe. He would go on to define Big Mountain riding and become something of a backcountry guru, developing specialized gear for

Burton and working as a guide, especially on the big peaks of Alaska and Canada. But running gates no longer appealed to him.

My friend Kris Jamieson was another who had gone a different direction. "Enters the nineties, time to make decisions," he remembers. "Take the racer route and do the gate-chasing thing. Go film/free-ride guy. Go freestyle half-pipe guy. I chose the party/free-ride/drugs/beer/girls route. Karol and Klug took the full racer route. It was anyone's guess which route would be the most cost-effective."

I was disappointed that those guys weren't around any more; they'd had so much to do with the sport's early years and my own development, as well as being my friends and mentors. But at the same time, I was making new friends with racers from all over Europe and North America who still loved running gates. Guys like Austrian Sigi Grabner, Richard Richardsson from Sweden, and Nicolas Huet and Mathieu Bozzetto, two up-and-coming French racers for Club Surf de Neige de Val d'Isere.

Thanks to my new friendships and travels, I became fluent in French and somewhat proficient in German. I'd actually studied French quite a bit in high school, including spending a summer in France during my junior year, living with my friend Vincent Weber and his family outside of Paris, as well as studying French at Deerfield. In fact, I'd learned just enough to butcher the language when I first went to Europe and had the opportunity to try out my language skills on some unsuspecting French and Swiss riders, as well as the locals.

Parlez vous "redneck from Central Oregon?" It's a little embarrassing when just about everybody in Europe speaks English better than you do their language. But I wasn't afraid to keep trying, and pretty soon I wasn't getting reprimanded as much.

Not speaking the language never seemed to be a barrier with other snowboarders. I considered Davide Marchiandi, one of the top Italian racers, to be a great friend, though I didn't speak his language and he knew only a few words in mine. Somehow we communicated with gestures and expressions and always seemed to end up laughing together until our sides hurt.

I think it was because we all loved what we were doing. I even loved the autobahn and rodding the rental cars at one hundred miles an hour. We'd get up the morning after a race—many of my teammates nursing hangovers—hop into whatever vehicles Rob had arranged for, and be off for the next event, sometimes one or two countries away. The only thing slowing us down was the gas pedal meeting the floorboard. We called it "Euro–Cruise Control" (an expression Foley claims was his)—just press the gas pedal as far as it goes and keep it there.

We spent the season (when we weren't racing in Japan or North America) speeding through the Alps from Austria to Germany to Switzerland to Italy to France and a hundred combinations of that. We raced in the most famous resorts in Europe—such as Val d'Isere, Davos, Ischgl, Madonna di Campiglio—and some lesser-known ones as well.

Wherever we went, we managed to have a great time. The people were friendly and supportive, coming out by the thousands to cheer us on. There were even snowboard "groupies," who followed World Cup events, hoping to hook up with the racers. Of course, I was pretty young and oblivious to a lot of it.

Yet for all the fun I was having, I was suffering a lot because my feet hurt all the time. What concerned me most about that was that my dream of snowboarding becoming an Olympic sport was moving closer to reality, but I wasn't sure I'd be around to participate.

The previous year there'd been rumors that we might even be allowed as a demonstration sport at the 1994 winter games in Lillehammer, Norway (a decision had been made to move those games up two years so as to stagger the winter games from the summer games). It didn't happen. But as I watched the opening ceremonies that February from my Japanese hotel room en route to a World Cup race, I felt that there was a good chance that we'd get in at the 1998 Winter

Olympics in Nagano, Japan. However, with my feet hurting like they were, I didn't know if I'd make it four more years.

The pain certainly affected my racing and there were no more podiums after Val d'Isere. I was thankful when the season was over, which was a first for me and a sign of how bad things were with my feet. But I had no idea how much worse things could get.

Chapter 8

New Challenges

"Do you drink a lot?"

The question from the nurse caught me off guard. Even in the fall of 1994, I knew that the public's perception of snowboarders was still one of pot-smoking, beer-swilling party animals in baggy clothes. And as I've pointed out, that description wasn't always far from the truth; plenty of my friends, including riders on my team and others on the tour, smoked pot and drank themselves stupid whenever the opportunity presented itself.

I didn't care if they did. In some ways it was just part of the fun, laid-back, rebellious snowboarder culture that I still enjoyed. I just got there naturally. (High, I mean, not stupid.) I really was high on life. I know it sounds like a cliché, and my friends will probably kick my ass for saying it, but it's the truth. And who could blame me? I had an intoxicatingly great life.

It had been ten years since I cut up that hillside by myself at Sun Valley, and a lot had changed. I was making a living as a professional snowboard racer with sponsors that included Burton snowboards, Bolle sunglasses, and Aspen Skiing Company. I was getting paid to travel around the world, doing what I loved. I didn't need to get any higher.

I thought my foot problems were a thing of the past, though it had been a struggle. After the U.S. Open I'd gone surfing in Hawaii with my teammate Nelson Jensen. It felt so good to soak my poor feet in the ocean all day and be able to do a sport I loved without shoes— and without pain.

Surfing helped prepare me mentally for the surgery I had in May to remove the bone spurs. The surgery was performed in Bend at St.

Charles by Dr. Tom Carlson, a family friend, who then let me conva-
lesce at his home for two weeks.

However, I didn't know anything about rehab back then and had
jumped right back into training without giving my heels a chance to
mend properly. In fact, I was damaging the repaired area, and scar tissue
built up until I could hardly walk. If my heels had a chance to stiffen
when I was sleeping or sitting around, then walking would tear the new
scar tissue, which made it feel as if someone were sticking a hot fork in
the back of my feet. Only after I had moved around a little and got them
stretched out could I walk somewhat normally, though I still limped.

I struggled in Bend all summer. When Rob and the team began
training at Mount Hood, I couldn't join them. He was planning on conducting a special training camp in Breckenridge, Colorado, in
November to get us ready for the season, but I was beginning to think
I wouldn't be able to race at all that winter. Hell, I couldn't even stand
to put my feet in running shoes unless the backs were cut out of them.

I thought it might all be over anyway unless I got back to riding
soon. I was worried that I was going to lose my sponsorships. I'd
signed a new one-year contract with Burton, but what if I couldn't
compete, or if I tried and completely fell apart in the upcoming season
because of my feet? They were paying me to race and hopefully win,
not to hobble around like an old man.

At the end of my rope, I called my parents and told them it looked
like I might have to end my career. But Mom convinced me to load up
the Pooper and drive to Aspen. She said she had someone she wanted
me to meet who might be able to help.

My parents had settled comfortably into a condominium in town
and were happily involved with their jobs and their church. Dad had
started a Wednesday morning men's prayer group, and Mom helped
run the Sunday school. She was also teaching at Aspen Elementary.
Her efforts to help me learn to read when I was a child had inspired
her to pursue her master's in education so that she could help other
kids with reading problems.

Mom set me up with Chris Peshek, a physical therapist at the Aspen Club, the premier fitness club in town. Their staff of therapists had earned such a reputation that pro athletes from a wide variety of sports traveled to Aspen to rehab injuries and train with them. Chris began with painful foot massages to break up the scar tissue, followed by a carefully laid-out program to gradually strengthen and train.

It helped to be rehabbing in one of the most beautiful places in the world with some of the most hard-core local athletes I'd ever met. Located in the Roaring Fork Valley, surrounded by some of the most beautiful and rugged mountains in the Rockies, Aspen is perhaps better known to the outside world for attracting the Hollywood jet-set crowd during the ski season. However, most locals who live in Aspen aren't famous nor fabulously wealthy. However, whether they're investment bankers or restaurant waiters, most are there because they're into an active outdoors lifestyle.

Even after I started getting back in shape, I'd be riding up some trail on my mountain bike and think I was really hammering, and then some old fart clad head-to-toe in Lycra and a cycling cap that read "Aspen Cycling Club" would come along and dust me. Or I'd be hiking up Ute Trail on Ajax, the locals' name for the main ski mountain just a block from my dad's hotel, and an old ladies' walking club would blow by me like I was standing still. I was like, *"Damn, what's up with this place and these people?"*

I was never at a loss for new playmates, like Bill Fabrocini, another physical therapist at the Aspen Club whom I met while working with Chris. Short and muscular, "Fab," as he is called by his friends when we're not calling him something much worse, was a former junior Olympic hockey player. We did a lot of biking and hanging out—going out on the town, and feasting at Boogie's restaurant, which made the best burgers, fries, and malts in the world and was the 1950s-motif setting for the movie *Diner.*

By October my feet were feeling a lot better. I could actually walk in the mornings without pain. I was back to training like an animal in the weight room and on the bike and looked forward to a pain-free racing season. I was so fit and not the least bit worried about passing when I went in to a medical clinic for a routine physical. I was going to change my insurance coverage and thought I'd just breeze through the qualifying checkup.

So I was stunned when I got a call the next day from the nurse at the clinic. She said my blood work indicated that I had "elevated liver enzymes, which could be serious." I was still digesting that when she asked, "Do you drink a lot?"

When I said no, I wondered if the nurse was thinking, *Yeah, right, a snowboarder who isn't a sauce monster . . . kind of like a fish who doesn't like water.* And what in the heck were elevated liver enzymes? It sounded like a commercial for Tide detergent, only scarier.

"This has to be a mistake," I said. There was no way I could be sick. I took great care of myself—worked out constantly, was a freak for a low-fat, raw fruit and vegi diet, and never put anything bad in my body. I still carried my asthma inhaler, but I rarely used it unless I'd been hanging out with someone's pets. Who could have been healthier?

Thinking there had to have been a problem with the tests, I called my regular physician and went in to have the blood work repeated. But the next day I got the call again, my enzyme numbers were high. My doc recommended that I go see Dr. Gerald Tomasso, a specialist in gastroenterology in Glenwood Springs, forty miles down the valley from Aspen.

Mom was teaching and couldn't get off, but my dad and Missy went with me. On the way to Glenwood, we all agreed that this liver enzyme deal couldn't be much of anything. I had no symptoms of anything being wrong. Heck, I didn't even know I had enzymes, or what they did.

I expected Dr. Tomasso to assure me that there was nothing to worry about. Instead, he explained that high liver enzyme numbers were often an indication that the liver wasn't functioning properly. And that, he assured me, could be very serious.

The doctor explained that if the heart was the body's pump house for circulating blood, the liver could be thought of as the filtration system, where bad things were removed from the blood and good things added. The liver regulated the body's metabolism, including energy levels, and its cholesterol. It stored sugar and took toxic chemicals—among them alcohol and drugs—and changed them into nontoxic substances, then got rid of them. The liver also produced bile, which was carried by bile ducts into the small intestine. Bile, he said, was necessary in the digestive process for nutrient and vitamin absorption.

Heavy drinking, drug abuse, and viral infections—such as blood-borne hepatitis viruses—could damage the liver and lead to cirrhosis or liver cancer. Without a functioning liver, death was certain.

With that uplifting message firmly planted in my mind, Tomasso quickly ruled out the usual suspects for my liver giving me problems. I could count on one hand the number of times I'd actually been drunk, and even a beer was a once-in-a-while event. I didn't use drugs, had never even tried pot, and the blood tests showed there was no hepatitis infection. This was going to take some detective work, he said. In the meantime, he said, I should just go on with my life.

Go on with my life? On the ride home, we all agreed there was nothing to worry about. In fact, I was more worried about somebody knowing I had a "liver problem" than actually having one. After all, I thought, alcoholics and drug addicts were the sort of people who had liver problems. Not healthy, athletic people who took care of their bodies.

I didn't want whatever was going on with me to contribute to the public stereotype of snowboarders. Competitive snowboarders were still trying to gain acceptance in the sports community, and the old stereotypes weren't helping. Yeah, some guys still smoked weed on the tour, even on the race hill, but most of us—even some of those who were smoking after races—still wanted to be taken seriously as world-class athletes.

Sure, some of it was financial. We knew that we needed to clean up the sport's public image if we wanted to attract more corporate sponsors for events and support so that we could continue doing what we loved and bring more people into the sport. There was also the little matter of getting snowboarding into the Winter Olympics.

We'd been shut out at Lillehammer. But the International Olympic Committee had since announced that two snowboard events—the half-pipe and an alpine giant slalom race—would be part of the 1998 Winter Olympics in Nagano, Japan.

At last we were going to get a chance to "shred" the image of snowboarders as just a bunch of stoned dudes who couldn't ski. This was our chance to show the world that we belonged on the same world stage as any other sport. But wouldn't people wonder if it became known that I had a liver disease? Was I doing drugs? Did I hit the bottle too much and do it to myself? The IOC was conscious of its public image. What if they heard and decided that snowboarders still weren't ready for prime time?

Yet, I hadn't done anything wrong. It didn't seem fair. I thought it best to keep my secret from everyone but my family.

When I arrived in Europe to race after Rob's Breckenridge training camp, I tried to forget about the liver problem. I had other things on my mind to help me do that. One was Missy. She'd been a great friend when I was dealing with my heel problems in Bend, taking me out to dinner or a movie or—and she hated this—helping me pass the time with board games. Then she'd come to visit me that fall in Aspen and we'd had a great time hiking. I could honestly say she was my best friend. It was so easy to talk to her, and the same things made us laugh . . . not to mention she was hot. But she'd made it clear when she left that she still just wanted to be *friends*.

I decided, *That's it, I'm done chasing her.* I climbed on the plane and took off for Europe determined to concentrate on my life as a professional snowboard racer.

Even that didn't work out like I planned, however. My feet were fine heading into the season, but the problem that caused the injuries in the first place was still there; the forces on my heels and the damage caused by poor-fitting boots hadn't magically disappeared. My feet started hurting again almost right away, especially my left, or rear, foot (I'm a "goofy footer," meaning my right foot is forward in my stance).

I was also having a hard time ignoring "the liver thing" too. Whenever I came back to the States during the season for a race or to visit my family and could make it to Glenwood, Tomasso would want to see me for more tests. He was on a fishing expedition, he'd say, but so far the net was empty.

My mind, of course, had gone all over the possibilities on the spectrum from "There is nothing wrong with me" to "I have liver cancer and am going to die young." It was really hard going out and competing at an elite level, racing against the best alpine snowboarders in the world, wondering what was going on with my body.

I was scared and wanted to talk to someone who knew about my "secret" but would look on the bright side of things. I started calling Missy, who, like me, is an eternal optimist, and talked to her for hours at a time. Our conversations soon turned to reminiscing about what a great time we'd had that fall and how much we missed each other. I decided to ask her to meet me back in Aspen during the Christmas holidays, when the World Cup tour took a break and she was out of school.

Missy remembers asking her roommate, Heidi Boyd, with whom she'd grown up in Sisters, "Why am I not with this guy? He's perfect."

"I'd gone out with a lot of jerks, while at the same time I was telling myself that Chris was too nice," she says. "But as he and I talked on the telephone, I finally realized that he was the greatest, purest, nicest person I had ever known, and it clicked that someone with all these great qualities was really what I wanted for my future. I told myself that when I got off that plane this time I would kiss him, and he would know that my feelings had changed. But I was a big chicken and couldn't do it."

Kiss or no kiss, we figured it out pretty quick. Missy and I were like kids, laughing all the time—sometimes even at the weirdness that so much had changed between us. We had fun exploring Aspen in the winter. Aspen Skiing Company owned four ski mountains in the vicinity—Buttermilk, Highlands, Snowmass, and right there in the heart of town, Aspen Mountain, or as the locals refer to it, Ajax. We ripped it up at the first three on the list—Missy on skis and me on my board, even though my feet were killing me—but not on Ajax. Snowboarders still weren't allowed on the flagship mountain's slopes (with some of the old-school skiers threatening it would happen only over their dead bodies). But then the week was over and I had to go back on tour and Missy had to return to Sisters.

I was happy that Missy and I were finally together. But it was hard to enjoy being in Europe racing, because my foot problems were getting worse again. I wanted to stop. It was no fun anymore training or racing in constant pain. But I'd made a commitment to my sponsors to compete, and I saw it through and even finished on a positive note, winning the Canadian Open giant slalom in Silver Star, British Columbia. But when I walked off the hill that day, I wasn't sure that I'd be coming back to the sport I loved.

I skipped my spring surfing trip to chase Missy around Europe for a month. My favorite place was Cinque Terre in Italy—five villages along the Mediterranean coast, where we swam, kayaked, snorkeled, hiked, drank red wine, ate cheese and fresh bread, and I read *East of Eden*.

I made up for missing the spring by surfing as much as I could the rest of the summer after Missy and I went back to Sisters for part of the summer. The water felt good on my feet, and I otherwise took it easy to see how they would respond.

At one point Dr. Carlson took me over to see Scott Peterson, a pedorthist who specialized in custom orthotics. "This is Chris Klug, a future Olympian. He needs help," Carlson said, introducing me.

Peterson had great credentials as an athlete and as a second-generation pedorthist. His father, Bill Peterson, had been a top-rated U.S. ski racer and at one time had been hailed as the best powder skier in America. He'd moved to Lake Placid, New York, and took up custom-fitting foot orthotics to correct foot, knee, and leg problems, a relatively new technique that might have saved his own career if he'd been born later. But at least he was there when the U.S. Ski Team turned to him for their problems.

Scott had followed in his dad's footsteps (sorry, another bad pun) and as a professional water-skier himself knew the mindset an athlete has to have to compete at the top level. We worked all summer with all sorts of insoles and custom liners and it seemed to help. But as soon as I started training hard on Mount Hood in late August, I knew I wasn't going to make it through another season.

My feet were so inflamed and sore, I couldn't imagine putting them into snowboard boots and then through the torture of cranking turns. I called Rob and told him I was going to take the year off. Then I sent a letter to Eric Kotch, my team manager with Burton, and David Schriber, head of Burton marketing, and told them.

I tried to act upbeat, like I would be back for sure the next season, no problem. But privately I was not at all positive. I'd already tried it all—punching out the plastic boots' shells, surgery, physical therapy, taking it easy, orthotics, and custom liners. But it was clear that as long as things remained as they were, the bone spurs and the pain would just intensify. I didn't want to ruin my feet and end up a cripple.

I was worried about how the guys at Burton would take the news. I mean, why stick with a young rider who had yet to really prove himself but was already having injury problems? But they replied, "Don't worry, we'll continue to support you. Just get better."

It was great to hear, but I still began to prepare for the possibility that my snowboarding career was over. I enrolled at Colorado Mountain College in Aspen and carried a full load of classes, including English, psychology, comparative religions, and speech.

To earn money, I bused tables at Mezzaluna restaurant in Aspen, the same place I'd eaten with the Burton Europe team in 1992. (My family jokes that this was my first real job. They seem to forget that I once bagged groceries at the Green Mint Market in Bend for two whole weeks before quitting because it was getting in the way of my skateboarding. And later, Jason and I were employed for a short time at the Inn of the Seventh Mountain, although all we did was rally the Cushman motorized worker's cart around the property.)

I'd certainly come down a few notches from pro athlete dining at Mezzaluna to the busboy cleaning up scraps. I did my best to convince myself that I'd be fine without snowboarding, but it wasn't true. I was miserable, especially when the snow began to fall and the mountains around Aspen turned white. Everybody was talking about their new skis they couldn't wait to try out, or maybe hiking up one of the Elk Mountain Range peaks with their boards and getting an early start riding some extreme line.

I was lucky to have friends to keep my spirits up. Missy moved to Aspen and got a good job teaching at the elementary school. It was great to have her around with our relationship on solid ground. But she couldn't help me with my feet other than to commiserate and tell me everything would work out fine.

Help arrived from an unlikely source. One of Bill Fabrocini's lesser-known patients was Gary Albert, a really old—fifty-something—Aspen Jewish Mafia Kingpin and the world's biggest crybaby, with the skinniest stick legs you've ever seen. Nicknamed "The Toymaker," he'd retired to Aspen at age forty after making a fortune as one of the marketing "geniuses" behind the Cabbage Patch Kids doll craze. He'd supposedly slipped in the club's shower after "working out" (a misnomer in this case) and hurt his back, so Fab was humoring him back into shape.

(Note to all the fitness buffs out there: The "Gary Workout" is famous. It consists of touring the entire gym for hours in workout attire, acting like you're interested in pumping some iron but in reality just flapping your jaws. However, historically speaking, the Gary Workout was modeled after the famous "Boogie Workout," developed by Lenny "Boogie" Weinglass, the owner of the Aspen restaurant by the same nickname.)

Despite the huge age difference (remember, I was only twenty-three), Gary and I became good friends at the club as I worked on my legitimate medical problem and he whined about his "ouchie." (In all honesty, don't tell him this, but I hope I'm half as fit as Gary, a hard-core bicyclist, when I'm his age.) One day, Gary told me about a friend of his who'd had foot problems and recommended that I see Dr. David Strom, an orthopedic surgeon in Denver who specialized in foot problems.

Hopeful, but not expecting a miracle, I went to see Dr. Strom, who persuaded me to have more surgery. However, he thought I should fix just the left heel, which experienced the greater pressure and hurt the most. He believed that the right heel was actually doing well and would continue to get better.

I felt like someone had given me a reprieve from a prison sentence. I was still going to have to take the rest of the season off, but now it would be to give my left foot a chance to "heel" properly. And I could still make it back for the next season, which would be much more important with the 1998 Winter Olympics in Nagano getting closer. I felt that if I had the surgery and spent the next nine months or so resting and rehabilitating my foot, I'd be ready, back in form, and ready for the push to make the U.S. Olympic team. Everything was falling into place . . . then it was just falling.

I'd had the heel surgery and was still on crutches in December when Dr. Tomasso called and asked me to come to Glenwood Springs for a new test. The request wasn't alarming. For a year he'd been on his fishing expedition without finding anything. He'd even performed a biopsy, looking for liver cancer—one of the most deadly and difficult to cure, I'd learned by reading up on it. But to my relief, that test came back negative too.

In early January my dad and Missy again accompanied me to Tomasso's office. When we arrived, he said he wanted to try an "exploratory" procedure called an endoscopic retrograde cholangio-pancreatography.

"An end-o what?"

"An ERCP" for short, the doctor explained. He would sedate me, then run a fiber-optic "laparoscope," a sort of tiny camera on the end of a wire, down my throat, through my stomach to the small intestines, where the bile ducts entered from my liver.

Tomasso didn't go into what he thought he might find, but he didn't seem any more worried than he had with the other tests. In fact, he seemed much less concerned than he had when he told me he wanted to do the biopsy. This endo-retro-camera-thing didn't sound pleasant, but it was just another test. I thought it was great that they could go in and look at my liver without having to make an incision.

After the procedure, I was still a bit loopy and trying to catch what my dad and Missy were chatting about when Tomasso walked into the room. He said he'd been looking for evidence of inflammation and scarring in my bile ducts—"and I found it." He wasn't 100 percent sure, he said, but he thought I might have a rare disease called primary sclerosing cholangitis—PSC for short.

No one knew what caused it—"it may be genetic," he said—but it had nothing to do with the few times I'd had alcohol.

The bad news was that there was no known cure and it could kill me. The problem, he said, was that after a period of time the scarring would cause the ducts to plug and the bile would pool up in the liver. Infections would be a problem, as well as liver failure and the strong possibility that even before that I'd have liver cancer. There was no good news. The fact of the matter was that if I had PSC, I was going to need a liver transplant someday.

I laughed. This was just too much. This guy Tomasso had to be some kind of quack. "You sure you got the right guy?" I asked. "I feel like a million bucks."

Tomasso didn't smile back. He repeated that his diagnosis wasn't a sure thing, but he wanted me to go see a real expert on liver disease, his friend Dr. Gregory Everson at University Hospital in Denver.

This time when we left Tomasso's care, we were mystified. What kind of a screwed-up disease had no symptoms? No symptoms, but according to Dr. Quack, I was going to need a liver transplant someday or die young. It didn't make sense. There still had to be a mistake.

That's what Mom said too when we told her about Tomasso's theory. She reminded us about the neonatologist who after I was born told her to hold off on the birth announcements. "He didn't know what he was talking about either." She was angry with Tomasso for scaring me "over nothing."

Nevertheless, we made an appointment with Everson, the medical director of the liver disease program at University Hospital. My dad pointed out when we got there that Rose Medical Center, where I'd been born, was right next door. I hobbled in wearing a big cast on my left foot.

Everson raised his eyebrow at the cast but didn't waste a lot of time with pleasantries. He said he wanted to perform an ERCP, like Tomasso had; only this time, if he found what he suspected he would, he'd insert a tiny balloon-like object on the end of the laparoscope into my bile ducts and inflate it to open them.

Even though I would be under anesthesia, he warned that the ERCP was not going to be a comfortable experience. If Tomasso's hunch was right, the procedure would release bile that was pooling up in my liver behind the scarred ducts. It would be like dumping a load of poison into my guts, and I would probably feel nauseated when I woke up.

Nauseated? I woke up sicker than a dog, vomiting a foul green slime. The stuff kept coming up for hours and left me as weak as a puppy.

Just when I thought I could not feel any worse, Everson came into the hospital room and delivered the bad news. Tomasso's hunch was right—I had PSC. It affected about one in ten thousand people, he said, most of them young men and an unusually high percentage of them living in the Colorado Rocky Mountains.

The immediate danger was from infections. But he said they could control those for the time being with antibiotics. They'd also dilute my bile with a new drug made of bear bile called Actigall to allow it to get through my ducts easier. The next step would be to perform ERCPs every six to eight months to drain what couldn't get through.

As if that didn't sound bad enough, the ERCPs would do less and less as time went by, he warned, until finally they would do no good at all. There was no cure, and eventually I would need a liver transplant or die.

One of us asked how long before I would need the transplant. "No one knows," he said. The disease didn't progress the same in every person. It might be three years; it could be twenty, even thirty years. But I shouldn't worry about it, he said, I would be in good hands when the time came. Everson pointed out that University Hospital was an early pioneer in liver transplants and now had one of the top programs in the world.

Everson was a bit more matter-of-fact and more of a realist than I was used to, and it scared the hell out of me. My voice seemed a little high and tight when I asked him about continuing my snowboarding career. He seemed skeptical about how I was going to accomplish that at a high level. As the scarring continued, my liver would begin to fail, and I would grow weaker. But he had no problem with me trying for as long as I was physically able. I had to understand, he said, this was a serious, perhaps fatal disease.

"One thing is certain, PSC will change your life."

We sat there stunned, then reacted in different ways. All three of us had listened to the same lecture but had heard different things about when a transplant would be necessary. Missy heard three years and burst into tears. Dad heard twenty and started to pray.

Being the eternal optimist, I latched on to thirty years. *Good,* I thought, *it won't get in the way of my snowboarding, and by that time they'll come up with a pill or something that will cure this without a transplant.*

Later that spring I decided I needed to go on my annual surf trip and come to terms with all I'd been told. I needed to find a place to store my "secret" so that I could concentrate on my goals of making a comeback in my sport and snowboarding in the Olympics. I could think out on the waves, removed from everything except the water and my board.

However, I didn't have much money working as a busboy at Mezzaluna, so Missy and I drove the Pooper to San Diego. We stopped in Vegas long enough for Missy to win some more money for our trip and for me to bankrupt the casino at the $3.99 "All You Can Eat" buffet.

When we arrived I hit the water as fast as I could get my Rip Curl 3/2 wetsuit on and my board out of the Pooper, which seemed to groan with relief. (Missy had continued to abuse the poor old Poop all the way across the desert, slamming and hanging all over the doors like a damn monkey.) The ocean worked its miracle on my body and my head. Nothing like eight hours of battling currents and drawing lines on overhead waves to cleanse the soul.

"He barely knew how to surf at this point. He was still learning. He did not get really good at the sport until we started to go to Costa Rica," Missy says. But what would she know—she was asleep on the beach. The waves were double-plus overhead, and I was riding 'em like the second coming of legendary surfer Jerry Lopez, who was also a friend of mine from Bend.

The point is . . . I got myself back to believing that I could beat this PSC thing. I'd been battling medical emergencies since I was a baby, and winning. If this disease wanted to race me for my life, we'd find out who was the better competitor. Unfortunately, the salt air did nothing for the Pooper, which lost the use of one cylinder and turned into a three-banger.

After more than a week in the water, tanned, rested, and confident that my body was in great shape, I was wondering if Tomasso and Everson really knew what they were talking about. I didn't trust them. But there was a doctor I did trust—the one who'd helped me face my fears and took care of me when I was gasping for breath as an asthmatic child, Dr. Peter Boehm.

Dr. Boehm and I had stayed in touch over the years, and whenever I was in Bend, I still went to him for any medical problems. After the surf trip Missy and I went to see her folks, eat them out of house and home at Papandrea's, and hang out with our friends in Sisters for the summer. Part of my routine now was to get blood work done every month or so to keep tabs on how my liver was doing. So I called Boehm's office to make an appointment for blood work. When I went in, I casually told him what was up. He listened like he always had when I was a kid and then asked me how I was handling the diagnosis.

"Well, there's not a lot I can do about it," I replied with a brave shrug. "It's the hand I was dealt. I'm just going to play it and continue my life as I know it. . . . Maybe they don't know everything about this disease." I was looking for him to agree, to tell me not to worry and that everything would be all right. But he couldn't.

"This is way out of my field, Chris," he said. "I do know enough that you're going to have to trust them."

I didn't want to hear it. He was telling me that I had to accept that I had a life-threatening disease. Still, I believed what I wanted to believe about PSC. Nothing to worry about for thirty years. I'd cross that avalanche chute when I came to it. And it would be long after my racing career was over.

Long after I won my Olympic medal.

Chapter 9

Sore Dogs

Modern medicine had thirty years to find a cure for PSC, a miracle pill or maybe some nasty-tasting drink that I could plug my nose and chug. Problem solved. In the meantime, I was going to see if I could beat it myself through diet and exercise. So I was able to push the idea of a liver transplant into a small dark cave in my mind and went back to trying to save my snowboarding career. Recovering from foot surgery was the medical obstacle, I thought, not my liver.

I started training with Fab, who designed a snowboard-specific program to make me bigger and stronger overall, not just my feet. Before we started this program, I had loved to hammer on my bike forever, but too much of that was making me scrawny. So Fab lowered the aerobic intensity of my workouts and focused on developing muscle mass and strength in my legs and trunk, as well as on my foot speed through plyometric drills and quick feet routines.

Training had never been a problem for me. I loved it, especially if I could do it with my friends. It helped now that I was around so many active people and had tons of playmates.

Missy was always up for a ride or a game of tennis, but she was often working when I wanted to do something. So I played tennis with Gary regularly, rode bikes with a crew that included Gary, Fab, Jon Gibans, and Marco Chingolani, a crazy Italian who managed L'hosteria restaurant and, like a lot of Europeans, loved cycling.

For some reason, I seemed to attract doctors for buddies like moths to a flame, or maybe, like sharks, they just smelled blood in the water and knew I'd be good for some outrageous medical bills they could hit my insurance company with. Most of them were cycling enthusiasts I'd met through Fab. They also seemed to have useful specialties considering how injury prone (or just old and fragile) our group was: Jon Gibans, the ER doc; radiologist David Hollander; and Tom Pevny, an orthopedic surgeon. There was also Kenton Bruice, an OB/GYN who was obviously in the wrong field to help any of us; and Thos Evans, a local boy and only a medical student, so he was sort of like a grom doc.

That was the tight group, but the town was full of fun and interesting people who loved the outdoors. Sooner or later you were bound to know most of them, at least to say hi or maybe meet on a trail somewhere and hammer along together for a while. People like Charlie Tarver, whose goal it was to eventually break one hundred miles per hour on skis and bikes, and Ginny and Bob Wade, who owned the Ute Mountaineer, an outdoor gear and clothing store, and whose eleven-year-old son, Robbie, was a typical Aspen kid ripping around town on his skateboard. He reminded me of me when I was growing up in Bend.

It was no accident that we mostly met each other while rehabbing our various injuries with Bill. As a result of the sort of constant injury report, a type of "ball busting" evolved that, while seemingly rude, was meant with a great deal of affection and for a good reason. We often referred to each other as "you big pussy."

Any sort of injury—being sore from a hard workout to broken bones to my heel surgery—was known in general as a disease called "puss-itus." More specifically, it might be "puss-itus of the femur," or "puss-itus of the back," or "puss-itus of the heels." There was no known cure (other than to never, ever admit to any injury or pain, even if you were bleeding to death or suddenly missing an arm or leg). The disease, according to our medical staff, could be treated only with a certain feminine hygiene product, so tubes of the stuff had a way of showing up in the oddest places. You might be on a killer single-track ride and get a flat, reach into your bike repair pack to look for a tire lever or tube, and instead find a rock meant to slow you down and a tube of "the treatment."

The ball busting of course served a higher purpose. My feet might be hurting, and I would get down and whine about the end of my snowboarding career, but my so-called friends would have no mercy. I'd be called a big pussy and someone would offer to rub the treatment on my heels. In other words: *Stop feeling sorry for yourself, Klug, and get back to work.*

I swear they gave me the hardest time of anybody in the gang and made up all sorts of lies about me. Take "Klug Time" for instance. They claim that I am always late—that if I say I'll meet them at 6 P.M., it's guaranteed to be 7 before I show. They even exaggerate and say that they purposefully tell me to show up at one time and then arrive an hour later . . . and that I'm still usually the last one in the door. They never buy my explanation that it's all Missy's fault and that left to my own devices, I am Mr. Punctuality. Instead, they point out that I am late even when Missy's out of town, as if that matters.

"Ha, ha," Missy laughs at that one. "He has always been on his own time, and always will be. The ONLY thing he is on time for are his races, and that is simply because he has to arrive two hours early on race day."

They also say I'm cheap just because I sometimes made Missy pay for her own bagel and coffee at the Ink Coffeeshop even if she had to write a check for a buck seventy. They harangue me endlessly because I got mad at her for slamming the door on the Pooper so hard that it broke the hinges and fell off. I wanted her to pay for it, but my friends, even my sister, Hillary, came to her defense and said it wasn't her fault, that the Pooper needed to be put out of its misery.

In the interest of being fair, Missy says my account isn't the truth. "The Pooper no longer had hinges on the doors that would work, and I just happened to be driving it when the door finally gave out," she says. "Hillary Klug was with me, and we looked at each other like, 'I will NEVER hear the end of this' . . . and here I am being blamed still.

"I might add that the Pooper was down to two or three cylinders out of four. We could barely make it to Denver over the mountains.

Maybe it will spark Chris's memory to mention that we averaged twenty miles an hour many times up the hills."

I still believed that there was plenty left in the old Poop if she hadn't been mistreated. She was the epitome of reliability until Missy started slamming the doors. I put a new engine in her, and she was ready for a couple hundred thousand more miles and adventures.

I was just careful with my money, that's all. It wasn't like I was making a ton of money working at Mezzaluna, though I got a glimpse at those who did, delivering focaccia to the likes of Don Johnson, Ivana Trump, Dean Cain, Kevin Costner, and Jennifer Aniston.

For all the unfair things said about me by my friends, I wouldn't have traded them for all the movie stars and other famous people. I didn't know yet how much I would come to rely on them and the crap they gave me.

Maybe it was the tubes of the treatment, or it could have been Fab's abilities as a physical therapist, I'll never know, but by the spring of 1996 I was feeling pretty good about my feet. I wrote Eric and David at Burton and asked if we could meet at Burton's headquarters in Burlington, Vermont, to discuss my return and the renewal of my contract. I was nervous about the meeting. I wasn't really sure what they would say. I'd been the top American finisher the previous two years and ended both seasons with wins, but it wasn't like I was dominating the tour when I took the year off. They might have decided I wasn't worth it or was a medical liability. Also, snowboarding, especially in the United States, was now dominated by freestyle, not racing, and that's where most of the money went.

When we sat down, I explained to them that I was 100 percent healthy and ready to race. To my relief, they said welcome back and agreed to honor my existing contract for another year.

I didn't tell them, or anybody else for that matter, about the PSC. I didn't see why I should. There was still nothing to indicate that I was sick. In fact, except for two things, it was as if the disease didn't exist.

The first reminder was the twice-daily dose of Actigall. The bear bile product (think of that in the morning over breakfast) was an experimental drug; they weren't sure if it did actually do the job. However, it didn't do any harm besides giving me the runs and making me have to seek an emergency hopper all the time.

The second reminder was that summer when I had to go back to University Hospital and let Everson and his team "roto-root" my bile ducts. When I woke up, I was as sick as a dog again, puking green slime. Missy and Dad did their best to ignore it and talked about how the doctors had shown them a cool video of the procedure while I was still out. This time the docs didn't keep me long but sent me home to Aspen, a four-hour car ride punctuated by having to pull over and vomit every fifty miles or so. The next day I had to take it easy, but then I was back to normal eating and exercising.

In August I showed up at Mount Hood ready to train with Rob and the rest of the team. After just a short time back on the snow I was winning runs against the other riders and knew I was stronger than ever. But then my feet started to hurt again. Surgery had fixed the immediate problem, but it had not resolved the cause—carving turns in racing boots.

Over the next couple of months, I tried everything. I spent thousands of dollars testing every foam, silicone, and Thermoflex liner on the market. I even drove a few hundred more miles several times to see Scott Peterson, who had moved to Klamath Falls in southern Oregon, to have special orthotics built. I eventually got enough relief on my front, or right, foot, but the forces were greater on the rear heel and nothing helped. I just hoped I could put up with the pain to get through the season.

I was back on snow in November at the now-annual team camp in Breckenridge. But after a few days of riding, I'd had it. The pain was intense, and I just wasn't willing to do more surgeries or risk being crippled. I called my dad and told him, "I quit. I've exhausted all the possibilities. I can't ride like this any more."

Hearing that frightened him. He would later say it was almost worse than dealing with the trauma of my premature birth and my asthma attacks. Telling him that I was going to leave the sport I loved and quit short of achieving my goal of being in the Olympics—with the possibility so near—was completely out of character for me and showed him how down I was.

Dad talked me into staying in camp another day to think about it. I shrugged, why not? It would take me a day to pack the Pooper and get organized anyway. I didn't know that Dad was really just stalling for time. He was determined that this wouldn't end my career or dreams. He got on the telephone to Scott Peterson back in Klamath Falls.

"Scott, you've got to help," he said. "My son just called and he wants to quit. That's not like Chris . . . he never throws in the towel. I have an idea."

They talked for a long time, going over different possibilities. The trick, they thought, would be to take the pressure off my backside heel and spread it evenly over the rest of the foot. Finally, they came up with the answer.

The next day, Scott called me. I was pretty resigned, but he said, "Don't give up until we've tried this." He told me to go to an orthopedic clinic in the town of Frisco, nine miles away from Breckenridge. "I want them to make a cast of your foot."

Scott called the clinic after I arrived and talked the entire time to the technician who was making the mold. He wanted to make sure he got my foot at the appropriate angle, as it would be in the boot, and had the technician measure the forward lean and measure my ankle bones and area of pain on my heel. I overnighted the mold to Scott, and he went to work.

I felt like a kid at Christmas opening the package I received from him a few days later. Inside was a prosthetic brace that slipped onto my left foot like a tight plastic slipper that fit to just above my ankle. I went down to a local ski shop, A Racer's Edge, and had a Thermoflex liner molded over my foot with the new brace on. The whole contraption then went inside my boot.

The next day, I was out on the slope early to try it out. After just a few runs, I knew that my foot problem was a thing of the past. The brace wasn't perfect, it hurt my foot in other areas, but my heel was free of pain. It was already so much better than what I was used to, and I knew it could get even better with a few adjustments. (Before we were finished, Scott had made, and discarded, hundreds of prototypes before getting it just right.) My career had been saved by my dad and a friend, who'd both refused to let me give up when it seemed so hopeless.

From that day forward, I treated the brace like gold. I never left it anywhere it could be stepped on or stolen. I never checked it at airports but always carried it on the plane with me. I got a lot of funny looks when the security folks X-rayed my carry-ons and saw what appeared to be a human foot, but no one stopped me either. Maybe they just didn't want to know. Just in case, Scott kept the mold back in his office under lock and key and my request that he guard it with his life.

I entered the 1996–1997 season pumped about the possibilities. My feet were happy, and I was riding fast and having fun again. About the only thing I didn't like were the politics surrounding the selection process for the U.S. Olympic Snowboard Team. In fact, it was just plain ugly.

The International Snowboarding Federation had been the original governing body for professional World Cup snowboarding before most North American ski resorts even allowed us on their property. The ISF established the sport and invented the competitive disciplines— including half-pipe and alpine—with the riders' input.

The Federation International de Ski, or FIS, had been around much longer, of course, but as the governing body for skiing, including Nordic (cross-country), alpine, and freestyle (the bump monkeys and aerialists). The FIS controlled the World Cup ski competitions, as well as ski events in the Olympics with the approval of the International Olympic Committee.

However, the FIS wanted nothing to do with snowboarding until the mid-nineties, when they climbed into the arena because of snow-boarding's growing popularity. In the United States skier participation had continued its steady decline from more than twelve million participants to nine and a half million in 1996; meanwhile, snowboarder participation had climbed to nearly four million over the same period of time. More than a third of the snowboarders were considered by the ski industry to be "frequent" riders, buying tickets more than ten days a year, a much higher percentage than frequent skiers.

In reality, snowboarding's mass appeal was going to someday force the IOC to accept it into the Olympics or risk alienating (further) a huge and growing winter sports crowd. The FIS decided that if snow-boarding was going to get in, then they and not the ISF would be in charge. The FIS said that it would sponsor snowboarding as a "discipline of skiing," and their longtime buddies on the IOC agreed and made them the official governing body for our sport.

However, this raised two major questions. First, would the best riders, most all of them on the ISF tour, cross over and legitimize the Nagano snowboarding events? Second, how would the teams be selected?

The second question was answered first. The FIS announced that it would sponsor its own World Cup snowboarding tour. Participants would then accumulate points for doing well at the events, which would count toward their selection for their countries' Olympic teams.

The first question was answered more slowly, but ISF riders began to switch allegiances. The FIS bought legitimacy—literally—in some cases paying ISF riders to come over, and by putting on events with more corporate sponsors and bigger purses. It was hard to resist and hard to blame anybody for going over. It was tough to make a living as a snowboarder, and there was the great carrot of the Olympic experience being dangled.

Still, it was hard for those of us who'd grown up with the ISF to stomach being forced to participate in FIS events or skip the Olympics. Nor did we like being suddenly labeled a "discipline of skiing" by the people who had ignored, or discriminated against, us until snow-boarding got big enough to be worth a lot of money.

As one of the pioneers of alpine snowboard racing, I had real reservations about getting in bed with the FIS mafia. To make matters worse, all sorts of new racers were coming out of the woodwork to join the FIS World Cup tour. People I'd never heard of were claiming to be "the U.S. Snowboard Team." *Huh?* I had been racing on the ISF tour for more than five years to prove that I was one of the top American riders, and here was a whole new group claiming they were the best in the United States. I thought it had to be some kind of joke.

I wasn't the only one who was angry, and it led to an ugly incident in Pitztal, Austria at the kickoff of the FIS-sponsored events when three top, longtime Austrian ISF riders—Martin Freinademetz, Dieter Happ, and Max Ploetzenader—showed up to protest wearing vintage ski clothes and equipment (a slam at snowboarders willing to race as a "discipline of skiing"). The drunk Austrians jumped Mike Jacoby and started beating on him with their ski poles. Mike's a big guy and got his shots in, and in true snowboarder fashion, the three Austrians later snuck into the FIS après tent and partied into the early morning hours with the FIS racers. But everywhere you looked, old allegiances and friendships were being frayed.

Peter Foley had retired from racing the season after he snapped his ankle but had come back as an assistant coach for Rob. He and I had patched our differences—mostly because he realized that I'd had some growing to do when I first joined the tour and had done enough groveling. He'd been a great coach but then left us to become the head coach of the new U.S. Snowboard Team. It was a great opportunity for him, but it strained his relationship with Rob, who saw the FIS and U.S. team as basically trying to put him and the ISF out of business.

I hated what this was doing to my sport and my friends. I would have never thought that politics and animosity would enter into a world created by a bunch of fun-loving rebels who grew up together when our main concern was finding fresh powder and getting to ride at ski resorts.

A lot of us were facing tough choices. If I wanted to race in the Olympics, I would have to join the FIS tour at least part-time. I was still loyal to the ISF; however, if I waited until the 1997–1998 season to make my push for the Olympic team, I would be low man on the FIS totem pole. That meant I would be seeded low for starting numbers. As I mentioned earlier, seeding is extremely important in snowboard racing. The more racers who have gone before you, the more rutted and thrashed the course becomes, making moving up in the standings more difficult.

Rob and I talked it over and decided that for the 1996–1997 season I would continue to race primarily on the ISF tour but participate in enough FIS races to get good seeding the next year.

It was a good year. Not a lot of podiums on either tour, but I was the top American finisher again and in the top ten riders on the ISF and FIS tours (thanks in part to a concession by the FIS to lure ISF riders by giving us two top-seed starts).

I finished the season on a great note by winning the U.S. Open in the parallel slalom. And I did it by beating two of the top slalom riders in the world at the time—Austrians Martin Freinademetz in the semifinals and Dieter Happ in the Big Finals—on Sundowner, the same hill Jeff Brushie had schooled me on a decade earlier.

I could hardly wait for the next season. Beating the best at the 1997 U.S. Open convinced me that I could go to the Olympics and do something special, like win a medal. Nothing was going to bring me down that spring, even when I was told to report for another ERCP.

The first couple of ERCPs had taken about ninety minutes. While I was still out from the anesthesia, the doctors would tell Dad and Missy what the team had been able to accomplish. They even had videos to illustrate which ducts they had been able to open and which were too scarred to do anything with.

After each procedure, I'd have to take it easy the next day as far as food and training, but then I'd be good as new—polishing off whole pizzas and maybe a quart of ice cream, hammering up mountains on my bike, or charging down slopes on my snowboard. It was more like having the twenty-four-hour flu twice a year than a life-threatening illness.

In fact, I was otherwise healthier than I'd ever been, thanks to the help of a new friend I'd met in Aspen in January, Dr. Carlon Colker. Carlon had come to town and stayed at the Aspen Square Hotel with his girlfriend and her family. They all had dinner with my parents one night, where Mom told Carlon about me.

Along with being a top-notch internist at Beth Israel Hospital in New York City, Carlon specialized in nutrition and training for pro athletes. He told my folks that he'd like to meet me, so we met up the next day after his snowboard lesson and went to the Aspen Club to work out. On the way, he started asking me about my diet. I was pretty confident that I'd impress this city slicker. I was 6' 3'' and about 185 pounds of pure muscle. I would have liked to have put on a couple of extra pounds but was having difficulty, so I complained that I couldn't seem to gain weight "no matter how many salads I ate." When he finally stopped laughing, he explained that my diet and training needed serious work.

Carlon wasn't exactly impressed with my finely tuned body. "Suffice it to say that, while I was impressed with his spirit and liked him a great deal even from the first moment we met, I was puzzled by his wispy physique," he says. "I mean, here was a guy who was introduced to me as a world-class snowboarder but looked more like a runway model."

Snowboard racing, Carlon thought, clearly required a rugged physique, big thighs and glutes to push out of the turns yet maintain speed, and as much lean muscle weight as possible to exploit gravity to help pull me down the hill. "He had none of this, but instead looked like he would have been more appropriate strutting on the catwalk in a little black dress, a Versace cravat, Burberry hat, with a Prada handbag, and some stiletto heels. To hear about his diet, you'd think a gerbil was talking—whole-grain pancakes and some kind of alfalfa sprout, hippie-shit Aspen concoction.

"Anyway, he asked me a great deal of questions. I actually did not expect this, because what I had heard about the pro-am snowboarders at the time was that they were really just a bunch of pot-smoking, floppy-topped, party-boy grunge dudes who did not care at all about taking the sport seriously and striving for athletic excellence. Chris was clearly different."

Carlon told me that he thought that with my height and build, I needed to get my weight up to about 220 pounds to be an Olympic champion. I was shocked—that would mean gaining 30-plus pounds, and I already had a difficult time keeping weight on. "No way," I told him, "you're frickin' crazy."

Carlon put me on a high-protein, low-carb diet and worked at improving my lifting technique and honing my strength exercises. A former bodybuilder and wrestler, he was also a sarcastic smart-ass who fit right in with my other friends and was soon calling me derogatory names along with my other so-called friends.

So now I had two trainers: Fab and Carlon complemented each other's efforts and became good friends. Before I knew it, I was getting bigger and stronger.

In fact, I was going to be Superman on a snowboard . . . but then the ERCP hit me like kryptonite. Dad and Missy knew from the videos of each procedure that the doctors were able to open up fewer and fewer bile ducts each time. I had experienced more infections too. It was apparent even to them that my liver condition was deteriorating faster than we'd hoped.

This time Everson came into the room as I was still trying to wake up, so he spoke directly to my dad. "I want to put Chris on the transplant list now," he said. "Low priority, but on the list."

Missy looked alarmed, but Everson held up his hand. "This is just a precaution so that he has a history of being on the list." The importance, he explained, was because there were far too few donated organs for the number of people who needed them. At that time, there were more than seventy thousand people on the waiting list in the United States alone, but only about five thousand donors— less than half the number of people who could have been following their deaths. The result was that as many as fourteen people were dying every day who could have been saved.

Organ donation agencies and transplant hospitals had to find a way to decide who would get the chance to live and who would not. There were several factors that were weighed to determine who had a higher priority for receiving donated organs. One was the probability of success: people who needed a liver but continued to drink or use drugs were a poor risk. Also at risk were patients who were already too sick and weak and not likely to survive the surgery or recovery, as well as those who developed liver cancer that spread beyond the organ before the transplant. Another factor was need: someone who needed the organ immediately was a greater priority than someone who could wait a little while. However, all of those people were tied into a third factor, and that was the length of time they'd spent on the waiting list.

Everson was concerned because PSC was different from other diseases that attacked the liver. As he'd explained before, it might take twenty or more years, or it could take three. But until the bile ducts actually closed up and the liver failed, infection set in, or cancer showed, PSC patients were often healthy and usually didn't qualify to be on the lists. Then when their liver failed, they would be on the bottom of the lists and maybe too late. Everson said he had to seek special permission to place a PSC patient on the list early, which is what he intended to do with me, since it was obvious that my disease was progressing.

Still, he said, there was nothing to worry about at the moment; he just wanted to err on the side of caution. But I got mad.

A little more than a year earlier, this quack Everson and that quack Tomasso told me I had twenty, even thirty years before I had to worry about a transplant. I'd been taking good care of myself with diet and exercise. Something had to be wrong with *them,* not me. "Are you nuts!" I yelled. "Aren't you jumping the gun a little? I'm fine."

Everson let me spout off, then nodded. "Yes, you're fine," he said. "I just want to play it safe."

"But the Olympics . . . ," I said. Suddenly my dream seemed in jeopardy; I couldn't be in the Olympics with a liver transplant.

"Don't worry," Everson said, "we're going to get you to the Olympics."

Everson seemed so sure of himself that I calmed down and held on to the thought: I'm going to get my shot at the Olympics before I have to worry about any of this. I looked at my dad, who shrugged and said he thought we should do what the doctor said was best. I nodded and gave in, "Okay, let's get on the list."

Mom, however, was furious when she heard the news. The world's gnarliest soccer mom can be a real mother bear when her cubs are threatened. At that moment, she saw Everson, not PSC, as the threat. Couldn't that damn doctor see that I was fine? Why was he trying to scare her boy?

Later that night as they lay in bed, my parents kept trying to figure out: *Why Chris?* The disease wasn't something I'd brought upon myself through poor lifestyle decisions I'd made. They didn't believe that anyone *deserved* to die. And certainly many people contracted liver diseases through no fault of their own, such as blood transfusions or accidental contact with the blood of a person infected with hepatitis. But those who used drugs or drank excessively had contributed to their health problems, and my parents wondered if their choices would impact me when I needed a liver transplant.

Even before we knew I had a liver problem, Mom had been incensed when she heard in June 1995 that former baseball great Mickey Mantle had received a liver transplant.

Mantle had destroyed his liver with decades of alcoholism. Yet, while fourteen people were dying every day waiting for transplants, many of them on the lists for months, he'd received a new liver just two days after being diagnosed with a liver tumor and cirrhosis caused by his drinking and hepatitis C. I'd been told that the presence of liver cancer could make me ineligible for a transplant because it wouldn't do any good; but Mantle had the tumor and then died anyway from cancer just two months after the transplant. Officials at the Dallas hospital where he got the transplant denied that he'd received any preferential treatment. But the public, including my mom, was still suspicious. *How dare he?* she thought. What about some young person who needed that transplant, and hadn't ruined his own liver, but died on the waiting list?

Now that it was her son who was going to need a liver transplant, Mom worried if I would also die because of some unfair decision. I had played by the rules. I worked hard, didn't do drugs, rarely drank alcohol, and treated my body with respect. I did everything I could to be in top physical condition, yet I was in the same boat as any heroin addict with hepatitis or a famous baseball player who drowned his liver in booze. But all my parents could do at night was pray.

"Chris had no real symptoms, so we were all incredulous," Dad remembers. "There is this impression that bad things happen to others, not to us. . . . I think we were all confident that things would work out just fine; he would continue his medication and yearly ERCPs and *way* down the road we would face what we had to. Chris was in our prayers every day, and we were confident that God had not brought him through so much when he was younger to see him fail now."

After the meeting with Everson, I needed to get away from it all, and there was no better way to do it than surfing. Missy and I decided to fly to Costa Rica and meet up with Shannon Melhuse and Robbie Morrow. I wore myself out on the waves and spent evenings laughing and relaxing with bonfires on the beach, lying in a hammock reading, or working my friends in chess.

The fear created by all that talk about long transplant lists and people dying while waiting slowly receded. I remember, however, one particular afternoon sitting on my board off the Osa Peninsula. I was looking at the jungle as scarlet macaws flew in pairs across the canopy and howler monkeys shouted to each other over the crash of the surf. *What a beautiful world and what a great life I have,* I thought. But then it struck me, this life that I loved might be a short one.

Chapter 10

Makin' the Team

The wind screamed like a jet engine on takeoff, whipping the snow horizontally while the temperature plunged into negative numbers. I was in the starting gate but could barely see more than twenty yards in front of me and was only guessing that the dark shapes moving around on the slope below were race course officials, coaches, and spectators. In other words, it was a typical day in January on Mount Bachelor, and I felt right at home.

I admit, I would have been more comfortable free-riding in the trees and out of the fifty-mile-an-hour-plus gusts than racing on the Thunderbird run under the Pine Marten quad lift. But I wasn't complaining; the weather was practically a home-field advantage for me over most of the other riders. After all, I'd started out thirteen years earlier riding in those conditions.

Bring it on! I thought. A little snow and wind wasn't going to stop me now. I was on the verge of realizing a dream I'd had since I was a grom chasing guys like Craig Kelly and Chris Karol all over that mountain. Back then, everyone thought I was nuts to talk about it. But when I got to the bottom of the course, I would know if I had made the first U.S. Olympic Snowboard Team and would be going to the 1998 Winter Olympic Games in Nagano, Japan, now less than a month away.

I'd had to sell my soul to the devil to be there, but I'd had no choice. The FIS was in charge of the Olympic snowboard events, and you had to play the game their way if you wanted to go. In some countries that all but shut out ISF riders, like my friends Nicolas Huet of France and Davide Marchiandi of Italy, who'd been screwed out of the opportunity to compete for their countries' teams even though they were top riders.

However, in the United States, the Ted Stevens Olympic and Amateur Sports Act, named for the Alaskan congressman who sponsored the legislation, required that some sort of provision be made to ensure that all amateur athletes—regardless of their affiliation—had a fair shot at making a U.S. national team.

In snowboarding that meant they had to figure out a way for ISF riders to compete for spots on an FIS-affiliated team. First, we had to get an FIS license, which cost fifty dollars, and register with the FIS-approved national governing body for snowboarding in the United States, which in this country was the United States Ski Association.

The USSA came up with the idea of three "Grand Prix" competitions—one in December 1997, one in January, and another in February, just a week before the Olympics—to determine the U.S. Olympic squads in both the half-pipe and giant slalom events. There were fourteen positions total. In alpine snowboarding the top three men and top three women would be chosen according to how they finished in two of the three Grand Prix races; the pipers also competed to pick their top three men and top three women. That left two "discretionary" positions—which could be split between the two disciplines or both assigned to one squad or the other—to be filled after consultation between Coach Foley, the USSA, and a group of coaches that included Rob Roy. Their decision would in part be based on riders' chances of medaling as determined by their international ranking.

You had to have FIS points and a FIS license to compete in the Grand Prix events, but you didn't have to be loyal to the FIS tour, which I wasn't. I'd done well at the FIS events the year before, which got me a top-seed starting position when the 1997–1998 season began. But I now concentrated on the ISF events and raced in just enough FIS competitions to keep my top seeding—out of loyalty, not practicality, as FIS events were worth a lot more money.

Winning the U.S. Open that past spring seemed to have taken me to another level, and I was enjoying my best season ever. I placed seventh at an FIS World Cup race in Tigne, France, and then eighth at an FIS World Cup at Whistler, British Columbia. I followed that with a sixth-place finish in the ISF race at Kaunertal, Austria.

With my feet no longer causing me pain, I was having a blast touring Europe with my teammates, including new faces Pete Thorndike, Ian Price, Adam Smith, Travis McLain, and Rosey Fletcher. Like the rest of us, the newbies were a typical bunch of snowboarders, fun-loving and ready to light Europe on fire.

Because I didn't drink, my teammates thought it was cool to appoint me "designated driver" so that they could chug German beer from one destination to the next, getting rowdier and more obnoxious toward the driver with each bottle. My revenge was to refuse to stop at rest areas and make them pee in their pants or in a bottle. Of course, they would turn that around on me if one of them was in the driver's seat; then they'd drive past the *Rosenberger* and *Movenpick* truck stops, laughing as I plastered my face against the back window and ignoring my pitiful cries. Meanwhile, as we streaked down the highway in Euro–cruise control, Thorndike, a redneck from New Hampshire, would be yelling out the window at the road hogs in the left lane. "The right lane is for savin' gas, the left lane is for haulin' ass, so get the hell out of the way!"

One night during a snowstorm in Mathon, Austria, a quiet village neighboring the ski resort of Ischgl, Thorndike, Price, McLain, and I decided to do a little sled-skitching. We tied three ropes to the bumper of our rental car, and then while one person drove, the other three sat on plastic sleds and hung on to the ropes for dear life. As the car slid and spun down the streets and around corners, the sledders tried to avoid getting slammed into immovable objects, like parked cars, street signs, and buildings, as well as each other.

Mathon was another typical alpine village walled in by peaks so high that the sun makes only a brief appearance each day. The Austrian

Alps formed a natural amphitheater, so no sound escaped without first bouncing back and forth from mountain to mountain. Especially the sound of a racing car and laughter at midnight. Someone was bound to notice.

We'd made a few passes down the main street and had paused in front of our pension when the proprietor came out, yelling, *"Nein, nein!"* We thought we were in trouble—maybe he was going to toss our gear and us out in the snow—but to our surprise, he brought us better sleds. A typical Austrian, he knew that the proper equipment was necessary to completely enjoy the snowfall. However, not everyone was so accommodating.

Betsy Shaw thinks it was my laugh that got us in trouble. "I could hear it from bed—distant but still distinctly Klug—then it would get closer and closer until it was right outside the window of my pension," she says. "I can remember thinking, 'What in the hell are they doing?' letting my envy take the form of annoyance. His laugh could be heard from one end of the town to the other, bouncing from mountain peak, to church tower, to barn in the sleepy community."

The residents of Mathon had been cool about our little escapade, or perhaps just too tired to call the cops. It was only after we decided to do the marathon slide to Ischgl, five miles away, to find a bar that we got in trouble. The Austrian cops pulled us over and pulled Ian (who was driving) out of our car and put him into theirs, and then drove off with him without saying a word. We considered just going to bed, but then Pete, Trav, and I decided that Ian would get pissed, so we decided we better follow the cops. They drove him to the station and put him in a holding cell until we paid the "fine" of about fifty bucks (which probably never made it to the city coffers).

Betsy remembers being impressed that I wasn't able to talk our way out of trouble. "That didn't happen too often," she says. "He had this way of kissing up and getting his way from the ugliest of authority figures, pouring on the charm, naivete, and prep-school manners. His bag of tricks didn't work on the blockheaded Austrian *polizei* this time though."

In between all the fun I was having, I was also getting stronger with each race. The hard work with Fab, Carlon, and my coaches paid off at the first Grand Prix in December at Sugarloaf Mountain in Maine. I placed second to Canadian Mark Fawcett, one of the Cross-M crazies. More importantly, I was the top American, which gave me a first place as far as qualifying for the U.S. Olympic team. I knew that if I placed in the top two or three spots at either of the next two Grand Prix events, I would sew up an Olympic berth. I thought it was a great omen that the next qualifier was going to be in my old stomping grounds on Mount Bachelor.

However, first there were more World Cup races in Europe, and I was on a roll. I started it with an eighth-place finish at Innichen, Italy, then followed that with a second-place podium finish at an ISF World Cup in Laax, Switzerland. I capped it all off by winning the FIS giant slalom in Grachen, Switzerland.

"This is a great win for me," I told a reporter from the *Aspen Times* who called after the win. "I'm beginning to peak at the right time. My goal for this year is to be on the podium representing the United States in giant slalom at the Olympics in Nagano. I expect to be there and to medal."

When I arrived in Bend for the second Grand Prix, I was welcomed as the hometown hero with stories in the newspaper and friends calling up to congratulate me. I holed up at the Aprils' home in Sisters, where even Missy's brothers, Rocco and Hub, had decided that I was okay—for a snowboarder—so long as I was nice to their sister. (Actually, Hub was snowboarding some of the time by now, so he didn't have as much ammunition.)

The morning of the race, I looked outside and smiled. It had been snowing all night, and it was still coming down. By the time we reached the parking lot up on Mount Bachelor, the wind was howling and the snow was flying sideways. *Perfect,* I thought.

In fact, everything was working out better than I could have hoped. The night before, the coaches and team captains attended a meeting to draw bib numbers for the top fifteen seeded riders. Rob drew bib number 1 for me. In soft snow conditions like we were going to have, holes and ruts develop fast, but I would get a fresh, relatively smooth course for my first run.

We waited in the lodge at the top of the Pine Marten lift for the competition to begin. Although normally we all would have gathered in the start area, nobody wanted to go outside in the blizzard until the last possible moment. I found a corner to be alone in and kept repeating my game plan in my head. *Take advantage of the good start position, and bury the field on the first run. Carve your board clean, and be balanced in the soft snow.*

At last it was time to go. I hurried through the blizzard, got into the starting gate, and snapped into my bindings. I wanted to get the qualification process over with. There would be another opportunity in Mammoth, California, the next weekend, but something could go wrong. I could fall and not finish; I could be sick or get hurt; some piece of equipment might break.

The real motivation, however, was that I wanted to qualify for the 1998 games there on Mount Bachelor, where I had learned to ride and first dreamed about riding in the Olympics.

So much had changed from my days on a Burton Performer or my Terry Kidwell Pro Model. I was riding a 185-centimeter board (almost six feet long and much longer than a half-pipe or free-ride board) built especially for me by Burton. It had an aggressive, hourglass-shaped sidecut so that I could carve, and a squared-off end (rather than curved, as racers try to avoid going backward and it meant more edge on the snow). My boots were fire-red Burton hard-shell racing boots especially designed for a sideways stance (as opposed to straight forward like a ski boot) that locked into Burton race plate bindings for a quicker toe-side to heel-side transition.

Some things had remained constant, however, such as the love and support of my family and friends, who were braving the blizzard that day to cheer me on. I wanted to qualify for the Olympics in their presence, on my hill. I leaned over and picked up a handful of snow and placed it on my neck. It was time.

I went out aggressively, even though I could hardly see from gate to gate, and had a great first run. It was so good that by the time the other riders finished, I was a full second ahead of my nearest rival. The dream was within my grasp.

Again I waited in the lodge to stay warm and focused. This time it was the waiting that was hard. I'd gone first in the first run, but now the top fifteen positions were reversed and I would be racing fifteenth. I never watch my competitors ride before a run, but we were getting reports of riders biting it in the gnarly weather conditions. The course was only going to get worse as more riders went ahead of me—making bigger holes and enormous troughs in the turns. I'd have to hit them just right or they'd eat me up.

The call came for me to head to the starting gate. I tensed my body as hard as I could, even my facial muscles, and then let it all go as I stepped out into the storm. Buckled in at the starting gate, I reached down for a handful of snow to rub onto the back of my neck and looked down the course. *This is my hill,* I thought. *I've done hundreds of turns here. I'm going to get it done . . . now!*

It was impossible to see beyond the first few gates. Nearly a foot of snow had fallen between the first and second runs, and more was coming down, whipped by the wind. The course itself was somewhat scraped off from previous riders, but I knew that if I swung a little wide on a turn and got into the powder, it would be like jumping into quicksand. Still, I couldn't be too cautious—that's when you make mistakes or get caught by riders willing to lay it on the line.

At the signal from the start referee, I pulled out hard and headed for the red object that I had to assume was the gate. Suddenly the weather didn't matter, nor did the fact that I could barely see out of my goggles. I was riding strong, in rhythm with the banked turns, and pushing off them to build speed but not forcing anything.

Three-fourths of the way down the course everything was still going as planned. The spectators who were lined up along the bottom third of the course screamed, clapped, and rang cowbells as I went by, but I barely heard them as I focused on the gate ahead of me.

Then, a near disaster! I juiced a turn and shot wide around the next gate into a foot of powder. I felt my speed dumping and had to muscle my board back on track. I couldn't see and had to feel for the rut and get back in rhythm for the last few gates.

As soon as I stopped in the finish area, I looked up at the leader board. I was worried that I'd blown the race, but there I was, still on top. The non-seeded riders had yet to race, but I wasn't worried. I knew I'd won. And more importantly, I WAS GOING TO THE OLYMPICS!

Everyone freaked at about the same time. My dad, Missy, and her dad, Ray, were all crying and hugging. My friends were jumping around in the snow like they were on pogo sticks. I'd definitely had the biggest cheering section on the mountain, and after the awards we all paraded to the Aprils' place for a party with my family and friends, including a lot of the people who had helped me get there, like Scott Peterson, the Pattersons, and the Jamiesons. In a way, I was going to be competing in the Olympics for all of us.

With two first-place finishes among American riders, I was the first male snowboarder ever named to the U.S. Olympic Snowboard Team. But I wasn't the first snowboarder: that honor went to Rosey Fletcher, an Alaskan native and one of my World Pro Snowboard teammates, who'd finished her winning run just before me.

The state and local media were all over the hometown kid who was going to Nagano. The Bend and Portland papers ran front-page stories, and I got a full-page spread that week in *USA Today*. The big surprise was that *Ski Racing* magazine put me on its cover, standing on the podium and spraying the crowd with a bottle of champagne (nice guy on a bitterly cold day, but, hey, it was a tradition and I had to celebrate). That cover was a first for a snowboarder.

The day after the win at Mount Bachelor, I flew to Mammoth for the last of the Grand Prix events. It was mostly a victory lap and money stop for Rosey and me, but for all the other American riders, the remaining spots on the team were still open.

I finished second in the race to a Canadian, Jasey-Jay Anderson, which meant I'd swept all three qualifiers as the top American. I thought my WPST buddies Pete Thorndike and Ian Price would make the U.S. Men's Olympic Alpine Team with me, but in the end it was Jacoby and Adam Hostetter. Rosey, Lisa Kosglow, Sondra Van Ert, and Betsy Shaw all made the first U.S. Women's Alpine Team.

After the race at Mammoth we had one of our traditional wild snowboarder parties. Those who weren't going to Nagano pretended that it didn't matter, but it was pretty obvious that they were disappointed. They were all good sports about it. One of the Cross-M riders, Jeremy Jones (now-legendary Big Mountain rider famous for "Jonesy Lines" extreme off-piste snowboarding) came up to me after Mammoth and said, "I'm psyched to watch you in Nagano, Klug. You're going to win it!" I thought that was a real compliment coming from a member of the "rival" American pro team.

The qualifications pretty much proved what the ISF riders had been saying about which tour had the superior talent. Of the seven alpine riders on that first team, five of us still rode on the ISF tour, and a sixth, Joker, had been with us until he switched. The WPST had also done well placing riders on the team with Rosey, Betsy, and me (plus Michele Taggart, who had been with us in the beginning but now focused solely on half-pipe, which is the team she qualified for); and Ross Rebagliati had squeaked onto the Canadian team. The Cross-M team had placed Joker and Hostetter on the U.S. team, as well as Jasey-Jay Anderson and Mark Fawcett on the Canadian.

We left straight from Reno for Osaka, Japan. On the flight over, I couldn't help but feel a deep sense of satisfaction. Ten years earlier, I'd been laughed at when I talked about snowboarding in the Olympics. Seven years had passed since the headmaster at Deerfield told me that snowboarding wasn't going anywhere and that I was making a big mistake.

Well, there'd been no mistake. Snowboarders were going somewhere—we were going to the Olympics. Only now the dream had changed slightly. I didn't want to just go to the Olympics—I wanted a medal.

Chapter 11

The Rising Sun

Maybe because I'd been dreaming about what it would be like for a good chunk of my life, walking into the Olympic arena for the opening ceremony in Nagano had dreamlike qualities to it. I don't particularly remember the sequence of all the events; they come to me in images and feelings.

Those of us on the first U.S. Snowboard Team, and probably many of the other winter sports athletes, were accustomed to competing in front of only a few hundred people. Sometimes it seemed like the "crowd" was mostly our friends, fellow competitors, and families. But now there we were, strolling along in our cowboy hats and Western-style blue dusters, waving to forty thousand stoked spectators, who cheered nonstop from the moment the guy from Albania walked in with his country's flag to long after the team from the host nation, Japan, brought up the rear.

I felt like I was in the Super Bowl . . . still that kid who brought all the lamps out of the house and made his grandmother run patterns so he could imagine what it was like to play in the big time under the lights. I was walking next to Rob Roy, who just smiled as he soaked it all in. I think he'd been as pumped as I was at the win on Mount Bachelor, and again when he'd been invited on board as a U.S. Snowboard Team assistant coach because he had three athletes on the alpine squad. I felt good for him; twenty-five-plus years racing and coaching and he was finally at the Olympic games, the biggest event in skiing and now, for the first time, in snowboarding.

I was also happy that the moment was finally here to get the Olympics rolling. Up to now it had been a madhouse—first the wild scramble just to get to Japan (even worse for our families, who suddenly had to find hotels and air tickets), then the crush of a zillion little things to do and demands of the media.

A lot of it had been fun. There's nothing an old snowboarder loves more (except free food and a party) than *swag* . . . free stuff. After we checked into the hotel in Japan that had been reserved for the U.S. Olympic team prior to going to the Olympic village, we were instructed to meet downstairs in a gymnasium-sized conference room with a lot of little booths around the sides and up the middle. We were each given a shopping cart and told to stop at each booth. My cart was soon filled to the top with Olympic wear and paraphernalia—race suits, jackets, socks, dress shoes, as well as the cowboy hats and blue duster jackets for the opening ceremonies. They even gave us luggage to pile it all in, and I left with three oversized duffels crammed with all the things I was supposed to get and whatever else I could get my hands on.

Some of us weren't too happy, however, about having to wear X-Nix gear, the "official" clothing sponsor of the U.S. Olympic Snowboard Team. Most of us wanted to wear our own gear and represent our sponsors, who'd believed in us and paid the way to even get to this point. But the Olympics are big business and its sponsors pay a lot of money to have their logos (and no one else's) displayed. We were told that every sticker and logo on our equipment—boards, helmets, boots, and clothing—had to be measured and approved by Olympic and FIS officials. If these emblems weren't already part of the equipment—and of regulation size—they would be covered with duct tape. Oh, the irony of duct tape being used against us.

Of course, the press got wind of The Great Clothing Rebellion and ate it up. It was just one more reason for the more than eight thousand accredited members of the media on hand—six thousand of them broadcasters—to love the snowboard crowd. We were the extreme punks who didn't want to wear the team uniforms and dyed our hair red (my buddy Mathieu Bozzetto from France) or green, wore spiked dog collars even when competing (party-boy Mike "Kildy" Kildevaeld of

Denmark), were always good for a colorful "dude" quote, and dropped F-bombs at press conferences (Ross Powers).

I think some of us got caught up in trying to live up to the press's stereotype of snowboarders, as if we had to prove that even though we were at the Olympics, we were still outlaws at heart. The press dug it, too, especially when word got out that those lovable, rebellious shredders were having a family squabble because some of the big names in boarding were knocking those of us who were participating in the Olympics as "sellouts" to corporate commercialism.

Obviously, those of us who were competing didn't agree. I loved the backcountry-soul aspect of the sport as much as anyone and had embraced it since I was a kid. But I also loved to race my snowboard and see how fast I could go when matched up against the top alpine riders in the world. I'd done both for longer than a lot of the critics had even been on boards. Now, here they were—many of them making a pretty good living from corporate sponsorships—making up the rules about who were the real snowboarders and who weren't.

As far as the media were concerned, I was pretty tame stuff. Sporting a long ponytail was about as controversial as I got. I was just trying to stay focused on what I wanted to accomplish.

The Olympic race—a two-run, combined-time giant slalom—suited me. I would have liked it even better if it had been a parallel giant slalom, because I enjoyed being pitted against another rider instead of just the clock and there was more room for error. I also thought the head-to-head competition was more fun for spectators. But the standard GS was the next best thing.

Keeping my focus wasn't easy with all the hype. I was used to preparing for my races in small alpine communities and resorts. The Olympic village was in the heart of downtown Nagano, a pretty big and definitely bustling city. So I was more than ready for the opening ceremony, after which we'd take off for Shiga Kogen, the village in the mountains near the snowboarding venue.

The opening ceremony was held during the daytime—a chilly

afternoon but beneath blue skies. Just watching everybody lining up to enter the arena was an amazing sight—the colorful uniforms and flags of 72 nations, 2,176 athletes, competing in 68 events.

I was proud to be marching in behind the U.S. flag, representing my country and my sport. As we walked up to the arena, Rob and I reminisced about how it seemed so unreal that snowboarding had gone from backcountry obscurity, a novelty like the hula hoop, to the international spotlight. We were stunned when we entered the arena and felt what it was like to hear forty thousand people cheering. Then we looked up at the huge Jumbotron screen, and there for a moment were our faces. We laughed and pointed like two kids in Disneyland.

Most of my immediate family was there—Mom and Dad, Jim, Hillary, Nanny, and Missy (Jason stayed home to watch on television). They'd all been cheering from the beginning and amped it up when the U.S. team appeared. Then they about passed out from excitement when Rob and I appeared on the big screen.

"Jim and I just kept looking at each other and saying, 'I can't believe we're here. Do you realize we're in Japan . . . at the Olympics!' And then Chris's face showed up on the screen," Missy recalls. "He had this huge grin on his face and was obviously so happy . . . which meant I had to start crying because I was so happy for him."

The next morning we left for Shiga Kogen. It was time to get serious about what I came there to do.

I rode well in training and was as confident and strong as I'd ever been. Even my liver problems seemed like just a bad dream. There was so much that was unknown, and I wasn't going to let it stop me from enjoying the moment.

I'd kept my illness a secret from all but my family and closest friends, and certainly didn't discuss it with the press. It was none of their business. I didn't want bad press for me or my sport, or for people to misunderstand why my liver was failing. *Oh, there goes Klug—needs a new liver, you know . . . a snowboarder. Need I say more?* As Everson had promised, my liver had held out long enough to get me to the Olympics, and I didn't want to think about much further down the line.

The day of my race dawned with bright blue skies, a setting for showcasing alpine snowboarding. In fact, we received exciting news during our training runs—we were going to be the first televised event of the 1998 Olympics. It was supposed to be ski races, but a cold front that brought with it snow and wind had canceled the ski events at Hakuba, sixty miles away. So we would be on center stage when people all over the world tuned in.

Snow conditions were perfect—grippy spring-hero snow; the warm weather and sun had softened the top layer, making it perfect for carving. So I'd selected a stiffer board than I would have if conditions were icy, and was carving turns like I was riding on rails.

I felt so relaxed that during one of my inspection runs (we were allowed to slip down alongside the course to inspect the layout of the gates and the terrain), I rode over to where I saw my family tromping up the hill to get a good vantage point next to the barrier fence above the finish area. They looked nervous—Mom was already hyperventilating—so it was me who had to give *them* a pep talk. I had assured them I was riding well and feeling confident when an Olympic volunteer buzzed past on a snowmobile with Nanny clinging to his back, smiling and waving; at least she wasn't worried.

As I turned to go, Dad reminded me to "plan your race, and race your plan." I smiled at that—it had been a long time since he'd first coached me with those words, and though I'd heard similar strategies from other coaches, including Rob and the U.S. team coach, Peter Foley, it was Dad's version that played in my head before every race.

On the way back up the hill, I looked around behind me. I couldn't believe the size of the crowd. There were thousands and thousands of people already filling up the stadium-style seating or pressed up against the fences on the side of the course, with more people trudging up like ants to a picnic.

With that sort of energy building, I was stoked not just for myself but for my sport. About the only bummer was the logo and sticker police from the FIS and Olympics who were lurking in the starting area, carefully eyeballing every piece of clothing and equipment. If something aroused their suspicions, they jumped with their little tape measures, and any deviation from the rules was immediately covered with duct tape.

They made me cover up my little Aspen Ski Company and Bolle sunglasses stickers on my helmet. The overkill on the logos ticked me off so much that I just started placing duct tape all over my equipment and clothing whether there was anything beneath it or not. Then I wrote "KLUG" in big, black letters on the pieces I'd placed on the front and back of my helmet, figuring they couldn't object too much to self-promotion. I had so much duct tape on me and my gear that I joked with my teammates that I should find out who made the stuff and see if they wanted to sponsor me.

Finally, it was time to race. I had an early start number and knew I would have a clean course to attack when I got in the starting gate. Down below there were ten thousand (so we'd been told) Japanese, Americans, Germans, Italians, Canadians, Austrians, Swiss, French and God-Knew-Who-Elses waiting to see the first-ever snowboard race in the Winter Olympics. Fortunately, I couldn't see them, because after an initial flat beginning there was a pronounced drop to the steep section, or I might have freaked. But I could imagine they were getting really pumped up.

I'd planned my race with Rob's help. Attack the top half of the course, where my strength would help me gain precious tenths of a second in the flats, then dive into the turns on the steeps, maintaining an aggressive high line but with quicker edge changes.

My gaze lifted from the course to take in the scenery. Sometime after coming back from my heel injuries, I had added a new ritual to my starting-gate preparations, and that was to take in the grandeur of my surroundings. Whether it was the Alps or the Rockies or the Cascades or Japanese volcanoes, the sight took me back to the beginnings and reminded me of why I got into snowboarding in the first place. I guess it was a way for me to put it all in perspective. Maybe it was just the size of the mountains, but it helped me realize how unimportant this race was in the grand scheme of things and that I should just relax and enjoy being in the starting gate with all the possibilities of the day still ahead of me. I loved that moment and had a smile on my face as I leaned over, grabbed a handful of snow, and placed it on the back of my neck. It was time.

The first run of our event turned out to be one of the tightest ever. Conditions were perfect and we could really go for it. When it was over, the top ten riders were all within one second of the leader, Jasey-Jay Anderson of Canada. I was tied for second place with Thomas Prugger of Italy, just seven hundredths of a second out of first. Seven one-hundredths . . . you couldn't snap your fingers that fast.

This is perfect, I thought. I was close enough that I wouldn't have to take chances. Just make another good solid run and let the chips fall. But the feeling wouldn't last.

For some reason, the race officials delayed the second run for two hours. In that time, the front that had canceled the ski races at Hakuba had moved in, bringing with it snow, fog, and a bitterly cold wind that almost instantaneously dropped the temperature fifteen degrees, into the single digits Fahrenheit, and severely limited visibility. Our beautiful springlike day had turned into a nasty blizzard, transforming the formerly soft snow into an ice skating rink.

The field was down to the top fifteen riders from the first run, with the fifteenth rider going first and then the rest in reverse order. The first five racers went down the course but had such difficulty that the race was halted for twenty minutes.

Then the weather eased up a little. It was still snowing and blowing, but not quite as bad. The first rider to race after the delay was my WPST teammate Ross Rebagliati from Canada, who'd been in eighth place. He was a talented and experienced racer, but wasn't having his best year. Still, he took advantage of the small break in the weather and ran a good, solid race, taking the lead. Ueli Kestenholz of Switzerland followed him and also rode well, landing in second place until Thomas Prugger, who was tied with me, bumped Ueli to third.

By the time I got into the starting gate, the weather had taken another turn for the worse. I'd had our technician put a little extra on my edges to make them razor sharp, but I was concerned that the board I was riding might be a little stiff for the icier conditions. I peered down the course but couldn't see farther than the first couple of gates. It was going to be tough to race any plan that afternoon.

I wasn't going to complain about the weather, however. I've always felt that one of the cool things about our sport was that we were all at the mercy of Mother Nature. Sometimes you lucked out and got a sunny window, and sometimes you got a gust of wind that practically blew you back up the hill. But everybody was rolling the same dice on what conditions they'd get.

I knew that a solid run still would have me in medal contention, with only Jasey-Jay to follow. This was the race I'd dreamed about for half of my life, and I wasn't about to let the gold medal get away from me because I was too timid. Besides, I'd never entered a race thinking I'd be satisfied with a second- or third-place finish.

Ten thousand people had come for a show, and we were sure giving it to them. Suddenly I felt like laughing as I thought, *Hey, you're at the Olympics, dude, and in position to win the gold medal! Go for it!*

So with the wind stinging my face with ice particles, I rubbed a handful of snow on the back of my neck and grabbed the rails, rocking back and forth as the start referee counted down. "Ten seconds . . . five . . . three, two, one . . ." I exploded out of the gate and assumed a crouched, low-profile, aerodynamic position into the flat pitch at the beginning, picking up speed as I reached the break-over onto the steeps.

This was what it was all about—a life on edge, carving past the gates, my body angled thirty degrees above the snow, my hand lightly brushing over the surface on my toe-side turns, trusting my board and my strength to hold. I flew around each stubbie as close as I dared, the material popping like firecrackers as I thwacked them going by.

I reached the halfway point with the clock showing I was on pace for the gold medal, though I didn't know it and could concentrate only on trying to see ahead to the next gate. My stiff board was getting bounced around on the icy surface, and I was struggling to see in the flat light and blizzard conditions. Between gates I briefly swiped at my goggles to clear the ice.

Battling, I made it three-fourths of the way down the course. Then, as I crossed over onto a heel-side turn on the lower pitch, my right arm got tangled in the gate for just an instant, spinning me slightly sideways, dumping my speed, and sending me off line. I had to fight just to get around the next gate. I made it but had lost my momentum.

Down at the bottom of the hill, my family and friends had just about exploded with joy when the halfway split on the timing board showed that I was on a gold medal pace. Their eyes went back to the huge television screen, trying to will me through the last few gates. Then they saw the mistake—a small one, but they knew it could cost me the race.

On the course, there was no time to dwell on the error, I just had to ride as aggressively as I could and try to make it up. I took chances and gained some ground, but it wasn't enough. I crossed the finish line and looked up at the results board. My heart sank into my racing boots. Sixth place. I'd lost my Olympic medal.

I was really disappointed and muttered a few F-bombs under my breath. I was so close and knew that this had been one of those opportunities that seldom come along. Who knew if I would get another chance? I was close to tears and didn't want to talk to the CBS television crew that was running toward me.

The media was already filming my family, capturing the look of disappointment on the face of my father, as well as the tears rolling down the cheeks of Missy and Hillary.

"We saw him hook his arm on the gate, but in my head I was still thinking he would be on the podium," Missy says. "When they said sixth over the loudspeaker, I thought, 'How could that be? His mistake was not that huge.' I was so upset for Chris; my heart was aching for how disappointed he would be. Of course I burst into tears, and Jim grabbed me and hugged me for a long time. The cameras were relentless. I tried to be encouraging and waved to let Chris know that sixth in the Olympics was still great, that we were all so thrilled just to be there and proud of him."

I felt like crying myself but smiled and waved back at my family. Then I noticed the crowd again. The fans were going crazy, jumping up and down and dancing as if they were at a big party. *Oh man, I don't believe this,* I thought when I realized what the fans were now up to. *They're doing "The Wave."* Then in the middle of the pandemonium, I spotted my brother, Jim, holding up a long staff with a huge American flag on it that he began to wave back and forth like we'd just won some battle.

The F-bomb that had formed in my throat now came out as a laugh. I was heartbroken that I'd come up short, but at the same time I was stoked just to be there with the crowd going nuts and my family acting like I'd taken the gold. I just stood there and couldn't quit laughing.

The CBS crews converged on me, and I raised my arms above my head to acknowledge the crowd, who were cheering for all of us who'd come from our backcountry roots, who'd ignored the wisecracks, who'd found our own hills when *they* wouldn't let us on the ski slopes. "I just want to thank the Japanese people for this experience," I yelled into the microphones. "This is great! Thank-you, Japan, you're awesome!"

At that moment, even as I waved one last time to the crowd, my dream shifted once again. I promised myself that I was going to return to the Olympic games in 2002 when they were held in Salt Lake City, Utah, just a six-hour drive from my home in Aspen. *And then,* I swore, *I'm going to win my medal.*

My little speech for the cameras might have been longer on enthusiasm than eloquence, but I did better than my mom. When the CBS crew jammed a camera in her face and asked for her reaction, she froze, then tried to salvage the moment by saying, "I'm just happy he wore his helmet and he brushed his teeth."

Mom tries to explain herself. "I was glad he was smiling," she says. "He has such a great smile, and I think that is what cued me to say something about brushing his teeth. I felt his future was so uncertain and unpredictable with the PSC that I wanted it then and there for him. Although I am the queen of singing songs of hope and optimistic expectations, I was holding all that medical info inside and just crushed for him when he came up short. I think I wanted to say something so 'away' from the loss that I focused on the Mom things: he wore his helmet, brushed his teeth, and had good manners. What else could a mother ask for?"

That's classic! Her son was in the Olympics and had just missed a medal by a few tenths of a second, and she's happy I brushed my teeth? We've given her a hard time about that one ever since and banned her from doing any more interviews.

I'd be less than honest to say that the pain of the loss disappeared in the roar of the crowd. But their response in the finish area and their continued best wishes when they saw me on the streets afterward helped me get over the disappointment when later that evening at the medal ceremonies they played "O Canada" instead of "The Star-Spangled Banner."

The standings had remained as they were when I made my run. Jasey-Jay fell in his second run and didn't complete the course. Ross Rebagliati won the gold, Thomas Prugger took the silver, and Ueli Kestenholz went home with the bronze. The women's alpine saw the favorite, Karine Ruby of France, win the gold; Heidi Renoth of Germany, the silver; and Brigitte Koeck of Austria, the bronze.

All in all, snowboarding put on quite an exhibition for its debut. The half-pipe event proved to be one of the most popular events at the games. My own finish had been less than I'd hoped for, but I felt that snowboarding had proved that it belonged. We certainly partied like it afterward.

My brother, Jim, remembers the party in the hotel as one of the greatest all-time parties, and he ought to know. "Everyone—all of the racers were having a great time," he says. "It was as if they were celebrating the coming-of-age of their sport. Somehow their Olympic debut legitimized what they all had been doing for so many years."

On the other hand, the Japanese had never quite figured out how to set up a party for snowboarders—that is, a large padded area with unbreakable furniture and nothing made out of glass. In Europe there was always a bar or disco—most of which had seen plenty of winter sports athletes in action and knew how to handle them. Japanese hotels, however, including the one we were staying at, have vending machines in the lobby with everything from beer to whiskey but no place to go with it.

So we partied in the lobby. There was lots of drunken karaoke, and I vaguely remember Jasey-Jay and Martin Freinademetz commandeering a snowcat and doing laps in the parking lot. The party lasted until someone threw a beer bottle through the window of the gift shop, which was definitely not cool. Thank God for the U.S. Hockey Team trashing their hotel rooms or we'd have gotten worse press than we did.

The press got bad enough a couple days later when the International Olympic Committee announced that Ross Rebagliati had tested positive for marijuana and would be stripped of his medal. I heard about it while eating in the athletes' cafeteria and was bummed. After all the years of work and then putting up with the bullshit of FIS politics in order to legitimize our sport as something other than a playground for pot-heads and part-time athletes, in my eyes Ross had literally just pissed it all away in his urine test.

As the scandal unfurled, Ross protested that he hadn't smoked pot in months. But, he said, he'd attended a pre-Olympics party where he might have inhaled "secondhand" smoke. Those of us who knew Ross rolled our eyes; he was practically Bob Marley on a snowboard, but it was tough to point fingers. Plenty of snowboarders, including some who'd tried out for the games and even those riding in them, smoked pot on a regular basis.

In the end, Ross got to keep his medal. It turned out that there was nothing in the IOC drug-testing regulations that prohibited weed. It wasn't considered a performance-enhancing drug. We even began to hear rumors that medalists from other sports, including skiers, had tested positive, and rather than throw gasoline on the fire of scandal, the IOC decided to back off and hope that the matter went away quietly.

In snowboarder fashion, we all laughed about it and saddled Ross with new nicknames like "Secondhand Smoke Rebagliati" and Ross "Buy Me a Bag-liati." We even kidded him, saying that he won because he was the most relaxed guy on the mountain, and therefore pot could be considered a performance-enhancing drug.

I considered Ross a friend; we'd been teammates since 1992, and I respected him as a competitor who'd won his medal by being the best rider that day. But inwardly, I—and a lot of other riders—seethed.

"What little reputation snowboarding worked so hard to get is ruined. This really sucks," Norwegian rider Anne Molin Kongsgaard told the press, speaking for a lot of us.

It did suck. And it played right into the hands of the same press who'd loved that wild side of snowboarding for a good quote and colorful stories.

"The Olympics invited Beavis to the Winter Games, then busted him for smoking pot," said one columnist in the *Denver Post*. "Wherever there's a halfpipe, there's smoke. Marijuana is as much a part of the snowboarding culture as baggy pants."

In fairness to Ross, wacky weed was never listed as a prohibited substance; he didn't know he would be tested for it. And I personally believe that the IOC was just out to embarrass snowboarding. Otherwise, why did the IOC try to make an example of Ross and our sport when they knew they couldn't enforce it legally?

Still, how could we expect to have our sport taken seriously when the gold medal winner became a joke for late-night talk shows and commentaries in newspapers? Ross even added to it after the games by going on a media tour as the public's poster boy of pot-smoking shredders.

After my race I stuck around for a week to see some of the sights and events with my family. I went to Hakuba to cheer for Katie Monahan, an Aspen skier, in the Super-G and watched Picabo Street win her gold, then took in a few hockey matches. But my heart wasn't in it anymore, and I took off before the closing ceremonies.

I was eager to head to Hawaii for a week of surfing before resuming the rest of the competition season. Jim and Missy traveled with me from Japan, and we met up with Fab and his friend, pro tennis player Mia "The Croatian Sensation" Buric. (And just to set the record straight about me being cheap, I paid for the house we stayed in.)

We still had more than a month of the racing season left, and I just wanted to decompress from the Olympics. As usual, surfing and being with my friends and brother did the trick.

I finished up the season on both a high and low note. I traveled to Vermont and took the North American giant slalom championship at Mount Snow, Vermont. The race was held on one of the longest courses ever, and I remember other riders collapsing in the finish area and crashing into the promotional banners because their legs were wiped.

Then I drove to the U.S. Open at Stratton, where I placed fourth. The Open that year was more significant for two other reasons.

One was that it was the first time I entered a boarder-cross race. For those who have never heard of a boarder-cross, it's sort of a gladiator-style Chinese downhill (where everybody lines up on top of a run and then bombs their way to the bottom) through an obstacle course with four riders at a time, six in the X-Games (with a few elbow and shoulder shots along the way). There's lots of carnage, which made it popular as a televised event.

However, I never even made it to the actual race. During a training run, I thought I could "double" the first two jumps (rather than go off one, land, and then go off the next, I wanted to fly off one and come down on the back side of the second). In fact, Kildy and I decided to have a contest to see who could do it first. I pulled out of the start as hard as I could and popped the takeoff but came up short on the landing and pancaked into the up side of the second jump. I ended my season riding back down the hill in a ski patrol toboggan and then off to the hospital for X-rays, which revealed a severely sprained ankle and heel bruise.

The second reason that U.S. Open was significant was because it was the last time for alpine racing. For the next two years, Burton would sponsor boarder-cross events, but after that all racing was dropped. Only the legendary half-pipe and freestyle events survived. Just more of an indication that racing was in trouble in the United States.

Chapter 12

Death of a Hero

After the season, I flew back down to Costa Rica with Missy for my annual surf trip. Riding the waves, I quickly got over my disappointment with my finish at Nagano and "Weed-gate." Hearing from old friends, like Tad Dobson, after I got back helped me put it all in perspective as well.

"We'd lost touch over the years, but seeing him on TV in Nagano," Tad says, "doing exactly what we had dreamed about all those years, filled me with a sense of accomplishment despite the fact that he was there and I was not. I chose the corporate desk-job path, and he had chosen to follow his dreams. I was proud of him."

Along with Olympic skiers Katie Monahan and Alex Shaffer, I was made a grand marshal for the annual Fourth of July parade in Aspen. I still enjoyed Central Oregon and looked forward to spending time there each summer with my friends, staying with the Aprils at their beautiful log home on Indian Ford Meadow, outside of Sisters. But I'd also fallen in love with Aspen and had made it my primary home during breaks and in the off-season.

The town is as close as you get in the United States to a Euro alpine community. Plus my family was there, including Jason, who'd moved to town, although not Jim, who'd done well for himself in the business world but didn't like it and "retired" to Bozeman, Montana, with his golden Labrador, Bo. He started Yellow Dog Flyfishing Adventures, which arranges wild-ass fishing trips all over the world.

One would have thought that after the Olympics my friends would have stopped verbally abusing me, but if anything the ball-busting only got worse. A favorite was to unfairly accuse me of being overly competitive.

"Chris absolutely can't stand to lose at anything, whether it's on a bike or a game of Scrabble," Gary "The Toymaker" Albert claims. "The funny thing is how much he loses, which is all the time. Fab schools him in racquet ball, I beat him at tennis and Scrabble, Boogie waxes him in basketball, and Gibans beats him at chess and ping-pong. A few years ago, he tells me he's going to crush me in tennis. Well, the game ends with him smashing his racquet on the court and yelling, 'You don't respect me.' And I'm, 'What's wrong?' He says, 'You're just standing there hitting the ball, and I'm running from corner to corner.' And I say, 'Well, Chris, you're not making me run.' . . . He was so angry about it and I made him even madder by asking him, 'Why's it so important for you to beat a fifty-seven-year-old man at tennis? What's that going to prove?'

"He'll stay hacked off for a half hour, then something will make him laugh, and he'll realize how ridiculous he is. . . . What's different about Chris is that he likes to brag about all that losing stuff too . . . it's part of his humility, his ability to laugh at himself. It's what makes us laugh about him—his successes and his failures, he thinks it's as funny as we do. But then he won't stop with that goofy Scooby-Doo giggle. . . . He's lucky we're willing to be his friends with a laugh like that."

Despite the constant harassment, most of the time my life just seemed to keep getting better. After the Olympics, I signed a new two-year contract with Burton, my first multi-year contract with the company. It gave me financial stability, enough to start looking around for a home to buy in Aspen. I had a great family, a great girlfriend, an exciting, wonderful career as a professional athlete, and okay friends.

However, all that just meant I was due for a dose of my parents' old warning that no life was without obstacles. My reminders came in the form of ERCP roto-rootings at University Hospital.

In late July I was in Oregon on a bike ride over McKenzie Pass with my friend Brad Boyd, who owned Euro Sports in Sisters, when I realized that I was going to have to cut my visit short. I hadn't had much of an appetite over the past few days, and when I did eat, I couldn't digest my food very well, which meant bile wasn't moving from my liver into my intestines.

Normally I would have hammered Brad climbing the pass, but I wasn't feeling well and he smoked me. He was waiting at the top of the pass with a question on his face. He didn't know about my liver problems, but I knew I was going to have to go back to Colorado for an ERCP and decided to tell him that my liver was "acting up" and that I "might" need a transplant "sometime in the future." He was concerned, but I told him it was no big deal.

I went back to Denver, got the ERCP, went through the usual two days of "bile flu," and returned to Oregon. But something still wasn't right, my energy just wasn't at its usual levels. Again, Brad and I were on a ride and started talking about how I was looking to buy a place in Aspen. He asked why I wasn't looking in Oregon.

I considered Aspen my home by this time, but there was a more practical reason. I told Brad that I couldn't have lived anywhere but Colorado, because I needed a liver transplant and was on the waiting list at University Hospital in Denver.

"That's when Chris first really told me about the disease and how serious it was," Brad recalls. "Before that it was sort of 'Yeah, yeah, I may need a liver transplant someday.' Now I was like, 'Wow, this is not a maybe thing. I could lose my friend.'"

I tried not to let my health problems get to me. Whenever I started to worry, I remembered and was inspired by a new sports hero who'd been through hell and back. I first saw him in late July when Brad and I went out to watch the Cascade Cycling Classic, a weeklong road-bike stage race that went through Central Oregon.

The CCC had been a yearly event since I was a kid, and was considered one of the premiere road-bike stage races (a new stage each day) in the United States. It was the race serious bikers and domestic race teams competed in if they weren't competing in the Tour de

France. This year we were particularly interested in seeing a relatively unknown—at least outside of biking circles—American racer named Lance Armstrong.

Lance was a top-flight rider who'd won big races in Europe, though the Tour de France victory had eluded him. As we were now learning from the press, Lance had survived testicular cancer that had spread to his brain and lungs. It should have killed him, but here he was, recovered from his battle and racing in the CCC to train for the next year's Tour.

Road-bike racing is a team sport. To win it usually requires the support and effort of "domestiques," who take turns riding ahead of the team leader to break the wind resistance or wear out other teams' riders. But Lance was on his own, having been dropped by the French racing team when he became ill. He'd told the *Bend Bulletin* newspaper that he didn't care if he won the CCC, but then he went out, took the lead, and never looked back. No one, including well-supported teams, could keep up with him.

Like many other people, I was inspired by his story of overcoming his illness to return to his sport. It helped when I had to return to University Hospital for another ERCP in September, only two months after the last one. I didn't like the implications.

It wasn't that I tried to stay in the dark about the disease. Dad and I had done a lot of research on PSC and liver diseases in general, including looking into the various research and hospital programs around the country. That's how we learned that University Hospital's liver disease and transplant program was considered one of the best in the world and that the very first liver transplant had been done there.

The University Hospital liver transplant program had been started in the 1960s by Dr. Thomas Starzl, the first surgeon to perform the operation. Back then the transplants could buy patients a few more years, but long-term survivors were few. Some didn't even make it out of surgery. A liver transplant was more complex than any other transplant surgery—including heart—and massive blood loss was common.

However, the biggest threat was after the surgery. The body's immune system is designed to attack dangerous "invaders" like viruses and bacteria, but the same defense would reject the new organ. The only way to suppress the immune system in the early years had been with steroids, which had their own negative health effects, including damaging the kidneys. Nor were they always effective and tended to get less so over time.

However, I learned that the outlook for transplant patients had improved greatly over the years with better surgical procedures and improvement in antirejection drugs. Some of the drugs still had to be used with steroids, or had unwanted side effects of their own, but long-term survival had greatly increased.

By the time I started going there, Starzl was gone, but the program had flourished. Dr. Everson was especially great to me. The hard thing during this period of uncertainty was that if I started running a fever or felt achy, I didn't know if it was a common cold or if my liver had suddenly tanked. Sometimes I would be convinced it was the latter and hit the panic button and call Everson's assistant, Cathy Ray. She'd track him down, and he'd talk me through it—assuring me that I was still getting relief from the ERCPs and that the frequent tests showed no signs of liver cancer. When the day came that I needed a liver transplant, he said, the wheels had already been set in motion and I would be okay.

After the procedure in September, I decided that two ERCPs in as many months was an aberration. I wanted to remain in denial that my liver was a time bomb ticking away faster than I'd initially believed. I turned my attention to the racing season, ready to pick up where I'd left off as one of the top riders on the ISF and FIS tours.

I was still loyal to the ISF, but the disintegration of that tour had continued and there weren't enough events or money to compete solely on the older tour. Coupled with the rise in sponsorships and number of events on the FIS, it was obvious that to remain a professional snowboard racer, including getting enough exposure for my sponsors—Burton, Bolle, and the Aspen Ski Company—I was going to have to race in FIS events.

In November the World Pro Snowboard Team reconvened in Breckenridge for Rob Roy's traditional camp. I was riding great and was anxious for the season to start when we met at the Breckenridge Recreation Center for an afternoon dry-land workout. I remember the date, November 18, because it was my twenty-sixth birthday and Adam Smith, Ian Price, Pete Thorndike. and Travis McLain had organized a sushi dinner party for me later that night. In a couple of days we'd leave for Europe and the first World Cup races of the season.

We were wrapping up the workout with gymnastic floor exercises such as flips and handsprings to improve our balance, agility, and strength. In retrospect, the flooring wasn't ideal, as it was made up of unconnected mats that had been shoved together. But I'd made several exercises without any accidents, so I wasn't worried about it when I decided to go for a round-off back handspring. I'd done a few of them already; they weren't pretty, but I was getting better and gaining confidence.

I took off running and lunged into the round-off when my right foot went between two of the mats and was trapped. My momentum continued forward, however, bending my knee almost completely in the opposite direction than it was intended to go.

My teammate Travis McLain had sprained his ankle playing hoops with all of us a couple of days earlier and was on the sidelines about five feet away and saw—and heard—the whole thing.

"I heard the mat slide and then this loud 'POP.' His leg bent in entirely the wrong direction; he looked sort of like a cartoon character," Travis remembers. "Then he got this huge wince on his face and screamed like some kind of wounded animal as he fell to the ground. It was gnarly, dog. His knee got broke up like a high school kegger."

My knee started swelling. I've never to this day seen a ruined knee swell up so big so fast. Within ten minutes my knee was the size of a watermelon . . . a big watermelon. Rob and my teammates helped me to the car, and we headed down to a medical clinic to get X-rays. The doctor who examined me and looked at the X-rays wasn't sure—he thought it was possible that I'd just slightly torn one ligament and maybe stretched another—but he still recommended that I get an MRI to determine the true extent of the damage.

Travis and I returned to my hotel room, where he packed my gear. In the meantime, I called my dad, who tried to reassure me that it probably wasn't as bad as I thought. "No, Dad, this is serious," I said. Then I called Missy.

"When Chris called me from Breckenridge, I could tell how scared and worried he was," Missy says. " I tried to reassure him that his knee would be okay. He said, 'You don't understand, it looks like a basketball. It's over. My career is over.'"

Missy and my parents rushed over from Aspen to get me and saw for themselves that this wasn't a knee "sprain." I was on painkillers, so the only hurting I was doing was psychological. Meanwhile, poor Travis, who was alternately freakin' and trying to be supportive, had been drinking steadily to get past the sight and sound of my knee bending in the wrong direction. They loaded up the Pooper and we headed home to Aspen. Missy drove my car, while I lay down in the back with my leg propped up, screaming anytime she hit a bump as the painkillers wore off.

The next morning I went to Aspen Valley Hospital and saw my friend Dave Hollander for an MRI. After the MRI, Dave and I sat down and looked at the images together. He confirmed that I'd torn my ACL (anterior cruciate ligament), LCL (lateral collateral ligament), MCL (medial collateral ligament) and the biceps femoris, part of the hamstring muscle group. That alphabet soup of capital letters meant it was bad, really bad.

I asked Dave who he thought I should have fix it. I was leaning toward my friend Tom Pevny. Tom was an athlete, and if anyone understood what it would take to get me back on snow, it was him. What might work for a weekend snowboarder wasn't going to be good enough for me. The limits I had to push my legs to with the kind of

G-forces I experienced in a high-speed racing turn were many times greater than in recreational riding. It wasn't just repairing the knee surgically so that it would hold up to the stresses, either. It was going to take rehabbing at the highest level.

Still, I wanted Dave's opinion. He cemented my decision when he replied that there wasn't anybody better than Tom.

Later that afternoon, Tom looked at my MRI. He knew immediately that the damage was severe. In fact, Dave and Tom both thought that my career was over when they looked at the MRI. But they didn't say that to me.

In surgery the next morning, Tom thought his first impression that the injury was severe was actually optimistic. I'd managed one of the worst knee injuries he'd ever seen. The ACL, MCL, and biceps femoris had been torn completely off the bone where they attached; the LCL had actually "avulsed" when it tore, meaning that it took some of the bone with it.

Dave Hollander watched the surgery for a little while and then reported back to my family and Missy in the waiting room. "The only way I can think to describe it is a turkey drumstick after Thanksgiving . . . bare bone, nothing's attached." He'd also gathered, from the way Tom was talking, that there was a chance I might not ever walk normally again, much less snowboard professionally.

What concerned Tom wasn't so much the ligament and tendon damage. He could repair the damage, although he had concerns whether I'd ever regain the full range of motion for the joint. What worried him more, however, was the damage I'd done to my peroneal nerve, which runs the length of the leg and is what allows us to flex our ankles and toes. If the nerve had been permanently damaged, I might end up having what in layman's terms is called "drop foot." I'd be unable to raise my toes as I stepped and would have to walk by swinging my foot out and around.

The good news was that the nerve had not snapped. But Tom could see that it was badly bruised and stretched, which could have also been crippling. Nerve tissue does not like to be messed with and sometimes will not respond after being injured.

After the two-and-a-half-hour surgery, Tom acted optimistic when he saw me. I peppered him with questions about what I would need to do to resume my career. I understood that I was out for the season. Fab had torn his ACL a few years earlier, and just about every hard-core skier in Aspen had the scars to join that club, so I knew what it meant. But as for the future, all Tom could say was that the surgery had gone well and if I worked at rehabilitation "appropriately," I might be on snow again by the next season. What he didn't say but was definitely on his mind was: *Or no matter what you do, you may never snowboard again.*

The worst piece of news he gave me was that I was going to have to stay off the leg entirely for eight weeks. My knee was going to be totally immobilized so that I couldn't bend the joint. I was going to be given crutches and could get around on those, but even then I was going to have to be really careful that there were no accidents to put stress on the knee.

I was sent home to recover, which in this case meant one of the condominiums at the Aspen Square Hotel. The Aspen Square was great, and it had an elevator, which would be a big help during my recovery. I had been working with a realtor since September trying to find a place to buy that I could afford. I'd located a tiny condo (and I mean tiny, 499 square feet) for $185,000, but Missy and I weren't going to be able to move in until the first week of December.

I wore the full leg brace only when I went out. When I was in the Aspen Square condo or later at my own place, I didn't have to wear it, but several times a day—and all night—I got strapped into a motion machine that would slightly flex and straighten my knee to prevent it from stiffening up and to break up the scar tissue. I also had an icing machine—called a Cryo Cuff—that surrounded my knee with ice-cold water and another brace I had to wear at night that kept my foot flexed up to guard against drop foot.

The inactivity was making me nuts, and I immediately began driving everyone else insane by wanting to play board games to pass the time. There were marathon battles of chess with my dad or Gibans. (And I mean marathon—I grew old waiting for those two to move. Man, were they slow.) Gary, and sometimes his wife, Kathleen, spent hours whipping me in game after game of Scrabble by scores of like 380 to 65. It had to be painful for him, but he'd show up almost every day to play whatever I wanted.

Missy was the real trouper. Not only did she have to try to fill my waking hours with diversions when my friends weren't around, then sleep next to my creaking, whirring machinery, she also had to empty my urine bottle a couple of times a night. Getting me unhooked from the motion machine was such a lengthy procedure that sometimes I would have already peed in my bed.

I started rehabbing with Fab within a week after surgery; however, initially it was just massage and leg lifts. After two weeks I had regained some movement in my foot and toes, but it was questionable if the nerve would ever come back fully.

Only after eight weeks had passed was Pevny willing to let me start working with Fab on a more aggressive rehab program. I was eager to get going even though I had pretty much concluded that my racing career was over. I had maybe a couple degrees of motion in my knee, my leg muscles had atrophied to the point where my injured leg looked about half the size of my other leg, and I could hardly move my right foot.

At that point I was just hoping I would be able to walk normally again. But while Tom didn't say it, he was still pessimistic about a full recovery. He was initially encouraged by the foot movement, but it would have to improve dramatically or I'd still have drop foot. It was also a toss-up whether I'd ever regain the strength in my leg or the full range of motion in my knee.

Still, he knew I had to try. At eight weeks, when he was convinced that the surgical repairs were healed sufficiently, he turned me over to Fab for what quickly became twice-daily torture sessions.

When Fab started in on me, I had only a 2 percent range of motion in my knee and could move it maybe a couple of inches. But I'd show up at the Aspen Club, lie on my stomach, bite into a rolled-up towel, and then scream while Fab wrenched my heel toward my butt. It was the most intense pain I've ever felt. After a few of these sessions, someone brought in a bottle of whiskey and offered me a shot as a joke, but I obliged, just before Fab said, "Are you ready for this?" and then jumped on my leg again.

It took a week of Fab's gentle persuasion before I had the flexibility to even turn the pedals of a stationary bike one complete revolution. We worked twice a day, every day, for two to three hours at a time, fighting for another degree of flexibility.

Progress was slow, but after the first month or so, I began to think about the possibility of racing again. Maybe my Olympic medal dream wasn't dead.

With the excitement of that thought, however, I also began to worry that my sponsors, who'd been understanding and supportive when I got injured, would drop me if I didn't get back by the next season. I was thankful that I'd signed the two-year deal with Burton before buying the condominium, but they and Bolle and the Aspen Ski Company were paying me to race and promote their products, not to learn to walk. I renewed my dedication to rehab, practically living at the Aspen Club.

The torture sessions went on month after month as Fab put me through a rigorous program to first regain motion, then my balance, and finally the strength in my leg. We got to where we could get my heel within a few inches of my butt (though I still can't touch all these years later). The knee itself healed tighter and stronger than ever.

I was still nowhere near where I would need to be to get on a snowboard, much less compete. In fact, I went ahead with Plan B by taking a full load of classes at Colorado Mountain College. I planned to go on from there to a good four-year institution (and was eventually accepted into Middlebury College in Vermont). Missy and I even enrolled in a ceramic class together; I loved throwing clay on the wheel, although everything I made was either an ugly, misshapen pot or a spittoon (not on purpose).

My friends were incredibly supportive, as always. "You big pussy," Gary Albert would say as Fab ground away on my knee and I screamed. I, of course, had to put up with the ribbing and "jokes" like reaching inside my gym bag for my shoes only to find a tube of "the treatment."

Still, while I hate to admit it, because it will only encourage them, my friends and family kept me going. There were times, I'd confess to Missy, I wanted to take it easy. Times when I began to doubt myself, or at least doubt that I would ever return to pro racing. I was sure my sponsors would drop me as damaged goods and that my friends would find better things to do.

Missy would just assure me that she believed in me and that I would be back if that's what I wanted. She was my rock and my nurse.

The amazing thing was that no one gave up on me. Not my sponsors. Not my friends. Not my family. One particularly down day, my mother dropped by the apartment and caught me moping around and feeling sorry for myself. I'd just been through a particularly rough session with Fab and felt like I'd taken two steps backward and maybe none forward. "I'm done," I told her. "My career's over."

Mom heard the frustration in my voice and asked me a simple question. "What do you love about racing, Chris?" she asked.

I stopped complaining and thought about her question. "I love the starting gate," I replied. "I love the possibilities at the start of every race."

"Well, then," she said, "you have two options. Cry . . . give up . . . find something new to love doing. Or you can do everything you can to get back on your board."

Oooh, talk about tough love, but then she hit me with the kicker. "If I remember correctly, there's a promise you made to yourself to win a medal in Salt Lake City in about three years."

With my ass still smarting from the psychological kick in the pants, I rededicated myself to my rehabilitation. The lessons I'd learned from a lifetime in sports helped a lot. When it hurt and I felt like I couldn't do any more, I kept driving my legs like I was fighting for one more inch on the football field, only it was a hundred more revolutions of the pedals on the stationary bike.

At three months Tom Pevny thought that I was doing really well and that the rest would depend on how hard I worked and how dedicated I was to returning to competition. "It wasn't long before I'd see him at the Aspen Club every time I was over there," Tom remembers. "It had to hurt and cause a lot of discomfort. Most people would have been too discouraged, but instead he worked a hundred times harder than most people—even those I'd see in Aspen who were completely dedicated to returning to active lifestyles.

"I've seen pro athletes whose injuries were a lot more minor than Chris's injury start feeling sorry for themselves, get lazy about their rehab, and never make it back. But Chris had the best attitude I'd ever seen toward rehabbing his knee. He never seemed to doubt that he would not let this alter his life."

Well, I had my doubts, but except for the few times I broke down to Missy and the time Mom slapped me out of the self-pity mode, I kept them to myself. I believed that I could make it happen and made sure that I surrounded myself with positive people. My feeling was that if you're going to tell me I can't do something, then I don't need you around.

One thing I was thankful for during this time was that my liver didn't act up. Maybe God had decided to give me a break, but after two ERCPs in two months, I didn't need another throughout this period of recovering from the knee injury. It allowed me the time to concentrate on one problem, and I was proud of how I'd responded.

However, I couldn't completely get away from the specter of PSC. In fact, I was reminded of just how serious the disease was one night in February 1999 as I tuned in to a news report. There on the screen was my old football idol Walter Payton holding a press conference. He looked terrible—thin and scared—then he started crying as he disclosed that he had a rare disease called primary sclerosing cholangitis and needed a liver transplant or he would die. "I ask those who care for me to pray," he said and buried his face in his hands.

It unnerved me to see him so upset. I couldn't reconcile it to the image I had of my hero; he'd always been so strong and tough. I was frightened and angry when he broke down and wept. Why was he so distraught? PSC sucked, but it was curable with a transplant. I wanted to yell at the television: *"Hey, I've got the same thing. It's not that bad."*

Later that night, I did my best to forget about the image of Payton crying and asking people to pray for him. I wrote him a letter, saying that I had PSC too, but that we would both get a transplant and go on with our lives. I never heard back.

In March I talked Tom into letting me hit the slopes to carve a few turns. His surgery on me and Fab's tough program had strengthened my legs until they were probably stronger than they had been before the injury. I had a scar that ran eight inches from the top of my knee, but that was the only physical evidence of what had appeared to be a career-ending injury.

Still, he was apprehensive. On a scale of one to ten degrees of severity, he figured I'd scored a nine. (I guess your leg has to come off to score a ten.) With most patients he would have preferred a few more months of rehab. He even suggested that I think about postponing getting back on the board until the next season. But he knew how desperate I was to get back on track and gave me the go-ahead. "But take it easy," he warned.

It was a sick powder day at Buttermilk Mountain, and I wanted to venture into the trees on the more challenging Tiehack side. But for once, I did the smart thing and let myself be satisfied with a few runs on smooth groomers. I can't begin to describe the joy I felt as I carved long flowing turns and knew that my legs would be up to the challenge ahead of me.

I moved back to Bend, Oregon, in May and started working with Rob at Mount Bachelor. We spent about three weeks on snow getting the feeling and strength back. There were days when my knee would ache, but I wasn't going to use my injury as an excuse to slack off. I wasn't going to let other people make excuses for me either. How could I when half a world away, Lance Armstrong didn't let his nearly fatal battle with cancer stop him from winning his first Tour de France. Poor Missy, if she slipped and made a reference to my "bad knee," I'd snap at her. "I don't have a bad knee!"

Three months later, on November 2, 1999, I was more worried about snowboard politics than about my knee or the PSC as I was driving from Aspen to Salt Lake City to participate in physical testing with the U.S. Snowboard Team. Obviously, some of the nerves were due to my trying to make a comeback after a full year off due to a knee injury. But the bigger stress was that I was trying to make this comeback as "the new guy" on the U.S. Snowboard Team.

My longtime coach and friend, Rob Roy, had decided to quit in October. The ISF had been gasping for air during the Olympic year and had all but collapsed during the season I was injured. Former ISF riders, as well as newcomers, were all going over to the U.S. Snowboard Team, which could provide a cheaper training alternative and was also in charge of who got named to the national team. Rob was down to Adam, Trav, Ian, Pete, Ben Fairchild, and me, and simply couldn't afford to go on. I understood why he had to get out, but it left me feeling adrift. The World Professional Snowboard Team had been my snowboarding family for nearly ten years. I needed to find someone else to train with, and the U.S. team was it.

I was eligible to join the team as a full-fledged "A" team member, but then I wouldn't be able to represent my sponsors and my contracts and would have to represent U.S. team sponsors. I couldn't see doing that—my sponsors had stood by me through my injury, and I wanted to repay the loyalty. So I worked out a deal that allowed me to join as a "training team member." It meant that I would be charged eighty-five hundred dollars a year for coaching and training with the team, as well as having to pay my other expenses, such as travel. But I could still represent my own sponsors and continue to solicit my own support.

Now I was going to have to find a way to fit in on a team where I knew most of the other riders but none of them well. Some of those I did know, I didn't particularly like, such as Anton Pogue, a seemingly overly loud, obnoxious, party animal who ran with Danish Olympian Mike "Kildy" Kildevaeld, one of the biggest goofs on the circuit. Pogue and Kildy had managed to add to Ross's legacy when a couple of months after the Olympics, they and Canadian pro Brett Tippee got pulled over in Nevada doing well over a hundred miles an hour and were busted for grass. Actually, Pogue didn't get in trouble, because he was asleep in the back of the truck. When the cops finally saw him, they pulled their guns, with Kildy yelling, "Don't shoot! Don't shoot!" Of course, the newspaper headlines were all over: "More Olympic Snowboarders Busted for Pot."

I was confident that my knee was strong and ready to prove that I was more fit than any rider on the U.S. team. However, I was wondering what my reception was going to be like in Salt Lake City. The physical test—a sort of pre-camp measurement of agility and strength—would be the first time I was going to join my new teammates and coaches. There was still some lingering animosity between the old ISF riders and the FIS, though personally I was over the politics and, after missing a season and wondering if I would ever ride again, just wanted to get back on the race course.

All the various scenarios were going through my head as I drove through the barren Uintah Mountains between Price and Spanish Fork, Utah. I figured the sooner I got there, the sooner I would know what it would be like, so I kept it on Euro–cruise control and rocked out to Blink-182 and Green Day.

As I started my descent from Soldier Summit, I got tired of listening to CDs and switched over to the radio instead. A moment later, I nearly veered off the road when the news broadcaster announced that "football great Walter Payton" had died the night before from liver cancer. I pulled over to the shoulder of the road and began to cry. I knew that it wasn't just liver cancer that killed Payton—the liver cancer was the result of primary sclerosing cholangitis.

After Payton's press conference that past February, I hadn't had to deal much with my illness, except for a "routine" ERCP in May. I knew the doctors were saying that they were having difficulty finding bile ducts they could open, but I still felt fine as I'd worked on my knee rehab and physical conditioning.

I continued to cling to the belief that anything like a liver transplant would be years down the road and that when I needed one, there'd be no problem. By then, I figured, they would be growing organs in Petri dishes or cloning them from my own cells. I wouldn't have to count on someone else dying and someone else making a horribly tough decision in the midst of their worst nightmare so that I could live.

I had noticed that there'd been no more word about Walter, so I figured he'd already had a transplant and was living happily ever after. But now he was dead at age forty-five. He'd been as tough an athlete as there ever was, and it scared me—if it could kill him, it could kill me. Suddenly it hit me why he had cried at his press conference just nine months earlier. *He already knew he had cancer,* I thought, *and wasn't eligible for a liver transplant.*

It had been nearly three years since I'd been diagnosed, and back then Dr. Everson hadn't said much about the possibility of liver cancer. In subsequent years the possibility of cancer had entered the conversations, but always as sort of a bogeyman on the fringe of reality. I was aware that it was bad and that getting the disease essentially meant you were probably going to die, because it spread rapidly to other organs and even a transplant wouldn't save you, so they wouldn't even try.

I looked around at my surroundings. The bleak, dry landscape of eroded rock and the sparse vegetation that seemed to be barely clinging to life mirrored the bleakness of my thoughts. "Why me?" I asked. But there was no answer in all that emptiness.

I got my cell phone out and called my dad. "Did you hear about Walter?"

There was a slight hesitation, then he replied, "Yes."

"What does this mean for me?" I asked. "Am I going to die?"

A few hundred miles away in Aspen, my dad flinched at the words. What guarantees could he offer me when there were none? "I think we had felt that Walter was on a path similar to that of Chris," Dad recalls. "Some sickness episodes, but he would get them cleared up and with the transplant, he would be fine.

"We saw parallels: both were relatively young, both in great physical shape, both seemed to have a strong faith in God, and both were athletes and used to overcoming hardships. We just expected similar paths to health. When Walter died, we were all hit by surprise. How could this happen? It reminded us all of the seriousness of the illness and the finality of it if a transplant was not forthcoming. It was a strong wake-up call."

Dad did his best to console me. He pointed out that there were substantial differences between Walter's case and mine: Walter was older and probably wasn't diagnosed until much later in the disease's progress.

On the other hand, my dad reminded me, I had been lucky that a routine blood test had turned up the problem and led me to Dr. Tomasso. Dad noted that Tomasso was a real hero for sticking with his medical fishing expedition until he found an answer. Because of him, I was in the care of Dr. Everson and the team at University Hospital—"the best liver specialists in the world"—and they were monitoring me closely.

"You know," Dad pointed out, "it turns out it was a pretty good idea that Everson put you on the transplant list way back when he did."

I recalled how angry I'd been with Everson when he suggested putting me on the list. *Are you nuts?* And that my mom had been ready to tear him to pieces for scaring her son.

My dad had taken to calling me "the bounce-back kid." He said it was because every time I got knocked down—whether it was fighting for my life as a child, or on the football field, or the chronic heel problems, and most recently, the knee injury—I'd bounced right back up, ready to have another go at pursuing my dreams. Now, he said, I needed to bounce back from Payton's death and not accept his fate as my own.

I knew Dad was right, Everson had it under control. But this was hitting me like a head-on car accident. There was nothing the doctors had been able to do for Walter . . . what made me different? I needed to touch base with Missy.

"Chris called me from the roadside and broke down," Missy says. "He told me over and over how Walter died of the same disease that he was now fighting. I think this is when Chris really realized that PSC was a serious disease and, yes, he could die. I just kept telling him that Walter was at a different stage in the disease, and he was a different case. At that moment, Chris was a little panicked, and I really just tried to separate him from Walter in his own mind. I told him he would not die from this. . . . That we would have a life together."

I was more scared than I had ever been in my life, but I couldn't just sit there in the middle of the Utah desert and cry. Starting the car, I pulled back onto the highway and pressed the pedal to the floor. In no mood to listen to music, I just cruised and reflected on what the news of Walter Payton's death meant to me.

I said good-bye to my childhood hero out there where the skies are so clear and limitless, the land so open and honest. And I thought about how I was going to deal with PSC and the suddenly large and menacing shadow of cancer. Again, the simple philosophies I'd learned from football and racing gave me strength. It wasn't over until the last second had ticked off the clock, and in the parallel giant slalom (PGS), you never gave up, because anything could happen.

A couple of hours later, I arrived in Salt Lake City somber but determined to not let this disease win without a fight. I was going to worry about the things I could control, which at the moment was my comeback.

I checked in with the team at our hotel. Now the fact that I didn't know anybody worked in my favor. I didn't want to have to make attempts at lighthearted conversation with someone, or have them think that I was being aloof if I couldn't bring myself to be outgoing. Most of the rest of the team had paired off in the rooms, but I was given one of my own, giving me time alone with my thoughts.

Early family photo before the arrival of my sister Hillary. I'm on the far left. Vail, Colorado, 1970s.

Here I am at age thirteen with a snowboard I received as a Christmas present.

I'm attempting a hand plant in the U.S. Open halfpipe competition in the late 1980s.

All photos are courtesy of the author's collection unless otherwise noted.

My grandmother, Nanny, and me at the 1998 Olympics.

Carving a heelside in the 1998 Olympics at Shiga Kogen, Japan. (Photo courtesy of the *Los Angeles Times*.)

Walking past "the Man," Dr. Igal Kam, the day after my surgery.

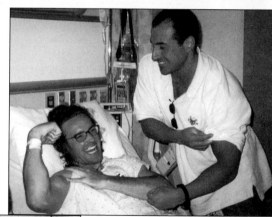

Carlon is checking my guns after my liver transplant surgery.

Left to right: Pat, Carlon, Missy, me, Khalif, Dad, and Brad. My first walk outside after surgery. August 2000.

My first time back in the saddle. My buddy Marco is checking out my new twelve-inch long "tattoo."

(Opposite page top) Pat and Ray April cheering hard in 2002.

(Opposite page bottom) Arcing a toeside in Park City, Utah, site of the 2002 Olympic Snowboarding events. (Photo courtesy of Dennis Schroeder, *Rocky Mountain News*.)

The Klug family in the U.S.A. house in Park City, Utah.

A photo of Lance Armstrong and me at the opening ceremonies of the 2002 Olympics in Salt Lake City.

2002 Olympic Medals Presentation. (Photo by Tim Mutrie, *Aspen Times*.)

(Opposite page top) My family and friends from Aspen. From left to right: Jon, Boogie, me, Missy, Gary, Fab, and Dave.

(Opposite page middle) Meeting my donor family for the first time in Salt Lake City.

(Opposite page bottom) Aspen homecoming 2002.

Congratulations With Love, From Your Donor Family
2002 Winter Olympic Bronze Medalist

Opening the stock market with halfpipe gold medalist Kelly Clark on March 13, 2002.

Lighting the torch to open the 2002 Transplant Games, Walt Disney World, Florida.

I slept surprisingly well that night, and in the morning I was ready to be tested. I did really well, which I'd counted on, and was pleasantly surprised that my new teammates weren't as big a group of obnoxious jerks as I thought. Of course, I was the guy from the ISF who'd been vocal about the politics before the Olympics, so we were all a little more tolerant than instantly accepting of each other. But I quickly learned that snowboarders are essentially the same whatever team or tour they came from—fun-loving, irreverent, and, well, different. My kind of people.

I experienced this early on in the testing when Anton Pogue, Pete Macomber, and I were sent to one end of the big gym where we were being evaluated. This test was called "box jumps." Essentially, you're jumping from one side of a platform raised twenty-four inches off the ground to the top of the platform then back down on the other side, then back to the top and back down again. We were told to do as many as we could in ninety seconds while a young female trainer kept count.

Anton went first. He was dressed only in his surf trunks and a T-shirt and, typical Pogue, was free-balling with nothing underneath. About halfway through his test, his trunks started to loosen and then dropped to his ankles. The young woman looked up and got an eyeful of Anton flopping around and for a moment couldn't quite seem to figure out what to do next, so she kept staring. Of course, Pete and I were rolling on the floor laughing (the first real introduction of the Scooby-Doo giggle for my new teammates, though it was coming out now as almost a shriek).

Anton was unfazed and kept jumping like nothing had happened. The young woman finally dropped her gaze and kept her eyes on the platform for the remainder of the test as she dutifully kept counting.

Grabbing at his shorts for the last couple of jumps, Anton got them as far up as his knees when the trainer said it was time to stop. Blushing and trying not to crack, the trainer turned to us and asked who wanted to go next, which brought on another round of shrieks, this time joined by Anton, and it was ten minutes before we could resume.

I packed my car and was ready to leave Salt Lake City that afternoon with a different perspective on my teammates and my life. Between Anton's Full Monty and their love for snowboarding and surfing, I thought, *This team can't be that bad, at least they're fun to hang out with.*

They'd certainly made me forget about Payton's death, at least until a conversation I had with Stacia Hookom, one of the women riders from Colorado. As it turned out, she was a big football fan and Walter Payton had been one of her heroes too. We were talking about his death when she said the liver disease was probably caused by steroid use.

I liked Stacia, but the comment made me angry. "You don't know what you're talking about," I said, but dropped the subject. What she said had also frightened me. What would my teammates think; in fact, what would the public think if they knew I had a liver disease? Would they assume it was because of drugs or drinking? It made me more determined than ever to keep my secret.

However, thinking about what my dad and Missy said about not having to share Payton's fate also made me determined to participate in my own destiny. I could choose how to face this obstacle, and it wasn't going to be lying down. I wasn't dead yet, and in the meantime there were waves to ride, laughter to be shared, turns to carve, and an Olympic medal to win in Salt Lake City in two years.

I got into my car, started her up, and cranked the tunes. Climbing back over Soldier Pass, my eyes were on what lay ahead, not looking back over my shoulder.

Chapter 13

Never Give Up

After I recovered from the initial blow, I think Walter Payton's death was hardest on my folks, especially my mom, who hadn't really accepted the seriousness of the disease until then. My dad had not given her all the details, and she really hadn't wanted to know them. But now they had no choice.

"Warren and Chris had sheltered me from the reality of PSC, but that day in November I got my first sense of the danger of all of this medical stuff," Mom recalls. "When Warren called me, he said Chris cried when he heard it, and all I could think was that my little boy was facing the reality of a possible death sentence all by himself on some nowhere back road in Utah. . . . That was another moment of asking for God's grace for my children. I could not be there, but God could and was."

Payton's death frightened me, but it also made me more determined than ever to enjoy what I had while it lasted. Even if I didn't share Walter's fate and received a new liver when it was time, no one knew if I would be able to return to my sport. No professional athlete to my knowledge, or to that of anyone else I had spoken to, had ever made such a comeback.

When I talked to Dr. Everson about it, he was skeptical. Transplant patients had a lot to deal with, such as the drugs they had to take to keep their bodies from rejecting the new organ. Also, returning to a sport where there was a risk of high-impact crashes might not be wise. I wasn't used to people telling me I couldn't do something, and it ticked me off when he did. It became a goal to prove him and any other doubters wrong.

My first task, however, was fitting in with the U.S. Snowboard Team. I was coming off a knee injury that a lot of them had heard was career-ending, and I hadn't proved I could come back from that. However, I would be starting with good seeding, because when I got injured, I'd written letters to USSA and FIS requesting my points be frozen, a standard practice for injured athletes. Therefore, my points from the Olympic season were frozen, and I got to return to my same top seed. The system was designed so that a veteran who got injured wouldn't have to start at the bottom of the totem pole—sort of like a pro football player not losing his position on the team, and his livelihood, due to injury—but it wasn't the sort of thing that went over well with some of the FIS regulars whose seeding was affected by my return.

I didn't really know my coach, Jan Wengelin, other than thinking he was this strange Swede. He was a former ski racer who'd coached the Canadian Snowboard Team leading up to the 1998 Olympics, but politics and missed paychecks caused him to leave before the games. He'd been replaced by the dark master of the Cross-M'ers, Jerry Masterpool, but was later hired after the games by Peter Foley to take over the U.S. Snowboard Team's alpine squad.

Jan had something of a reputation as a wild partier on the FIS tour. But when I met him for the first time at the U.S. Snowboard training camp at Copper Mountain that October, I had no idea of what kind of coach he'd be.

I got through training camp and was riding strong as we entered the season. However, I quickly discovered that even Fab's rehab wasn't a magic pill that made my knee the same as it was before. I started off in December with a respectable sixteenth place at the World Cup race in Sestriere, Italy, the site of the 2006 Olympic ski events. I then hopped into a car and drove to Kaprun, Austria, with team trainer Kyle Wilkens. When we arrived, I could barely move, and my knee stayed so swollen and stiff I had to sit out the race.

Except when I simply couldn't race because the knee wouldn't let me, I refused to use my injury as an excuse for a poor showing. I had some dark moments when I wondered if I'd ever regain my form, but then I'd get angry and just kept working through it.

All the sweat and pain paid off when I took third in the World Cup giant slalom at Whistler, Canada. I followed that by winning the Grand Prix at Breckenridge. With the podium finishes, I noticed that a trend seemed to have developed: every time I had a medical setback of some kind, I followed it up by coming back faster and stronger than ever.

In 1992 I had broken my arm and then placed fifth at Rusutsu, my best World Cup finish after leaving Deerfield. Then I had sat out a year after my heel surgery and came back to win the most important race of my life to that point, the U.S. Open, which was followed by my best year ever, culminating in the Olympics and the U.S. Nationals championship. My knee injury cost me another year, but here I was with a third and a first already, as well as being the top American finisher in the other races I'd entered. And it was only halfway through the season.

In retrospect I believe that the breaks were blessings in disguise. I don't think I realized how hard I pushed myself physically and mentally during a racing season. The breaks gave me a chance to recover, but they also gave me space to realize how much I loved what I was doing and how lucky I was to have the opportunity.

After the shock of Payton's death wore off, I even began using the "liver thing" (as I sometimes thought of it) as a motivational tool. Every season, every race, every wave, every snow-covered hill—hell, every turn—seemed more precious than the last, and I didn't want to waste any of it. It was back to: *Enjoy the moment and the people around you, because you never know when it will be your last game together.*

I was brimming with confidence and psyched when I went to Berchtesgaden, Germany, for the first World Cup races of the new millennium. Then I got the bad news. I was going to have a roommate.

As the season had progressed, I started to be accepted a little more by my teammates. At least they had to respect that I was winning. Still, no one wanted to room with me, which was fine because I didn't want to room with any of them. Then again, no one wanted to room with Anton Pogue, either, which is how we ended up together.

There was a reason no one wanted to share a room with Pogue. He was crazy and more than a little weird. He liked to establish "encroachment lines" in the hotel rooms by using duct tape to split the place in two. If there was only one bed, as sometimes happened in Europe, he used the duct tape to cut it in half as well. As soon as he got in a room, he'd completely redesign it—moving beds, tables, and televisions to create his own little carnage pit to trash, while demanding that his roommate "stay on your side of the room and don't touch my stuff." He was also famous for "Shamu-ing" the room. You know, Shamu, the famous Seaworld killer whale, who liked to jump out of the water and splash everyone in the audience? Well, Anton would fill the tub to the brim with water, then jump in and start splashing around, soaking the room with several inches of water. He'd even been known to jump in with his clothes on so that he could do his laundry at the same time.

At Berchtesgaden, Peter Foley or Jan finally decided it was time I got over being "the outsider" by making me room with someone. They asked for volunteers. The rest of the team volunteered Anton, who said, "You can't make me." But they did.

When I learned of the plot, I thought, *This is going to be a nightmare.* The box jumping, free-balling incident with Pogue in Salt Lake City had shown me that we shared the same sense of humor, but it didn't make us friends. In fact, I thought he was an idiot.

While on tour, Anton usually ran with Kildy the Dog-Collar Boy, and both were known to be hard-core ragers who thought the party wasn't over as long as they could stand up. And sometimes that wasn't even a requirement. When old-school skiers want to frighten their children with horror stories about what happens to people who snowboard, they show them photographs of Anton and Kildy at après race parties.

Pogue wasn't too thrilled with me, either. He still resented the ISF riders who'd come over to FIS events to make the Olympic team and knocked his seeding way back. Plus, I didn't drink at all or smoke weed, which immediately made me suspect in his book of fun people to hang out with.

Funny thing is, after a few days of rooming together at Berchtesgaden, we were inseparable. With his mop of curly blond hair and surfer's tan, Pogue is the poster boy for the Peter Pan syndrome . . . he'll never grow up. He's probably the only guy I know who's as intent as I am on playing 24/7. In fact, now that I think about it, Anton's kind of like my mischievous twin.

When not on tour, Anton lived in Hood River, Oregon, on the banks of the Columbia River, because it was one of the wind-surfing meccas of the world, a thirty-minute drive to Mount Hood and a two-hour drive to the Oregon coast for surfing. But he's not always a rabble-rouser. Most people only see the wild-child side of Anton, but he's also someone who will do anything for a friend.

Anyway, we had a great time in Berchtesgaden leading up to the day of the race. The event itself, however, didn't begin as well as I'd hoped. I placed a disappointing eighth on my qualifying run, but at least I was in the final sixteen and would get to race the head-to-head competition.

I won my first heat and then the next by comfortable margins, and felt like I was getting stronger with each run. I then sailed through the semifinals to advance to the Big Finals for first and second place against Stephen Copp from Sweden.

On the first run, I was in the red course and Copp was in the blue, which had generally been the faster course during the day. So I knew that if I finished close or tied with him, I would have the advantage for the second run.

Copp and I were neck and neck on the top part of the hill. If you'd been at the bottom looking up, it might have seemed that our movements were choreographed, as together we'd lean into our turns, pop up, and then lean into the next one.

We got to the flat pitch near the bottom at the same time, and it should have been over right there. Normally, I have an advantage in the flats because I'm bigger and stronger than most other riders and have a smooth touch around the gates on the flats. But this time, I was a little cautious and crossed the finish line fifty-two one-hundredths of a second behind Copp.

When I got back to the top of the course, one of the team technicians handed me a two-way radio we use to communicate with the coaches up and down the hill. The next thing I heard was a loud, sarcastic voice with a Swedish accent. "Are you a stamp collector or a snowboarder?" Jan yelled so loud I could have probably heard him without the radio.

Now, you have to understand that Jan spoke what the other riders called "Swenglish," a sort of Swedish version of English that didn't always translate. Some of his more famous race-day sayings included (you have to imagine the accent):

"Don't slow down until you're there."

"There's no danger on the roof."

"You looked like a retarded pig coming out of the barn." (That one said to Anton as he tried to hike back onto the course after a fall in a boarder-cross race.)

"Fly at her like a bat on acid." (Reserved for women riders.)

You might be in the starting gate and suddenly he'd yell something like, *"Your momma's a badger. Your momma's a badger."* Like that was supposed to inspire us? Now he was wondering if I was a stamp collector or a snowboarder? Okay, okay, I got the picture. I handed the radio back to the technician.

I got in the starting gate determined to win or to crash and burn trying. No one calls me a stamp collector (or retarded pig) and gets away with it. The blue course was faster, and I knew that if I made a clean, aggressive run, I could still beat Copp. I reached down and picked up a handful of snow and placed it on the back of my neck. The act seemed almost like a sacrament—a way of saying thank-you for the opportunity— as was the moment I took to absorb the beauty of the German Alps in front of me. Without thinking about it, I whispered a prayer, *God, give me the power and strength to do my best.*

The start official counted down, and I jumped out of the gate. We got to the midway point, and I knew I was having a sick run. But I wasn't ahead by as much as I felt I needed and took an even more aggressive line, carving right on top of the stubbie, risking getting tangled or even disqualified if the edge of my board went on the wrong side of the pole.

I thought I'd gained a little more as we crossed the finish line. But was it enough? Copp raced well and hadn't made any mistakes. Then I looked at the race board. It read: *Klug .01 Winner.* I'd won my first World Cup since my knee injury by one one-hundredth of a second! There was no cutting it closer than that, but a win was a win.

I'd followed the win in Germany with a third-place finish in a PGS in Ischgl, Austria. But in February, while back in Breckenridge to race, I had to break from the tour to return to Denver for another ERCP. I'd been feeling poorly, like a mild flu, which Everson attributed to bile duct infections from bile pooling up.

After I woke up from this ERCP, Everson entered the room, and I knew from the grim look on his face that the news wasn't good. They weren't able to open much up, he said, and he wanted to see me back again in two months. I looked at my dad and Missy. Without saying anything, we all knew what it meant—my liver was failing. I was going to need a transplant much sooner than I'd ever envisioned, which scared me. But then I thought of Payton, and suddenly the idea of surgery didn't frighten me as much as the possibility of liver cancer.

Every time the doctors performed an ERCP, they also did a "scraping" of cells from my liver, looking for changes that would be the first warning signs of cancer. Getting cancer was practically a death sentence; I wouldn't even be eligible for a transplant if the cancer spread outside the liver.

"Why wait?" I asked. "I don't want to die before we get this fixed."

Everson just said that it wasn't time yet. I was still not a high priority on the transplant list. "There's still time," he assured me.

It just didn't seem fair. I was young, in the prime of my life, a world-class athlete and having a phenomenal year . . . but I was dying. Something was wrong here. However, I was also about to get hammered by the lesson that life isn't necessarily fair, no matter how young, or strong, or talented you are.

We returned to Europe, where I competed at an FIS World Cup in Schonried, Switzerland, where I finished seventh, and then rode with my friend Mark Fawcett to the ISF World Series race the next day in Leysin, Switzerland. Leysin had been one of the regular stops on the ISF tour for years and the biggest event for the few ISF racers left. The rest of my team were skipping the event, but it had always been one of my favorites, and I wanted to support the mostly Swiss riders and a few other friends who continued the ISF tour.

The PGS in Leysin ran over two days. The qualifying race was the first day to narrow the field to sixteen, which I qualified for easily, and the next morning I was paired against Daniel Loetscher, a young Swiss rider.

I didn't know Daniel well other than to nod and say hello. He was an up-and-comer who had mostly been competing in Swiss Cup races and was just starting to come on strong at the next level.

I remember I was a little envious of him that morning, because his girlfriend, family, and a lot of friends were there to cheer him on as the home-crowd favorite. I missed my family and Missy. While I loved my life and recognized that a lot of other people had it worse than I did, a lot of the "glamour" of being a professional snowboard racer evaporates on the long plane rides and in the lonely hotel rooms between races.

The scene at Leysin was typical for alpine snowboarding in Europe. A couple of hundred people partied around the course, cheering and dancing as Euro-techno favorites blared from the loudspeakers. Over the music, the race announcer excitedly gave the play-by-play descriptions of each run in English, French, and German: *"Sigi Grabner takes the lead in the blue course, but Gilles Jaquet is coming on strong in the red . . . they are neck and neck."*

The course had been laid out a little strangely, with a slight veer to the right near the end that obscured a straight-on vision of the finish line. During my inspection run, I noted that it would be easy to get confused and go through the wrong finish.

When it came time for my first run, I got off to a great start against Daniel and had more than a gate lead on him when I crossed the finish line, so I had time to look back. I wish I hadn't.

Apparently, Daniel got mixed up and started heading for my finish line before realizing his mistake at the last moment and swerving back toward his. However, he ran straight into a metal pole that held the timing device and separated the two finish lines. He went down hard.

As other people rushed over to Daniel, I headed to the lift and back up the hill. We all wore helmets, and I thought that Daniel had just had his bell rung. Concussions were common from hard impacts on snow, so I knew there was a possibility he might not make our second run. But I was shocked when I got to the top of the course and looked down. People were still crowded around Daniel, who had not moved.

Then a medical helicopter arrived and landed in the finish area. I couldn't believe this was happening. Race days were supposed to be all about fun and competing against friends, not the body of a young man lying motionless in the snow.

Pretty soon, those of us waiting at the top were told to go back to the bottom for a meeting. I rode down the course to the finish area. Daniel still lay in the snow, partly shielded from the crowd by plastic sheeting. Instead of disco classics and the voice of the animated race commentator, a strange Gothic sort of chanting music was playing over the loudspeakers as his family, friends, and Swiss teammates stood holding hands and crying. That's when I learned that he was dead—a result of massive head injuries. It was horrible.

The race was canceled, and later that afternoon we got together at a local church to share stories about Daniel's life and pray for him and his family. Those of us in alpine snowboarding were a small group— despite our competitiveness and the occasional personality conflicts, we were a family and now there was an empty place in our ranks.

That night, Mark Fawcett and I drove to Munich in one of the worst snowstorms I've ever been in. The ride was a somber one; instead of the usual jokes and music and demands for pit stops and food, we were both lost in our thoughts, watching the snowflakes dashing themselves against the windshield. We arrived late that night and found a pension to stay at, ironically named Gasthaus Daniel. When we got into the room, we turned on the television and there was Daniel and me racing up to the moment of his accident. His death was big news, but all I could think was that it wasn't right, snowboard races weren't supposed to end that way.

I hadn't gotten past Daniel Loetscher's death when I heard that my friend and former competitor Davide Marchiandi had been killed in an avalanche. It didn't seem possible. I had just seen him a couple of weeks earlier at a trade show in Munich. He'd stopped alpine racing after the FIS political mess in Italy kept him out of the 1998 Olympics and was now focusing more on boarder-cross.

Apparently, he'd been out free-riding off-piste—which means out of the ski area's boundaries—near his home of Aosta in the Italian Alps. The avalanche caught him and dragged him across a field of rocks, killing him. I just felt so sad as I recalled the times I'd been around Davide. We always laughed so hard trying to communicate with our hands, and even with those limits, we were able to establish a friendship based on a shared love of what we were doing. I wished I'd learned enough Italian to tell him that I valued his friendship, and hoped that he knew anyway.

Our sport had lost two family members in a short period of time, and there was a sort of emptiness at the end of the year. Yet, in a strange way I was a little envious of Daniel and Davide as I thought about what I was facing. At least they died doing what they loved, and it had been quick. If I had to go, I wanted it to be while surfing or snowboarding, not wasting away in a hospital bed from cancer or waiting for a new liver when mine gave out.

There wasn't even anybody on the team I could talk to about it. Jan knew I had a "liver problem." It would have been impossible to hide it, as I had to fill out forms for race drug-testing officials that spelled out what medicines I was taking. But he didn't know the severity.

Although we were roommates and best friends, I didn't even tell Anton. He too knew I had a problem with my liver, because he saw the array of pills I was taking and I'd had to explain (if for no other reason than to turn down his offer to "sample" them for me. I considered giving him Actigall, which along with thinning my bile acted as a laxative, but he already had enough issues with parasites and bacteria he'd picked up on surf trips in Central and South America, and I had to live with him. He says, "I just wanted the pills that made Klug fast." Yeah, right.).

However, I still kept the true extent of the disease from everybody but a few friends and my family. Stacia's comment about Payton still had me spooked about what people would think. But more than that, I wanted to concentrate on living, not answering questions about how I got the disease, or having people feel sorry for me because I might die.

After the tour stop in Japan, I stopped off in Hawaii with Pogue to surf en route to the race in the States. Our teammate Adam Smith joined us one morning to go surfing on the North Shore.

Adam had never been out before and borrowed a long board, but we lost track of him getting through the breakers. Anton and I surfed for the next three hours without seeing him and figured that he never made it beyond the break and had given up and headed to shore.

Anton and I headed for the beach. We kept trying to catch waves to help push us to shore and both hooked into the same one while lying on our bellies. Unfortunately, the wave was a little messy and tossed me right into Anton. In fact, I rode right over his head and gashed him pretty good. I was so bummed and kept asking him if he was okay as he bled all the way to shore, but he just kept telling me to shut up and paddle.

We were almost to shore when we heard faint cries behind us. "Help! Help!"

I looked back and saw Adam drifting out to sea a half-mile beyond the break and heading for Maui. He'd been caught in a riptide and was trying to paddle against it, not realizing he needed to go sideways to get out of it.

I left Pogue and swam out to Adam, who was almost in tears when I arrived and couldn't even lift his arms. He'd thought he was going to die. I had him hold on to my surfboard leash and towed him in as he thanked me over and over again.

We arrived at the shore, where Adam could barely struggle to make it to where Pogue was waiting with blood still pouring from his melon. I reached in my pocket for the rental car keys only to realize they'd been lost in our surf session. It was a fiasco. Adam nearly drowned, Pogue sliced, and keys lost. Fortunately, Adam's friend Sasha showed and we got a ride to the ER, where Anton got a dozen stitches and the car rental guy came by with a new key. Pogue has never let me forget running him over, but the way I see it—yeah, I almost killed him, but I saved Adam, so it was pretty much a wash.

After a week of surfing we flew back to Lake Placid, New York, for the Goodwill Games, sort of Ted Turner's answer to the Olympics. I surprised everyone, including myself, by taking third in the Super-G. Then it was back west to a World Cup giant slalom race in Park City, Utah.

I hoped to do well in the race, because it was being held on the same hill where the Olympic event would take place in two years. It was a two-run, timed GS rather than a PGS, but a good showing would help me psychologically when I returned for the Olympics. More importantly, I wanted to get to know the slope and the terrain.

However, the course was especially challenging (some would say poorly laid out), with a steep drop, or breakover, a few gates out of the start. The first seven seeded riders, including me, caught air off the break and flew right past the gate below. The competition was over for us.

I quickly put the Park City race out of my mind and headed to the U.S. Nationals at Okemo, Vermont, where I took the national title.

Not a bad way to end the season when a little more than a year earlier I was learning how to walk again.

The end couldn't have come too soon, as I wasn't feeling very well. It was pretty normal to feel drained by the end of a long, hard season that included more than 25 events, 150 days of riding (which didn't include off-snow training camps), flying four times to Europe—rallying on the autobahn between several events and towns with each trip—and back, another round-trip to Japan for two events, and crossing the United States several times. The last half of any season I seemed to run mostly on adrenaline, and everybody else on the team seemed to have a cold as well, so I wasn't worried about it. I figured the cure was to go home, relax a little, then dust off my surfboards and head to warmer climates.

So I came back to Aspen, did a little free-riding, and helped usher in a milestone in the history of snowboarding. Aspen Ski Company was finally opening its crown jewel, Ajax, one of the last holdouts, to snowboarding!

Some of the old-time skiers grumbled, but most of Aspen celebrated the big kick-off ceremony to welcome snowboarders along with snowboard industry folks and lots of media coverage. As a sponsored athlete for Aspen Ski Company, I'd been taking VIPS and media types out on the mountain all week long and on the town at night. So it happened that on the big morning of the "official" ribbon-cutting ceremony preceding a mad dash by snowboarders to be the first, I sort of slept in. Unfortunately, I was supposed to help with the ribbon cutting. But it wasn't entirely my fault; it was the weekend we switched to daylight savings time and I forgot to "spring ahead" with my clock. The bummer was that I missed the event and showed up an hour late . . . almost lost my Aspen Ski Company sponsorship over that one.

The last days of April arrived, the slopes closed, and I made plans to join my teammate Pete Macomber in Maui for a few weeks of surfing. But first I planned to stop in Los Angeles with Missy and surf with my friend Mike Croel, who with his wife, Cassey, had invited us spend a few days.

Mike and I had to be the odd-couple pairing of the decade. He's a huge former professional football player who'd been an outside line-backer out of the University of Nebraska and the 1991 NFL Rookie of the Year when he was with my favorite team, the Denver Broncos. Or, more accurately, he was a Hummer-drivin', giant black dude with tribal-looking tats, and I was a scrawny, white-as-a-ghost snowboard punk with a ponytail. But other than that, we had a lot in common.

A talented artist who was concentrating on graphic arts now that he wasn't playing ball, Mike had been into snowboarding from the sport's early years. He'd learned in high school back in Boston at Nashoba Valley when snowboards still weren't allowed on the slopes and he'd had to carve his first turns after hiking up hills in the countryside.

Mike's other passion was surfing, which was how we connected in 1997 when Fab introduced us at Eric's pool hall when he was in Aspen training just before Missy and I left for that trip to Costa Rica. It turned out that Mike and Cassey had just returned from a surf trip there, and we spent the night playing pool and talking about surfing and Costa Rica.

In the spring of 1999, while still rehabbing my knee, Fab and his girl, Susan, and Cassey, Mike, Missy, and I all went to Kauai for a few weeks of sun and surf. That trip nearly ended in disaster one afternoon when we hiked to a waterfall. Fab and I were sunbathing below the falls, while the others were swimming in the pool created by the water-fall. Missy was in the water when Cassey jumped in and came up yelling for help. Missy grabbed her and was pulling her to shore when Mike jumped in to save his wife.

Funny thing about Mike is that he's a great surfer, but a lousy swimmer. We used to razz him all the time about it and tell him there was no way we could haul his 240 pounds to shore if he got in trouble. Only, this time it wasn't funny. He looked at Missy and said, "I'm going down."

Missy was flabbergasted. "What! I can't save the two of you!"

Fortunately, Missy was able to get Cassey to shore, and Mike made it on his own. Needless to say, we were great friends and looking forward to seeing them in California.

I know, it sounds like a lot of surfing. *Poor baby, no wonder he's tired.* But the sport was becoming more important to me, not because of the cross-training and conditioning, but because of the way it helped me recharge the batteries and appreciate what I had after a grueling race schedule. By comparison, surfing was so simple and laid back. All I needed was a board and a wave, maybe a wetsuit in colder waters, and, of course, friends to enjoy it with.

However, I was starting to worry about not being able to shake the end-of-the-season crud. It was lasting longer than normal, plus my appetite was off and I seemed to be running a constant low-grade fever. Dr. Everson had warned me that the persistent fever was a sign that the antibiotics weren't able to control the infections in my bile ducts. The thought scared me, because the infections cause scarring in the ducts, which in turn increases the chances of cancer.

I think I knew then that time was running out. So even though I wasn't feeling well, I was determined to head out to California to see the Croels and then off to Maui to meet up with Pete.

Mike and I surfed our brains out for two days. I didn't want to come out of the water, almost like I was afraid I might not ever get back in. I remember sitting on my board at the end of the second day, just taking it all in, trying to capture the moment, the sights and sounds and smells. I loved my life and felt so lucky to be able to do what I wanted for a career and to have friends like Mike and the crews back in Aspen and Central Oregon. I didn't want to give all that up any more than I was willing to give up on that day . . . until it grew dark and I had to go in.

Missy was worried. She didn't understand how I could surf from morning until sunset but not be able to eat at night. Then I'd lie in bed all night burning up with fever. But she had to return to Aspen, where she was teaching school. I assured her that the fever was just some bug I'd picked up because I was so worn out by the season, and she finally allowed herself to be convinced that if I could surf all day, I couldn't be too sick.

I was sleeping the night she left when suddenly I was ripped out of my dreams by a searing pain in my abdomen. It felt like someone had just stabbed me in the right side of my stomach with a dagger. I gasped in pain and looked at the clock; it was 2 A.M.

The pain wouldn't go away, and I knew then that I was in trouble. I hadn't wanted to admit that I was getting sicker. I wanted to go to Hawaii. If I could just surf in Hawaii, everything would be all right. But now I knew I wasn't going anywhere but home. I saw what lay ahead of me—I was going to need a new liver, and soon, or I was going to die. I started to cry in the dark. I'd never felt so alone.

Still, I didn't want to alarm the Croels, so I waited until morning to ask for a ride to the airport. Mike knew I had a liver problem and had to take some pills, but I hadn't told him that I was going to need a transplant or I might die. What could he do except say that he would be there for me as a friend, give me a hug, and put me on a plane for Denver.

Dad and Missy met me at the airport and drove with me to Everson's office. He rushed me off for another ERCP.

Normally the procedure took about ninety minutes. After they wheeled me off, Missy and Dad went down to the hospital cafeteria to get a snack and some coffee. They came back, prayed, talked, read their books, talked some more, and waited. And waited. After more than three hours, Dr. Roshan Shrestha, who performed the ERCPs, walked into the waiting room.

Dad knew that my health had been going downhill and that this latest episode had to be particularly bad if I was willing to cut my surfing trip short. "However, we expected they would pull him in, clean him out with the ERCP, and we would go back to living our lives," he recalls of that day in the waiting room. "Normally the doctors would report how they had done, how much they opened up, and they would show us video of the bile ducts and the progress they'd made. There were no smiles this time, and no pictures of progress to show. The doctor shook his head, and said, 'We couldn't do anything for him.'"

Missy frowned. "You mean you couldn't do much?'

"No," the doctor said. "I mean we couldn't do anything."

My bile ducts were completely closed. Bile was pooling up in my liver. Everson came in to check on me, but because I was still loopy from the anesthesia, he said I should come back in the morning to discuss what came next.

The next day we met with Everson and another physician who he introduced as Dr. Igal Kam, the chief of liver transplant surgery at University Hospital. Without wasting any more time, they explained that a failed ERCP meant only one thing: a liver transplant.

I didn't cry or react, except to say, "I know." The dagger in my abdomen had told me.

"We want to move Chris up to status 2b," Everson continued, which meant that I needed a transplant as soon as it could be arranged but was not in danger of dying at that time.

Moving up in status was important. Transplant hospitals belong to the United Network of Organ Sharing, or UNOS, which back then listed transplant patients according to their medical status.

In 1997 Everson had placed me on the list as a status 3, which meant I was receiving ongoing medical care for my liver but was a low priority as far as immediate need for a transplant. Status 2b, where they wanted to move me now, was the next level up.

The next two status levels were 2a and 1, both of which were reserved for critically ill patients. A status 2a patient was a patient with chronic liver disease whose disease had progressed to the point where he or she had seven days or less to live. Status 1 was reserved for patients without underlying chronic liver disease, but who had sudden liver failure, say from acute hepatitis or liver injury. Children under eighteen years old with chronic liver disease could also be listed as status 1 if they had severe deterioration in their condition.

UNOS divided the country into regions. Each region had a panel of doctors at transplant sites who had to approve moving a patient up on the lists, according to medical criteria and other factors. Within a status group there were other factors determining who would get a donor liver, such as worsening of liver function, complications of liver disease, matching blood types, and body size. There were also some caveats. For instance, someone who continued to use alcohol or drugs after they'd been diagnosed with liver disease might not be eligible. Or someone with hepatitis could have the liver only from a donor who also had hepatitis because of the risk of reinfection by the virus.

In my case I was moved from status 3 to status 2b because my liver tests were worsening and I was having repeated infections in my bile ducts, which couldn't be controlled by the ERCPs. Another key factor that determined allocation of donor liver to a recipient under the UNOS status system was the length of time you'd been on the transplant list. (Today the system of organ allocation has changed; now, only the sickest patients receive deceased donor livers, based on a system of priority score, called the MELD [Model for End-Stage Liver Disease] score. The range of MELD scores is 6 to 40, with the sickest being 40. Currently, the average MELD score at which patients receive liver transplants is approximately MELD 25.)

It was now that Everson's brilliant foresight to put me on the list in 1997—despite my protestations—became apparent. If a liver became available, a 2a or 1 critically ill patient would trump a patient with a 2b status. However, all other things being equal, the next "tiebreaker" between people in a status group was the length of time they'd been on the list.

Back in June 1997 Everson had to seek permission from the Region 8 panel of doctors, which oversaw transplant lists in Colorado, Wyoming, Nebraska, Iowa, and Missouri, to put me on the list as a PSC patient. Now he and Kam were confident that they would get approval to move me up to status 2b, and with the time I had already spent on the list, I would be near the top.

"How long will I have to wait?" I asked. Now that the time had come, I wanted to get it over with.

The doctors said it depended on when a donor could be found. But University Hospital had been performing liver transplants at a record pace over the first part of 2000. The average waiting period was thirty to sixty days. But organ donations seemed to be on the rise, and they thought I might get one sooner.

"What about a living donor?" my dad asked. He'd been doing a lot of studying and knew that the liver is the only organ in the body that can regenerate. A portion of a liver can be taken from a living donor—usually a family member for the best blood type and DNA match—and transplanted into the patient, and both pieces will grow to normal size.

My brother, Jim, had already volunteered to be my living donor. He was pretty funny about it. "Sure, you can have my liver, but I'm not sure you want it; it's been a little abused over the years."

However, Everson explained that they generally preferred whole deceased donor grafts, and would do a living-donor transplant only if the deceased-donor supply were inadequate. He noted that there was a higher rate of complications in recipients of living-donor grafts, even though overall outcome is excellent and equivalent to deceased-donor grafts. "We didn't pursue the living-donor graft with Chris, because we thought it was likely that he would get a deceased donor in time," Dr. Everson says.

A living donor was a last resort, the doctors said. Personally, I was glad we'd put Jim's offer to rest, at least for the time being. I loved my brother, and while it was the sort of gesture I knew I could have counted on him to make, I didn't want him to take that risk unless there was no other alternative.

In the meantime, the doctors said, it was going to take a week to ten days to hear whether I had been approved to move up on the status list.

Everson had to leave. But Kam invited us to stay if we had more questions. We had a bunch.

Kam was an interesting character. He was barrel-chested with wavy, combed-back silver hair and piercing brown eyes. A native of Israel, he spoke with a thick accent. But what stood out the most was his air of supreme confidence, the sort I usually only saw in world-class athletes who know they are at a level above most, if not all, of their peers.

I put him to the test and fired off question after question. What if I developed a blood clot? What if my body rejected the donor organ? What affect would antirejection drugs have on me and my ability to compete? What if I started showing signs of cancer before a donor could be found? What if there were no donors who matched?

Kam showed the patience of Job as he answered the medical questions. But when I kept envisioning bad scenarios, he stopped me. "Chris, I don't want you to go into this thinking that something is going to go wrong," he said. "If something does, I know what to do, and we'll handle it."

"But how many patients do you lose in surgery?" I asked.

I was feeling a little desperate. I'm sure our faces, especially mine, were all masks of the fears and doubts racing around in our minds. But Kam just smiled. He leaned forward, looked me in the eyes, and said, "Chris . . . I don't lose any PSC patients."

I couldn't help but smile back. This guy was a winner. Still, I had one more question, something that was really weighing on my mind. "Since I won't be moving up on the list for a week, can I go surfing?"

Kam arched his dark eyebrows. I don't think he'd had that request from too many of his patients. "I don't see why not," he said with a shrug. "Go . . . surf . . . I'll see you when you get back."

Chapter 14

The Long Wait

After I returned to Aspen from Denver, I called Pete Macomber to tell him I couldn't join him in Hawaii. I didn't even really give him a reason, just telling him I couldn't make it. He must have thought I was a flake, but I still didn't want the word getting out.

However, I went back to Los Angeles and surfed long sessions for a week with Mike. The docs had put me on a new regimen of powerful antibiotics to control the infections, so I felt better and tried to pack as much as I could into every day.

Getting out of the water on that last day was the toughest. I kept thinking, *This might be the last time you ever surf.* Walking across the sand to the car with my board under my arm seemed to take forever.

Not long after I returned home, I learned that I had been approved to move up to status 2b. I reported to University Hospital, where Missy and I were given a tour and educational lecture about the transplant program and what I could expect. The lecture was both reassuring and alarming.

While antirejection drugs had improved greatly, I was told that some had pretty bad possible side effects—such as kidney damage, high cholesterol, and diabetes—and at times had to be used in conjunction with steroids. Some side effects sounded more gross than dangerous. For instance, one of the leading drugs for transplant patients could cause abnormal gum growth that in some patients required having surgery to cut the gums back. And the commonly used steroid Prednisone could cause abnormal body hair growth, even for women and children.

Another drawback to taking antirejection drugs was that they worked by suppressing the immune system, which meant I would be more susceptible to common diseases like the flu. I could expect to heal more slowly, and I would be more prone to get sunburns. On the other hand, the alternative to taking the drugs was worse.

I was told that I was going to be given the latest drug for liver and kidney transplant patients, Prograf, which was made by a small Japanese pharmaceutical company called Fujisawa Healthcare, Inc. Developed in 1994, Prograf worked so well on its own that steroids could often be eliminated or taken in very low doses. So far, studies seemed to indicate that the side effects for liver transplant patients were milder than with other drugs, or nonexistent.

After the lecture and tour, I was sent home with a pager by Tracy Steinberg, the transplant coordinator at University Hospital. "Stay in range," she warned. I had to be within a four-hour travel time to the hospital, and Aspen was right on the edge of that if I had to drive. If a potential donor was located, Tracy said, she would page me three times and then try to locate me through the list of phone numbers I gave her of family and friends. If they couldn't find me, I might lose the liver.

Tracy had told me they'd been performing liver transplants at the rate of one or two a week, so I was convinced that the call would come soon and followed the rules for the first few weeks. The idea of the surgery scared me. I might die on the operating table or from complications afterward. But every time I started freaking about it, I'd remember that Walter Payton would have been happy to take that risk.

In the meantime, my dad, Missy, and I did a lot of homework about transplant programs around the United States and the world. After Tom Starzl left University Hospital in the mid-seventies, the transplant program had come to a halt. As a result, Colorado transplant patients had to travel out of state, many of them to the large program at the University of Nebraska. But in 1988 Dr. Kam and Dr. Fritz Karrer had reinstituted the liver transplant program at University. With their skill and the new antirejection drugs, I was assured, they soon had one of the best records in the world for long-term survival of transplant patients.

We had a good family friend, Dr. Jeff Rank, at the Mayo Clinic in Minneapolis, with whom we talked about different programs and the progression of my disease. When we asked about the transplant program at Mayo, he put us in touch with the surgeons.

"Who are you seeing now?" the doctor asked.

"Dr. Kam at University Hospital in Denver," I replied.

There was a sort of laugh and he said, "Don't worry, you're in great hands. Dr. Kam trained us."

With that issue settled, it didn't matter to me if Kam or the other liver transplant specialist at University, Dr. Michael Wachs, did the surgery. They rotated who was on call, and it just depended on when a donor became available.

Older and more experienced, Kam was king. Since the transplant program's reincarnation at University, more than five hundred livers had been transplanted, and Kam had done most of them. Missy agreed with me that he was a man either one of us would trust with our lives. But he was always a little too honest when answering my questions about whether I would be able to return to championship form. "We don't know," he'd say. "We've never had an Olympic snowboarder before." It was possible, that's about all.

On the other hand, Wachs, who was younger and athletic, didn't hesitate to tell me what I wanted to hear. "Of course you'll be back." He didn't quite have Kam's royal presence, but he made up for it in self-confidence and optimism. I liked that, because I wanted to surround myself with positive people who supported what I wanted to do, not tell me what had never been done.

Yet, no one could really promise me that I would survive the wait or the surgery, much less be able to return to professional snowboarding after being cut open, having a major organ removed and replaced, and then sewed back up again. The staff at University Hospital tried to help me understand what I would be going through by putting me in touch with other transplant patients. But after I'd talked to a few of them, there were a couple of things that still bothered me.

Many of them had ruined their livers with drinking or got hepatitis from intravenous drug use, and I couldn't identify with that. But more troubling to me were those who seemed to have accepted that having a transplant meant they were invalids—that they shouldn't try to get in shape, change their habits, and take advantage of their second chance at life. To me, idea of ending up alive but unable to enjoy the things I loved was almost more frightening than death.

Even some of the liver program people, including Dr. Everson, questioned whether I would be able to participate in contact sports (including those where you might hit the ground at a high rate of speed). Others made it seem like I'd have to be so careful because of my suppressed immune system that I might as well live in a sterile bubble.

One person who believed I could come back to my former life was Bill Fabrocini. As a physical therapist, Fab saw no reason why he couldn't whip me back into shape to compete professionally. It had never been done with a liver transplant recipient, but he knew of a recent case of a professional athlete who had a kidney transplant but was competing at the same level again.

Fab trained professional basketball player David Robinson of the San Antonio Spurs at the Aspen Club during the off-season and they'd become friends. One of Robinson's teammates, Sean Elliott, had received a kidney transplant in 1998 and was now back playing for his team.

Knowing that I was having ups and downs about my chances of a comeback after a transplant, Fab asked Robinson if he could get Elliott to call me for a pep talk. One night, my telephone rang. I answered it and it was Sean on the other end of the line. This was the sort of guy he was. The Spurs were in the middle of a playoff series against the Phoenix Suns, and he had just finished playing, but he took the time to call me.

I jumped at the chance to ask a professional athlete about the difficulties he'd faced making a comeback, especially whether the anti-rejection drugs had hindered him. I didn't know if he was telling me the truth or was just trying to keep my spirits up, but Sean was completely optimistic. He'd done it, no problem, he said, and I could too. The drugs were no big deal, I just needed to keep my spirits up and stay in shape as best I could prior to the surgery.

That was exactly the sort of encouragement I needed to hear. From that point forward, the way I saw it, I had a choice while I waited for the transplant. I could be a victim, or I could participate in my own destiny. No, it wasn't my fault that I had PSC, and there was nothing I could do about it, but I could train for what lay ahead just like I trained to compete. Only now I was getting ready to race for my life.

I figured that the secret to a quick recovery was staying in top shape right up to the moment of surgery. A typical day, usually with Missy or at least one of my other friends, would include a five-hour bike ride up a mountain, followed by a sand volleyball game, or wakeboarding on Ruedi Reservoir, then a weight-lifting session, and maybe a round of golf with my parents to "cool down."

The worst part was the waiting. The month of July rolled around, but the days kept ticking by without the pager going off. I kept calling Tracy to see if the pager was working properly. She'd check and say, yes, it was working. But she was as perplexed as I was by the length of the wait.

For some reason the number of organ donors had dried up, but it was hard to say why. My research had revealed that the numbers weren't in my favor. There were more than seventy-five thousand Americans on transplant waiting lists—more than a thousand of them just in Colorado. Some were waiting for help with non-life-threatening medical issues, such as cornea transplants and skin grafts. However, most needed organs to save their lives, and the majority would wait in vain. There were less than six thousand donors annually nationwide—a number that had remained static for the previous four years. A new person was added to the national lists every fourteen minutes. But the scariest number was that an average of sixteen people were dying every day as they waited, and that was just in the United States.

I was going crazy waiting for that damn pager to go off. Sometimes, as if to tempt fate, Missy and I would "cheat" and go fishing or hiking out of range of the pager. Then we'd hurry home and call Dad to see if maybe the hospital had tried him at the hotel or home when they couldn't reach me.

We couldn't help but read the newspapers and see where someone had been killed in an automobile accident and wonder if I would get a call that night or the next morning. After the Fourth of July holiday we read that a dozen people had died in car accidents in Colorado. But there'd been no calls, and we were left to wonder if the victims' internal injuries had been too severe, if they simply had not wanted to be donors, or if their families couldn't make that difficult, but lifesaving, decision.

My family and friends did their best to keep my spirits up. The former prayed while the latter stuck with their longtime strategy of harassing me to keep things light and distract me from my plight. Only those guys could watch their friend dying in front of their eyes and then smile as they diagnosed me with "puss-itus of the liver."

I still hadn't told everybody, especially the media. However, it wasn't so much because I had a "dirty secret" any more. Yes, some people might have contributed to their liver problems, but they didn't deserve to die any more than I did. And I'd learned that there were a lot of people out there with liver problems who were no more responsible for their condition than I was. They may have been infected with hepatitis after contact with someone else's blood—from sex or blood transfusions or something as innocent as placing a bandage on an injury. Quite a number were health professionals who came into contact with the virus while helping care for sick people. In fact, I learned that a lot of medical corpsmen in Vietnam who'd had to save guys on the battlefield had come home carrying the virus and didn't even know it for twenty years until their livers started to fail. Others simply suffered because of some genetic bad luck, like me. The point was that I came to understand that we were all in the same boat, dependent on the courage and kindness of strangers for our lives.

No, I wasn't worried any more about someone finding out I had liver disease and jumping to conclusions. The main reason I was still keeping my secret was that I didn't want to spend what might have been the last days of my life answering questions from the media or having to explain over and over to well-meaning strangers and acquaintances. I was making it a point to concentrate on positive things, like my training program, and spending all of my time with my family and friends.

Some of them found out only after the opportunity presented itself. Anton Pogue just couldn't understand why I wasn't in Oregon surfing with him as we'd talked about at the end of the season. Every time he got a report of six-foot waves on the Oregon coast, I'd get a call.

"You bragged you were going to surf with me all summer," he'd complain. Or, "You're blowing it, summer's over and you're not even out here yet."

This went on for a month or so until he finally hit me with a really low blow. "Your girl won't let you. It's okay if you like mountain biking and weight lifting better than surfing, but just admit it."

That was it. I liked mountain biking, but there was nothing I would rather do than surf, except for snowboard. I had to tell him. "Sorry, buddy, but I have to hang out here. . . . I need a liver transplant."

I filled him in on the entire story and waited for the shock to sink in. The silence on the other end of the line told me that for once in Pogue's life he wasn't sure what to say. *Gosh*, I thought, *he's taking it pretty hard*. I should have known better.

"Well, then hurry up and get it done, dude," he replied a moment later in pure Pogue. "The summer's almost over." There was another pause and then he added, "Uh, I hope you don't die."

See what I mean about his sensitive side?

Anyway, by mid-July, I could tell that my body was failing. The antibiotics kept the worst infections at bay, but I seemed to run an almost constant low-grade fever. Most days, I didn't have the energy to ride my mountain bike or lift weights. My outdoor activities were mostly limited to golf or fly-fishing. Some days, it was all I could do to sit up on the couch at home and play chess. If I went to the gym, I mostly did a Boogie Workout, sometimes varying it with a Gary Workout—walking around talking, then going hard at the tri-bath-alon (a demanding circuit training event that began in the Jacuzzi, followed by the steam bath, and ending in the sauna).

I was fortunate to have friends and family. My sister, Hillary, was especially accommodating.

"Chris is a lot to handle, especially when everyone else keeps growing up (read maturing) and he stays young," she says. "That's where I come in. I always look forward to the time I get to spend with Chris.

"During the months before his transplant, he was at home a lot, and we got to hang out. Missy and Mom and Dad worked, so it was fun for both Chris and me to have someone to play with. Although I couldn't keep up with his daily routine, even when he was slowing down, we would usually catch lunch, or play chess (he only plays me in chess right after Dad has beaten him, because he knows he will win against me, and that will boost his ego), or watch scary movies that both of us hate. It was a difficult time before the transplant, because nothing was certain and no one ever knew what was going on or what would happen in the future. But as Fozzy Bear and Kermit the Frog say, we just kept 'movin' right along!' That was the most important part."

As my strength faded, however, my faith in God grew, thanks to the care and support of the congregation at Christ Episcopal. Some of the support was a helping hand. Early in my diagnosis, when my medical bills had threatened to overwhelm my resources before my insurance coverage kicked in, our church friends, the Baileys, had contributed money to help cover costs. I needed the money, no doubt, but what I needed more was the knowledge that other people cared and wanted to help.

Some of the support was spiritual, like a "laying on of hands" prayer session at the church, where the other members kept their hands on me as they prayed, sharing in the power of prayer. With their love and wishes, I accepted what my dad was always saying about God having a plan for me, or he wouldn't have brought me through so much already. "Hang in there, Chris," he would say when my faith wavered. "God knows where you are and what you need."

It wasn't a guarantee. I had to do my part, but the more I thought about it, the more I clung to the idea that maybe God's plan was for me to live and champion the cause of organ donor awareness, much as Lance Armstrong had championed cancer awareness and funding. I promised that if I lived, I would do everything I could to spread the life-saving message of organ donation.

Yet, even my faith couldn't keep me from worrying. After all, God might have had another plan that didn't include me surviving.

As my situation grew more desperate, our sense of humor became more twisted. We'd see someone riding a motorcycle without a helmet and say, "There goes a future donor." Or Missy and I would joke about going to a particularly dangerous cliff area on Independence Pass frequented by rock climbers and bringing along an ice chest and a scalpel. It seems strange to write about it now, but back then black humor helped me keep my sanity.

I confess that I really didn't give much thought to what had to happen to someone else for me to live. In some ways it didn't seem real that someone else would have to die. When I joked about helmetless motorcycle riders or climbing accidents, I didn't see any faces or think about what their loved ones would be put through. I would just go into the hospital, be put to sleep, and when I woke up I would have a new liver . . . and I would live. When I did allow myself to think about it, I knew that I didn't want to wish for something bad to happen to someone else just to save my life. But deaths happened and nothing I wanted, or didn't want, could change that.

I was upbeat most of the time around other people, because that's my personality and I didn't want to be treated like I was ill. But privately, my spirits plunged up and down like the alpine roads Lance Armstrong was riding in pursuit of his second Tour de France victory that summer. Even my subconscious got involved. Some nights I would wake up covered in sweat, my sheets soaked as if I'd wet the bed, after dreaming that

I didn't make it. Other times I'd wake up from a dream that I'd received a new liver and was back racing and loving it.

As more time passed, the plunges were harder to pull out of, the soaring didn't rise quite as high. Every day that passed increased the danger that the antibiotics would stop working—my white blood cell count was tested every two weeks to monitor whether the infections were gaining the upper hand. Every minute that passed was an opportunity for a cancer cell to take root and grow.

One sign of how low my spirits had sunk was my reaction to the death of the Pooper. We were driving down the valley for a mountain bike ride but had only gone a few miles out of town when the old girl kicked the bucket. Her engine had seized and there would be no more fun trips. I was devastated. I loved that car, and it was like losing a member of my family. But Missy, Fab, and Gary practically died laughing. What they didn't understand was how it affected me in what I was going through with the PSC. The Pooper and all the good times it represented were gone—maybe I was next. I could have bought another car but decided to wait, because in a month or two I might not have needed one ever again.

As hard as the wait was on me, it was also wearing my family down, although they tried not to show it. I remember one "Klug Family Outing," as my parents liked to call them, in mid-July to the golf course on the outskirts of Aspen. My parents were almost desperate to fit these outings in as they felt time ticking away, but that afternoon it had quickly become apparent that we wouldn't be getting any golf in.

The storm clouds that had been building up all morning behind the Maroon Bells peaks were now crowding toward where we stood on the driving range. Lightning flashed and thunder rumbled down from the high country. I was getting more concerned as the sky darkened—lightning is nothing to ignore, especially in the high country. But Dad, a cardigan sweater draped over his shoulders and tied at the neck, dismissed the approaching storm with a wave and a smile. "Five minutes and it will be gone," was all he said.

The words were hardly out of his mouth when a bolt struck the summit of Buttermilk Mountain, followed shortly by a rolling boom less than a mile distant. "I'm outta here," I said as the lightning flashed again, only closer.

My parents protested. The storm would pass, they said, and the sun would come out again. "Come on, wait just a few more minutes," Dad pleaded. "This is going to blow right over."

Sometimes it seemed to them as if there were a conspiracy to rob us of our time together on Earth. Lightning storms, birth complications, childhood ailments, and now I needed a liver transplant or it was clear I wasn't going to live to see my twenty-eighth birthday in November.

However, I wasn't going to wait for the storm to pass. The way I was feeling, there was no time left to waste waiting for anything. I was competing in the biggest race of all, and I was falling behind.

I hugged them. "I love you," I said and hoisted my golf bag onto my shoulder and walked off toward the car my parents had loaned me. I was off to join my friends for a movie and then, later, to watch Armstrong's performance in that day's leg of the Tour.

My parents knew I was right. They couldn't wish away a Colorado thunderstorm any more than they could wish away the disease that was killing me. "We love you, Chris," I heard them call after me.

As I got in my car, Mom lamented to my dad that I had been on the top of the transplant list much longer than the doctors anticipated. She usually managed to put on a brave face, but the strain was wearing her down and her voice cracked. "Tomorrow will be day number seventy-two since he got moved up on the list," she whispered.

Dad put an arm around her shoulders. "There's time," he said. He reminded her that my friend Thos Evans, who was now doing his residency at University Hospital, had just completed a stint with the liver transplant team and had assured them that the surgeons were waiting for the perfect donor.

Mom and Dad reached their car, but she suddenly turned back to where I had parked. "I want to tell him something," she said to my dad. But I was gone.

My parents went home. Home to another night of prayers and jumping every time the telephone rang. *Is this the one? Who died?*

They wanted to pray for a donor but wrestled with the moral dilemma of what that would mean to someone else. They had believed in the power of prayer all of their lives. They'd asked God to watch over us and prayed for divine intervention when I was an infant with an aura but sick lungs, and when I struggled to breathe as a child. But how could they pray for someone else's child to be killed in a terrible accident so that their son could live?

The dilemma struck home when the eleven-year-old daughter of friends from our church was killed in a car accident on the highway north of Aspen. Even if she had been a good blood-type match, there was no thought of her liver being used for me—her internal organs had been too badly damaged.

Yet, during the funeral services, acutely aware of the girl's grieving parents, my dad realized with horror that this was the other side of what I needed. They couldn't wish that on any other family . . . not even to save me. So they prayed for "a miracle" and then left it in the hands of God and those of the surgeons at University Hospital.

Everybody was trying to handle the pressure in his or her own way. Jim called daily, ready to fly in at a moment's notice if I needed part of his liver.

My sister, Hillary, had gone to Europe, a trip she'd planned for a long time. After I was moved up on the transplant list, she said she wasn't going, but my parents insisted that she keep her mind off my predicament. Every morning, Mom would call my apartment and ask me or Missy if I was okay.

"God wasn't the only one we had faith in; we had faith in Chris too," Mom remembers. "Sometimes I think we were the ones who were clinging to his supreme confidence in himself. He told us he was not only going to survive, but he would also be back on his snowboard racing this season, gearing up for the Winter Olympics in Salt Lake City. He was going to win his medal.

"There were plenty of tears and sleepless nights, but when things were at their grimmest, I would remember who I was fearful for. Wasn't this the struggling infant who'd gripped my finger so tight I knew he wasn't leaving any time soon? Wasn't this the teenager who'd told anyone who would listen that he would be in the Olympics someday, when snowboarding wasn't even an event? Who was I to doubt him now? . . . We needed him to be strong for all of us, and he was."

When I wasn't so strong, Missy was again my rock. We were committed to each other and best friends. She was there for every tough day and night. It wasn't as bad physically as having to empty my pee bottle every few hours in the middle of the night; this time it was more mental—preparing herself for the possibility I might not make it.

"All the talk about Chris's racing career is what drove me crazy," Missy says. "Chris didn't want to talk about what might happen, except the occasional, almost offhand comment he would make when we talked about the future, saying something like, 'I might not make it.' But he was constantly worrying that every day that went by was another day he couldn't be training for the racing season.

"As he grew weaker, he worried that it was going to be harder and take more time to rehab. And all I could think was, 'I don't give a damn about snowboarding. I just want you.'"

It just wasn't as frightening to worry about whether I was going to resume my career and make the Olympics than if I was going to live or not. Instead of death, I worried about whether my sponsors would stick by me, or like Armstrong's French racing team, drop me. If I couldn't get back this season, it would be the third I'd missed for health reasons. And if that prevented me from another run at the Olympic podium, would they still think they were getting their money's worth? I shouldn't have worried, though, as they all let me know that they would be with me through this too.

"We do try to stand behind our athletes, and Chris was always up front about his issues," Jake says. "He never tried to hide or minimize them, even if he was always optimistic about his chances of making a comeback.

"After the knee injury, there were never doubts that we would stick with him. I've broken my leg twice, and it's clear to me that it's all about the type of individual. You'd be surprised how minor injuries have ended some careers and, at the same time, how other athletes have overcome incredible injuries.

"We knew that Chris gave a high priority to taking care of his body and was a great competitor . . . one of the best competitors I've ever known . . . and determined to succeed. When the liver thing came around, he was very communicative. It wasn't like I caught wind of it and asked to see him. . . . I was definitely caught off guard, but he seemed to have done his homework on what was going on, and how he was going to deal with it and come out the other side. I knew it threatened his career, or worse, but he was also very upbeat, and there was no question he was still our rider."

I may have been upbeat with Jake, but I continued to be troubled by the fact that for me to live, someone else had to die. I loved life so much, it was hard to come to grips with the idea that someone had to lose theirs so that I could go on and enjoy all those things the donor would not. Before I was diagnosed, my family and I had all signed the back of our driver's licenses to indicate that we wanted our organs donated in the case of our death. Now, in the rare moments when I was willing to acknowledge that I might die, I told Missy that I felt better knowing that I'd taken such good care of my heart, lungs, and kidneys so that someone else could enjoy their use.

I tried to keep up my spirits and forced myself to work out as much as I could. But by the end of July, I was sure the race was nearly over and I'd lost.

"I'm finished," I told my parents and Missy. "I'm done. I'm done. I'm done." The concession frightened them; it was so unlike me. But I wasn't quite through fighting. The next day I rebounded a little and assured my mom that I still intended to win my Olympic medal.

On the morning of July 26 Missy spotted an article in the *Denver Post* about a thirteen-year-old boy who'd been shot the night before by another teen in a Denver-area trailer park. The story said the youth had been shot in the head and taken to St. Anthony Central Hospital in Denver. She wondered if this would be the day I got the call, but knew I wouldn't want to talk about possible donors so didn't bring it up.

The clock felt like it was ticking really fast. The next day, my friend Marco invited us to Ruedi to go waterskiing. Running late (as usual), I was leaving the house in a rush when I saw a notice on the refrigerator. It was a summons for jury duty, and I was supposed to report that morning. I went to the courthouse and told the clerk that I was sick and couldn't participate in jury duty.

"You don't look sick," she said. "You'll need a note from a doctor."

I wasn't going to explain my situation, nor was I going to spend what might be my last days in a courtroom. I ran over to my doctor's office and returned with the note. Excused, I jumped in the car with Marco and Missy and headed to the reservoir, where I followed my doctors' orders to "take it easy" by waterskiing until the sun went down. We then returned to Marco's and built a huge bonfire and hung out with friends. There was a sense that I was saying good-bye to the people and things I loved.

The pager had stayed quiet all day, and there were no telephone messages when we got home that night. So Missy dismissed the shooting victim she'd read about.

The next morning, I reported to the clinic for my now-weekly blood tests. The news wasn't good, as my white blood cell count was way down—my immune system was being overwhelmed. The doctor at the clinic decided to give me a pneumonia vaccine while my immune system was still strong enough to benefit, in case I was called to the hospital.

I was complaining that the vaccine made my arm sore and that my back was stiff from the previous day's waterskiing when I arrived at the Aspen Club to work out with Marco and my brother Jason, who'd recently moved back to town to be with me. Actually, I was doing a combo Gary/Boogie Workout with Fab and just waiting for them to finish so that we could do a tri-bath-alon.

While I talked up a sweat, Missy decided to go for a hike up Ute Trail, which climbed up the mountain above the Aspen Club. At the top, she sat down on a rock cropping to take in the day. She was enjoying the sunshine, but then started thinking that maybe she'd been gone too long. She headed back down and had just about reached the bottom of the trail when she saw Marco sprinting toward her.

"Hurry," he shouted. "Chris got his call." As they ran back to the club, Marco filled her in.

I had just walked into the locker room when I heard my cell phone ringing. It was Dad. "Tracy wants you to call her," he said. For confidentiality reasons, Tracy wouldn't tell him why—"just that it's urgent."

I was puzzled; my pager hadn't gone off. But I immediately called Tracy at University Hospital. "We have a possible donor, and you need to get down here," she said.

I couldn't believe the moment had arrived . . . I had to contact people, get my stuff together . . . Tracy told me to calm down. If I could get there in the next six hours, that would be great. She was about to hang up when my stomach reminded me of another question. Strangely, my appetite was back, and I'd had only a bowl of Cream of Wheat for breakfast. "I was just about to go get a smoothie," I said.

"Don't," was Tracy's reply. "Just get down here."

I hung up and looked down at the pager in my hand. The only call I ever got on the damn thing was a wrong number in the middle of the night. A moment later it was bouncing in several pieces off the asphalt in the Aspen Club parking lot. Then Missy and I were off for our apartment, where our bags were already packed (and had been for months).

On the way, I called my dad and told him what was up. He'd already arranged for tickets and called the airport to find out that the next flight left in an hour and a half. We had plenty of time to get ready . . . and to get more nervous.

"I've been waiting so long and thought I'd be excited," I confessed to Missy, "but now that it's happening, I'm really nervous." Would I survive the operation? Would I get an infection? Would I need a blood transfusion (which frightened me because of the possibility, however low, of picking up a disease like AIDS)?

Missy assured me that everything was going to be okay. Drs. Kam and Wachs were the best in the business. "Besides," Missy cautioned me, "we shouldn't get too excited." Tracy had told us before that we might get the call, only to have it be a false alarm because there was something wrong with the donor liver, or someone with a higher priority status might come in to the hospital before I got there.

I started calling friends like Gary (Fab had learned at the club), and Brad Boyd in Oregon, who said he'd be there as soon as possible. "You don't have to come, dude," I said.

"No, this is one of those trips you have to make," he said.

I called Carlon Colker, and he said he'd be on the next plane too. I didn't know that he'd already been making arrangements to come spend what he thought were going to be my last days.

"He was high up on the liver transplant list, but we all knew that it could be getting too late," Carlon says. "His health was fading fast. No doubt, death was approaching. I had actually planned to fly out to Aspen to be with him. I had no other plan other then to pray with him for a liver donor. As a friend I planned to be with him and make him laugh and smile as much and as long as I could. . . . Luckily, my 'home hospice' plans were cancelled and hope shined anew."

When it was time, Missy and I drove to the Aspen airport, where we met Dad and boarded the plane. Mom and Hillary were going to follow in a car so that we'd have one available in Denver.

After all that rushing around, however, we ended up just sitting on the runway. It was a hot summer day and it seemed like we didn't move for an eternity. It was probably more like a half hour, but I finally stood up and said to my dad, "We should get off the plane and start driving."

Dad told me to sit down. He then got up and went to see what the problem was and explained my situation to the pilots. They assured him we'd take off in minutes, and they'd get us to Denver in plenty of time.

Soon we were in the air. I was a bundle of nerves and only wanted to stare out the window, lost in my own thoughts. But Dad and Missy were huddling over a story in that day's *Denver Post*.

There on the front page was another story about the teen who'd been shot; he wasn't expected to survive. The other boy had been arrested, but he was claiming it was an accident.

Dad and Missy looked at each other and nodded. But they kept the story of Billy Flood and the boy who shot him, Patrick Random, to themselves.

Chapter 15

Crossing Paths

wo days earlier, Patrick Random had crawled out of bed about noon, rolled a joint of marijuana, and left his parents' mobile home to visit a friend. He was just fourteen years old, but he'd been smoking pot, drinking alcohol, and running with an older crowd for years. So far, he'd had only minor brushes with the law, all juvenile stuff like trespassing and criminal mischief. His parents told law officers that they had trouble controlling him and making him go to school.

The trailer park where they lived was in an unincorporated part of Adams County just north and west of Denver. It was an older park with mostly vintage single-wides, many in need of paint and repairs. A mix of tenants lived there. Some were retirees on fixed incomes who tended to keep their homes and the strips of tiny yard separating them from their neighbors well maintained. Some residents were young, low-income working couples with toys in the yard and hopes for the future, just trying to get by. But the park also had a reputation with Adams County deputies as "transitional" housing for those either just out of, or soon to be heading to, the big new jail down the highway.

Patrick spent the afternoon at his friend's house getting high and playing with a .38 caliber revolver called a Titan Tiger, a cheap, evil-looking thing with a short barrel; it was not much good for anything except shooting people at close range. About 9 P.M., Patrick left his friend and walked over to another dilapidated mobile home. He knocked on the door, which was answered by thirteen-year-old Billy Flood.

Most of the year, Billy lived with his father, Rob, in California. But he'd been in Colorado for a week visiting his mother, Leisa Flood, and grandmother, Evelyn. A pretty typical adolescent, he liked radio-controlled toy cars, riding his bike, swimming, skateboarding, and he'd told his parents that someday he'd like to try snowboarding. The neighbors had complained to the sheriff's office about Billy and Patrick trespassing and smoking pot on their property. But most of them thought Billy was a good kid, a likable, quiet, follower type who was spending too much time with the older boy.

Leisa had stepped out, saying she was going to run to the store for cigarettes, so Billy was alone when he let Patrick in. A short time later, there was the sound of a gunshot. Patrick ran out of the house, but then he remembered something and went back in, but only for a moment before he came out again and fled into the dark.

Leisa returned to the trailer not long afterward. At thirty-three years old, her own choices in life had brought her into contact with the law, although not for anything major. She didn't have custody of her son, but she loved him and had looked forward to this summer visit. She opened the door of the mobile home expecting to find him playing video games. Instead, she saw him slumped on the blood-soaked couch. He'd been shot through the eye.

Billy was still breathing, but just barely. Frantic, she called 911 for an ambulance, thinking there might be hope. But the bullet had entered Billy's brain and he was already dead—his body just didn't know it yet.

An ambulance arrived and whisked Billy off to St. Anthony Central Hospital, where he was placed on life support. Arriving at the hospital, Leisa was distraught and blamed herself. If only she'd been home. If only she'd lived somewhere else. If only . . .

Back at the trailer park it didn't take detectives long to identify Billy's assailant. A neighbor reported that Patrick had stopped by and told him, "I shot that kid." The fourteen-year-old was then located at a local pool hall and arrested.

At the police station, Patrick told the detectives that he and Billy had smoked pot and played video games before moving on to something more realistic: the gun with a single bullet in the chamber.

"I said, 'Hey, take the bullet out of the gun.' And he said, 'All right'. . . . I was smoking pot at the time," the suspect told the detectives. "And then I said, "Well, let me see it.'"

Patrick said he pointed the gun at Billy's head believing that the bullet had been removed. Billy grabbed for the gun, he said. "It just went off, you know," Patrick said, crying a little. "And it, it just . . . it was all bright, and my ears were ringing."

Patrick said he left his friend bleeding on the couch and ran from the mobile home. But then he thought about the marijuana pipe and the gun he'd left behind and worried that his fingerprints would tie him to the shooting.

Patrick said he then ran back to the house of the other kid he'd hung out with that day. It was this friend, he told police, who'd loaned him the gun. The pair discarded the spent shell, and then he hid the gun in a field behind the mobile home park. He'd then smoked some more pot before considering his next step.

Only after he'd gotten high again, Patrick said, did he think to summon help—but not an ambulance. Instead, he'd called his mom, who was at her job as a cocktail waitress.

The day after the shooting, Patrick was charged as a juvenile with reckless manslaughter and weapons violations. It would be up to a judge to hear his version of events and determine his fate.

In the meantime, Billy lingered on life support through that first night and through the next day. But there was no chance that he was going to recover. The sole purpose of the machinery that kept his heart beating and his lungs functioning was to prevent his organs from deteriorating until his parents had been contacted and asked to make a difficult decision in the midst of their anguish.

Immediately after the neurosurgeons declared the boy brain-dead, Leisa Flood was approached by a representative of the Denver-based Donor Alliance, a nonprofit agency that coordinated the recovery of organs and helped match organ and tissue donors with recipients. Gently, yet with urgency, the representative expressed her condolences but said that there was something good that could still come of this tragedy. Billy's heart, his lungs, his kidneys, pancreas, and liver could save the lives of others. His father, Rob, had given his permission, now they needed hers.

In a perfect world, my path and Billy's would have never crossed, unless maybe it was ripping it up on a snow-covered hillside. But in an imperfect world, Leisa and Rob Flood were asked to set aside their grief for a moment to make a heroic decision on the behalf of a stranger. With broken hearts, they reached out and gave the one thing their own child had been denied—the gift of life.

Leisa would later tell Alan Abrahamson, a reporter with the *Los Angeles Times,* "The hardest thing I ever did was when I walked out of that room knowing they were taking him down to surgery."

I knew nothing about him or how he died, but Billy had come to Colorado in August 2000 and died violently, and so his fate became woven into my own.

In the meantime, Dad, Missy, and I were flying to Denver. We arrived at the airport and hopped into a cab driven by Khalif, an Ethiopian immigrant. Dad explained why we were in Denver, and when we got to the hospital, Khalif waved away his money. "No charge," he said. "I will pray for you."

The act of simple human kindness at that moment meant more to me than I was able to express with my simple thank-you. But I told him to come visit me in a couple of days. "I will do that," he said. It seemed to be an act of faith on both our parts that I would even be alive in a couple of days.

A few minutes later, I stepped out of the elevator onto Floor 7 West at University Hospital. It was the transplant floor, and the walls near the waiting room were adorned with plaques from organ recipients and their families thanking the doctors and nurses for "the gift of life." Just as I didn't know anything about Billy's life, I didn't know what was going on now behind the scenes.

Immediately after Billy's mom gave her consent to Donor Alliance, the care of his body was taken over by one of the agency's coordinators, all of whom are registered nurses. The boy's vital statistics, such as age and blood type, were fed into the UNOS computer, and a regional list was run. There were no status level 2a or status 1 patients who qualified for the liver, so the computer began ranking the patients on status level 2b. My name had popped up at the top of the roster, thanks to the three years I'd spent on the waiting list.

As I was led to my room, a nurse asked how I was feeling. "A little sore . . . we water-skied our brains out yesterday," I told her. "I'm excited but nervous—excited to get split open like a trout."

Dad and Missy hovered nearby as the staff rushed around, each person doing his or her job like worker ants, highly trained worker ants. Dad commented about how efficient everyone seemed. A nurse hesitated long enough to reply, "Well, we've done twenty-eight of these since last October. We've got it down pretty well."

First-year resident doctor and Aspen buddy Thos Evans showed up. He told me that after his plastic surgery rotation was over, he'd be qualified to help hide the scar I was going to have on my abdomen. "We'll get you fixed up for those underwear commercials," Evans joked.

I laughed one of my goofy Scooby-Doos. I'd been working extra hard on my abdominal muscles during my wait, hoping it would help speed up my return to snowboarding. Now I looked down at my stomach and made a sad face. "Good-bye, abs. See ya next year."

Dr. Josh Goldberg walked out of the elevator. Short and dark-haired with a goatee, the third-year resident already exuded a surgeon's confidence. He was going to be assisting Dr. Kam.

"Kam wants to roll," Goldberg announced. The procurement team—"We don't say 'harvest' any more"—was at St. Anthony Central Hospital preparing the donor.

"Do we get our money back if this doesn't work?" Dad quipped.

"Yeah, and do I get a two-thousand-dollar rebate for my old liver?" I asked.

The humor may seem odd now, but at the time I wasn't thinking about the donor. I was scared and trying not to freak over what was happening.

Goldberg went right along with it, replying, "If you're not happy, return the liver and we'll give you a full refund." Then it was back to business as he explained that the entire procedure would take five to six hours. Using his own body to demonstrate, he described how the incision would be made starting just below the sternum, run straight down four inches, then off at an angle for another eight inches toward my right hip.

"If you added another cut to the left, it would look like a Mercedes symbol," I said of my impending scar.

"Or a peace sign," Goldberg acknowledged. He then reviewed the steps of the surgery, rattling off the parts that would be getting sliced: the vena cava, the hepatic artery, the portal vein.

"I don't want to hear any more," I said, making a face. "I might leave. Let's just do it." I wanted to keep this light; otherwise I was going to need a heart transplant too.

Goldberg ignored my complaint. He said I needed to know that there was a possibility of postsurgery pain, infection, and bleeding. Complications could lead to another operation. Or death. Such problems were, he noted, very rare with Kam.

"That's why they're the best liver-transplant team in the country," Thos assured me.

"The world," Dad added.

"That'd be my vote too," Goldberg said, "but I haven't worked with them all."

"The infection risk is low, right?" Missy asked.

Goldberg nodded. "The whole trick postsurgery is finding a balance between enough immunosuppression, to keep his body from rejecting the liver, and too much immunosuppression, which invites infection."

I wanted off this subject and on to one that interested me, my comeback. I explained to Goldberg what Sean Elliott had told me about returning to his sport without any setbacks.

"Well, he's the man," Goldberg agreed. "But you're going to have to take it easy for a while." Everybody in the room who knew me laughed at the suggestion.

"Six weeks before you do much activity," Goldberg cautioned.

"Hear that?" Missy asked me.

"Enough of negatives," I replied. My nerves were frayed, and I was getting a little testy.

I asked Goldberg what he knew about the donor liver. He hesitated because of confidentiality issues—the donor's identity was protected. But a nurse overheard me and noted that according to the hospital grapevine, the donor was a thirteen-year-old boy who'd been shot in the head. "Otherwise, he was perfectly healthy."

I sat there blinking my eyes without knowing what to say. It was like I couldn't quite understand what it all meant. "I hate to think that some poor kid died," I said finally as tears clouded my vision. "His mom and dad are damn generous to do this for me."

Missy and Dad immediately thought of the newspaper article they'd read on their flight to Denver. Dad now wondered aloud if a thirteen-year-old's liver weren't too small. But Goldberg assured him that a young person's liver would adapt to a new body even better than an organ from an adult.

Goldberg left, then returned a few minutes later. There was a complication that might delay the surgery, he said. Apparently, there was a problem finding a proper recipient for the donor's heart; they thought they had one, but the match was no good. And they couldn't take the liver until they were ready to take the heart.

I felt let down. I'd gotten fired up for the big game, like in high school, but now the game was being postponed. Not knowing really what to think, I walked with Missy down the hall to a row of windows that faced the west. The sun was setting, painting the sky with a brilliant display of reds, oranges, pinks, golds, and purples over the shadowed mountains. There was a row of stationary bikes lined up facing the windows, and I climbed up on one and began pedaling.

Now that the initial excitement had died down, I was feeling guilty about having felt so happy that my wait was over. I thought about how my life would be going on—that I would get to see more sunsets like this one—but the donor wouldn't. I thought about how my family would now still be whole, but somewhere out there a family was grieving for a thirteen-year-old boy. I thought about how my mother would feel if the places had been reversed and imagined what his mother was going through. *Her life,* I thought as I spun the pedals of the bike faster and faster, *will never be the same.*

The thought evaporated when Goldberg rounded the corner. It was official—the surgery was being delayed until morning. By that time they'd have a recipient for the heart, he assured me. In the meantime, I was free to check out of the hospital, get some dinner, and spend the night in a hotel.

Goldberg left. I gave the pedals one last shove and jumped off the bike as the sun dipped behind the silhouette of the mountains. I wished I were in Hawaii, sitting on a surfboard as waves gently lifted me up and lay me back down. Out there I felt closer to God, closer to answers.

Chapter 16

The Operation

A little before 6 A.M. on July 28, we gathered in the waiting room on the transplant floor. I sat on the couch, trying to lose myself in a *Surfing* magazine. Missy sat next to me, quietly leaning on my shoulder.

Hillary and my cousin CC sat together in a chair nearby reading. They'd recently returned from France, where they watched Lance Armstrong take his second Tour de France victory spin through Paris and brought me back a *maillot jaune,* a replica of the yellow jersey worn each day by the tour leader, usually Lance.

Hillary had arrived the night before with Mom after I was released from the hospital. Apparently, it had been quite the trip over Independence Pass and its twisting, narrow road and then the rest of the way through the mountains with my mom at the wheel. I think Hillary was still trying to recover.

"When Dad, Missy, and Chris flew down to the hospital, I was charged with getting my mother to Denver in one piece, physically and mentally," Hillary recalls. "She was in rare form, an absolute tornado of emotions. I can't believe I let her drive! She was anxious, and fearful for her 'baby boy,' but that was combined with happiness and the sense of relief that was pouring out of her. She was making up songs about the liver and how thrilled she was to know it was for Christopher.

"I felt like I was watching a 'Lifetime' original, made-for-TV movie in fast-forward. But she kind of summed it up for all of us. We did not know what to expect, but we knew this was what we had been waiting for."

Mom and Dad stood and sat and stood again. False bravado hung in the air like fog off the Oregon coast. Dad noted that the record number of laps around the transplant floor for a liver-transplant patient in the first twenty-four hours after surgery was thirteen. Mom responded with a strained laugh. "Let's not turn this into another sporting event."

I didn't even look up from my magazine. I was scared shitless, excuse the French, but trying not to let any of them know how much.

Missy shut her eyes but kept her thoughts to herself as she leaned closer to me. She wrote a note on the page of my magazine, realizing, she said, that nothing about that day was guaranteed. *"I can't imagine life without Chris."*

No one had managed to get much sleep the night before. After my release from the hospital, we'd gone to dinner, where I stuffed myself with chicken and dumplings and topped it off with a piece of peanut butter cheesecake.

About midnight, we returned to the Holtz Hotel (since renamed the Magnolia) in downtown Denver, a really classy hotel managed by a friend of my father, who'd offered us a place to stay, even for my recovery. We said a prayer in the hallway and hugged each other before heading off to our rooms.

Missy and I stayed up watching television and calling friends until about 2 A.M. We finally turned off the television, but sleep was difficult. Instead, we lay there and talked about what would happen in the morning.

I was stressing that someone would come along with a higher status level and snake *my* liver. I tried to say it lightly, but Missy knew I was truly afraid of the possibility.

Tracy Steinberg had warned me back when I went up on the transplant list that even after going through the preoperation preparations, the organ could still be rejected by the surgeons or given to a patient who was more suitable for reasons such as age, size, or medical necessity. As a status 2b patient, and not in danger of dying at that particular moment, I could just about be on the operating table and lose the liver at the last minute.

To keep my mind off the bad scenarios, Missy and I went over the updated schedule for my comeback now that—if everything went well—I could start planning for the future. I figured I'd be out of the hospital in record time, because I was in decent shape coming in. Then I'd start rehabbing as soon as the doctors said it was okay (and maybe a little earlier if my body said go for it). Fab had already talked to Kam, and they'd formulated a plan. I thought that I might even still make the late September training camp with the U.S. Snowboard Team on Mount Hood.

Exhausted, Missy and I finally fell asleep sometime after three, only to be awakened at five to go back to University Hospital. On the ride over, I didn't say much but just listened to my dad talk about my being in God's hands now. I agreed. I'd done everything I could to prepare myself, and I knew the surgical team would do a great job—everything else was in God's hands.

At six, a nurse arrived with a gurney to transport me down to the pre-op room. Dad quickly gathered the family in a circle, and we held hands as he prayed. "Thank-you, God, for this miracle, while our hearts go out to the family of the young man who died." Dad got a little choked up there, but still finished with, "Yea, God! Amen."

Out in the hall, I didn't want to get on the gurney. "Can I walk?"

No, the nurse shook her head, hospital rules wouldn't allow it. I reluctantly climbed aboard.

My family and Missy escorted me down the elevator and into the pre-op room, which was large, dark, and as chilly as a morgue. They put me against one wall, the light above my bed the only one in the room. A row of beds without any patients on them were lined up in the shadows against the other wall. I didn't like it—the emptiness of the place scared me.

At 6:10 A.M. anesthesiologist Tom Henthorn arrived. "The liver's here," he said. "It looks good."

I perked up. I'd been thinking about Tracy's warning that not every donated organ was a good enough match. "Really? Is it perfect?"

Henthorn backtracked a little. He said it would be up to the surgical team to inspect and approve the liver. Nevertheless, that was the report he'd heard from the recovery team who'd gone to St. Anthony to get it.

The chief of transplant surgery, Igal Kam, strolled into the room wearing green surgical scrubs. He appeared to be in no hurry as he looked around like a king surveying his subjects.

"God has entered the building," a nurse standing next to my mom said under her breath. "Chris is lucky. He gets the boss."

Kam announced that he had performed a visual inspection of the donor liver, and the team was ready to proceed. I was getting sleepy from the pre-op drugs, but I wanted more reassurances. "Does it look perfect?" I asked again. But Kam would say only that it "looked fine," and then he was gone to prepare for the operation.

More nurses arrived to wheel me off down a long, bright corridor to the operating room. Up to this point, I'd tried to appear nonchalant. But now as the nurses paused at the door beyond which my family couldn't follow, I struggled not to cry. I looked up at my mom, and my voice cracked as I asked, "Am I ready for this?"

Mom stroked a stray hair off my face. She was thinking about all those times she had looked down on me lying in some hospital bed. Her infant with pneumonia . . . *and an aura*. The ten-year-old Captain Hook with asthma who she'd stood next to and willed to *breathe in, breathe out*. She thought about the day she found me crying about my knee and asked, *What do you love, Chris?* and was told, *I love the starting gate, Mom. I love the possibilities.* She knew then how to answer my question.

"Chris," she said quietly, "your whole life has prepared you for this."

My eyes were wet with tears, the drugs were kicking in, but I managed a smile. She was right. All my life I had been training for this moment. "I'm ready," I said, and the nurses wheeled me past the door.

I heard my family and Missy say, "We love you, Chris," and then they were gone.

Back at the elevator, Missy stifled a sob. Mom's voice wavered as she cautioned her, "The floodgates, Missy. The floodgates." She was afraid that if one of them started to cry, they would all be bawling.

I don't remember much from this point on, but I learned about it all later. I do remember Dr. Henthorn saying that the lights were about to go out. I tried to fight it, but then the world faded to black.

I lay naked on my back on a steel table. My head and shoulders were shrouded beneath a blue half-tent, my face visible only to the anesthesiologist. Electrodes had been placed on my chest to monitor my heart rate. Other electrodes were attached to my head to measure my brain waves, which would help Henthorn assess my level of consciousness.

On the other side of the blue tent was the rest of my body. I was covered from my hips to my feet with another blue sheet, but my torso, from my rib cage to my hips, had been wrapped in a thin, yellow plastic covering called Ioband, which was impregnated with iodine to cut down on infections. The blue sheets represented areas that were not to be touched by anyone or anything that was not sterile; the yellow Ioband was where the surgeons would operate.

Kam stood at my right side wearing an odd pair of glasses called "loupes" that had what looked like microscope lenses attached. To Kam's right was a large tray bearing a wide assortment of instruments—forceps, scalpels, and curved needles already threaded. Surgical nurse Anthony Adams hovered over the tray, counting and recounting the supplies, making sure that all was in order, while other nurses bustled about assisting him. Josh Goldberg, also wearing loupes, stood across the operating table from Kam. Ignored for the moment in a corner of the room was a small plastic basin covered with a sterile blue towel.

There was a momentary pause, like a symphony orchestra between tune-up and that first note of Beethoven's Ninth, then Kam spoke a single word—"scalpel." Adams handed over the instrument and noted the time of the first incision: 7:47 A.M.

Kam started at the middle of my abdomen and made a diagonal cut through the skin toward my right hip. From his original starting point, he then cut up toward the sternum.

Instead of continuing through the next layers of fat and muscle with the blade, he handed it over and called for a "bouvie." The pen-like instrument, which cuts by using electricity to quickly burn through flesh, has the effect of also cauterizing severed blood vessels. With it, Kam proceeded through the fatty layer beneath the skin—a very small layer on me, thank-you very much—and then through several layers of muscle to reach the abdominal cavity.

Kam placed retractors along the sides of the cut to spread my abdomen, creating a gap that revealed my internal organs: pink-gray intestines and stomach and a large, dark purple liver.

Reaching deep into my abdominal cavity to move the organ aside, he began what would be hours of work to free my liver by first cutting the bile duct where it exited the liver. Inside the liver, the bile ducts branch out like vines before joining the right and left hepatic ducts, which then merge into the "common" duct that carries bile from the liver into the intestines; it was this common duct that Kam severed. The duct was then tied off near the intestines.

The team then began working quickly, but methodically, to cut off my liver from its complicated blood-supply system. Almost all organs have arteries that bring oxygenated blood from the heart and veins that return "used" blood to the heart to be pumped into the lungs for oxygen. But the liver also has a third "portal" system that brings nutrient-rich blood from the digestive tract—intestines, stomach, and spleen—into the body's "chemical factory," the liver, where the nutrients are altered and stored for use.

Using forceps, Kam first clamped and then cut the hepatic artery. (About the size of a drinking straw, this artery brings oxygenated blood from the heart to the liver via the aorta, the biggest artery in the body.) He then repeated the procedure with the portal vein, a white tube about the size of an adult's pinkie finger. Cut off from the hepatic artery and portal vein, my liver began turning a blotchy gray-brown. Next in line was the hepatic vein, which carries blood back to the heart.

Finished with these chores, Kam lifted the liver to get at the connective tissue that attached the organ to the abdominal wall. Doing so revealed the purple-pink muscle of the diaphragm that separated the organs in my abdominal cavity from my heart and lungs, which could still be detected by their regular movements. Goldberg followed along behind Kam with a bouvie to cauterize blood leaks with a blue arc of electricity and a buzzing sound, then tiny white wisps of smoke.

The next step was the diciest part of the operation: separating the inferior vena cava from the liver. *Vena cava* translates rather undramatically from the Latin as "hollow vein," but it is responsible for returning the blood from the lower part of the body to the right atrium of the heart. It carries a lot of blood, and puncturing the vein could result in death within fifteen seconds.

The team worked with few words, but a radio in the operating room was tuned to a local rock station. The chief surgeon began freeing the vena cava just as Jimi Hendrix launched into Bob Dylan's "All Along the Watchtower," which had an opening verse that was probably what I might have said if I'd been awake. *There must be some kind of way out of here . . .*

Goldberg's head bobbed to the beat as Kam began working from the bottom of the liver up. As he lifted the organ away from the large vein, he and Goldberg found the "on ramps," which Kam cut and passed a suture through that his assistant promptly tied off.

If all went well, Kam wouldn't have to clamp the vena cava and cut off the blood supply to the heart, except for a brief time when he would have to tie the ends from the donor's vena cava into my system.

After about a half hour, the vena cava was no longer attached to my liver. Paul Simon's "Graceland" was playing when Kam, his scrubs smeared with traces of blood and the band of his surgical cap dark with sweat, asked nurse Adams to make sure there was enough ice on the donor liver.

I may be obliged to defend / Every love, every ending / Or maybe there's no obligation now, sang Simon as Adams hopped down from his perch, walked over to the plastic basin, and looked under the blue towel. He added more ice and returned to his post.

Thos Evans entered the operating room but hung in the back, where he could not see my face or much of what the surgeons were doing. He'd have preferred not to be there at all—this was just too personal—but he knew that my family and Missy were in the waiting room, anxious for any news.

Kam assured him that everything was fine, and Thos risked a peek. "Would you look at those abdominal muscles?" Thos said with admiration.

Kam deadpanned his response, "This is a liver, not muscle."

"Thank-you, Doctor Kam, for pointing that out to me," Thos said with a laugh as he turned to walk back out the door.

"You're welcome," Kam replied. The surgeon glanced up at Goldberg. His mouth was hidden by a surgical mask, but his eyes were smiling.

For several hours the surgical team of Kam, Goldberg, and Adams worked as one organism with six hands. Goldberg, who had assisted with ten liver transplants, anticipated Kam's next moves with only the occasional correction or guidance. Adams was even more automatic.

At 10:02 Kam announced that my old liver was out. He handed it to a nurse, who placed it in another plastic basin.

Billy's liver was smaller than mine. Devoid of blood, it was tan in color as the surgeon slipped it into my body. With hardly a pause, Kam began to reverse the steps he'd been taking for the past two and a half hours by attaching the vena cava ends from the donor liver to my vena cava, which he clamped.

With the donor liver off the ice and still lacking a blood supply and with my heart under stress, it was important at this point to work as quickly as possible. "You can have the vena cava back in four minutes," Kam told Henthorn. The longer my heart was without that blood, the greater the risk of a heart attack or stroke.

At 10:25 he released the clamps on the vein, and the anesthesiologist immediately reported that my blood pressure was climbing back to normal, while my heart rate was slowing. "The heart's happy to see all that blood," Henthorn said.

Next, Kam began to attach my portal vein to its counterpart on the new liver. Using thread so fine it was hard to see with the unaided eye, he began to sew the two severed ends together using one continuous suture. It was like sewing the mouth ends of two balloons together into a single passage, except balloons are made of stronger stuff. He made pass after pass with his needle, each pass perhaps a thread's width apart, around the circumference of the vein ends.

No one remarked on the irony when the band Dada came on the radio singing, *I just saw a good man die / I'm going to dizz knee land* . . .

After the portal vein was sewn together at 10:40, Kam asked how long the donor liver had been out of the ice. "Thirty-five minutes," Adams replied. Kam released the clamp on the portal vein, and almost immediately my new liver regained a dark purple color as blood rushed in.

Kam didn't wait to admire his handiwork. He started right in on the hepatic artery. Fifteen minutes later he released the clamps, and the artery turned a bluish purple and began to pulsate to the rhythm of my heartbeat.

Throughout the operation, Kam's cell phone had rung and was answered by one of the nurses, who relayed the messages. One call suggested that my fear of someone snaking my liver had almost been realized. A higher-status-level patient had been brought in during the night, and the family was asking questions having heard there was another liver transplant under way. But Kam unemotionally explained that the patient had been running a high fever and therefore was too sick and weak to survive the operation.

After he dealt with that call, Kam began lifting my intestines out of the abdominal cavity and piling them on top of my groin area. The surgeon deftly handled these slippery, ropelike parts, cutting here, stapling there, and burning a small hole at one spot just as the funky bass lead to Stevie Wonder's "Superstition" got the heads of Goldberg and the nurses moving in unison. The mood in the room was lightening; they all knew the operation was almost at an end.

Kam connected the donor liver's bile duct to the hole he had burned in the small intestine rather than to my tied-off bile duct. The duct could not be attached to the new liver for fear that whatever caused PSC might find its way in from the old duct. (Even with that precaution, there is a chance that the PSC could return someday, but such cases are rare.) With that step completed, the surgeon plopped my intestines back into place.

At 12:20 Kam removed the retractor that had been holding my belly apart. The yellow Ioband was stripped off, after which Kam used the bouvie to burn a hole through the skin and muscle near my navel. A tube was inserted in the hole that would serve to drain any fluid, including blood, from my belly while I recovered.

Kam began closing the enormous wound in my abdomen by stitching a suture through the muscle layers as Goldberg followed behind tying the sutures into knots. Finally, there was nothing left for Kam to do but staple the outside of my skin together while Goldberg stitched around the drain tube to hold it in place.

At 12:50 P.M., five hours after the first cut, Kam threw up his hands like a concert pianist finishing a recital. "Thank-you," he said to the staff in the room, then walked away from the operating table, removing his gloves, gown, and mask. He carefully placed the loupes in a felt-lined wooden box.

As Kam spoke into a tape recorder, making notes about the operation, Henthorn began waking me with different drugs. A nurse bent down near my head and called my name. My eyes flew open, uncomprehending, then closed again. I began to shift restlessly and attempted to pull the intubation tube out of my nose.

"Chris, you're doing okay," a nurse assured me. "Can you try to move your leg?"

The request was perhaps a mistake. I began moving too much and struggled to get up as the nurses tried to hold me down. "Chris, you've had your operation," the same nurse said. "You've got a new liver."

I mumbled something back but calmed down. I was satisfied in my semi-stupor to flex and straighten my legs.

Kam left the room to go talk to the family as I was moved onto a gurney for transport to the recovery room.

In the waiting room, Missy, Hillary, CC, and my folks were getting antsy. Evans's report had been hours ago.

To pass the time, Missy called Gary, Boogie, Bill, and Gibans to give hourly updates. She also kept up with her journal on the pages of my surf magazine. *"It hurt me to see him so frightened,"* she wrote of the moment before I was wheeled off to surgery. *"I told him to dream of waves and our next surf vacation. I hope he can.*

"I love you so very much, honey. My life is so incomplete without you. I can't wait until you wake up, so I can see your smiling face again. . . . I look forward to spending the rest of my life with you. Thank you God for Chris's new opportunity for life. He will make it worth the effort."

As Missy, the girls, and my parents waited and prayed, they were reminded again of the price that had been paid for the new opportunity. An older man sitting in a wheelchair near them had been listening in on their conversation while he read the newspaper. He finally asked if they had a family member who was getting a liver transplant. When they told him, the man nodded and held up the newspaper he'd been reading and showed them a headline and story.

"Boy Wounded by Gunshot Dies: Police Investigating to Determine if Handgun Shooting Was Accidental," read the headline. The story began, "A thirteen-year-old boy, allegedly shot by a fourteen-year-old friend, died Thursday at St. Anthony Central Hospital."

"This is all a nightmare," the boy's grandmother, Evelyn Look, was quoted. "I'm just hoping it was an accident."

"The fourteen-year-old could face charges ranging from first-degree murder to criminally negligent homicide," the story went on.

"'I think people should be more aware of what's going on in their household, and if they have guns, lock them up where children can't get hold of them," Evelyn told the newspaper. "Nobody's been exposed to guns in our family. I don't allow them."

Billy, she said, was "a typical teenager. . . . He was just a lovable kid. Everybody loved him."

According to the article, "The family was left to find solace Thursday in those memories and the knowledge that he might help others to live because his organs were donated."

My parents admired the compassion the boy's mother had demonstrated in the midst of her grief. They were signed up to be organ donors in the event of a tragedy, but they knew how devastated they would be to lose one of their children and couldn't imagine having to make such a decision. It was hard to fathom the courage that had moved this woman to reach out to strangers. They would have to try to find a way to thank her someday, but they had no idea of what words would be adequate.

Kam walked into the room and over to them. "It went as smooth as could be," he said, as if he'd done nothing more than change the oil in their car. "Everything is fine. He's awake."

Still, he warned, there could be bleeding; the sutures might not hold. They would have to wait and see. "The first twenty-four to forty-eight hours are critical," he added.

When Kam was done talking, my parents and Missy gave him a standing ovation. Then everyone else in that large, busy room, who all knew why we were waiting, stood and applauded too.

Caught off guard, Kam blushed. "Thank-you," he said with a little bow. "That was new for me."

Mom left to take Hillary and CC to the airport; they were flying back to North Carolina for the annual family get-together on my mom's side. Mom then flew out to Seattle to get Jim and drive back with him to Denver.

Two hours later, Dad and Missy poked their heads into my room on the transplant floor. I had my eyes closed but opened them at the sound of their voices in the doorway. It was so good to see them. I raised my hands like a boxer who'd just been declared the winner and shouted, "I rule!"

Dad and Missy each moved to different sides of the bed and reached for my hands. "Thank-you, God," my dad began to pray. "Thank-you for this miracle."

When he finished, I joined in with "Amen." I was happy, but then I remembered that while this had been a miracle for me, it was a tragedy for someone else. My smile faded and my eyes filled with tears as I looked at my dad and said, "I just wish that kid didn't have to die."

Chapter 17

Back on Snow

Patrick Random also said he was sorry that Billy had died. But not everyone believed him on the day in September when he was sentenced for reckless manslaughter.

The prosecutor told the judge that counselors at the juvenile jail reported that he'd been "bragging about what he did. . . . He's shown the remorse of someone who stole a candy bar." The defense attorney countered that his client was "a very sad child, who was having a very difficult time dealing with the fact that his actions led to the death of one of his best friends."

Billy Flood's dad, Rob, then addressed the court, noting that his ex-wife was still too upset to attend the sentencing. "While Patrick gets to go on with his life, it will still be in my heart every day that my son is not here."

The judge was unmoved by Patrick's mumbled apology. "Your irresponsible behavior, your criminal behavior, has destroyed the lives of two families. . . . Frankly, I don't think that you're remorseful at all. And that's consistent with what your behavior has been like throughout your early life."

The judge turned to Patrick's parents. "I don't mean to be disrespectful, but I have to say that I believe that you folks bear some of the responsibility, because he didn't have the life that kids deserve."

Looking back at Patrick, the judge continued, "This case screams for the maximum sentence. If I could give you a longer sentence, I would." But because Patrick was a juvenile, all he could legally hand out was two years in a juvenile corrections facility—and one more unusual requirement, based on a request from Rob Flood.

"I will make it a condition of this sentence that every Father's Day," the judge said and nodded to Rob, "you send him a Father's Day card."

On that same morning, I sat in the snow on Mount Hood, Oregon, basking in the sun and soaking in the view of the Cascade Mountains. I was looking in particular at the jutting volcanic peaks that guarded my old hometown of Bend: Three Sisters, Mount Washington, Mount Jefferson, and, of course, Mount Bachelor. *Where my road began,* I thought.

As my mom had predicted, I'd turned getting out of the hospital into a sporting event with the help of the staff, my family, and my friends, who visited mostly to harass me while I was unable to defend myself. In the first couple of days, dozens of friends called or came by, like Marco, Travis, Gary, and Fab. Brad Boyd flew in from Oregon and Carlon Colker from Anaheim, California, where he'd been in the middle of giving a lecture when he got the message that a donor had been found.

"I remember the moment when I got the call," Carlon says. "I felt a tremendous sense of relief that now he would either live or die. You see, he has the freest spirit I have ever come across; seeing him as sick as he was made me cry, it made him cry. I just assumed when I got on the plane to Denver that he would either make it through or die trying, but the call sent my heart racing with nothing but joy. I don't know how that sounds. I don't care. It's my truth. Get through it, or die. No more slow suffering."

Carlon got off the plane and drove straight to the hospital, where he walked into my room and hugged me. But the kinder, gentler Carlon didn't last long.

As a doctor, he knew that hospitals are germ factories, and he wanted me out as fast as I wanted to be out. The way to do that was to get me back to functioning on my own as soon as possible. He instructed my friends and family not to coddle me; he even ordered them not to empty my bedpan. "You want to take a piss, get up and go to the bathroom," he told me.

I quickly set the record for laps around the transplant-floor hall-ways, often parading around with an IV pole in the company of family and friends who'd driven or flown in. The day after surgery I was able to go outside and walk around a little and get some fresh air. We were joined by Khalif, the taxi driver who'd met us at the airport and drove us to the hospital for free, and who now used his lunch hour to come over and see how I was doing. I thanked him for his prayers and we took great "family photos" with him.

I'd felt like a new man from the moment I woke up from the anes-thesia. Gone was the low-grade fever, inability to eat or digest, and struggling to breathe because my blood was losing its ability to absorb oxygen. Yeah, my abdomen was sore—after all, I had thirty-six staples across my midsection. I was also slow getting around, and it hurt like hell if I coughed, laughed, or sneezed. But I just felt whole and healthy for the first time in maybe years. It was as if the surgeons had opened up the hood and given me a brand-new engine. I seemed to have more energy than anyone around me, and even remember lying in bed one morning, ready to go, wishing somebody would come along to play because my wuss buddies Brad and Carlon were passed out in chairs on either side of me.

Of course, for the first couple of days I was pretty loopy on painkillers. Missy says they made me nicer, because every once in a while I'd blurt out some emotional statement with tears in my eyes, like, "I have the best friends and best girlfriend in the whole world."

Sometimes my remarks were a little on the crude side, however, like when I first really noticed the catheter. "Dude, there is this thing in my Johnson," I complained to Brad.

Or when the nurse told me I should report any bodily functions so that they could tell when I was getting back to normal and that there was nothing wrong with my digestive system, like a twisted intes-tine, so I told her, "I think I'm going to fart." Pause. "Okay, I did fart." Everyone laughed, including the nurse who said, "Good, but I needed to hear it."

Fart jokes definitely meant I was getting back to normal. But the return of my sense of humor was dangerous in other ways.

The day after the surgery, a nurse told me I should take a shower, but I had to have someone help me. She said I had a choice: I could either shower with a nurse I didn't know, or with a friend. I went for the known evil and picked Brad, who'd taken over the Chris watch that morning after Missy spent the night babysitting me. I took the shower sitting on a chair and was lathering up when the bar of soap slipped out of my hands. I couldn't bend over to pick it up, so I had to say something to Brad, who hadn't noticed.

"Dude, I dropped the soap, could you pick it up?"

It was a like a line from a bad prison movie, and the look on his face was priceless. We both started to laugh, which hurt so bad I wondered if I was going to blow my stitches apart. I'd been warned to try not to laugh. Yeah, right.

Missy's mom, Pat, showed up the day after the operation. She was going to spend a week and was there mostly for Missy's mental health. Missy had been so strong throughout the ordeal that in a way she needed to recover now too.

My mom also showed up with my brother, Jim, on the second day. They'd driven straight through from Seattle and had plenty of time to talk. Jim says the conversations were pretty upbeat. "I remember my mom talking a lot about us as young kids, particularly about Chris being so sick when he was little and how far he had come," he says. "We kept telling ourselves that Chris would be fine . . . that he was the strongest kid we knew . . . that he would dominate the transplant surgery with the same attitude he took with everything else."

I was sure going to try. I'd been told that the average stay for a liver transplant patient after surgery was twelve days. I could have been out in three, but the doctors made me stay until the fourth just to be sure there were no complications from infections and that my body wasn't showing signs of rejecting my new liver. They said I had to remain within a half-hour drive so that I could have blood work done

242 | To the Edge and Back

every few days to make sure the new liver was working properly and to gauge my reaction to the antirejection drugs.

Dad even got a limousine and had it take us all to lunch and then on to the Holtz Hotel, where I would be recuperating. Opening the door of the room, I walked into an absolute jungle of flowers, as well as a hundred cards, from sponsors, friends, and family members.

"Look forward to seeing you on the hill soon. Feel better fast," signed Jake and Donna Carpenter.

The family holding the reunion in North Carolina signed theirs, *"Some people will do anything to get out of losing at volleyball."*

I heard from friends in Bend whom I hadn't talked to since elementary school. Even some of the guests at the Aspen Square Hotel, where Dad was telling anyone and everyone the good news, sent me get-well cards.

My story was finally out there in the public as well, as I'd started talking about the disease and my ordeal with the media the day after my surgery. The long wait for an organ had given me a new perspective and made me more determined to fulfill a promise I'd made that summer.

I thought it was terrible that less than 50 percent of those people who died in accidents, or of natural causes, and whose organs could have been used to save lives, were donors. In the meantime, sixteen people were dying every day, hoping that someone would make a decision that would save their life.

When the press came to talk to me, these were the numbers they heard. My message was that I was alive only because some grieving family, some mother and father, had made a courageous decision to offer a stranger this wonderful gift. Everybody was treating me like I had done something heroic—and I was proud of myself for how I'd faced the challenge and hoped that my story might inspire someone else to keep fighting—"but the real heroes in stories like mine," I told reporter after reporter, "are the donor families."

Articles quickly appeared in the big Denver dailies, as well as other papers around the state, and on television stations. My story also went out on a dozen Web sites, my own and those of sponsors, friends, and organ donor organizations and transplant centers.

My mailbox and e-mail were soon flooded with responses to the stories, many from people who were either suffering from PSC or another liver disease, or who had a loved one who was. I answered every e-mail I got, and as many letters as I could until there were simply too many. I was particularly moved by those who said they found renewed hope for themselves or someone they loved in my story.

With their encouragement, I rededicated myself to my career—only, my motivation was changing and maturing. In the past, racing my snowboard and getting into the Olympics had mostly been about me and my love of competition. I won't lie—I still wanted an Olympic medal for myself as an athlete, but I also saw it as a way to fulfill my promise that if I lived, I would do everything I could to promote donor awareness. Just from the little bit of media coverage I'd already received, I knew I could do that best in the spotlight provided by the Olympic podium.

With that in mind, I knew I had no time to waste getting back on the slopes. Points earned at World Cup and Grand Prix races during the 2000–2001 season wouldn't specifically determine who would be on the team, but they would determine seeding at the first few races the following year when the run for the team began in earnest.

In those first few weeks, I did what I could at the Holtz Hotel—climbing on a stationary bike and doing light arm lifts in the workout room just seven days after my operation. One day I was riding the stationary bike with my shirt pulled up to avoid irritating my stitches when an airline pilot came into the weight room to work out. He took a look at the huge scar and asked what happened.

"I was attacked by a shark," I said with a straight face.

"My God, you're lucky to be alive!" the pilot exclaimed.

His reaction was so classic, I didn't have the heart to tell him the truth. Besides, I did feel lucky to be alive.

When the medical staff let me out of the hospital, they told me the best thing to do was walk. They didn't really put a distance limit on it, so as always, I figured more is better and walked all over Denver every day with whoever thought they could keep up.

Golf was a big part of my early rehab. I couldn't play (I might have torn myself in two swinging a club), but I could stroll the fairways and watch others. One day it was laughing (painfully) as my Dad and Missy hacked a course to pieces. Another day, only the tenth since the operation, we went to the international tournament at Castle Rock (also illegally off my leash). I walked all eighteen holes following Vijay Singh and Sergio Garcia, although I had to lie down on the edge of the ninth hole to catch my breath.

Three weeks after I got out of the hospital, Kam said I could go home to Aspen and hook up with Fab. As a physical therapist in a ski town, Fab was used to assisting people recovering from knee injuries or broken bones. This was the first time the prescription for his services read "liver transplant."

There wasn't much in the way of literature or experience that Fab could turn to in planning my rehab program. Sean Elliott was the first professional athlete to return to his sport after a transplant. But a liver was a much more complicated, and larger, organ than a kidney (no disrespect, Sean). Kam told Fab what to avoid, but that didn't tell him how to get me back in shape for the rigors of racing a snowboard at fifty miles an hour on ice.

Although I was anxious to get back in shape all at once, I knew enough to stick with the schedule Fab and Kam devised. For the first few weeks, the regimen stayed pretty gentle. We started in with the stationary bike and light repetitions with weights on isolated arm and leg muscles, always conscious not to strain my abdomen.

Fab massaged the wound, sometimes using ultrasound, to break up the scar tissue and keep me limber for the gut-wrenching, twisting maneuvers involved in snowboard racing. Slowly, we also worked on regaining my balance by walking forward and backward on a narrow beam—first with my eyes open, later with them closed—and then trying to stay upright while standing on a board with a wooden roller underneath.

I began hiking in the mountains around Aspen with Missy and other friends to regain my aerobic capacity. Within a couple of weeks, I was on my mountain bike, hammering up and down trails, getting my legs back and also getting used to charging through a narrow space at high speeds to condition my mind and body to act together quickly in such circumstances. The first bike ride was with Gary, Marco, and Missy. She snapped a photo of me lifting my shirt to show off my scar while Marco leaned over with a sort of "*paisan* (Italian for dude), that's gnar" grin on his face.

In the meantime, my appetite had returned, and I was quickly gaining back the twenty pounds I'd lost during the summer. I was a freak for hydration—I only put the best in my body. Unfortunately, Missy's parents had retired and sold Papandrea's while I was wasting away on the transplant list. It was one of the saddest days of my life, one that I'm sure set my weight recovery back weeks, if not months.

Seriously, thanks to all the docs, my friends and family, the nutritionists, physical therapist, nurses, coordinators, and especially the donor family, the starting gates of the world and the possibilities they represented were mine to enjoy again. The only downside was thinking about the boy whose liver was now inside of me.

Others knew Billy Flood's name, but I didn't yet. In fact, I still didn't know how to handle the idea that because a boy died I was alive, and until I did, I didn't want to know his name or much about him. I was aware that he'd apparently had some rough times growing up, coming from a broken home and all, and that he'd died violently.

It made me think about how fortunate I'd been. My mom might have driven me crazy sometimes with her exuberance, and her mother-hen hovering. But she also knew how to say exactly the right thing at exactly the right time—such as at the hospital when she told me that my whole life had prepared me for that moment.

My dad could be pretty conservative (though he also likes to have fun and has been known to enjoy a fine wine on occasion), but he'd always been there for me, helping me achieve my dreams. When it felt like my life was being swept away in a swift current that summer, his faith that God would not abandon me had been a rope for me to hold on to.

As I thought about the boy who died and heard bits and pieces of the circumstances surrounding his death, I was reminded of my brother Jason's childhood and how his life might have turned out differently if my parents had not changed its course. Yet, that also taught me an important lesson that would become part of my message about organ donation. In the midst of their grief, Billy's parents had made a decision every bit as life-affirming as my parents had made when they took Jason into their home. It didn't matter where you lived, how much money you made, the level of education you had, or what your family situation was . . . anyone could be a hero if they respected and loved life enough to make that kind of decision for someone else.

Near the end of September, Dr. Kam gave me the green light to get back on my board. As soon as I could arrange it, I was off for the U.S. team snowboard camp on Mount Hood.

I was looking forward to resuming my career like never before and had no doubt that I could. I'd just survived the "race for my life"— compared to that, the rest was going to be easy. But I'll admit to a few anxious moments.

I showed up at Mount Hood a day earlier than the rest of the team was scheduled to report, because I wanted to take my first few runs without anybody watching me. I just wanted to enjoy my first days back on snow.

Driving up to the ski area, I experienced a mixture of eagerness and fear. I was excited to be back, but I was also afraid. *What if I fall?* Would I literally burst open at the purple seam that stretched across my abdomen? Might some organ tear loose or twist inside me, and I wouldn't know it until I wound up in a hospital again?

I took it easy that first day, free-riding to get a feel for the snow and staying out of the racing gates. I was a little rusty, but I made ten runs and felt physically strong. The old joy of setting an edge and allowing the board to carry me through an arcing turn was there from the first moment.

The snowboard team showed up the next day, and I watched jealously as my teammates ran gates while I stayed off to the side free-riding. This went on for about a week until I couldn't stand it any more.

One morning I was riding next to the course when I decided to drop in and run the gates. It felt great to find that rhythm again, and I was maybe feeling a little cocky and going too fast on my approach to a toe-side turn. I loaded the nose of the board too much and sprung myself into the air, ejecting out of the course and landing on my head. Then I was flipping over, twisting and turning as I tumbled down the slope. I felt a tearing in my abdomen as I came to a stop.

I lay there in the snow, afraid to get up. Mentally, I searched my body, waiting for some pain or strange sensation to tell me that my comeback would be short-lived. Gingerly, I felt my midsection with my hand, afraid that the force of the impact had split me open. But after a minute, I realized that I didn't feel any worse than a similar fall would have caused before the operation. *I'm okay,* I thought. *I'm really okay!*

I stood up and made my way off to the side of the course. Because I'd been free-riding, I wasn't wearing my helmet and the blow to my head had me seeing stars. I also wasn't wearing my speed suit and ended up with a few yards of snow crammed down my baggy pants. I dropped my pants to get the snow out.

My coach, Jan, had seen the crash from the other side of the course. When it was clear that I was all right physically, he guessed that I'd scared myself half to death.

"What'd you do?" Jan shouted. "Shit your pants?" He and the rest of the team started laughing.

I realized the image I must have presented—squatting over with my pants down—and started my hyena giggle. But my laughter was only partly in response to Jan. It had more to do with how relieved I was that I'd taken a hard fall and survived. It would have happened sooner or later, and until it did, the fear would have weighed on me. Now, I knew I had nothing to be afraid of on the slopes.

Later that afternoon, I sat on the snow looking south over the Cascades. I loved my life and was so grateful to the donor family for giving me a second chance. Yet, I was also overwhelmed by how to express that gratitude in some way that measured up to the gift they had given me.

Chapter 18

A Simple Thank-You

It would take more than three months for the words to come to me. But it was no surprise that I would again be on a snowboard and looking out over a beautiful mountain range.

The season had begun well enough. I'd placed second in one race and then won the next at the Continental Cup races at Copper Mountain held at the end of training camp. A step below World Cup races, the events were more of a tune-up for veteran racers and a way for young riders trying to make the pro tour to show their stuff. They were significant to me because the second race fell on November 18, my twenty-eighth birthday, and my parents were there to watch.

It was an emotional moment for all of us, and I remember my dad getting choked up at the end of my run. Then there were more tears again that night at my birthday party at Jimmy's restaurant in Aspen (where I was predictably an hour late).

"There was a time, of course, when we were not sure that Chris would see his next birthday," my dad explains. "But there we were, celebrating with him not only another year but a very amazing, blessed, terrific year that included the miracle of another family saying 'yes' at a time of tragedy. A year of amazing medical professionals doing their work, and a year of Christopher hitting the bottom with his health and coming back from it all in an almost unbelievable way. And yes, still when I think about it all I get choked up, tears come, and I say again, 'Thank-you, God.'"

I'd given myself an early birthday present that reflected as much as anything else my new outlook on life. I hadn't replaced the Pooper, because I wasn't sure I was going to need another car. But now I treated myself to a brand-new, black Chevy Blazer.

As I entered the main part of the season, I continued to participate in television and newspaper interviews whenever I was asked. I had one rule about the interviews—they had to include the life-saving message of organ donations. I continued to educate myself about the cause and knew the statistics by heart. One donor could save the lives of more than a half-dozen people and improve the quality of life for as many as fifty. But the number of Americans waiting on the transplant lists was climbing every year and approaching eighty thousand; yet the number of donors had been stagnated at about six thousand, which was about the same number of people who died annually while waiting.

I spoke to the press about the importance of people indicating their intentions on their driver's licenses and registering with their state's donor registry. Part of the problem was that families often don't know what their loved one would have wanted and can't bring themselves to make that decision in the midst of their grief.

My message was an early beneficiary of the U.S. press starting to gear up for its Winter Olympics coverage. They were looking for human interest stories, and I had a pretty good one.

On December 7 *USA TODAY* gave me the entire front page—under the headline "Klug's Salt Lake Dream Alive"—of its special sports section, "Olympic Glory," which named "10 to Watch for Salt Lake." (USSA president Bill Marolt had promised that U.S. skiers and snowboarders would win ten medals at the games, which would be a record for Americans.)

Missy told the reporter, Vicki Michaelis, "I've never heard this year, 'Oh man, I'm tired of training' or 'I wish I didn't have to go out there.' It was like, 'Let's go, I'm ready to get on that board and go and compete and prove to myself and everyone that I'm back and I'm stronger and better than ever.'"

But Vicki also noted that I was still struggling to write a letter to the donor family, having started, stopped, and torn up a couple dozen attempts already. "It's pretty humbling, I have to say," I told her. "They're the real heroes in this deal."

That same week, the ESPN show *Outside the Lines* aired a segment on the death of Walter Payton and the efforts of his wife, Connie, to promote donor awareness. I'd been honored to take part in the show as "one of America's best hopes for an Olympic medal." I smiled when they showed that segment of Walter running up that hill in Chicago that had motivated me so much when I was a high school player. But it was so sad to watch the replay of his emotional press conference when he announced that he had PSC and asked everyone to pray for him.

However, I thought the most moving segment was when Stacy Bacon, whose ten-year-old daughter, Brianne, died from a brain tumor, was asked if it was hard to donate her dead child's organs. "I put myself in the place of parents whose child needed an organ to live," Stacy said. "No, the decision wasn't hard."

Stacy and Brianne were the first real faces for me on the other side of the equation that had spared my life. I wondered if my donor's parents had felt the same way. I'd been receiving hundreds of messages thanking me for my efforts on behalf of donor awareness, but it was Stacy's courage and compassion that I admired.

If I wanted to be the first Olympian to compete after an organ transplant, the physical part wasn't going to be a problem. In reality, the rehab following my knee injury had been a lot more painful and challenging than the liver transplant recovery had been. The knee was brutal, and there'd been times when I thought I'd never walk again. It took me a full year before I was 100 percent, and even then it would swell randomly and keep me from racing.

On the other hand, practically from the moment I woke up from the transplant surgery and felt like the Energizer Bunny running on a new twelve-volt, I knew I could physically return to my sport. I'd trained for the transplant, and it paid off with a quick recovery.

About the most difficult change in my lifestyle so far had been remembering to take my medicine. I only had to be on Prednisone for one day, which was great. But I had to take three milligrams of Prograf twice daily, morning and night. Even that was no big deal once I got in the habit; it came in a small easy-to-swallow pill. (It was sort of amazing to me that Prograf even existed. It had been developed by Fujisawa Healthcare, Inc. from a substance—*tacrolimus*—found in a fungus that lived in only one place in the world, the soil of Mount Tsukuba in Japan.)

I'd done so well—with no "rejection episodes," indications that the body was trying to get rid of the donor organ and controlled by upping the drug dosage—that Kam had already cut the Prograf back once. I hoped that over time I would be able to wean myself off the drug even further, although I realized that I would probably have to take some amount for the rest of my life.

So physically I was doing fine. But mentally, while stoked to be back on snow and confident of my ability, things just weren't clicking yet. Following the races at Copper Mountain, my comeback had been less than spectacular.

I'd fallen in the first few races in Europe. I'd be riding strong, but then I'd make some small mistake due to a moment's loss of focus, and I'd be sliding across the snow on my butt instead of my board.

Finally, at the PGS World Cup in Ischgl, I'd stayed on my feet and finished twelfth. Not great, but respectable, and at that point I was satisfied. We returned to North America for the World Cup in Whistler, Canada, a two-run, timed giant slalom. I hoped to at least repeat my 1999 performance when I placed third. However, another mistake put me in twenty-second place after the first run. A fast second run moved me to eleventh, but that was little consolation, although it did mean some money plus points toward my seeding in future races.

I did better the next day on the same slope when I placed second in a Continental Cup PGS. It wasn't a World Cup, but it was against many of the same great racers, and it felt good just to stand on a podium and listen to my dad ring his cowbell. It was such a small thing, but I had learned to treasure small things.

My standings and my morale continued to climb when I followed the Whistler races with a third-place finish at the FIS World Cup on

Mount St. Anne in Quebec, Canada, an event won by Canadian Jasey-Jay Anderson. Two days later, I beat Anderson for first place at a Grand Prix event in Okemo, Vermont.

I'd known that regaining my mental edge before making my run for the Olympic team was going to be as tough as rehabbing my body. Waiting for my transplant had put me in the loneliest, scariest place on the planet. After the fear and worry of those months, I was going to have to switch from survival mode to the competitive focus needed to become a champion again.

I owed a lot of my progress in that regard to the support I got from family and friends, the medical staff at University, the e-mails, calls and letters of encouragement from hundreds of people I didn't even know. It was also great not to have to stress over finances because my sponsors—Burton, Bolle, Aspen/Snowmass, and the Aspen Club—had kept their word and stuck by me. I will never be able to fully express my appreciation for that, and they still weren't even sure I would race again, at least not at the level I had in the past.

Derek Schuman, Bolle Team Manager, says the company was well aware that there was uncertainty that I would be able to come back from my liver transplant. "We could have looked at this from a simple business perspective and opted out of our sponsorship," Derek says. "But he had stood by us and believed in us and our product for a long time, so we viewed it as a no-brainer to stand by him during this trying time.

"The longstanding relationship we have with Chris is much more than a marketing relationship. Yes, Chris is a visible athlete and does a great job helping us promote the Bolle brand, but Chris is also regarded as a friend, which makes everything that much more meaningful."

I owed a lot of people more than I could ever repay. But there was one debt that weighed on me more heavily than the others. I still had not thanked the donor family.

I don't know if that was what was messing with my concentration. I didn't consciously link the difficulty I was having in coming up with the right words to express my gratitude to the mental mistakes I was making on race courses. I do know I was troubled by my inability to write a simple letter and didn't want the donor family to think that I wasn't grateful.

It still wasn't an easy concept to grasp. Lying in bed at night, I sometimes felt as if there were something inside of me that wasn't really mine. I wondered what the boy had looked like, what he liked to do, what plans he may have had for the future. I wasn't ready yet to put a face or a name to him. That would have made it too personal. But what could I say to his parents that would be as meaningful as what they had given me?

Even my father had been able to write a letter in September expressing how he and Mom felt. There were confidentiality rules that kept donor families and recipients and their families from contacting each other directly until a certain period of time had passed. After that, both sides had to agree to contact. My situation was different, because the media attention paid to me had also found Billy Flood's family.

Still, my dad honored the rules as set forth by Colorado Donor Alliance and gave them his letter to pass on to the "anonymous" donor family.

Dear Family,

There are times in our lives when paths cross, totally unplanned and unexpectedly. Sudden events change things forever, or something happens that brings a drawn-out story to conclusion.

I believe firmly that God does not cause bad things to happen to us, but of course, we all go through bad things at times, and it seems that God allows it. We do not know why. But I also believe that God does step into our lives at times.

I am the father of a boy who received a liver transplant in late July. The transplant saved his life. Even as we traveled to Denver from our home in the mountains, we were well aware that the gift our son was about to receive had come through great loss to another family.

*In your grief and sorrow, please know that the other side of
your tragedy is that there are parents like me who are grateful
for your gift. . . . Thank you so much. You helped save our son's
life.*

A Grateful—Very Grateful—Dad

Back home in Aspen for Christmas, I looked forward to the next
Grand Prix race in Breckenridge, an event I'd won in 1999. But then
I fell on my first run.

I left for Europe but continued to struggle, falling in the first two
races of the new year. I was riding so fast in training runs before the
races, but I just couldn't stay focused and avoid mistakes long enough
to put it all together.

I was getting discouraged when we arrived in Olang, Italy, in mid-
January for the last World Cup PGS before the World Championships
in Madonna di Campiglio, Italy.

The day before the race I took my customary two runs through the
gates and felt good about how I was riding. In fact, I was enjoying being
on my board so much that I decided to go free-riding in the afternoon.

As I took the chairlift to the top of the ski area, I got out my
camera. Northern Italy has always been one of my favorite regions for
racing because of its beauty. The jagged Dolomite Mountains are
famous in mountaineering circles for their spectacular climbs, and that
day they were sparkling in the sun beneath a layer of new-fallen snow.
I snapped a few photographs and got off the lift.

Cruising down the hill, I couldn't keep from smiling as I carved
long, graceful turns in the clean corduroy, acutely aware of how strong
and in sync my body felt. The snow was perfect and I got back on the
chairlift, soaked in the view, and took another run. And then another
and another. It was more than I would have normally done on the day
before a race, but I was just so happy to be alive and doing what I
loved that it was almost like I couldn't stop myself. I wanted to shout
and laugh like Scooby, and probably did, but I don't remember.

Riding cleared my head of doubts, and the chairlift gave me time to think. When I arrived at the top for a final run, I knew at last what I would write to the donor family. I'd been trying too hard to say too much. Every turn, every laugh, every moment that I was alive to enjoy days like this one, or to feel the love of my family and friends, I owed to them. There were no words that could match their gift to me; because of them, I'd won the only race that really mattered. All that I could do . . . all that was required, really . . . was a simple, heartfelt thank-you.

I got back to my room that afternoon, sat down, and wrote my letter on my laptop computer:

Dear Donor Family,

I am over in Europe doing my favorite thing in the world, snowboarding. I thank God every day I'm back on the mountain, and I thank you every day for your gift of life. You have given me a second chance to pursue my dreams and to enjoy life to its fullest.

I love my family and I love my girlfriend very much. They are as thankful and as grateful for your gift as I am. . . . I am forever grateful and humbled by your decision. And I am truly sorry for your loss.

It is impossible to express with words my gratitude. I hope through my efforts, I can spread the good news on my successful transplant and someday save someone else's life.

Sincerely, Chris

I sent the letter via e-mail to University Hospital that night to pass on to the donor family. The next morning I woke up feeling like an enormous weight had been lifted off my shoulders. The thought struck me that perhaps like the letter to the donor family, I had been trying too hard to win again. I just needed to go out and have fun.

That morning in the starting gate, I placed snow on the back of

my neck and then straightened to look out over the Dolomites. . . .
God give me the strength to do my best today.

Like I said, I don't know if there was a link between words of
thanks and racing a snowboard. But when the day was over, I had
beaten the top riders in the world for my first World Cup win since
being given a second chance at living.

Chapter 19

Changing Times

I celebrated my win at Olang with the first sip of alcohol I'd had in eighteen months. The transplant team at University had told me I should, of course, avoid things that could damage my new liver. The occasional social drink was okay, they said, but nothing in excess.

Especially no grapefruit—grapefruit really was my kryptonite—something about enzymes in the fruit that could mess up my anti-rejection drugs. I'd been told that transplant patients had died from eating grapefruit.

Anyway, the party started right after the race when I gave in to Anton's insistence that I climb aboard the new Ducati 750 Dark Monster motorcycle that I'd won and take it for a spin. Anton, who along with Kildy and Swedish rider Daniel "Bive" Biveson had been drinking and gambling since their early exits from the competition, started demanding that I "get on it now, because you're never going to see it again!"

I got caught up in his excitement and jumped on, still wearing my racing boots and speed suit, turned the key, kicked it into gear, and opened the throttle. Spinning donuts, I sprayed the cheering, ducking crowd with slush while the Ducati representative ran after me yelling in Italian something to the effect of, "No, no, that's not the bike you get!" And Anton running after him screaming, "Rod it! Rod it! You'll never see it again!"

The Ducati rep was really fuming by the time he got me to stop. I don't speak Italian, so I'm not exactly sure what he was muttering, but I'm sure it wasn't nice. (I never did get the bike and eventually had to accept cash for it.)

Anton, on the other hand, drunkenly told me how proud he was of me and led the way to the party in the restaurant at the bottom of the slope. There, head coach Jan Wengelin was going for it in classic Swedish style. He danced over with a shot of something alcoholic in a glass with one of those little umbrellas. I hesitated. *Ah, what the hell* . . . I figured that one little umbrella drink couldn't do much harm, so I gulped it down.

However, Jan wasn't through leading me down the road to ruin. He had in tow one of his friends, Italian snowboard coach Alexa "Lisko" Grisa, a short, wild-mountain gnome of a man with a foot-long gray goatee. He held up a bottle of clear liquid with something long and dark inside that I couldn't make out at first.

"Viper Grappa," Alexa yelled over the throbbing music and shouts of the other riders and spectators who'd joined the throng. He shoved the bottle into my hands.

It took me a moment to realize what I was looking at. *Grappa* is a super-strong schnapps, and *Viper Grappa* is, well . . . a nasty-looking snake floated in the bottle, staring back at me with angry yellow eyes. Closer inspection revealed that the snake had lost some of its scales and skin, which were drifting around in the liquor.

Viper Grappa was definitely the gnarliest thing I'd ever seen in my life, and there was no way in hell I was drinking it. The rest of the crowd, however, had a different idea.

"Take a sip! Take a sip! Take a sip!" they shouted in unison.

I looked again at the snake in the bottle. I thought about the scales sliding down my throat and almost gorked.

"Take a sip! Take a sip!" The crowd was going nuts. Alexa and Jan grinned evilly at me. It was clear that I wasn't going to get out of this one without losing all respect from my fellow riders and gaining years of verbal abuse.

I looked again at the snake in a bottle. I figured the liquor was probably pure alcohol and had to be pretty much germ free and therefore somewhat safe. I raised the bottle to my lips . . . *"Take a sip! Take a sip!"*

. . . closed my eyes so I wouldn't have to look at the snake . . . *"Take a sip!"* . . . and drank. It wasn't bad, if you like the taste of turpentine, but it took a real effort to keep it down when I felt what I was sure were scales and skin sliding down my throat.

I managed not to spew the stuff all over the triumphant Alexa and Jan, who were capering around in a funny sort of Euro dance. But at least my encounter with *Viper Grappa* was over with and I was okay . . . or so I thought.

On the team bus on the ride back to the hotel, I freaked when I started seeing everything in triplicate. Only later did someone tell me that they'd heard that *Viper Grappa* was hallucinogenic because of the snake venom. I decided that was it for drinking *Viper Grappa,* or much of anything else; the little incident in Olang reminded me that I better take care of the gift I'd received.

So I didn't join Anton a week later for his "$30,000 Funding Dance" after he podiumed at the World Championships in Madonna di Campiglio. I'd arrived at the championships brimming with confidence. There were three alpine events on three consecutive days at the World Championships.

The first event was a two-run, timed giant slalom, in which I placed sixth. I was riding better than ever and was stoked for the PGS the next morning. I lost a contact lens four gates into the qualifying run, but I still had the fastest time—more than a second better than that of my closest rival.

After my name had been left at the top of the leader board all morning, I thought I was going to be seeded first for the head-to-head competition, but the technical director of the race disqualified me. He said the edge of my board had crossed over a stubbie gate (the short side of the triangular panel that you were required to go around). To be honest, with only one contact lens I was half blind and wasn't sure. I knew I'd taken an aggressive line and was right on top of the stubbie, so it was possible. But I didn't think so and asked Foley to protest. He did, but the video analysis was inconclusive and, unfortunately, the ruling stood.

I really stunk it up on the slalom course the next day. However, I was happy for Anton, who placed third, a huge deal for him as it qualified him for the "A" team, which had all their expenses covered, including lodging, food, equipment, and transportation, as well as entry and coaching fees. It was a big deal for him.

By 2001 most American alpine riders were struggling financially; the money in U.S. snowboarding went to the freestyle side, where contracts in the six figures and up to a million-plus weren't uncommon. It was all about who was selling snowboards to kids, and most of them were into free-riding and the half-pipes and special terrain parks that 80 percent of U.S. ski resorts now had. Heck, so was I whenever I got a chance.

Alpine snowboarding in the United States was declining in popularity. As a sports culture, we don't support racing of any kind like they do in Europe, whether it's skiing, road biking, track, or snowboarding. U.S. athletes in team sports—football, basketball, baseball, hockey—get the lion's share of the attention, except every four years when the Olympics roll around and suddenly Americans get behind their Olympic teams. That's part of the reason why American athletes involved in the lesser-known sports place such importance on the Olympic games. It is our one time to really shine in front of a mainstream national audience.

Many European alpine snowboarders did pretty well for themselves, and Burton's Europe and U.S. riders were well-supported—though as my thirty-thousand-dollar annual contract demonstrated, not close to the salaries and endorsements of half-pipe specialists. I was lucky; most U.S. alpine riders maxed out their credit cards every season, then worked all summer to pay them off so that they could compete again. Even then they'd end up in the hole, sleeping on hotel room floors, begging for rides to the next event, and eating if they placed well enough. You had to love it or there was no reason to do it.

Sometimes the "A" snowboard team was made up of only one or two males and the same number of female riders. This paled dramatically to the U.S. Ski Team, which received enough money from the United States Ski Association (USSA), supposedly the national governing body for both sports, to fully fund even its "C" Team and development team skiers.

The annual package was worth about thirty thousand dollars to Anton and, for once in his career, meant no more money worries, at least for the next season. Let's just say that it threw another log on the fire that night that's always burning in Pogue, and of course Jan was ready to stoke the flames. Anton showed up for the party in nothing but surf trunks, accompanied by Jan, who was dressed up as a woman.

Jan makes for a very ugly woman, but not quite as ugly as the sight of a sweating, beer-covered Anton Pogue doing what he called the "$30,000 Funding Dance," a sort of frenzied tribal gyrating to the repetitive throbbing of Euro-techno music. All the while, he was sucking down free beers while the other riders poured more on him. Anton had a word or an expression for just about everything. But he'd never said much about my transplant. Mostly just "glad you didn't die . . . you missed an epic summer, dude."

After the European tour was finished, the World Cup circuit moved on to Japan for two races. I got back on the podium with a third-place finish at Sapporo, and a week later I took second at Asahikawa at a resort called Santa Present Park.

Then on the way back to the States, Anton and I stopped off in Hawaii, where we rented a house on the north shore of Oahu with Nicolas Huet and Mathieu Bozzetto from the French team. Nicolas kept complaining about Anton and me dropping in on him (cutting off another surfer and stealing his wave). If I'd known what a good sport he was going to be in the future, I might have cut him some slack. But we had a lot of fun running with the Frenchies, even if we did snake a wave or two from them.

The next race on the schedule was in Park City, Utah. The race was sort of a dress rehearsal for the next year's Olympic event. After crashing the year before, I wanted to demonstrate to myself and my competitors that I could win on that hill, and I wanted to get in as many runs as possible to get a feel for the hill.

I qualified for the head-to-head competition and easily blew past my first challenge, Dieter Krassnig of Austria. Then I did the same in the first run of the quarterfinals against another Austrian, Alexander Maier, the younger brother of ski racing legend Herman "The Herminator" Maier, beating him by almost a full second. I thought I had the hill figured out: a steep pitch at the beginning, followed by a short transition, then onto the flats, where my size and strength made me tough to beat.

In the second run Alex and I reached the transition to the flats at the same time. All I had to do now was stay with him and the race was mine. However, I took too tight a line coming into a heel-side turn, and my boots hit the base of the stubbie pole as I was leaning over the gate. The impact knocked my feet out from under me, and I crashed onto my side and slid past the next gate before I could recover.

Alex went on to win the competition, while I stewed over my seventh-place finish. I'd felt that the day had been mine to win. Still, as Missy and my family gathered around me in their protective cocoon, I had to concede that I'd learned a couple of lessons that might help me the next time I raced on that hill in the Olympics.

The first was to never give up in the PGS, because anything could happen in that second run. Of all the people on that hill, I knew about second chances. But it was Alex who had capitalized on his second chance, and it kept me from moving on to the semifinals. The second part of the lesson had been with me all of my life: nothing is ever guaranteed. Not winning with a one second lead. Not trips to the podium. Not making the Olympic team. Not life.

I left Park City knowing I could win on that hill. But I was going to have to work harder and stay focused from the first run to the last. I renewed my promise to myself that I'd be back in a year to get my medal.

My time in Park City had been well spent in a more important way. I'd been contacted by Ben Dieterle, the public relations manager for Intermountain Donor Services, which coordinated donor programs in Utah. The agency wanted to make a public service ad that would appeal to young people (that is, snowboarders) and get them to sign up for the Utah Organ Registry (similar to Colorado's).

Ben asked if I would participate and was sort of apologetic that they were operating on a shoestring budget and didn't have money to pay me. The money didn't matter—I was happy to help. After all, I had a promise to keep.

My season ended on a great note at the U.S. Nationals in Sunday River, Maine, with my taking first place in the PGS and fourth in the slalom. It had actually been one of my most successful years ever, and I would enter the next season as the top-seeded American rider and in the top five of the world standings—a great place to be for my run at the Olympic team.

Once again, I'd come back from a medical problem stronger than ever. This time I attributed it to a new perspective on life. Eight months earlier, I'd looked up at my mom from a hospital gurney, afraid that I was going to die, and asked her if I was "ready for this." Yet, despite the fear, coming so close to the brink was the most freeing experience of my life. I felt lucky—not just to be alive, but to really understand how precious life is. I didn't take a single day or race or turn on my board for granted, nor did I get caught up in the small stuff, including what the person racing next to me was doing. I'd already won the only race that mattered, the rest were just for fun.

After the season, I flew to California, where I was met at the airport by Mike Croel. We drove from there halfway down the Baja Peninsula to meet up with Anton and his Hood River gang of Joker and Mike Tinkler. We planned to spend the next two weeks surfing and camping on the beach.

My first mistake was not thinking it through when Mike told me not to worry about bringing any camping equipment. He said he'd take care of it, but I should have known better than to send a city boy to do a mountain boy's job. He went to the store and bought a cheap "two-man" tent . . . yeah, right, two-man if both "men" were small children.

Anton and his buddies had a great time watching the two biggest guys in our crew—both of us about 6' 3'', with me at 220 pounds and Mike at 240—squeeze into what they promptly labeled "the butt-hugger tent." We didn't get much sleep, but the surfing was great.

Surfing had continued to evolve for me. When I was younger, it was a new challenge and an adrenaline rush. Then I saw it as a fun way to cross-train for my snowboarding career. After that, it was to decompress with friends after an exhausting racing season. When I knew that I needed a new liver, that final surf trip to Los Angeles had been a way of saying good-bye to the life I loved.

After the transplant, there was still an element of all of those things—except I wasn't saying good-bye. Farewells had been replaced by a celebration of being alive in a way that I had never appreciated as much before.

The ocean was mysterious, always changing, and unpredictable, just like life. It could be dangerous and frightening, but more often it was beautiful and filled with life—creatures I'd sometimes see while floating on my board off the Oregon coast, the fish and seabirds and sea lions and orcas. I had received a new liver, but sometimes—especially when I was surfing or looking out over some mountain range—it felt like I had also been given new eyes to see how stunning the world really is and a new heart to appreciate what I had been given.

After the Baja trip, Pogue and I went on to Bachelor for an "A" Team Olympic training camp. We could tell it was an Olympic year because all of a sudden the USSA boosted our funding. We got a full-time tech, Jay Cooper, to tune our boards and keep the rest of our equipment in top shape, and a full-time sports psychologist, Bob Harmison, to work on our heads, while Jan and his assistant coaches, Nick Smith and Bjorn Almkvist (another crazy Swede), worked on our technique.

"Uncle Bob" Harmison spent a lot of time emphasizing the concept of teamwork. Although snowboard racers competed as individuals, he noted, it took the effort of a team—from coaches, to equipment managers and technicians, to the riders—to achieve winning results.

Bob also worked on individual programs to help with visualization— seeing yourself running the gates and winning (another version of my dad's "plan your race, then race your plan")—and focus. With me, he developed a sort of mantra to repeat in the starting gate as a reminder to run my own race and not get "tinned" by whatever the rider next to me was doing.

(*Tinning* was a Pogue-ism and referred to the old saying about being as nervous as a cat on a hot tin roof. It was what happened sometimes in a PGS to the rider who won the first run. The other rider has nothing to lose and will be charging, so you start taking chances yourself . . . and maybe make a mistake.)

Just put on the blinders and ride. We came up with "Blue is you, red ahead," for the colors of the gates on the PGS course.

After camp, I was ready to forget about racing and the Olympics for a while, but I had one more snowboarding obligation, although this one sounded like fun. NBC, the network that would be televising the Olympics for the U.S. audience, wanted me to star in a million-dollar, sixty-second promotional piece for the games. The purpose was to reach the eighteen-to-thirty-four-year-old audience in movie theaters. The spot was to be entertaining (snowboarding) while it promoted the games.

At last, after a long absence, my acting career, thwarted by an asthma attack when I was ten, was being revived. The producer, Barb Blangiardi, said it was going to be a sort of *James Bond/Mission Impossible* action movie trailer they wanted to shoot in British Columbia at the Whistler-Blackcomb ski area. They planned to show it in theaters in the fall. My newly acquired agent, Peter Carlisle, thought it was a good idea, so I said yes.

However, first I joined Anton for a kite-boarding session on the Columbia River outside Hood River, Oregon. Essentially, in kite-boarding you are harnessed to a large four-line foil kite that pulls you as you ride a modified wakeboard across the water. At least that's the theory. My first few times, I mostly got "tea-bagged" as I was dragged across the mile-wide river. I'd gotten better, but this time I managed to gash the bottom of my foot and needed twenty-six stitches.

When I arrived in British Columbia a couple of days later, I was trying not to limp. I probably shouldn't have been walking around, much less snowboarding, but I didn't want to blow my acting career for a second time.

Most of the footage was shot on the slopes of Blackcomb. But the coolest experience was climbing on board a helicopter that took me and Brian Savard—a Canadian Big Mountain free-rider hired to be my "double" for jumping through windows, over cars, and a backflip while jumping a road—into some of the backcountry behind the resort. We had the springtime corn snow, chutes, and snowfields all to ourselves (well, along with the film crew). Somehow I managed to keep the secret that every afternoon when we finished filming I'd pulled off a blood-soaked boot.

As for my acting career, I had only two lines . . . but they were important and I delivered them with real feeling. After eluding police chasing me in cars and snowmobiles (presumably for "speeding" on my snowboard), I rode up to a pretty young woman.

Me (cheesy grin): "Hey, what's going on?"
Her (sexy smile): "You in some kind of trouble?
Me (cheesier grin as I give her a hockey puck emblazoned with
    the five circles of the Olympic emblem): "Meet me in
    February in Salt Lake City."
Her (sexier smile): "Okay."

All right, already . . . so it wasn't exactly Oscar material, and I had had more lines as Captain Hook, but it was fun.

A few days after the filming in British Columbia, I boarded a plane for Bali with Anton, his wife (at the time), Jean, and Missy. I was proud of myself for having proved that as a liver transplant recipient, I could return to the life I'd left behind. In fact, with the approval of my transplant team, I had just dropped my Prograf dosage from three milligrams to two milligrams twice daily, and hoped that soon I could whittle it down even more.

I'm not saying my life wasn't impacted. I had to have blood tests every month to make sure my liver was still functioning properly. I got tested regularly by the United States Anti-Doping Association, which monitors drug use in U.S. athletes and can get you kicked out of competition, even in the off-season. I had to continually fill out "athlete location forms," detailing my daily schedule so that testers could show up unannounced at any time. It was sort of like being a criminal on probation; they'd find me on my road bike or after an afternoon of kiting on the Columbia and make me pee in a cup.

I didn't mind the testing and never had a bad result, but I hated filling out the forms and having to describe where I'd be every day four months into the future. I didn't know where I was going to be the next day, at least during the off-season, much less three months down the road.

It wasn't like antirejection drugs could be considered performance enhancing. In fact, if all of my competitors had to take them, it would have made my life a lot easier when it came to competing.

My overall health was generally great. In fact, I'd lived so long with my deteriorating liver and what it did to my energy levels and digestion that I couldn't believe how good I felt.

However, the same drugs that protected my liver by suppressing my immune system left me more susceptible to common illnesses like colds and flu. They also hit harder and lasted longer. I had to take extra care to wash my hands and not let myself get run down. I also had to be careful to avoid unguarded exposure to sunlight, because the drugs made me more susceptible to burning and, I was told, skin cancer down the road.

The drugs also opened the door for the parasites and gastrointestinal ailments that one encounters, especially in Third World countries, as I learned during my Baja trip, which carried over to desperation outhouse runs during the filming at Whistler.

Even some medicines for other health problems had to be avoided. I couldn't take antiinflammatories, like Ibuprofen, and pretty much avoided all over-the-counter home remedies when I wasn't feeling well, because I didn't want them to interfere with my meds or get me in trouble with the drug testers.

On our monthlong trip to Indonesia, I couldn't take antimalaria drugs, because they're hard on the liver, although we were in a part of the world where malaria was a concern. So I was in a panic whenever I thought I heard a mosquito buzzing nearby.

During the trip, we booked a weeklong boat excursion, along with seven other people, that traveled to the outer islands in search of perfect waves. We lived on the boat and surfed pristine coastlines all day long, then headed for the next area.

One day we arrived at a spot where we'd heard the waves were double-plus overhead (in other words, twice our height). However, the captain informed us, those waves were on the other side of a thin, jungle-covered peninsula and could be reached only by taking a path through the bush. I took one look at the trail from the boat and declared the place "Malaria Island."

That wasn't about to stop me. Instead, I covered myself with at least one big bottle of bug repellent and then put on every piece of clothing I owned, including long-sleeved shirts, a jacket, and topped it off with a blanket. It was a hundred degrees outside and 1,000 percent humidity, but I could have survived in the arctic.

Fully cloaked, I jumped off the boat and paddled to the trailhead on our side of the peninsula. Fearing swarms of blood-sucking, malaria-infested mosquitoes, I took off in a mad dash through the jungle, with Anton laughing his brains out behind me.

We arrived on the other side of the trail, where I was rewarded with the sight of a pristine coast with big, peeling double-high rights (even if I kept slipping off my board because of all the bug juice on me). Oh, and we never saw a single mosquito . . . but I know they were there, just waiting.

I suppose some people might ask why I would continue to take risks and not "play it safe" after coming so close to dying. But ripping it up on a wave off some remote island was my way of saying thanks to God and to my donor family.

Unfortunately, not everyone feels life is as precious as I do.

After the Continental Cup races at Copper Mountain kicked off the 2001–2002 season, we headed to Valle Nevado, Chile, for the first FIS World Cup ever in South America, where I took third in the PGS. It was a good start to the season, which got even better when we then surfed for a week off the coast of Chile. The water was cold, but the waves were huge, with only penguins in the lineup with us.

I was thinking that life was just about perfect when I caught a flight from Santiago to Miami and then boarded an early morning flight to Denver. Once airborne, Missy and I settled in for what was usually a four- to five-hour flight to Colorado.

The plane was half empty, so Missy was lying down across several seats and I was engrossed in a surfing magazine when the pilot came on the public address system and told us to stow our tray tables, return our seats to their upright position, and fasten our seatbelts. "We'll be landing in five minutes."

Five minutes? I looked at the little map on the chair in front of me that shows the plane's progress; we were over the Gulf of Mexico near Alabama. I looked around, and that's when I saw the stewardess and realized with shock that she was crying.

We're crashing, I thought.

The woman behind me noticed her, too, and became hysterical. "What's wrong!" she screamed in my ear. "Oh, my God, we're going to crash!"

I was scared to death but tried to calm her. "You know there's a lot of high winds in Denver," I told her. "That's probably why we're being diverted."

The pilot came back on and told us that the FAA was forcing us to land, but he still didn't explain why. Soon it was clear that he was trying to bring us in for a landing, and I assumed there had to be something wrong with the plane. Maybe the landing gear wasn't working or an engine had failed.

As we approached the ground, I took out my cell phone and called my dad. I know you're not supposed to, but I figured I was about to die and to hell with the rules. When Dad came on the line, I told him the bad news before he had a chance to say anything. "Dad, I think the plane is malfunctioning, and we're about to crash."

There was a pause on the line. "You haven't heard?" he asked, and I could tell that he was choked up about something. "A jet just flew into the World Trade Center in New York. . . . I think they're grounding flights all over the country."

The day was September 11, 2001.

We landed at the airport in Birmingham, Alabama, and walked into the airport just in time to see the second hijacked plane fly into the WTC. It was like being in the twilight zone or a far-fetched Tom Clancy book. Bewildered people shuffled around or stood staring up at television screens with tears running down their faces. Nobody seemed to know what to do or say. Thank God we were with Foley, who took charge and found us a place to stay, because rental cars were disappearing and the hotels were filling up.

Like everybody else, I couldn't believe the evil it took to do such a thing. I loved life so much, I couldn't understand how anyone could hate enough to kill so many innocent people. All I could do was wait, pray, and hold on to Missy through that long, empty night.

Chapter 20

Proud to Be an American

Five months later, fifty-five thousand people waited in the dark around me, looking on silently. Occasionally a camera flash went off, but no one was cheering, and I didn't understand why.

The people in the stands had come to Salt Lake City from dozens of countries to watch the opening ceremony of the 2002 Olympic Winter Games and root for their favorite athletes. I thought that they would erupt when we walked onto the field carrying the American flag that had been found in the rubble of the World Trade Center. I didn't expect them to cheer for us—the eight U.S. athletes who had been chosen for the honor—but for the flag itself and what it represented, as well as for the uniformed men and women from the New York City police and fire departments who filed in next to us.

Instead, the crowd was as silent as the snowflakes that fell on Rice Eccles Stadium on that bitterly cold night. *"What's wrong with these people,"* I wondered. The only sounds were the ominous *thwok-thwok-thwok* of the helicopters hovering over the stadium, searching for signs of danger, and the wind rippling the flag.

I looked over at Frank Accardi, a New York Port Authority officer whose partner had died on 9/11 trying to save other people. Tears were streaming down his face. He noticed me and smiled slightly. "My partner would be so proud of us today," he said quietly.

Only then did I understand the silence.

Up to that point, the most evident impact of the terrorist attack I had faced was dealing with the additional security at airports. Flying didn't make me nervous; I wasn't going to stop traveling and competing, so the rest wasn't something I could control. Even then, the security precautions were more of an inconvenience for someone who travels one hundred thousand miles a year, carting eight to ten snowboards and two big "wheelie bags" full of clothes and gear.

I was proud to be an American and proud of how our country had come together. In Europe there was a great sympathy for Americans; it was as though they thought we'd each lost a relative, and in a way we had.

As if any of us needed more reminders of the fragility and uncertainty of life . . . a week before we were scheduled to wrap training camp and head for a race on the Kitzsteinhorn glacier above Kaprun, Austria, the Kaprun 2 "funicular"—a sort of ski train that carried skiers and snowboarders to the slopes—burst into flames inside a tunnel. About 170 people died, many of them young junior racers on their way to training camp for the first day of the Austrian winter season.

I had raced at Kaprun many times over the past ten years and had been in that train often. It always felt claustrophobic, especially with hundreds of Euros cramming it full and jockeying for position. I could only imagine the terror and helplessness of those who'd been trapped.

Our race was canceled, and we stayed home for Thanksgiving. I was glad to be with my family and friends. It seemed especially important that year. Racing on a snowboard just didn't seem important compared to what was happening in the world, but I also realized that racing was what I did. It did seem important that we go on with our lives; otherwise, we were giving in to the terrorists and fear.

Racing, for me, had always been a celebration of life. A life spent on edge . . . the edge of a snowboard, and right up to the edge of death. But now I was back and could do my part to balance the scales by using my sport to spread a message about saving lives.

The NBC promotional piece we shot in British Columbia started airing in movie theaters that fall and was a big hit. There wasn't anything in it about donor awareness, but it got my name out there as the public started to identify athletes who would be in the Olympics. Millions of people saw the promo, which in turn spurred interest from the media. I was besieged with requests for interviews, all wanting to tell my story, which gave me the opportunity to pound the numbers at them. Eighty thousand on the waiting list. Sixteen dying every day. *"Sign up . . . let your family know . . . be a hero and save lives."*

In December I even got a write-up in *People* magazine. But to be honest, I was much more excited to learn that the public service ads I'd done for Intermountain Donor Services had been a big hit, and not just in Utah.

"When other states saw the ads, they asked if they could use them to promote their registries or donor awareness," Ben Dieterle says. "We provided the PSAs, and the spots aired in Utah, Colorado, New York, Kentucky, Idaho, Oregon, and Alaska. We believe people of all ages responded favorably to the ads. Teenagers liked the fast-paced ads and Chris's charm and snowboarder personality. Adults liked the message and were equally taken by Chris's easy smile and good nature. The results have been that over one million people have joined the Utah Donor Registry, approximately sixty-five percent of driver's license holders in the state."

It felt good to learn that I was reaching some people. The way I looked at it—and I know it sounds cliché, but I mean it—if one person responded to something I said or did and that saved even one life, then it was worth the effort.

When I hired Peter Carlisle, I wanted him to assist me with developing my career opportunities and take over negotiations with sponsors and such. But I'd also told him that it was also my goal to find ways to promote organ donation.

We traded on the fact that if I made the team, I would be the first Olympian, and only the second professional athlete (the first being Sean Elliott), to have received an organ transplant and resumed his career. We tried whatever it took to get the message out, and it was working, including in one way I hadn't foreseen.

Peter contacted Fujisawa Healthcare, the makers of Prograf, and suggested that I would be a great spokesperson for the company. Sue

Ellen Knutson, the director of consumer marketing for Fujisawa, was unimpressed at first.

"I'd never heard of him," she recalls. "And what's snowboarding? I was a fifty-three-year-old woman whose children were already grown and out of the house. I knew nothing about the sport. But I saw his picture and a story about him and I said to myself, 'I don't know if he's going to the Olympics, and if he does, I don't know if he's going to win. But you know what, he's already a winner.' Anybody who could get a liver transplant and then go back to competing at that level had to be a very special human being. I decided right then to take a chance on how he would present himself and how he would speak."

As my story got out there, the number of e-mails and letters I received kept multiplying. Some of them were simply congratulatory, or were from people who identified with me because of some obstacle they faced in their lives, not necessarily even medical. Others were from people on the transplant lists, or their family members and friends, and recipients.

Many said something along the lines of the e-mail I received from Todd Coulston of San Ramon, California. Todd was twenty-nine years old and also had PSC. He'd read about my story in the *Contra Costa Times*.

"I was diagnosed in 1992. At that time, I ran track and field and cross country for USC–Irvine. . . . My disease path pretty much followed the same pattern as yours, and I had the same attitude about having the disease. I thought that by continuing to run 7–10 miles a day and keeping a solid spiritual faith, I wouldn't have to deal with the disease until I was 50 or 60, if ever. Your reaction to Walter Payton's death brought everything home to me. I can remember driving from work on the day he died in tears. . . . Earlier this year, it became apparent that I needed a transplant soon. However, the waiting lists here in California are jammed beyond belief. They seriously have people dying here left and right waiting for transplants. It was scary."

Fortunately, Todd's doctor referred him from Stanford Hospital to Shands Hospital in Florida, where on May 22, 2001, *"I received the gift of life. . . . It was even more special for me as it was only three weeks after my first son had been born. . . . I'm now just over six months post-transplant and doing great and back to running on a regular basis. I'm amazed and extremely pumped to see the recovery schedule you kept. In my eyes, for you to come back and compete at the level you have is just as impressive as what Lance Armstrong has done, if not more so."*

I realized from these letters and from talking to people like Sue Ellen and Ben that my message wasn't just about trying to get people to sign up to be organ donors and let their families know their wishes. I was living proof to those who were waiting or had already received transplants that they could lead normal lives again. Also, I recognized after hearing from donor families that I personified the results of the heroic decisions they'd made for the benefit of someone most of them would never know or see. It was a truly humbling realization.

Sometimes, though, all I could do was try to cheer someone up in a frightening time in their lives. And it saddened me to learn afterward that not all stories ended happily like mine or Todd's.

One of the e-mails I received was from my old friend Steve Shipsey, whom I'd first met on Mount Bachelor during my high school years. He'd been the one to counsel me not to let other people make me decide between football and snowboarding. He'd told me to follow my heart, and that's what I'd done. Now he was writing on behalf of someone else.

"I had not spent any significant time with Chris in person since 1990; however, like many of the friends I have from snowboarding, I enjoyed following his career," Steve says. "I was very proud of Chris, and the sport overall, as I watched his runs in the Japan Olympic games. Leading up to the SLC Olympic games I became aware of Chris's transplant saga.

"The story was not only of interest to me because it was Chris, but also because a friend of mine from law school had a three-year-old daughter awaiting a heart transplant. Particularly to everyone awaiting a transplant, Chris was/is a hero, inspiration, and role model. After not having spoken to him in so many years, and in the midst of his Olympic training, I contacted him by e-mail with a request (like I'm presuming he was inundated with) for a favor. I asked that he send a note of encouragement to little Eliza Cascade Jacobs as she waited for her heart far from her Eugene, Oregon, home at the UCLA Medical Center. Chris complied with that wish and brightened what proved to be Eliza's last days.

"Ultimately, Eliza did not receive the transplant that she required, a tragedy that affirmed in my mind just how special an accomplishment it is that Chris not only survived his transplant, but that he went on to continue his snowboard career."

I understood that some people were uncomfortable talking about death, as if being on a donor list might jinx them. Others had religious or philosophical objections, or couldn't bear the idea of someone they loved being a donor. But what would they have said about these objections if they had met Eliza?

I obviously saw the issue from a different perspective and had to respect their feelings. But I'd also met people who said they'd always intended to sign their driver's license or talk to their families, they just hadn't gotten around to it. I could only wonder what they were waiting for. After they died, it might be too late . . . too late for the next Eliza.

I don't want to give the impression that my goal of reaching the Olympics was just so I could promote organ donation. Yes, I hoped to use the podium to spread the word. Yet, I also had purely selfish reasons to be in the Olympics; I was an athlete and I wanted that medal. But even that, I thought, was an important part of the message: it is possible to go through a transplant operation and still keep your dreams.

There was only one problem with my dream. I was having a hard time even making the U.S. Olympic team. As late as January, I was still on the outside trying to catch the front-runners.

The rules were different this time around, because the USSA no longer had to worry about how to merge the FIS riders with riders on the essentially defunct ISF. Now Americans had to earn their way onto the team by competing at three FIS World Cups and two Grand Prix events. The strange part was that the selection would be taken from results of the qualifying runs, not the actual race results. In other words, a rider could win an event but still rank behind someone who had a better qualifying time.

The first qualifying World Cup was at Whistler in early December. I was the top-seeded American and started first, which should have been a significant advantage. But I fell at the fifth gate and didn't finish. That was one down and only four to go.

The next qualifying event was a Grand Prix a week later at Park City on the Olympic hill, and my results weren't much better. That was two down with nothing to show for them, except that now I was getting double-digit start numbers and had dug a hole for myself.

Usually I looked forward to Christmas break, but now it was just two weeks of stressing about making the team. There were three more qualifying events: a Grand Prix at Mount Bachelor in January, and then two World Cups in Europe. I was going to have to probably take one first and a second, or I was going to lose my shot at the Olympics. And at twenty-nine years old, who knew if I would be able to hang on for the 2006 Olympics in Torino, Italy.

I'd hoped that the Christmas break would fix the jinx that seemed to have taken over my season, but I fell in the next two races in Europe. Fortunately, they didn't count toward making the Olympic team, but my confidence was wavering when I flew to Oregon for the Grand Prix at Bachelor. I hoped a little home cooking on my old shredding grounds would turn the tide.

The good news was that I took second at the event. The bad news was that my qualifying run was slow, leaving me in the fourth or fifth spot for a three-man Olympic squad. I was going to have to perform in the last two qualifying races in Europe or was going to be watching the games from my home in Aspen.

The next event was in Bardonecchia, Italy, the site of Olympic snowboarding events for the 2006 Winter Games. Again, it was sort of a good news–bad news result. Only this time, it worked out in my favor. I placed seventh in the competition, losing to Philipp Schoch of Switzerland in the quarterfinals. That was the bad news; the good news was that I was the top American, so as far as the qualifiers went it was a first-place finish.

Bardonecchia had instantly become one of my favorite places to race, and it got me thinking a little ahead of myself. When I called my dad to tell him the good news about the qualifier, I said, "We're sticking around until oh-six. I love this hill!"

"Um," he replied, "that's great. But isn't there a race in Salt Lake City first?"

Oh, yeah, Salt Lake City. First place in the qualifier put me in a much better position going into the last one in Kreischberg, Austria. But I still needed to finish as one of the top two Americans to guarantee my spot.

At Kreischberg I wasn't worried about getting into the head-to-head competition. I just couldn't afford to fall or be disqualified in the qualifying run, so I pussyfooted my way down the hill and came in as the second American, behind Jeff Greenwood. I missed the main event but made the Olympic team.

Greenwood was the first to be named to the men's alpine team, with me second and Pete Thorndike third. Rosey Fletcher, Lisa Kosglow, Lisa Odynski, and Sondra Van Ert made up the women's team.

Although happy that I'd made the squad, I felt sorry for my buddy Anton, who just missed out as a fourth male rider. The worst part was that he had to wait for the finish of the women's races to learn if he or one of the women would be the "seventh" member of the alpine team.

It was between him and Sondra Van Ert. I'll spare you the convoluted details, but it came down to this: if Sondra advanced past Swedish rider Sarah Fischer in the first round of the PGS finals in Kreischberg, Anton would go. If Sondra lost, then Lisa Odynski got to go. Sondra was beating Sarah but then crashed with just a few gates left.

Poor Anton crashed with her. He was a good sport about it outwardly, but we all wondered if he was serious when he said he was going back to the hotel and jumping into the bathtub with an electric toaster. We commiserated with him, but of course being snowboarders our sensitivity only goes so far. From then on, whenever Anton lost a race, someone on the team would yell, "Unplug the toaster!"

The final two weeks leading up to the Olympics were a blur. First, the team flew to Salt Lake City and immediately headed for Park City thirty minutes away. None of the other teams were there yet, so we had the race hill to ourselves for three days of training before they closed it.

Even better was our "private Olympic pow" training ground. Above the race hill was an area encompassing about five or six slopes that had been cordoned off from the public. You had to have an Olympic athlete or coach credential to get into it. It had snowed a couple of feet just before we got there, and we had some of the best pow riding of the year.

The team then left for Sun Valley, Idaho, where our assistant coach, Nick Smith, had once been the area's snowboard team coach and had connections with the Sun Valley Lodge manager. Jan wanted to get us away from the media frenzy and Olympic circus for a few days, and Sun Valley welcomed us to train and stay there for the week leading up to the start of the games.

I was going to join them, but first I had something to do in Aspen. The U.S. Olympic Committee had designated the town as one of the stops for the Olympic torch as it made its way across the country to Salt Lake City. Members of the community had formed several committees working with local coordinator Linda Gerdenich to prepare for the event, which was to be a big party and send-off for Katie Monahan, Casey Puckett, and me.

My dad headed the committee charged with locating all the athletes in our part of Colorado who had participated in past Olympics. We knew quite a few just in the Aspen and Roaring Fork Valley area, but to get them all he called the U.S. Olympic Team headquarters in Colorado Springs and asked the woman who answered his call for a list of "former Olympians" who lived in Colorado.

"Hold it right there," she replied. "There are no 'former' Olympians. Once an Olympian, always an Olympian. Now, we have some Olympians from former years . . ." Once my dad got the wording right, she came up with a list of three dozen names in the area from Aspen to Grand Junction, all of whom he invited to the festivities.

The Olympic torch relay team arrived with a huge semitrailer that folded down into a big stage (and looked like an enormous billboard for Chevy trucks and Coca-Cola). They set up in front of the historic Wheeler Opera House in downtown Aspen, where thousands of people gathered—the largest crowd I'd ever seen in Aspen since John Denver's community service Christmas concert the year before he died. The whole town turned out and cheered as the people selected to carry the torch wound their way through town to the stage.

Local musicians supplied the music, including the Aspen High School choir, which led us in singing "God Bless America," as well as Bobby Mason and Jimmy Ibbotson. It was definitely a patriotic moment at a time when our country was still healing from the terrorist attacks.

Dad alluded to it in his speech welcoming the crowd: "We are here to celebrate the Olympic torch relay, traveling throughout this great nation and now coming through Aspen and the Roaring Fork Valley. On its way to Salt Lake City, the flame brings the Olympic spirit to communities all across the country, large and small—including Aspen, right here and right now.

"The theme of the Olympics this year is 'Light the Fire Within.' And it sure applies to all of us here. The nation has watched as heroes of all shapes, sizes, and colors have proudly carried the flame on its way to the Olympic games.

"As we watch the flame arrive here, and as it lights the Olympic cauldron in just a few minutes, we can celebrate together the strengthened spirit of unity that has come over our nation. And we honor the young people of our country and the world who will gather in Salt Lake in competition, sportsmanship, and high achievement. We honor, too, Olympians from our own communities who have competed in the past and those locals who will compete in the Winter Olympics in the days ahead."

Fifteen other Colorado Olympians from former years showed up and were introduced to the crowd by my dad. They were our town's Olympic legacy, and I was proud to be standing on the stage with them along with Katie (Casey was off racing).

After the ceremonies, Dad invited the eighteen Olympians (including the class of 2002) to a buffet at the Aspen Square Hotel. During the lunch he asked if the Olympians from former years would stand up and tell us about their favorite Olympic memory. I was really in awe of all the history in that room, and I can't remember the specifics of what anyone said. What stuck with me was how each of them said in his or her way that the Olympics had remained one of the defining moments in their lives. It was true what the woman had said about once an Olympian, always an Olympian.

I left the next day to join my team in Sun Valley, where we had several good days of training. When I got a moment, I went and looked at the wall of fame. This was the first time I'd been back since our first family trip. I gave Jack Sibbach, the manager of the Sun Valley Lodge, a hard time about the resort kicking me off the hill when I had first appeared with my Burton Performer. Then I asked him what it would take to get my photograph on the wall.

"A gold medal," he said.

I laughed. "No problem, Jack," I said. "Get the frame ready!"

At last we left for Salt Lake City to get ready for the opening ceremony, scheduled for February 7, 2002. Early in the morning—as in 3 A.M.—the day before the ceremony, I participated in a satellite media tour along with Tommy Thompson, the U.S. Secretary of Health and Human Services, to promote National Donor Day.

Sponsored by the Saturn Motor Corporation, its parent company, General Motors, and the United Auto Workers union, National Donor Day was slated for February 14, which, not coincidentally, was also Valentine's Day. The single largest donor drive in the country, National Donor Day had been launched in 1998.

Realizing that the 2002 event would coincide with the Winter Olympics in Salt Lake City, Eric Sherman and David Quick, the event coordinators for Saturn, asked the sixteen nonprofit partners in the event if they knew of any connections between the Olympics and organ donation. Guess whose name turned up?

They gave me a call, asking if I would volunteer my time. It seemed like a natural, not just because I was a liver transplant recipient, but also because the finals of my event were scheduled for February 14. I jumped at the chance (well, at 3 A.M. it was more like stumbled out of bed).

We did the media tour from a Saturn dealership in Salt Lake City, the first time the event had had a national spokesperson. It was very well received by major media market morning shows. (The 2002 campaign was the strongest ever—as measured by blood donor collections, which went up 23 percent over 2001.) After the media event, I agreed to be the spokesman for National Donor Day for the next four years.

"The agreement was formalized at Saturn's insistence," Dave Quick says. "One goal of Donor Day is to not focus on the process of donation so much as the result. I cannot think of a stronger example of the miracle of life-saving donation than the Chris Klug story."

At last the day of the opening ceremony dawned. I was looking forward to walking into the stadium with my teammates but wasn't aware that there would be an additional honor. After breakfast I was told that I would help carry the World Trade Center flag in to the opening ceremonies before the national anthem.

Eight athletes—one from each of the Winter Olympic disciplines—

had been selected by their teammates. I'd been chosen to represent the discipline of skiing—no small irony after our resentment of being so labeled before the Nagano games. (I later learned that my friend Katie Monahan had lobbied the skiers to vote for me, so I guess I have to admit that not all skiers are completely evil.)

That afternoon, the U.S. team reported to the Olympic village in our ceremonial uniforms. In Nagano it had been cowboy hats and blue dusters; in Salt Lake City it was berets and navy blue leather jackets. All the teams—2,399 athletes, representing 77 nations—paraded from the village to Rice Eccles Stadium, where the U.S athletes were separated and herded into a gym.

Once there, the eight "flag bearers" were taken out to a staging area beneath the arena, where I had a few minutes to chat with some of my new comrades, like Mark Grimmette, who was competing in the two-man luge, and speed skater Derek Para. Then we were introduced to the men and women from the New York Police, Fire, and Port Authority Departments who were there to represent their fallen comrades.

People were already starting to fill the stadium when we went out to rehearse our part. The stadium was already a madhouse of noise and commotion. Whistles were blowing, people were yelling and running around every which way. Olympic volunteers on bullhorns were telling the spectators when to hold up different colored placards: *"Okay, now Section 352, when the Indians enter the stadium that's when you hold up the yellow cards . . . and Section 142 . . ."* Meanwhile, Native American dancers were going through their dance routines, while ice skaters were making last-second adjustments to their programs.

We did a dry run without the flag, each of us being assigned a position. Mine was on the back left-hand side. We were then led back to the gymnasium for a pep rally with President Bush, baseball great Cal Ripken Jr., and now three-time Tour de France winner Lance Armstrong. The president was the only one who spoke, telling us how proud he was of us and honored to be there that night. America needed heroes now more than ever, he said.

When the president was finished, there was time for photographs and a quick word. I made my way through the throng that surrounded Lance. Back when I was struggling with my own disease, I'd identified with the way he stared death in the face and refused to give up. I wanted to congratulate him and thank him for the inspiration during my own tough time.

Lance was being mobbed by the other athletes, so it took a while for me to reach him. I shook his hand, posed for a photo, and told him that I'd had a liver transplant eighteen months earlier. "I just wanted to say what a huge inspiration you were."

Lance looked at me for a moment and said, "Oh, right on." Then someone else stepped between us and he was surrounded. I wasn't sure what I said had even registered with him, but then the eight flag bearers were summoned to take our places.

We were brought to the staging area and took our positions. A simple wooden box was opened and the large American flag was removed, gently unfolded, and handed to us.

I could see where it had been torn and charred. It was ripped from my corner almost to the stars, so I had to grab at two places to keep it from dragging on the ground.

It was such a powerful moment for me, and I was far more nervous than I'd ever been for a competition. This was about something much bigger than Chris Klug and my sport, or even the Olympics. *Oh, my God, the crowd is going to go crazy,* I thought and prayed that I wouldn't trip and fall.

The stadium was pitch black when we emerged from the tunnel. A stiff breeze rippled the flag and made it difficult to hold on to as we stepped into the spotlight. The announcer told the spectators who we were and where the flag was from, and I held my breath waiting for the roar from the crowd. But all I heard were the helicopters and the wind.

"What's wrong with these people?" I wondered. *"I could carry on a conversation with someone in the nosebleed seats."* I looked at Frank Accardi, embarrassed that this was the reception he and the others

were getting. But then I saw the tears, and he smiled at me and said, "My partner would be so proud of us today." And then I understood the silence. It was respect.

Five months earlier, almost three thousand people had died where the flag was found, murdered by animals who cared nothing for the sanctity of life. This was no time for cheering like at a football game. It was a time for silent remembrance, a time for good people of all nations to come together in peace.

I glanced at the other members of the honor guard. Frank and his colleague, Sgt. Tony Scannella of the Port Authority police, weren't the only ones choking up. Everyone was in tears—those who'd lost their friends and partners in New York City, and those of us who in the coming days would be competing for medals and glory.

I was proud to be an American, proud when we began to sing "The Star-Spangled Banner," and humbled that I'd been given such an honor. My tears felt hot on my cold face as I stood there and held tightly to that flag.

Chapter 21

A Life on Edge

When the national anthem was over at the opening ceremony, the reaction I'd expected when we first walked in erupted in full force. Fifty-five thousand people stood and kept cheering as they held up the appropriate placards at the appointed moments for the television cameras as fireworks lit up the sky.

The flag's honor guard quickly left the field to find our spots with the U.S. team, which, as the host country, would be the last to enter the stadium. It seemed everybody was as affected as I had been. Mark, Derek, and I kept laughing about how we had to keep reminding ourselves to bend our knees so that we wouldn't pass out and fall on the flag. But it was clear we were all deeply moved by the experience.

Rather than walk all the way back to where the teams were lining up near the gym, we waited at the tunnel entrance for the other nations' athletes to emerge in alphabetical order. That way I got to see and yell to many of my snowboarding friends from other countries— Sigi Grabner from Austria, Mark Fawcett and Jasey-Jay Anderson from Canada, Mathieu Bozzetto and Nicolas Huet from France, Walter Feichter from Italy, Daniel Biveson and Richard Richardsson from Sweden, Gilles Jaquet from Switzerland, and all the others who made up that wild, fun-loving crew. It was a great moment for me, as many of us had grown up together with our sport, and I expected we'd remain friends long after our careers were over.

At the end of the line walked the U.S. team. They'd seen the flag ceremony on monitors and were excited for us and kept asking how it felt. I kept smiling and saying, "Great," because once again any words I had would have been inadequate.

Near the end of the line was a pissed-off group of women hockey players. As they passed, I heard several derogatory remarks about snowboarders and wondered what was up. Turns out, the women's hockey players were the last ones in the U.S. lineup to enter the stadium at Nagano, where they eventually took the gold medal. Being superstitious, they'd made a big deal about wanting to walk in last this year too, which, of course, meant that the snowboarders just had to hide behind curtains until the women went by and then jump in behind them when it was too late to do anything about it.

I joined my crew, who were grinning and hooting while ignoring the venomous glances directed toward them by female hockey players. It was probably a damn good thing that the women didn't have their sticks with them or things could have turned really ugly. (Unfortunately, the 2002 U.S. Women's Olympic Hockey Team would go on to lose the gold medal to Canada and have blamed the snowboarders ever since.)

Somehow the U.S. team got to our seats in the stands without a fight breaking out. Then President Bush, "on behalf of a proud, determined, and grateful nation," declared the Winter Olympics open and, to our surprise, then came over and sat with us. He even talked to the mother of one of our teammates on her cell phone. *"Hi, Mom, I'm at the Olympics. Want to say hi to the president?"*

We stayed that night in the Olympic village but left the next day for Park City, where we'd rented two houses for the alpine team and coaches. I almost ran into a disaster right away when I picked up my bag that I'd put down on the bed in the room I was sharing with Pete Thorndike. It was covered with an inch—I kid you not—of white dog hair.

I ran out of the room but could already feel an asthma attack coming on. Dog hair was all over the house, and a minute later I was sucking on my inhaler, which I probably hadn't used in months (since the last time I hung out in a pet-infested house). I got out of there and went over to the coach's house. I told Jan I couldn't stay in the other place, so I ended up in one of the rooms in the coach's house.

I had a week before my event, so I spent the time training,

relaxing, and visiting my family. I tried to stay out of the limelight and watched other events only on television. I went out socially once for a USSA team dinner at the restaurant in downtown Park City that the association had rented out as a place for competitors and team members, as well as their families, to grab a bite to eat and get away from the media and crowds.

Hanging on the wall in the restaurant was a banner with the motto coined by Bill Marolt, the head of the USSA, "Ten Medals in 2002." He'd been telling the press for months that the U.S. Ski Team (and its little-brother discipline) would bring home ten medals, which it had never done before in a Winter Olympics. In fact, the highest U.S. medal total in a Winter Olympics, counting all sports, was thirteen.

I was actually pretty relaxed about my race in the days before the event. I'd given dozens of media interviews in the weeks leading up to the games and right up to the opening ceremony, but now I avoided the press and everyone else. I even turned off my cell phone and computer.

After I turned off the gadgets, the biggest stress for me was that the press had found Billy Flood's family, and some reporters and their employers were determined that we meet as soon as possible (so long as they had an exclusive).

It wasn't the family's fault. They'd never tried to contact me themselves. In fact, Leisa was home in Idaho and Rob in California. Billy's paternal grandmother, Kathy, and aunt, Mary, who lived in Salt Lake, wanted to watch my race in Salt Lake City, but they'd kept their distance as I prepared.

Even most members of the press seemed to know that this was a difficult time for me to be tugged in these different directions. Guys like Alan Abrahamson of the *Los Angeles Times* managed to do their stories—including helping me get the word out about organ donation—and even talked to the family for their response, without feeling like he had to throw us together for some Cinderella ending.

I wanted to meet Billy's family, and we'd expressed that to the people at Colorado Donor Alliance. But not until after my event, and when the time was appropriate, which didn't mean in front of a bunch of cameras and reporters. As much as I wanted to get the word out on organ donation, I wanted meeting the family to be a private moment between just us.

The day of our qualifying run finally arrived—February 14, 2002. So far, it was the U.S. snowboarders who were making Marolt look like a psychic by getting us almost halfway to his magic number. First, Kelly Clark took the gold in the women's half-pipe event; then Ross Powers, Danny Kass, and J. J. Thomas swept the men's half-pipe one, two, and three.

After fighting for so many years to win a spot in the Olympics for our sport, it was great to see snowboarders leading the way with four medals for the U.S. team, especially because we only got a tiny fraction of the USSA funding that the ski team received. Of course, maybe that's because the ski team doesn't send their boards flying through the windows of the houses they rent at their post-event parties, like the half-pipers did at theirs. Ross was still feeling the effects of the celebration the next morning when Peter Carlisle, who was also his agent, showed up to take him to the *Today* show. Peter finally gave up and called the show to cancel.

I didn't even think of going to the party. But Ross and Kelly let me wear their gold medals for a minute when I saw them at the team house. *I want one of those,* I told myself. *If they can do it, so can I.*

Unfortunately, I arrived at the Olympic hill for my qualifying run less than fully confident after the training runs I'd had the day before. Toe-side turns had given me fits on both practice runs at exactly the same spot on the hill—the transition from the steep pitch onto the flats. Both times I lost my edge coming around a turn, sketched, and missed the next gate. I didn't know why I was struggling there, but knew I had to try to put it out of my mind or I was finished.

The day began on a good note when I drew bib number one. I got to go first before anyone else messed up the course. However, the toe-side turn problem still haunted me, and I held back a little at the transition, so my time was slower than I'd hoped. I had to wait nervously and watch thirty-one more riders come down the course, some of them getting better times and pushing me from first to second to third . . . to twelfth.

At first I was disappointed with my spot for the next day's head-to-head competition. Then I thought about it and reached the conclusion that it didn't matter where I started. I'd lost PGS competitions when I was seeded first, and I'd won them seeded sixteenth. This was the Olympics and everybody was a great rider; if I was going to get a medal, I would have to face those who were riding the best sooner or later. I was in the show and that's all that counted.

Of my other teammates only Lisa Kosglow (who would advance to the second round the next day but was eliminated by eventual silver medalist Karine Ruby of France) made it past the qualifying runs. There were some other surprises. Jasey-Jay Anderson had been one of the top racers all year but didn't qualify, but Swiss rider Philipp Schoch, who'd never been on the podium in a FIS World Cup PGS and who started way back in the pack at number twenty-nine, and Jerome Sylvestre, a virtually unknown young rider from Canada who started twenty-sixth, both did. In fact, Jerome would be my first opponent the next day.

That night I had dinner with my parents, Missy, Hillary, Jim (Jason decided to watch at home again), Missy's parents, my Aunts Marion, Beth, and Barb, and Uncle Chuck, and a couple of other friends in a private home they'd rented in Park City. I wasn't the best company, as I had my game face on and was pretty focused.

I got up that morning ready to have fun. I had trained and prepared to the best of my ability. I'd run this one race in my head a hundred times, now it was time to do it for real. I thought it was awesome that my race was on National Donor Day. Now, if all went well, I would get a chance to tell the world about it.

When we arrived on the hill, the temperature was in the low twenties, with scattered clouds and a few passing snow showers. I took my inspection runs next to the course, amazed at the number of spectators who were lining up along the fence and filling the stadium-style stands at the bottom. We'd been told that the alpine snowboarding event was one of the first to sell out and that we could expect a crowd of twenty-five thousand.

"Doesn't matter," Uncle Bob Harmison reminded me outside the finish corral, "twenty-five thousand or twenty-five, you race your race. Focus on the performance, not the outcome. . . . Now concentrate—blue is you, red ahead."

I thought it was pretty cool when I looked around and considered the influence of that early Mount Bachelor shred crew and the World Pro Snowboarding Team. Pete Thorndike, Rosey Fletcher, and I had all raced for Rob Roy. Former WPST teammate Kevin Delaney was broadcasting the play-by-play of the race for NBC, while my old friend and teammate Kris Jamieson was working as the "live host" for the crowd on the public address system. And, of course, Peter Foley, whose boards I'd snaked, was the head of the U.S. Snowboard Team, in charge of both the pipers and racers. I was proud to have had a role with those people in the evolution of snowboarding.

"Anyone and everyone in the U.S. who chose the racer approach back in the early nineties made a bad investment . . . especially when compared to the sales and money numbers of the freestyle market," Jamieson says. "The only person who was able to make it happen was Klug. Not only did he pull it off, he took on the Euros. Racing is huge in Europe. They have big dollars, big support, and a big supporting media environment. Klug went in there as the full underdog in every aspect of the sport and kicked their asses.

"In fact, despite all the hurdles, all the financial woes, all the media blockades, the poor product sales, the horrible product support, and the overall shunning of racing by the U.S. snowboard market . . . Klug kicked everyone's ass. He is the only true American alpine success out there. Others may claim, but Klug is the only one whose actions have spoken for him. A person is ultimately defined by the actions they throw down. Klug threw down."

Of course, my family and friends were out in force. I remember when I got to the bottom of my first inspection run, I looked over to my right and saw a hundred big blue foam fingers and thought, *"What in the world is that?"* Then I smiled and laughed when I realized it was "Team Klug"—the blue fingers were a complete surprise supplied by my brother, Jim.

At last the sixteen riders, their coaches, and support staff gathered in the starting area. We were all nervous, but managed to smile and joke a little. After all, we were snowboarders and friends.

The first two racers took off. I could hear the roar of the crowd, but I didn't watch. Instead, Jan worked to keep me focused. "Remember, you don't have to win the race in the first few gates," he said. The first few gates were on the steepest, and most difficult, part of the hill—an error there and it could be over. "Make good, solid, high-percentage turns, then carry your speed into the flats."

Then it was my turn, and I entered the starting gate. I know Jerome did too, but to be honest, I didn't see him; I was too focused on the course in front of me. I leaned over and picked up a handful of snow and placed it on the back of my neck, then looked up and saw the Wasatch Mountains. I smiled. *This is what made me fall in love with this sport,* I thought, and prayed, *God give me the strength to do my best.*

I pulled hard out of the start determined to win, but it wasn't going to be easy. *"Who is this kid?"* I thought as I rode the chairlift up for the second run. The relatively unknown Jerome Sylvestre had beaten me by three-tenths of a second. I'd sort of eased into it, and he'd caught me by surprise.

I nearly blew it in the second run too. I slipped and fell behind in the top section and really had to turn it on, taking chances riding a straighter line than I wanted. When I crossed the finish line, I didn't know who won until I looked up at the scoreboard. I breathed a sigh of relief, I'd beat him by a mere five one-hundredths of a second (the smallest margin of victory there would be for anyone all day).

Next up were the quarterfinals, where I faced my friend Walter

Feichter, from Olang, Italy. I made another mistake at the top, lost an edge on a toe-side turn, and had to put both hands on the snow to regain my balance and stay on course. I crossed the finish line three-fourths of a second behind Walter.

The crowd that had erupted with chants of "USA! USA! USA!" every time my name was mentioned or rode through the finish area while racing Jerome was now more subdued. They looked worried. Except for my mom—the woman who once didn't know what an aura was now felt she had "special" powers. She recalls, "I was sitting in the snow trying to communicate with him by telepathy. I said, 'Okay, now what are you going to do? What do you remember about why you're here?' I think he heard me."

I don't know, Mom, maybe I did. I do remember, however, that I was pissed off. Angry at myself for the way I was riding—inconsistent and making dumb errors. *You can ride better than this. This is not you!*

Without a word to Jan, I got in the starting gate and grabbed the handles like I was going to rip them out of the snow. The rest of the world was quiet, I couldn't hear the crowd. I don't even remember the start referee's cadence, though I must have heard him. Under my breath, I chanted, *You can do this . . . You can do this . . . You can do this . . .* I felt possessed as I yanked myself out of the gate.

I didn't know where Walter was on the course. I didn't care. I charged that damn course from the top to the bottom, hanging on to my dream by the narrow edge of my board.

I crossed the finish line and quickly looked over my shoulder to see how close Walter was to me. But he wasn't there. When I looked back up the hill and spotted him sitting in the snow, it was one of the greatest sights of my life (sorry, Walter). I learned later that when I got out ahead of him, he'd panicked a little and started taking too straight a line to stay up with me. I'd tinned him, and he crashed halfway down the course.

The fans were going absolutely berserk, especially Team Klug. My mom was sitting in the snow, hyperventilating, asking her sisters what was happening, but the others jumped around with the blue foam fingers and waving American flags, alternately yelling "USA! USA! USA!" and "Klug! Klug! Klug!" I pumped my fist and yelled back at them, ready to carry the momentum into the next round. I was in the semifinals against Philipp Schoch, but still a long way from a medal.

Maybe I was too pumped up, because I took too aggressive a line in the steeps in my first run against Philipp and got locked down on an edge and rode it right into the fence on the side of the course. I sat there for a minute gathering my thoughts. Now I was in trouble. I'd be docked a penalty of 1.5 seconds for not finishing the run.

Still, the race wasn't over. *Not until the last second has ticked off the clock . . .*

I'd like to tell you that I went out and crushed Philipp like I had Walter. I certainly tried. I took enormous chances at the top to try to rattle him and was leading when we crossed the finish line. But it wasn't enough to overcome the deficit.

I was disappointed not to be in the gold and silver medal round, but I had to put it behind me if I still wanted a medal. My opponent in the bronze medal race, Nicolas Huet, was one of the stars on the tour and the only one that year who had won two World Cup races.

On the chairlift up the hill, I remembered how Jan and I had talked about the bronze medal being the most difficult race mentally. The conversation struck home now as I thought about the possibility of once again coming up short of my Olympic dream.

Jan remembered it too and immediately took me aside to keep me from thinking about the ramifications of winning and losing. "Be solid up top and don't give the race away," he said. "Carry your speed from the transition and then boo-ya the flats."

"Boo-ya?"

"Boo-ya," he nodded.

More snow on the neck . . . by this time the back of my speed suit was soaked. A look at the mountains and a swift prayer . . . *do my best.* Then Nicolas and I were out of the gates.

I was riding hard in the red course and had a slight lead on him as we started to come off the pitch. But then I slid out on a heel-side turn and had to bear down and rail a clean toe-side against some serious G-forces to get back on line.

Suddenly, I felt my front boot release, allowing my leg to flex much farther forward than it should have, and I nearly fell on my face. But somehow I held on to cross the finish line ahead of Nicolas, but only by one one-hundredth of a second. Less than the time it takes to blink your eye.

The spectators were rocking as we rode past. Some waved French flags for Nicolas, but most were chanting, "USA! USA!" and waving our flag and their blue foam fingers. I certainly had the home-field advantage, but I couldn't savor the moment.

Unsnapping my bindings, I took off my board and walked to where team managers Margie Peterson and Becky Wooley and Uncle Bob were standing behind the fence at the back of the finish corral. They realized that there was a problem by the look on my face, but none of us knew the cause until I lifted my leg and propped the boot onto the fence to get a closer look.

My heart sank. The instep buckle on my front boot—necessary to hold my foot firmly in the boot so that I could power through toe-side turns without falling forward—had snapped. If I couldn't get it fixed, winning the next run was going to take a miracle.

I asked Margie for one of the two-way radios the team used to communicate on the slope. "Coop!" I yelled for our team technician, who was waiting at the top of the hill. I explained the problem and said that I had replacement buckles in my Burton backpack.

"No problem," he assured me. "We'll fix it."

Cooper might have been relaxed, but I was stressing as I got on the chairlift. I kept trying to tell myself that everything would work out . . . that we had time to fix the problem when I reached the top. But I was losing focus. Instead of thinking through my race, I was wondering why this was happening to me.

"Three minutes," the start referee bellowed when I got to the top.

As Jay Cooper and Thanos Karydas worked frantically on my boot, I tried to focus on the course below me. *Blue is you . . . blue is you.* It was no use. Coop tried to back the remains of the buckle's screw from the boot with a drill, but the broken piece just spun freely and wouldn't come out.

"Two minutes, Klug!" Time was running out.

"Take off the boot," Coop ordered.

I groaned and shut my eyes. Taking off my boot was no simple matter. First I would have to remove the plastic guard that protected my left shin from the racing gates, then peel up the legs of my speed suit and unfasten the power straps that stiffen the top of the boot a little more. It might take five minutes to get it all off and back on again. Even if Coop could fix the buckle, I didn't have five minutes.

Thanos was dancing around saying in his Greek accent, "Don't worry. Don't worry." But I was more than worrying, I was losing it. I started to let the F-bombs fly. This wasn't fair, not after everything I'd been through. Why did it seem that time was always running out on me?

Then Jan grabbed my head with both of his hands and forced me to look into his eyes, which were amazingly steady. "They'll fix the boot," he said in a tone that left no room for argument. "It's not your concern. You need to focus on riding your board."

Jan was right, and about a lot more than he realized. Maybe it wasn't fair, but then again, there were a lot of unfair things in life and having a broken buckle wasn't the worst of them. It wasn't fair that Billy Flood died when he was only thirteen years old. And it wasn't fair that I had survived only because he died, a sadness that would be with me for the rest of my life. But at least I was alive and in the Olympics. Was I really going to complain about fairness because I might lose a race? I calmed down and nodded to Jan, prepared to accept whatever happened.

Jan went over to the French coach, Xavier Perrier-Michon, and explained the trouble. Now we can talk about fair. Xavier and Nicolas, who was already in the starting gate wondering what was up with me, could have insisted that I be ready on time or forfeit the race. But that was not the way they wanted to win. Xavier turned to the start referee and said, "Let them fix the boot."

When Jan came over and told me what had happened, I was humbled. Nicolas and I were buddies, but this was the Olympics. He wasn't just taking a chance with the honor of climbing the podium at the medal ceremony. He was potentially sacrificing a large financial windfall in endorsements and sponsorships.

Nicolas certainly had his reasons for wanting the medal as much as I did. He'd been robbed by a political decision having to do with the FIS rules in France of participating in the Nagano Olympics. "For me, it was the time to take my revenge. I had been thinking about that for the four years before Salt Lake. . . . But I was happy that Chris could fix his boot. That was fair," Nicolas says. "I just hope someone will do the same for me the next time. But to be really honest, I didn't make the decision, my coach did . . . me, I was at the start waiting to race. . . . I wanted to race him; after all, it is just games."

The French decision was what the Olympics were all about. But I don't know, maybe it was also part of snowboarding's "outcast" beginnings when we all had to look after each other because no one else wanted us. I couldn't imagine the same sort of offer being made in figure skating, which had already tainted and cast a shadow over this Olympics with its judging scandal. There it was all about winning, even if it meant cheating.

The start referee agreed to give me more time, but only three more minutes, then I would race or be disqualified. After all, the event was being televised live all over the world . . . and television waits for no man.

We got down to a minute left when Cooper gave up fixing the buckle and went to Plan B. He told me to put the boot back on as he reached into his bag of tricks and pulled out a pipe fastener—one of those metal bands used to hold two pieces of plumbing together. As soon as I got the boot on, he whipped the fastener around my boot, placed it under my instep, and then cinched it as tight as it would go with the drill.

In fact it was tighter than I would have probably liked it, but there was still a problem—the outside shell of the boot was slick with melted snow, and Coop worried that the fastener was going to slip down toward my toes as soon as I put pressure on it.

Coop stuck a hand into his bag again and brought out the last thing I thought I'd need that day to win an Olympic medal. It was a great, big, industrial-sized roll of duct tape.

I saw it and let rip one of my hyena yelps. The most important race of my life, and we were counting on the same technology I'd used when I first started ripping it up on Mount Bachelor.

"This is classic," I said and laughed again as Coop quickly wrapped duct tape around the fastener to hold it in place.

The laughter released the stress that had been building up as time ticked down. *You know what,* I thought, *if you're going to let a fifty-cent buckle take you out of this race, you don't deserve to win it anyway. . . . To hell with that, let's go win this thing.*

"Thirty seconds, Klug!"

I jumped up and sprinted for the starting gate, where Jan had my board all ready to go. "All right," I shouted to Nicolas, "Merci!" I grabbed a handful of snow, slapped it on the back of my neck, clicked into my bindings and . . . *oh, my God, I forgot my gloves.*

Jan saw it too. "Gloves! Gloves!" he yelled at Coop. The missing equipment flew over the wall, and I had just enough time to put them on before hauling myself out of the gate.

In hindsight, the distraction of the broken buckle might have been a good thing. It had kept me from thinking about the crowd at the bottom and the Olympic podium and Nicolas Huet. Now, as I entered the course, I heard nothing but the sound of my board on snow and saw nothing but the snow and the gates in front of me.

We both had minor problems at the top. First, I slipped and he gained; then he slipped and I struck back. We were neck and neck at the transition and as we entered the flats. At that moment, I knew I had him. A smile started to creep across my face. *Not yet, you idiot,* my brain screamed at me. *No smiling until you cross that line!*

I tucked the last couple of gates and crossed the line more than a second ahead of Nicolas with my arms raised in the air. I rode straight to the back of the corral and into the arms of my teammates, who were jumping over the fence. I turned back toward my family and friends. They all looked like they were jumping on a trampoline and trying to hug each other, cry, and laugh all at the same time. I touched my fist to my chest and pointed to them. I wanted them to know where my heart belonged.

When I could escape my teammates, I walked over to Team Klug. Dozens of arms reached for me as I dove into them. I hugged my father, who kept saying, "I'm so proud of you," over and over. Missy was bawling, while Jim, Carlon, Jon, Fab, Brad, Pat and Ray April, my Bolle rep, Derek Schuman, and the Saturn rep, Eric Sherman, pounded me on the back until I couldn't breathe. I looked for my mom, but she was up on a little hill above the bedlam, crying and telling everybody that she *knew* I was going to win. "He just wanted to give me a heart attack first."

The press was all over us. One eager reporter had picked up that my friend Kenton Bruice, an OB/GYN, was a doctor and asked him if he was the surgeon who performed the liver transplant. "No," Kenton replied with a laugh, "I'm his gynecologist." The reporter looked confused and sort of faded back into the crowd.

Jim handed me an American flag attached to Mom's ski pole, and I started parading back and forth across the finish area. If the opening ceremony was a time of quiet remembrance with the flag, now it was time to celebrate, and that flag was good for both.

Meanwhile, Nicolas was in the middle of the finish area and, déjà vu of me in Nagano, he was getting the crowd to do the wave like he was a cheerleader at a football game. I ran over and he reached out to embrace me. He congratulated me and said he was happy for me *en français*, "*Félicitations, Chris! Je suis très content pour toi!*"

"My best memory of the Olympics was when I finished. Chris won the medal and went to his friends. Me, I stayed in the middle of the finish area, and I played with the public. I asked them to applaud and they answered me. This time even if I didn't get any medal, I was the king!" says Nicolas, although he told me recently that he still has nightmares about coming in fourth.

It took a little while for us to realize that the race officials were trying to get us to clear the finish. There was still the last run of the Big Finals. *Oh, yeah, them.*

Philipp and Swedish rider Richard Richardsson, who'd beaten Nicolas to advance, might not have been the fastest riders that day. But they were the steadiest, kept their mistakes to a minimum, and deserved to go on.

Philipp took the first run. In the second, Richard had laid it all on the line and took enormous risks to come back but crashed. So Philipp Schoch won his first PGS and the gold medal.

After their final run, Jan skied down and grabbed me in a bear hug and then broke down in tears. A podium appeared in the finish area, and the medalists were reintroduced to the crowd, which had not stopped cheering and dancing. First the women: Isabelle Blanc, the gold; Karine Ruby, the silver, both from France; and Lidia Trettel of Italy got the bronze. Then the men: Philipp, Richard, and the kid whose prayers for a new Burton had been answered by Santa Claus nineteen years earlier.

We were all handed a bouquet of yellow flowers. When I got down from the podium, I walked over and gave mine to Missy. Dudes, pay attention—it was, perhaps, the greatest Valentine's Day save of all time.

The next few hours were a blur of urine tests for drugs (we were tested for weed, but no one came up positive), press conferences, and parading around Park City and up to the USSA house with my family. Then I was whisked down to Salt Lake City with Peter Carlisle for the medal presentation.

My medal was a big deal to the U.S. Olympic Committee, because it was the fourteenth for the United States, a record. It also got the USSA to five medals—half of Marolt's goal—all from that little "discipline of skiing," snowboarding. (The skiers would eventually kick in five to make everybody happy.)

When I arrived backstage at the Olympic stadium, I bumped into Mark Grimmette. He was grinning ear to ear. "No way," I said.

"Yep," he laughed. He and his partner, Brian Martin, had taken the silver in the pairs luge. (I don't know if carrying the flag at the opening ceremony gave us some special juice, but seven of the eight in the honor guard medaled.)

The medal ceremony itself seemed like a dream. It was certainly the culmination of one. The funny thing is that I had always believed I was capable, but now that it had happened, it was hard to comprehend. I choked up again as I watched the American flag being raised overhead, even if it was the Swiss national anthem being played.

We'd been handed another bouquet of yellow flowers—these were roses—which Schoch and Richardsson threw to the crowd as they'd seen other athletes do before us. But I got down from the stand and made another great Valentine's Day save.

The world's gnarliest soccer mom—along with her partner in crime, Dad, and my siblings and friends—had elbowed her way to near the front of the security barrier between the crowd and the stage. She really was the best mom in the world. I leaned over the stage and shouted to the fans who had their hands out for souvenirs, "Give these to my mom," and pointed to her. They carefully passed them back to Mom, and no one tried to keep a single bud.

After the medal ceremony was over, the rock band Smash Mouth, who I got to meet backstage, came out and the area in front of the stage turned into a dancing, jumping, twisting jumble of fans. I happened to look out at the crowd from the stage wings and started laughing. I nudged Richard and pointed. "Hey, there's my mom. She's crowd surfing the mosh pit."

Mom and Dad were getting absolutely carnaged in the front row at a rock concert. But you know what? Mom was dancing with her flowers in the air and Dad was bouncing around right next to her . . . and they looked like they were having the time of their lives.

No Friends on a Powder Day!

"When I saw Chris on the podium after he won his bronze, I was obviously extremely happy for him and his family. I thought the image would be engraved in my head for as long as I lived. However, although that day was special, seldom do I think of it when I think of Chris. I just think of Chris my friend who I go biking with, the friend I joke around with, and the family I have dinner with every Christmas and Thanksgiving. That's it, and that's enough."

—Bill Fabrocini, April 2004

As soon as I left the stage that night after the medal ceremony and arrived on "media lane," I began using my appearance on the Olympic podium to get the message out about organ donation. It seemed that reporters and photographers and television crews from every newspaper, magazine, and network in the world were there. A young woman escorted me from interview to interview. *"Mr. Klug, I'd like you to meet . . . with USA Today . . . with CNN . . . with the Canadian Broadcasting Corporation and the BBC . . . and the Japanese correspondent for . . ."* Each of whom got an earful about donor awareness. However, it wasn't all business.

After meeting with the press, Peter Carlisle escorted me back to our house in Park City. There were hundreds of people in the house, many of them old teammates from the early days, as well as friends and family from Aspen and Bend. Needless to say, it was a party as only snowboarders know how to throw them. One of the "highlights" was when Pete Macomber and our chef, Cheffy, got into a drunken fight over . . . uh, nobody remembers. They were trading punches until someone told Pete he was hitting the guy who put out the food, at which point Pete immediately stopped and apologized.

Before he left at about 11:30, Peter Carlisle made me promise that I wouldn't get so out of hand that I'd pull a similar stunt as the pipers and miss my appearance on the *Today* show. "I'll be here at 5 A.M. to get you," he warned. He didn't have too much to worry about, I wasn't drinking. But Missy and I still didn't get to lie down until 4:45 in a basement room away from where the holdouts were still raging.

Peter was there fifteen minutes later. "Get up, got to go, come on," he said tugging at me. I thought I was being strangled, then realized I'd fallen asleep with my medal still around my neck.

I was exhausted and don't even remember the show, except that I managed to say how grateful I was to have been given a second chance through organ donation . . . and my mom giving her official Olympic beret to weatherman Al Roker, who kept calling her Kathy Kl-ugh (rhymes with mug, instead of boog), but she was too hoarse from all her yelling and surfing the mosh pit to speak.

Peter got me back to the house, where I lay down again, but only for an hour before he showed up again to drag me off to Salt Lake City for more interviews. In fact, the next few days were a marathon of appearances and parties from the *Tonight Show* with Jay Leno to *Sports Illustrated* VIP bashes to meet-and-greet luncheons with deep-pocket Olympic sponsors to watching the men's Gold Medal Hockey Game with Vice President Dick Cheney and New York Mayor Rudolph Guiliani, with whom I talked organ donation and tried to convince to try snowboarding (he said no way).

I even gave a few speeches, including one for Olympic Aid, which helps kids in impoverished African communities, before the *NSYNC concert. That one was memorable because I was introduced to the crowd of screaming teen-aged girls (they were screaming for *NSYNC, not for me) by the great former NFL quarterback Steve

Young, who yelled into the microphone, "And now, the guy who can do flips and spins on a snowboard better than anyone else in the world . . . Chris Klug!" I guess he thought I was Ross Powers.

It wasn't all for charity. What I hadn't expected from winning an Olympic medal was the immediate financial windfall. I got paid for some of the luncheons with sponsors. Plus there was a check from the U.S. Olympic Committee for $10,000 ($25,000 for gold and $15,000 for silver) that I didn't know they handed out. Then I received a phat bonus from Burton for medaling. Everyone at Burton was pumped—two of their half-pipers, Kelly and Ross, won the gold. Now I had the bronze and was proud to have represented Burton, a company that had stood by me for ten years and three major operations.

"After his operation, it didn't surprise me how he came back," Jake says. "I knew he was a goal-oriented guy and a great competitor . . . in fact, one of the better competitors I've ever seen. I think part of it is how he approaches his sport. He is more determined to succeed than he is worried about beating the other guy. He's all about getting the most out of himself and then letting the chips fall where they might.

"He might not have been the best rider on that hill, and those Europeans were lined up to take him out, but the guy just willed it to happen."

Although I talked about the organ donor cause at these events, I also found time to contribute in a quieter way. A couple of days after my race, I visited the pediatric transplant center at the University of Utah to talk to the young patients, let them wear my medal, and sign autographs. It was important to me that transplant recipients realize that they weren't invalids, life wasn't over; in fact, it was beginning again. It was great to watch them light up when I told them that I was healthier and stronger than ever.

I was hoping that my message was getting out there, but I had no idea how many people were paying attention until I finally turned on my computer again a few days after my race. I thought there had to be some sort of mistake; there were nearly ten thousand e-mails waiting for me (later I'd receive three big plastic lawn bags full of mail). Many were from PSC or transplant patients and their families, or donor families—congratulating me and thanking me for showing the world what was possible because of organ donation. Some were just from ordinary people who wrote to say they were touched by my story; the most gratifying of these were those who added that they'd registered as organ donors as a result of learning of my story.

As I was scrolling through my e-mail thinking, *"Oh, my God, it's going to take me years to answer these,"* one jumped out at me. It had been forwarded by a friend from Lance Armstrong.

> Sent: Saturday, February 16, 2002 9:00 AM
>
> > Subject: Klug
>
> >
>
> >
>
> > Can you pass along my sincerest "Congrats" to the snow boarder named Klug.
>
> > The one with the liver transplant. I read the article in the LA times this
>
> > AM and was psyched.
>
> >
>
> > Another medical miracle!
>
> >
>
> > Things like this should be the story and not f*****g ice charades . . .
>
> >
>
> > LA

One appearance I made was strictly away from the cameras and reporters: just me, my family, and Billy Flood's paternal grandmother, Kathy, and aunt, Mary.

Billy's mom, Leisa, had cheered me on from her living room in Idaho. She'd placed two roses on top of her television—one for me and one for her son. "Billy always wanted to try snowboarding," she told a reporter for the *Rocky Mountain News*. "He never got to. But now he was in the Olympics."

Billy's dad, Rob, had also watched the race on television. When a reporter showed up at his home, he pulled out a box in which he kept the letter I'd written at Olang. . . . *I hope through my efforts, I can spread the good news on my successful transplant and someday save someone else's life.* . . . It didn't really make the pain of Billy's death go away—he still missed his son—but he took comfort in the fact that other lives had been saved.

I was nervous about meeting Billy's relatives and didn't know what to expect. How could I thank them for my second chance and the fulfillment of my dream, while they had lost their son?

They were kind and gentle as they congratulated me on my race. They showed me photographs of the family, and of Billy, and told me a little about him—that he liked being outdoors, they said, and sports, and that he laughed a lot and enjoyed being with his friends. He was a lot like me, and if he had to die, they were glad that he'd been able to save someone else. "Billy would have liked that." I was happy that they had shared in my victory.

After the closing ceremonies, I left right away for the World Cup races in Japan. So I wasn't available the next day when the U.S. Olympic Committee announced on the *Today* show the winners of the 2002 Winter Olympic Spirit Award, given to athletes who "best exemplify" the true meaning of Olympic competition. Vanetta Flowers, the first African American female Winter Olympic gold medalist, and her doubles luge partner, Jill Balken, won the award for women. I was honored to be the men's recipient.

After the race in Japan, I almost missed my return flight to Colorado and had to rush on board the airplane still wearing my speed suit. Then when I got to Denver, I rallied straight home to be in a parade through Aspen.

Three thousand people turned out in front of the Gondola Plaza even though it was minus-five degrees Fahrenheit. The mayor of Aspen, Helen Klanderud, declared that day, March 3, 2002, "Chris Klug Day," and Pat O'Donnell handed me a huge cardboard replica of a "Lifetime Pass" for Aspen/Snowmass. I don't think there was a dry eye on the plaza when one of Aspen's famous local musicians, Bobby Mason, led us in singing "America the Beautiful."

"Thank-you for believing in me. This is yours, Aspen!" I told them and stuck around for a couple hours signing autographs until the last person had left and my fingers were too cold to hold the pen.

My "Olympic Victory Tour" continued into the summer, although by the time I was done, there were some who might have preferred I'd stayed home. In March I traveled to New York, where I opened the New York Stock Exchange with gold medalist Kelly Clark. We were also introduced to the crowd during a break in a Knicks basketball game and a Rangers hockey match. I'm pretty sure it wasn't our fault, but the stock market plunged 150 points that day, the Knicks were trounced, and the Rangers got spanked.

But the most humiliating moment was throwing out the first pitch at a Detroit Tigers versus Cleveland Indians baseball game in May, as part of a Saturn National Donor Day event in Detroit. I took the mound with visions of sending the heat, but then I started worrying that I might rifle it over the catcher's head. So I took something off—in fact, a lot off—and one-hopped it to the plate. I'll never forget walking past the Indians' dugout as they were holding their sides laughing and shouting at me. "Hey, nice throw . . . for a snowboarder!"

It was all fun, and not all of it ended in disasters or losses. I even got to be myself as a Warner Brothers cartoon snowboarder on *Scooby-Doo*. I wanted to do the laugh, but they wouldn't let me. I think the dog has a copyright on it.

I also visited the White House with the rest of the U.S. Winter Olympians. (I kept thinking about my mom's lecture about our table manners when we were kids. *"What will you do when you visit the White*

House?" Now, two of us had been there—me and my brother, Jim, who had dined at the White House as part of the first President Bush's speech-writing team.)

I was also named one of the "Sexiest Men in Sports" by *Sports Illustrated for Women.* I was wondering if they were going to rethink their decision when I showed up as white as a ghost and pretty scrawny upstairs from only snowboarding all winter. They wanted me to pose in a "banana hammock" swimsuit for the shoot. I talked them into surf trunks.

The most moving of these post-Olympic events were the 2002 Transplant Games in Orlando, Florida. I was asked to participate in the ceremonies along with Sean Elliott and actor Larry Hagman (who also had a liver transplant). I was humbled to be selected as the torchbearer who lit the flame and keynote speaker at the games, where fifteen hundred athletes and hundreds of donor families marched in to the opening ceremonies. It was awesome watching little kids with new hearts running the 50-yard dash and for me to hand out the medals.

Along the way, I've also picked up a few new sponsors, including Fiji Water, as well as being named the new "Mr. Coffee," a position formerly occupied by the late, great Joe DiMaggio (glad he didn't see me throw that baseball). My last-minute technical problems on the Olympic hill also prompted Tyco Adhesives, a maker of duct tape, to become one of my sponsors (they promptly sent me cases of giant rolls in every color they make).

Since the 2002 Olympics, I have tried to live up to my promise to get the life-saving message of organ donation out there. I've visited about twenty transplant centers for my antirejection drug maker Fujisawa, given a hundred speeches, and participated in a couple dozen other events. I've also been Saturn's National Donor Day spokesperson for the last three years. It seems to help.

"One transplant surgeon summed it up this way," Fujisawa's Sue Ellen Knutson says. "He said that Chris visited one of his patients that morning and it was the best medicine she could possibly have. One thing that he perhaps didn't foresee is the positive impact that he has on the transplant physicians, surgeons, coordinators . . . and the Fuji-sawa people he has worked with. He reinforces the importance of what they do as well."

When I talk about my story to groups, I tell them that there were times when I wondered if my efforts were helping the cause. I was get-ting a lot of e-mails and letters of encouragement, including some from those who had signed up as potential donors, but I was missing a personal connection to the other side of the organ donation story.

Then I tell them the story of Robbie Wade, the smiling, energetic kid I'd first met when I moved to Aspen. He'd grown up to be a great young man. Something of a daredevil—whether it was doing flips on skis or skydiving or rock-climbing—he was a popular kid at Aspen High School, always surrounded by friends..

In May 2002 I gave my presentation to the students at Aspen High School. Not long afterward, Robbie told his father, Bob, that if something ever happened to him, he wanted to be an organ donor. He'd broached the subject before, but I guess my talk, where I asked the students to please register as organ donors, and to make their wishes known to their loved ones, reminded him to bring it up again.

Several months later, on a warm August evening, Robbie was skateboarding without a helmet at night down a long steep road. He'd made a couple of runs successfully, but then he wiped out going around a corner at high speed and struck his head, fracturing his skull.

Ginny and Bob Wade had divorced, and she was out of town this day. So it was Bob who got the telephone call that his son was being rushed to the hospital. The doctors in Aspen, and then in Grand Junc-tion, where he was flown, did everything they could, but there was no saving him. Recalling his son's wishes, Bob agreed that his organs be donated, but the doctors waited for Ginny to fly in from California.

"When I walked into the hospital room, except for the bandage on his head, it didn't look like anything was wrong," Ginny recalls. "I thought, 'Oh, good, he's just sleeping.' But he wasn't. The person with the organ donation team came rather quickly, it seemed, and asked for my permission. . . . I had only been there a little while . . . it was too quick. I asked to be left alone with him that night so that I could say good-bye to my son . . . I lay there all night with my head on his chest, listening to his heart beating so strong, and thought, *The next time I hear that heart, it will be in someone else's body.*

"It's the hardest thing I've ever done . . . to leave him. But it's what he would have wanted. Robbie was absolutely in love with life and lived his to the fullest. He would be happy to know that someone else could enjoy their life if he could no longer have his."

Robbie was well-loved by many people in our community, and his death stunned our little town. More than a thousand people turned out for his memorial service. I happened to be in town on that sunny afternoon and went to the service with my parents.

What I remembered most about Robbie was that he was always smiling, always in the middle of a group of friends. I was so moved when both Bob Wade and his friend and family doctor, Bill Mitchell, mentioned my story and Robbie's wishes.

I hadn't planned this—but I had a small bronze medal on a ribbon that my Fujisawa friends gave me to distribute to kids at the hospitals that I visit. I hung one around Ginny's neck and said, "You're the hero, not me." I've never said anything I meant more.

For me, Robbie's death and his decision and that of his parents to donate his organs to save other lives went beyond answering my doubts about whether my efforts were doing any good. Until his death, I don't think I had ever quite understood the courage and humanity of donor families. I knew Billy Flood's name and something about him, and I will always be grateful to his parents. But Robbie gave me not only a face, but a voice and a personality, and a family I knew to personify for me all of those other heroes.

When I talk about donors, I see Robbie Wade smiling, skateboarding, and carving turns on his skis. And in quiet moments when I stop and contemplate this gift I've been given, and give thanks for the courage of donor families, I think of my friends Bob and Ginny and the decision they made in the midst of their grief.

In a way, Robbie and I have become partners in getting the message out, so it's appropriate that large photographs of the two of us hang next to each other in the commons at Aspen High. Nobody among my friends and family takes my second chance for granted, either. They are all signed up to be donors, if the time ever comes, and every Valentine's Day, Mom, Dad, and Missy hold a National Donor Day drive at the Gondola Plaza in downtown Aspen with Mom's high school Outreach Club.

My parents once asked their minister how they could repay the kindness the church had shown them when Jim was born. He'd replied, "You'll know." When I think back, it strikes me that they've been "paying ahead" by the sort of people they are. I too feel that I'm trying to express my appreciation to the Floods and the Wades and all the other heroes by doing what I can to save others' lives in the future.

As for some of the main characters you've met in this book: Missy got her master's degree and has started a successful adolescent counseling business; Mom is finishing her PhD and (thanks to me) is a whiz at helping "nontraditional" kids get through school; Jim has his fly-fishing service and married Hillary Peterson in June 2004 (I guess the pressure's really on me now!); my sister, Hillary, is in her senior year at Colby College and is a competitive snowboarder; Jason went to Oregon State University to play football and, while he didn't make the NFL, won several national rugby titles as a member of the Gentlemen of Aspen and now has his own business; and Dad, well, he runs the best hotel in Aspen and still cheers for God.

Unfortunately, life will always have a way of balancing the ups and downs, and since the Olympics, two of my role models have died. A month after the Olympics, cancer claimed my grandmother, Nanny. I'll always remember her running pass patterns for me and her post-game advice. She'd told me that the trip to the Nagano Olympics was the best of her life, and I'd really wanted her to come to Salt Lake. But

Mom had to break down and tell me she couldn't—she was too ill but didn't want me to know until after the games. Nanny was a classic, and I miss her and have often wished I could call her and tell her about my latest adventure.

The other great loss was Craig Kelly, who was killed along with seven others in an avalanche in January 2003 while guiding a group of skiers and riders in the British Columbia backcountry. He was such a great influence on me and on the world of snowboarding in general; he epitomized the sport's spirit and the camaraderie. I'll always remember stalking him on the slopes of Mount Bachelor and how he'd let even a little grom like me hang with the legend.

So we come to the end of this book, although not my story. I'm still taking Prograf, although I've now tapered down to one milligram twice daily and hope to drop it still more someday. Otherwise, I'm still surfing, riding, playing with my friends and family . . . and dreaming. Only, now the dream has changed a little bit since the Salt Lake City Olympics. I finished strong last year, the 2003–2004 season, with a sixth national title and third-place finish at Bardonecchia, Italy—the site of the 2006 Winter Olympic snowboarding events.

I'll be looking for the podium this year and jockeying for position for the fall of 2005 and the race to make the U.S. Olympic team for a third time. But the dream doesn't end until I get to Bardonecchia and climb to the top of that Olympic podium.

In the meantime, I'm trying to grow my sport here in the United States with snowboard racing camps for kids in Aspen after the end of my competition season and with an online site I've developed in partnership with Burton specializing in alpine gear (www.klugriding.com). Yet, for me, snowboarding will never be just about medals, or making a living, or even a podium from which to champion donor awareness. It's about how I view life.

I remember a few days after the Olympic parade in Aspen. I was hiking up the ridge of Highlands Bowl with my friends Fab and Gibans when we came to the "lunch gate." The gate was actually just a rope across the trail to hold back skiers and riders until the ski patrol had finished setting off explosive charges to make the bowl safe from avalanches.

We walked up to where another seventy-five locals, all dedicated powder fiends, were milling about, waiting for the rope to drop. I moved through the crowd, stopping to talk and be congratulated for my Olympic race, but all the time working myself closer and closer to the gate.

One of the biggest storms of the year had passed through the night before, dumping two feet of fresh snow. The storm clouds were gone and the sun was out. As far as we could see, the mountains rolled away like enormous white-capped waves, and Highlands Bowl didn't appear to have a single track blemishing the new snow.

It was a spiritual moment, surrounded by well-wishers and two of my best friends. I was thinking that there's a lot I would do for a buddy . . . but not give up the first run in blower conditions on an epic day in the mountains. At the word from the ski patrol, I jumped over the rope ahead of everyone else and started scrambling for the top of the ridge on all fours with my board strapped to my back, all the while giggling like a mad hyena.

I paused to look over my shoulder. Fab and Gibans had this look on their faces like they couldn't believe I'd taken off on them. I laughed and yelled, "NO FRIENDS ON A POWDER DAY!" And kept climbing for the top.

Acknowledgments

From Chris Klug:

I want to thank my family for the great life they've given me and for all of their hard work and dedication helping with this book. Thanks to Missy, my rock when I needed one, for her endless proofreading and late night sessions picking out photos. Thank you Jason for watching my back and letting me include your story. I'm grateful to all of my teammates and coaches over the years who have shared their lives and skills with me and contributed greatly to this story. Rob Roy who has always been my coach and friend. My buddies in Aspen and Central Oregon for being there through the wins and losses and taking the time to remember the details. The April family for their love and hospitality. I'm forever indebted to Scott Peterson and Bill Fabrocini for never giving up on me. Carlon, Mike, Jon, Brad, and Anton for your humor and support, and Gary for your brilliant ideas and long-time friendship. Thank you to my team of doctors who have put me back together more than once and put up with the interviews and requests, especially Dr. Boehm, Dr. Carlson, Dr. Pevny, and Dr. Kam and Dr. Everson and the entire University of Colorado Transplant and Hepatology Teams. To my donor family for letting me share their courageous story and for giving me a second chance to realize my dreams. Thanks to the Octagon crew of Peter Carlisle and Morgan Boys, and Peter Sawyer at the Fifi Oscard Agency for steering me through this process. C & G, I'm stoked you gave this book a chance. Thanks to everyone at Burton for the fast boards and support the past thirteen years through it all; Derek Shuman at Bolle, Eric Sherman, and David Quick with Saturn's National Donor Day, Aspen/Snowmass for the support and epic terrain, and Fiji Water for keeping me hydrated. Thank you to Fujisawa for the miracle of Prograf and especially to Sue Ellen and her team. Finally I want to thank Steve Jackson for putting up with me the past four years as we wrote this book together. You are a true friend and an awesome writer! Thanks to all who have supported me and to all who have helped me tell my story!

From Steve Jackson:

I'd like to first of all thank my wife and daughters who put up with the long hours I sit alone in front of a computer or on the road. There's no greater treasure I could wish for than more time with you. And my parents, sisters, and brother—there's never been enough time. And my Boyz who keep me sane with our trips to heaven in the Colorado Rockies and the big lake in the desert . . . and Bronco Sundays. As always, my agent Michael Hamilburg of the Hamilburg Agency in Hollywood, California, is the very best there is as an agent and a human being, ably assisted by his consigliere, Joanie Kern. Thanks to my own consigliere, Robin Repass, lawyer and friend. I deeply appreciate the editors at Carroll & Graf for giving this book a chance when no one else would. I'd be remiss in not thanking Chris's version of the Boyz—Gary, Fab, Anton, Carlon, Mike, Josh, Brad—as well as his girl, Missy, for your friendship and for telling me the truth to counterbalance Klug's version. (Note to Klug: Marry her before she comes to her senses.) Thank you Ray and Pat for the warmth, the bed, and large pieces of beef hot off the grill. Second to last, I owe a deep debt of gratitude and affection to the Klug family, especially Warren and Kathy—for your kindness and hospitality, your openness and acceptance, and your dedication to your son and this book. Kathy, you may be the gnarliest soccer mom ever, but (except for my mom and mom-in-law) you may be the best mom ever. And Warren, you've been a friend as well as roomie, and The Aspen Square Hotel is second to none and will always be my favorite. Most of all, I'd like to thank Chris. He is one of those rare people who is exactly what he seems to be when you first meet him—open, funny, engaged in living life to the fullest, a great and loyal friend. This was fun, especially the part where they gutted you like a trout, but you still owe me the loan of your long board the next time I get to the coast.

Index

About the Authors

Chris Klug travels the world as a professional snowboarder, calling Aspen, Colorado, his home. He is a four-time World Cup winner, six-time U.S. National champion, a U.S. Open winner, and a two-time Olympian. In 2002 Chris became the first ever transplant recipient Olympian and medalist. He is focused on spreading the life-saving message of organ donation awareness through his snowboarding and speaking. The Chris Klug Foundation is dedicated to donor awareness and helping transplant patients. Chris can be found surfing, kiteboarding, mountain biking, or fly-fishing when not on his snowboard. He looks forward to competing in the next Winter Olympics in Torino, Italy, in 2006. For more information, visit www.chrisklug.com.

Steve Jackson is a *New York Times* best-selling author and award-winning journalist who lives in the mountains west of Denver, Colorado, with his wife and three daughters. His last book for Carroll & Graf, *LUCKY LADY: The World War II Heroics of the USS* Santa Fe *and* Franklin, won the 2003 Colorado Book Award for best history/biography and was the runner-up for the 2004 Admiral Samuel E. Morrison Naval History Award. Time well spent is time with his family, fly-fishing, hiking, camping, practicing martial arts, writing, playing in the ocean, spent with friends, and skiing (he leaves the snowboarding to Chris).

"When Dr. Caroline Leaf first appeared on *LIFE Today* in 2007, our viewers were captivated by her research on how humans think. Dr. Leaf connects the dots between science and Scripture—explaining how we can indeed be 'transformed by the renewing of [our] mind.' If you need a change in your thought life or overall attitude, *Switch On Your Brain* will convince you that your brain can be renewed by the power of God's Spirit and biblical truth."

—James Robison, president of LIFE Outreach International;
cohost of *LIFE Today*

"This book is the owner's manual for how our brains work. Caroline Leaf's first appearance on TBN's *Praise the Lord* program with Laurie and myself is one of the 'stuck' memories in my brain. Science in 2013 is actually catching up with the Bible! She has taught us more and more truth over the years now and is in production on an entire TV series that will air on TBN for years!"

—Matt Crouch, broadcaster, filmmaker

"Caroline Leaf has given us a real jewel, translating modern brain science into language accessible to everyone. She engages, educates, and encourages us to use science and biblical truths to improve our thoughts, relationships, and health. This book is a delight, and I highly recommend it to everyone interested in improving their joy and mental health."

—David I. Levy, MD, neurosurgeon; author of *Gray Matter*

"I resolved not to let twelve years of abuse destroy my mind and my life; I resolved not to let injustice flourish on this earth and instead to stand up and do something about it; I decided to make something out of my brokenness; I decided *to choose to change my mind*. Caroline helped me to understand the science behind what had happened in my brain when I made these choices in my life. She explains how our choices work scientifically, but in a practical way that makes something that is really hard to do much easier and more tangible. This book is so helpful that all the girls who go through our A21 program will be learning how to use these principles to help them renew their minds and give them hope so that they can get back into life . . . and change not only their lives but also their world."

—Christine Caine, founder of the A21 Campaign;
director of Equip and Empower Ministries; author of *Undaunted*

"Dr. Leaf has spoken at Gateway on many occasions, and we're so grateful for the impact she's had on our congregation. We've seen firsthand how her unique and groundbreaking message changes lives. She understands that your brain is fearfully and wonderfully made by God. We encourage you to act on the wisdom found in *Switch On Your Brain* and begin the incredible journey of thinking God's way."

—Robert and Debbie Morris, pastors of Gateway Church;
authors of *The Blessed Life*, *The Blessed Marriage*,
and *The Blessed Woman*

"Dr. Caroline Leaf's research allows for tangible understanding of the link between the Bible and the brain and shows us how understanding this develops us both emotionally and spiritually. Her teaching is not only life changing but life *saving* as it makes the renewing of the mind so real. I am so very grateful for the wisdom contained within these pages. Grow as you read."

—Darlene Zschech, singer-songwriter; author of *The Art of Mentoring*

"Neuroplasticity? Genetic research? Electromagnetic flow? Never in a million years did I think I could relate to, much less understand, topics like these. Leave me to my normal right-brained tendencies and I'd run as far and fast as I could at the first mention of them. But that was before I met Dr. Caroline Leaf. Some of the most life-transformative lessons I've learned have come from this incredible woman whose brilliance is upstaged only by her integrity and graciousness. Whether sitting in an audience along with twenty thousand other people hanging on to her every word, or just sitting across from her over a couple mugs of hot tea, I've heard her share deeply scientific data in a profoundly practical and simple way that every person can understand. Even me. *Switch On Your Brain* will show you how to turn on the part of your brain, and your life, that has been turned off for far too long. You'll emerge a happier, healthier, and more well-rounded human being."

—Priscilla Shirer, author of *The Resolution for Women*

"Dr. Caroline Leaf masterfully weaves brain science and the Word of God. Not only will *Switch On Your Brain* detox your brain, it will awaken your brilliance—so that you can be all that God created you to be and do all he fashioned you to do. Read it and renew your mind."

—John and Lisa Bevere, authors; cofounders of Messenger International

"I am neither a scientist nor a specialist in this field, but what I do know is that the fruit and influence of Dr. Caroline Leaf's ministry is inspiring people to see—from a scientific perspective—the genius of God's timeless Word and wisdom. Each of us is full of untapped potential when it comes to our ability to think and process our way through life. I pray that Caroline's years of research and passion in this realm of unfolding science will be a blessing to you as you discover what it is to 'switch on your brain.'"

—Bobbie Houston, senior pastor, Hillsong Church

"In *Switch On Your Brain*, my good friend Dr. Caroline Leaf shows us all how the science of thought is catching up with the Word of God. Featuring the 21-Day Brain Detox Plan, Dr. Leaf shares the brain-boosting secrets that she used successfully with thousands of her patients, teaching you how to literally rewire your brain. If you're looking to improve your memory, your focus, your concentration, or your very life, it's time to switch on your brain!"

—Jordan Rubin, NMD, PhD, author of *The Maker's Diet*; founder of Garden of Life and Beyond Organic

"Can you imagine the outcome of a collaborative effort between a brain scientist and a faith-filled believer with a deep biblical foundation? Fortunately, we have the benefit of such resources from someone who possesses an aptitude in both realms. Dr. Caroline's works have provided rare insight into the fascinating inner workings of both the natural and the spiritual. *Switch On Your Brain* underscores that the capacity for abundant living we have through Christ is directly linked to choice. Her teaching provides both exploration and exercises to enable 'the lights to come on,' helping the reader experience a new level of freedom. Her candid and authentic delivery is refreshing and uplifting. I'm grateful for this gift of hope supported by both biblical and scientific proof!"

—Colleen Rouse, pastor of Victory Church Atlanta

"*Switch On Your Brain* is such a marvelous revelation of how powerful the brain is. I love this! So many times we think, *Well, this is the way I've always been and I can't change.* Not true. No matter how we have thought in the past, we can change our present and future with our thinking. God has told us these things, but Caroline has researched them and proven them scientifically. I believe with all my heart that God wants to soak you in his love and to share the revelation of how to detox your brain from the lies of the enemy and switch it on to the love and truth of God's Word. Thank you, Caroline, for the years you have spent in study, for your commitment to Jesus, for your humility and wisdom, and for being a wonderful friend."

—Marilyn Hickey, president and founder of Marilyn Hickey Ministries

"If our teachers and students could really grasp the power that we each have to think differently, as described by Dr. Caroline Leaf, we could see a true change in education. When each individual, whether adult, teen, or child, begins to take personal responsibility for our own mental, physical, and spiritual health, it will change lives!"

—Angie McDonald, superintendent of Advantage Academy Charter Schools

"In this book Dr. Leaf provides you with the key to detoxifying your brain. She combines her years of expertise in brain research with the Word and wisdom of God to show you that you have the ability to rewire negative thoughts and habits that have led you to live a life of ill health, depression, and defeat. Dr. Leaf includes a 21-Day Brain Detox Plan that will teach you how to get the negativity out of your thinking, allowing you to recalculate your destination from down a negative road to one that leads to a happier, healthier, more productive you. We live or die by the choices we make; but if our brains are toxic from poisonous circumstances, events, and decisions from our past, we cannot make quality choices that will effect positive change until we correct our thinking. I encourage you to take advantage of Dr. Leaf's combination of the Word, wisdom, and science to learn how to 'flip the switch,' enabling you to do, be, and have all that God intended for your life."

—DeeDee Freeman, associate pastor of Spirit of Faith Christian Center

"Our thought life plays a critical role in the outward expression of our being. In *Switch On Your Brain* Caroline Leaf describes how advancements in cognitive neuroscience support biblical principles pertaining to a healthy thought life. She describes how a healthy thought life can have beneficial effects on our overall health and physiology. She provides a practical strategy to align our thought life with biblical truth to facilitate being continually transformed by the renewing of our mind (Romans 12:2). Dr. Leaf challenges us to see ourselves the way God sees us, through the perfect and finished work of Jesus Christ."

—Brian E. Snell, MD, neurosurgeon

"Dr. Leaf demonstrates to us that these breakthroughs in neuroscience are actually ancient, already referenced in the Bible. Neuroscience is actually confirming God's Word. Caroline's gift is her ability to renew our childlike wonder at God's wisdom and creation; we are truly fearfully and wonderfully made (Psalm 139:14). In the second part of the book Dr. Leaf explains how this knowledge can be applied to our lives in a way that even a child can understand. Drawing from her years in clinical practice, she is able to give us practical steps that can truly transform our lives: spirit, soul, and body. I have seen firsthand how these steps have revolutionized people's lives in family, church, and educational settings. Indeed, they have transformed my own life."

—Dr. Peter Amua-Quarshie, MD, MPH, MS, neuroscientist

"When I first met Caroline Leaf in Rwanda years ago, I knew I had met someone with a message that had to be shared with the world. As I leaned in to listen to her heart, her story, her wisdom, and her research, I felt hope rising within me. This is a book of wisdom, knowledge, and truth for everyone. Dr. Leaf's research and insights based on biblical truth give every reader practical keys to live a happy, healthy, and fulfilled life starting today."

—Helen Burns, pastor of Relate Church; author; international speaker;
cohost of TV show *Relate with John & Helen Burns*

"Caroline Leaf is such an amazing person, and her book *Switch On Your Brain* is super helpful for everyone because we all need help with our thinking! Dr. Leaf teaches us, in this book, some very essential techniques and insights to help us live a life of peace, health, and happiness. This book will be hugely helpful to you no matter your age or educational background!"

—Sarah Bowling, pastor; cohost with Marilyn Hickey

"I have had the privilege of working with Dr. Leaf when she taught at The King's University in Los Angeles. During the courses she taught, her books were reviewed, critically examined, and thereafter uniformly adopted by course attendees, college and seminary students, and myself. As you will learn, her teachings are on the cutting edge of research in neuroscience. I am enthusiastic about the material in her latest book, as its application can radically change lives and enhance our walk with Jesus. I recommend you read this book, study the material, and apply the teachings. It will begin a great journey."

—C. Fred Cassity, BSE, JD, professor of practical theology,
The King's University

"This new book by Caroline Leaf is a practical plan that helps you implement a technique that takes just seven minutes per day to rewire your brain and change your life. I can personally attest to the effectiveness of her methods since I have been healed now for over eight years of several incurable conditions, including autoimmune thyroid disease, acid reflux, fibroid tumors of the uterus, panic attacks, depression, and chronic fatigue syndrome. I was healed through the use of intentional thinking—meditating on the truth to combat the lies about myself and my life that had been programmed into my psyche. I'm not the same person because I have started to think differently. The simple and easy-to-implement concepts in this book can truly change your life. I encourage you to start today!"

—Jennifer Crow, founder of Beautiful Dream Society;
author of *Perfect Lies*

"Dr. Leaf has written a book that has the potential to change the life of each of us! Her research and study of the brain has shown that we do have the ability to change our future by changing how we think. In very practical ways she shows us how to do this. This is such an exciting book and I know will be a huge blessing to everyone who reads it!"

—Holly Wagner, pastor of Oasis Church; author of *GodChicks*

SWITCH ON YOUR BRAIN

The Key to Peak Happiness, Thinking, and Health

DR. CAROLINE LEAF

BakerBooks

a division of Baker Publishing Group
Grand Rapids, Michigan

© 2013 by Dr. Caroline Leaf

Published by Baker Books
a division of Baker Publishing Group
P.O. Box 6287, Grand Rapids, MI 49516-6287
www.bakerbooks.com

Paperback edition published 2015
ISBN 978-0-8010-1839-8

Printed in the United States of America

The Library of Congress has cataloged the previous edition as follows:
Leaf, Caroline, 1963–
    Switch On Your Brain : The Key to Peak Happiness, Thinking, and Health /
Dr. Caroline Leaf.
      pages cm
    ISBN 978-0-8010-1570-0 (cloth)
    ISBN 978-0-8010-1624-0 (pbk.)
    1. Thought and thinking—Religious aspects—Christianity. 2. Well-being—Religious aspects—Christianity. I. Title.
BV4598.4.L43 2013
248.4—dc23   2013014493

16 17 18 19 20 21 22   14 13 12 11 10 9 8

I see myself as a puzzle builder. And in writing my books, the pieces of the puzzles come together to tell a specific story of hope.

This book is dedicated to:

The ultimate Creator of the puzzles—thank you for honoring me with the task of building a few pieces of the "science of thought" puzzle. I am humbled by this task and will endeavor to bring only you glory through it.

My ever-loving, magnificent love of my life—Mac, my husband. You never seem to tire of listening to me teach on God and the brain with rapt enthusiasm. My sister once said to me that I wouldn't be able to do what I do if it wasn't for you, and this is so true. You are the epitome of loving husbands.

My four outstanding phenomenal children—Jessica, Dominique, Jeffrey, and Alexandria. When I look at you and listen to you, I know I am experiencing God's love and hope and joy. He has blessed me with the epitome of loving children as well.

Our life is what our thoughts make it.

Marcus Aurelius

Contents

11

Contents

Prologue

W hat would you do if you found a switch that could turn on your brain and enable you to be happier, healthier in your mind and body, more prosperous, and more intelligent?

In this book you will learn how to find and activate that switch. What you think with your mind changes your brain and body, and you are designed with the power to switch on your brain. Your mind is that switch.

You have an extraordinary ability to determine, achieve, and maintain optimal levels of intelligence, mental health, peace, and happiness, as well as the prevention of disease in your body and mind. You can, through conscious effort, gain control of your thoughts and feelings, and in doing so, you can change the programming and chemistry of your brain.

Science is finally catching up with the Bible, showing us the proof that "God has not given us a spirit of fear, but of power and of love and of a sound mind" (2 Tim. 1:7). Breakthrough neuroscientific research is confirming daily what we instinctively knew all along: What you are thinking every moment of every day becomes a physical reality in your brain and body, which affects your optimal mental and physical health. These thoughts collectively form your attitude, which is your state of mind, and it's *your attitude and not your DNA* that determines much of the quality of your life.

This state of mind is a real, physical, electromagnetic, quantum, and chemical flow in the brain that switches groups of genes on or off in a positive or negative direction based on your choices and subsequent reactions. Scientifically, this is called *epigenetics*; spiritually, this is the enactment of Deuteronomy 30:19, "I have set before you life and death, blessing and cursing; therefore choose life, that both you and your descendants may live." The brain responds to your mind by sending these neurological signals throughout the body, which means that your thoughts and emotions are transformed into physiological and spiritual effects, and then physiological experiences transform into mental and emotional states. It's a profound and eye-opening thought to realize something seemingly immaterial like a belief can take on a physical existence as a positive or negative change in our cells.

And you are in control of all of this. The choices you make today not only impact your spirit, soul, and body, but can also impact the next four generations.

The great news is that we are *wired for love*, which means all our mental circuitry is wired only for the positive, and we have a natural *optimism bias* wired into us. Our default mode is one of being designed to make good choices. So our bad choices and reactions were wired in by our choices, and therefore can be *wired out*. Our brain is neuroplastic—it can change and regrow. In addition, God has built in the operating principle of neurogenesis—new nerve cells are birthed daily for our mental benefit. This sounds like Lamentations

3:22–23, "The LORD's mercies . . . are new every morning." This book shows you how to *get back control* over your thoughts and renew (as in Rom. 12:2) and rewire your brain in the direction you were originally designed to go.

Based solidly on the latest neuroscientific research on the brain, as well as my clinical experience and research, you will learn how thoughts impact your spirit, soul, and body. You will also learn how to detox your thoughts using my practical, detailed, and easy-to-use 21-Day Brain Detox Plan.

The application is for all walks of life. You won't forgive that person, get rid of that anxiety or depression, follow that essential preventative healthcare, strive to that intellectual level you know you are capable of, follow that dream, eat that organic food, do that diet, be that great parent or husband or wife or friend, get that promotion, or make other changes to create a quality, positive lifestyle—*unless you first choose to get your mind right and switch on your brain.* After all, the ability to think and choose and to use your mind correctly is often the hardest step, but it is the first and most powerful step.

> If you realized how powerful your thoughts are, you would never think a negative thought.
>
> Peace Pilgrim

Acknowledgments

My inspiration for building these puzzles and the pieces of the puzzle have come from multiple sources:

The inspiration starts and ends with God, always.

The thousands of scientists whose brilliant work I have devoured and spent many thousands of hours pouring over, astounded at the truths God is revealing through them—many of whom I have mentioned in this book and in my references.

The dedicated, driven, and sometimes very broken patients and clients I have had the privilege of working with over the years. I see their mindful determination to succeed pull them up, often to beyond levels they thought they were capable of.

The wise Bible and science teachers I have sat under (and still sit under).

The wonderful Baker Books publishing team—efficiency, excellence, and speed describe their high-standard approach to completing a project.

My very special family, whose love and support have always been a scaffold to me.

My friends: There are so many who have encouraged me and spoken words of wisdom and prophecy over my life, and who contributed to this book in ways they perhaps don't even realize. Mentioning all of you would fill pages, but you know who you are, and I appreciate and love you all. In fact, it was hard to choose who *not* to ask to do endorsements because I wanted all of you in my book.

Introduction

Switch On Your Brain with Hope

Main Scripture: Faith is the substance of things hoped for, the evidence of things not seen. Hebrews 11:1

Linked Science Concept: Thoughts are real, physical things that occupy mental real estate. Moment by moment, every day, you are changing the structure of your brain through your thinking. When we hope, it is an activity of the mind that changes the structure of our brain in a positive and normal direction.

It was only a few decades ago that scientists—including those who trained me—considered the brain to be a fixed and hardwired machine. This view saw the damaged brain as incurable. They believed brain damage was hopeless and untreatable, whether the effects were from stroke, cardiovascular event, traumatic brain injury, learning disabilities, traumas, PTSD, OCD, depression, anxiety—even aging. All of these causes and conditions were seen as largely irreversible.

Because this was the presiding view of the brain, I was trained back in the '80s to teach my patients *compensation*, not *restoration* of function. I was trained in the conventional wisdom of the time that said brain normality was an impossibility for those with mental limitations or brain damage of any kind. Being a student of the Bible, however, I was deeply familiar with and constantly comforted by Romans 12:2: "Do not conform to the pattern of this world, but be transformed by the renewing of your mind" (NIV). I knew this famous and fabulous "renewing of the mind" passage was a truth I needed to apply to my patients' care to help them overcome their deficits. So my relentless search of this truth as a scientist began.

I was struck by how my patients, using the therapeutic techniques I was developing from my research, belied the negative picture conventional science presented of the human brain at that time. These results confirmed that the brain, far from being fixed in toxicity, can change even in the most challenging neurological situations.

I was in awe of what each patient displayed in terms of what you *can do when you set your mind to it*. Each new scientific study in this direction confirmed what I knew intuitively to be true: We are not victims of our biology or circumstances. How we react to the events and circumstances of life can have an enormous impact on our mental and even physical health.

As we think, we change the physical nature of our brain. As we consciously direct our thinking, we can wire out toxic patterns of thinking and replace them with healthy thoughts. New thought networks grow. We increase our intelligence and bring healing to our brains, minds, and physical bodies.

It all starts in the realm of the mind, with our ability to think and choose—the most powerful thing in the universe after God, and indeed, fashioned after God.

Healthy Memory: Adapted Graphic Sketch

Toxic Memory: Adapted Graphic Sketch

It is with our phenomenal minds that we understand the truths set down in our spirits. It is with our minds that we wire these truths into the brain, which is part of the body. It is with our minds that we choose to develop the spiritual part of who we are and "Therefore put away all filthiness and rampant wickedness and receive with meekness the implanted word, which is able to save your souls" (James 1:21 ESV). It is with our minds that we reject or believe the lies of the Enemy, the Prince of Lies. It is with our minds that we change the physical reality of the brain to reflect our choices. It is with our minds that we decide to follow God's rules and live in peace despite what is going on around us. It is with our minds that we choose to follow the lies of Satan and spiral into mental, physical, and spiritual disarray.

Thought changes the structure of matter. God said, "Let there be light" (Gen. 1:3), and his words produced the physical earth. And science, which, again, is just catching up with the Word of God, is confirming this reality in a tangible and thought-provoking way with eminently clear accounts arising from the burgeoning field of neuroplasticity research.

Neuroplasticity by definition means the brain is malleable and adaptable, changing moment by moment of every day. Scientists are finally beginning to see the brain as having renewable characteristics (as in Rom. 12:2); it is no longer viewed as a machine that is hardwired early in life, unable to adapt, and wearing out with age. With example after fascinating example, exceptional scientists talk about and demonstrate—using brain-imaging techniques and the evidence of behavioral changes—how people can change their brains with their minds. We can see and measure the activity of the mind through the firing of neurons. We can even predict the seeming elusiveness of the main functions of the mind—that of thinking and choosing—through quantum mechanics.

I continue to find myself moving in a world of engrossing truths, and my spirit leaps inside of me. The fact that the brain is plastic and can actually be changed by the mind gives tangible hope to everyone, no matter what the circumstance. I have been privileged to work with and see:

22

- autistic children cope in academic and social environments
- senior citizens sharpen their memories to the point that in their eighties they change careers and obtain degrees
- young men and women who grew up in abject poverty and a lifestyle of selling and taking drugs do a complete about-face in their lives, go back to school, and become leaders in their communities
- car accident victims who had been written off by neurologists as "vegetables" retrain their brains to the point that they complete their schooling up to a tertiary level and go on to become successful, contributing citizens
- students labeled as learning disabled with years of therapy and no hope left master learning and achieve grades they and their parents only dreamed of
- schools in some of the worst third-world areas in Africa, in which students could not pass to the next level, become schools on the minister of education's "most improved" list
- children with dyslexia learn to read and write and even help their parents study for exams successfully
- suicidal and emotionally traumatized minds set free
- entire schools improve grades across core subjects

And the list goes on.

Science is hovering on a precipice as we recognize the responsibility and impact of our thinking and the resultant choices we make, which have ramifications right down to the ways in which the genes of our bodies express themselves. Deuteronomy 30:19 is becoming a reality in the world we live in today as we begin to see the effects of choice in the brain and body: "I set before you life and death, blessing and cursing; choose life so that you and your descendants may live."

How we think not only affects our own spirit, soul, and body but also people around us. Science and Scripture both show how the results of our decisions pass through the sperm and ova to the next four generations, profoundly affecting their choices and lifestyles. The science of epigenetics (the signals, including our thoughts, that affect the activity of our genes) explains how this plays out. This reminds me of the Scripture, "he punishes the children and their children for the sin of the parents to the third and fourth generation" (Exod. 34:7 NIV).

That the brain is plastic and can be changed moment-by-moment by how we direct our thinking—in other words, the choices we make—is a top idea on the bestseller lists, and it actually is the key to switching on our brains. Add to this the fact that every morning when you wake up, new baby nerve cells have been born while you were sleeping that are there at your disposal to be used in tearing down toxic thoughts and rebuilding healthy thoughts. The birth of these new baby nerve cells is called neurogenesis, which brings to mind, "The LORD's mercies . . . are new every morning" (Lam. 3:23).

What a remarkable and hopeful portrait of the endless adaptivity of the human brain God has given us.

This book is divided into two parts, with the overall goal of showing you how to switch on your brain. Part 1 uncovers the keys to doing so. In part 2 you will see how all these keys work together in my 5-Step Switch On Your Brain Learning Process during my 21-Day Brain Detox Plan. Here I will lead you through a process of switching on your brain to achieve peak happiness, thinking, and health.

Here are some of the key points in this book:

- Your mind is the most powerful thing in the universe after God.

- Free will and choice are real, spiritual, and scientific facts (Deut. 30:19).

- Your mind (soul) has one foot in the door of the spirit and one foot in the door of the body; you can change your brain with your mind and essentially renew your mind (Rom. 12:2).

- You can develop your spirit through choices you make in your mind to be led by the Holy Spirit (Gal. 2:20).

- Your body is not in control of your mind—your mind is in control of your body, and your mind is stronger than your body. Mind certainly is *over* matter.

- You are not a victim of your biology.

- You cannot control the events and circumstances of life, but you can control your reaction to those events and circumstances (Matt. 7:13–14; Gal. 6:7–8).

- When you think, you build thoughts, and these become physical substances in your brain. "As he thinks in his heart, so is he" (Prov. 23:7).

- Good thinking = good choices = healthy thoughts; toxic thinking = toxic choices = toxic thoughts (Deut. 30:19).

- You are designed to stand outside yourself and observe your own thinking *and change it* (Rom. 12:2; 2 Cor. 10:5; Phil. 3:13–14).

- You are designed to recognize and choose the right things to think about (Josh. 24:15; Eccles. 7:29; Isa. 30:2).

- Each morning when you wake up, you have new baby nerve cells born inside your brain to use wisely as you remove bad thoughts and wire in new ones (Lam. 3:23). This is called neurogenesis.

- You have been designed for deep, intellectual thought (Ps. 139:14).
- You are wired for love, and fear is a learned and not a natural response (2 Tim. 1:7).
- You have the mind of Christ (1 Cor. 2:16).
- You are made in God's image (Gen. 1:27).

All this knowledge will help you realize these truths:

- Happiness comes from within and success follows—not the other way around.
- You can learn how to learn and deepen your intellect.
- You can overcome those learning issues.
- You can get the chaos in your mind under control.
- You don't have to walk around in guilt and condemnation.
- If you wired those toxic thoughts in, you can wire them out.
- You don't have to get stuck in bad habits; you can change them.
- You can overcome feelings of rejection and hurt.
- Forgiveness is not the battle you think it is.
- You don't have to worry about things that are out of your control.
- You are not a victim of the things you shouldn't be doing.
- You don't have to fear that if a condition runs in your family that you are going to get it (for example, Alzheimer's, Parkinson's, or depression).

- You can balance your over-thinking and over-analyzing mind.
- You can overcome and control depression and anxiety—some scientists are showing you can even control and overcome schizophrenia and OCD.
- You don't have to keep digging into the past to get free from it.
- You can be happy and filled with peace regardless of your circumstances.

If you have nodded your head at even one of these, it is time for you to be set free in your mind to pursue all God has for you. Read on. It is time for you to Switch On Your Brain and find the keys to peak happiness, thinking, and health.

In part 1, I explain through science and Scripture how the concepts described above come together.

In part 2, you will find my 21-Day Brain Detox Plan, which incorporates my scientifically proven 5-Step Switch On Your Brain technique based on my research, my years in clinical practice, and doing seminars and conferences around the world. This section is practical and filled with key, proven strategies that will help you develop a lifestyle of renewing your mind and aligning it with God's will so your divine sense of purpose can be released (Eccles. 3:11).

You are truly designed for peak happiness, thinking, and health.

Introduction Summary

1. It was only a few decades ago that scientists considered the brain to be a fixed and hardwired machine. This

view saw the damaged brain as incurable and the focus was *compensation*, not restoration of function.

2. We can change the physical nature of our brain through our thinking and choosing.

3. As we consciously direct our thinking, we can wire out toxic patterns of thinking and replace them with healthy thoughts. New thought networks grow. We increase our intelligence and bring healing to our minds and physical bodies.

4. It *all* starts in the realm of the mind, with our ability to think and choose—the most powerful thing in the universe after God.

5. Neuroplasticity by definition means the brain is malleable and adaptable, changing moment by moment of every day.

6. Scientists are finally beginning to see the brain as having renewable characteristics (as in Rom. 12:2).

7. Science is hovering on a precipice as we recognize the responsibility and impact of our thinking and the resultant choices we make, which have ramifications right down to the ways in which the genes of our bodies express themselves.

8. Neurogenesis is the birth of new baby nerve cells.

PART 1

How to Switch On Your Brain

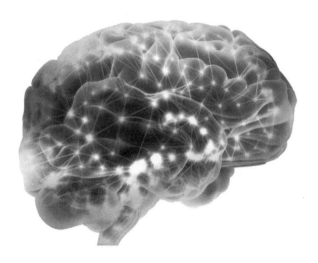

1

Mind Controls Matter

> **Main Scripture:** God has not given us a spirit of fear, but of power and of love and of a sound mind. 2 Timothy 1:7
>
> **Linked Science Concept:** Science shows we are wired for love with a natural optimism bias. This means exactly what the Scripture says above.

The debate in science is between the mind being what the brain does versus the brain doing the bidding of the mind. The position you adopt will impact how you view free will and choice.

The Mind Is What the Brain Does

The first argument proposes that thoughts come from your brain as though your brain is generating all aspects of your mental experience. People who hold this view are called the *materialists*. They believe that it is the chemicals and neurons that create the mind and that the relationships between your thoughts and what you do can just be ignored.

So essentially, their perspective is that the brain creates what you are doing and what you are thinking. The mind is what the brain does, they believe, and the ramifications are significant. Take, for example, the treatment of depression. In this reductionist view depression is a chemical imbalance problem of a machinelike brain; therefore, the treatment is to add in the missing chemicals.

This view is biblically and scientifically incorrect.

The Brain Does the Bidding of the Mind

Let's look at this from the other angle of the argument: The brain is what the mind does.

You are a thinking being. You think all day long, and at night as you sleep, you sort out your thinking. As you think, you choose, and as you choose, you cause genetic expression to happen in your brain. This means you make proteins, and these proteins form your thoughts. Thoughts are real, physical things that occupy mental real estate.

Eric R. Kandel, a Nobel Prize–winning neuropsychiatrist for his work on memory, shows how our thoughts, even our imaginations, get "under the skin" of our DNA and can turn certain genes on and certain genes off, changing the structure of the neurons in the brain.[1] So as we think and imagine, we change the structure and function of our brains. Even Freud speculated back in the 1800s that thought leads to changes in the brain.[2] In recent years, leading neuroscientists like Marion Diamond, Norman Doidge, Joe Dispenza, Jeffrey Schwartz, Henry Markram, Bruce Lipton, and Allan Jones, to name just a few, have shown how our thoughts have remarkable power to change the brain.[3] Our brain is changing moment by moment as we are thinking. By our thinking and choosing, we are redesigning the landscape of our brain.

Our mind is designed to control the body, of which the brain is a part, not the other way around. Matter does not control us; we control matter through our thinking and choosing. We cannot control the events and circumstances of life but we can control our reactions. In fact, we can control our reactions to anything, and in doing so, we change our brains. It's not easy; it is hard work, but it can be done through our thoughts and choices. This is what I focus on in the second half of the book with my 21-Day Brain Detox Plan.

For now, rest in the assurance that what God has empowered you to do with your mind is more powerful and effective than any medication, any threat, any sickness, or any neurological challenge. The Scripture is clear on this: You do not have a spirit of fear but of love, power, and a sound mind (2 Tim. 1:7). We are not bound by the physical; we control the physical. You just have to look at the many inspirational survival stories of those who have overcome impossible odds throughout history and in the current day to know this is truth.

Choices Are Real

You are free to make choices about how you focus your attention, and this affects how the chemicals and proteins and wiring of your brain change and function. Scientists are proving that the relationship between what you think and how you understand yourself—your beliefs, dreams, hopes, and thoughts—has a huge impact on how your brain works.

Research shows that 75 to 98 percent of mental, physical, and behavioral illness comes from one's thought life.[4]

This staggering and eye-opening statistic means only 2 to 25 percent of mental and physical illnesses come from the environment and genes.

Thinking Activates Genes

Every day scientists are discovering the precise pathways by which changes in human consciousness produce changes in our brain and bodies. Our consciousness—this phenomenal gift from God to be able to think—activates our genes and changes our brain. Science shows that our thoughts, with their embedded feelings, turn sets of genes on and off in complex relationships. We take facts, experiences, and the events of life, and assign meaning to them with our thinking.

We may have a fixed set of genes in our chromosomes, but which of those genes are active and *how* they are active has a great deal to do with how we think and process our experiences. Our thoughts produce words and behaviors, which in turn stimulate more thinking and choices that build more thoughts in an endless cycle.

Our Brains Are Shaped by Our Reactions

We are constantly reacting to circumstances and events, and as this cycle goes on, our brains become shaped by the process in either a positive, good-quality-of-life direction or a negative, toxic, poor-quality-of-life direction. So it is the quality of our thinking and choices (consciousness) and our reactions that determine our "brain architecture"—the shape or design of the brain and *resultant* quality of the health of our minds and bodies.

Science and Scripture both show that we are wired for love and optimism[5] and so when we react by thinking negatively

34

and making negative choices, the quality of our thinking suffers, which means the quality of our brain architecture suffers. It is comforting—and challenging—to know that negative thinking is not the norm.

Thinking Changes Our DNA

Taking this to a deeper level, research shows that *DNA actually changes shape according to our thoughts.* As you think those negative thoughts about the future—the week ahead, what a person might say or do, even in the absence of the concrete stimulus—that toxic thinking will change your brain wiring in a negative direction and throw your mind and body into stress.[6]

According to Dr. Herbert Benson, MD, president of Harvard Medical School's Mind-Body Institute, negative thinking leads to stress, which affects our body's natural healing capacities.[7]

Toxic thinking wears down the brain.

The Institute of HeartMath, an internationally recognized, nonprofit research organization that helps people reduce stress, discusses an experiment titled "Local and Nonlocal Effects of Coherent Heart Frequencies on Conformational Changes of DNA." This study showed that thinking and feeling anger, fear, and frustration caused DNA to change shape according to thoughts and feelings. The DNA responded by tightening up and becoming shorter, switching off many DNA codes, which reduced quality expression. So we feel shut down by negative emotions, and our body feels this too. But here's the great part: the negative shutdown or poor quality of the DNA codes was *reversed* by feelings of love, joy, appreciation, and gratitude! The researchers also found that HIV positive patients who had positive thoughts and feelings had 300,000 times more resistance to the disease than those without positive feelings.[8] So the takeaway here is that when we operate in our normal love design—which is being made in God's image (Gen. 1:26)—we are able to change the shape of our DNA for the better.

So when we make a poor-quality decision—when we choose to engage toxic thoughts (for example, unforgiveness, bitterness, irritation, or feelings of not coping)—we change the DNA and subsequent genetic expression, which then changes the shape of our brain wiring in a negative direction. This immediately puts the brain into protection mode, and the brain translates these poor-quality, toxic thoughts as negative stress. This stress then manifests in our bodies. But the most exciting part of this study was the hope it demonstrated because the positive attitude, the good choice, rewired everything back to the original healthy positive state. These scientists basically proved we can renew our minds.

Stress

Stress stage one is normal. This is our alert state that keeps us focused and conscious and is the state we are in when we are thinking in alignment with God. Stress stage two and stage three, however, are our mind and body's response to toxic thinking—normal stress gone wrong. Even a little bit of these negative levels of stress from a little bit of toxic thinking has far-reaching consequences for mental and physical health.

The dictionary defines *stress* as "a condition typically characterized by symptoms of mental and physical tension or strain, as depression or hypertension, that can result from a *reaction* to a situation in which a person feels threatened, pressured, etc."[9] Synonyms for stress include anxiety, nervousness, fearfulness, apprehensiveness, impatience, fear, tenseness, and restlessness.

Reaction is the key word here. *You cannot control the events or circumstances of your life, but you can control your reactions.* And controlling those reactions is the difference between healthy minds and bodies and sick minds and bodies.

Here are just a few statistics confirming that 75 to 98 percent of mental and physical illness comes from one's thought life:

- A study by the American Medical Association found that stress is a factor in 75 percent of all illnesses and diseases that people suffer from today.[10]
- The association between stress and disease is a colossal 85 percent.[11]
- The International Agency for Research on Cancer and the World Health Organization[12] have concluded that 80 percent of cancers are due to lifestyle and not genetics, and this is a conservative number.
- According to Dr. Bruce Lipton, a scientist who has made great strides in understanding the effect of our thinking on our brain,[13] gene disorders like Huntington's chorea, beta thalassemia, and cystic fibrosis, to name a few, affect less than 2 percent of the population. This means the vast majority of the world's population comes into this world with genes that should enable them to live happy and healthy lives. Lipton says a staggering 98 percent of diseases are related to lifestyle choices—in other words, our thinking.
- According to Dr. H. F. Nijhout,[14] genes control biology and not the other way around.
- According to W. C. Willett,[15] only 5 percent of cancer and cardiovascular patients can attribute their disease to hereditary factors.
- The American Institute of Health estimates that 75–90 percent of all visits to primary care physicians are for

stress-related problems.[16] Some of the latest negative stress statistics causing illness as a result of toxic thinking are eye-opening.

The main point of this chapter is that mind controls matter. If we get this right, we have enormous potential to reach peak health. If we get it wrong, we will be our own worst enemies.

Chapter 1 Summary

1. The debate in science is between the mind being what the brain does versus the brain doing the bidding of the mind.
2. The correct view is that the mind is designed to control the body, of which the brain is a part, not the other way around.
3. Our brain does not control us; we control our brain through our thinking and choosing.
4. We can control our reactions to anything.
5. Choices are real. You are free to make choices about how you focus your attention, and this affects how the chemicals, proteins, and wiring of your brain change and function.
6. Research shows that *DNA actually changes shape in response to our thoughts.*
7. Stress stage one is normal. Stress stage two and stage three, on the other hand, are our mind and body's response to toxic thinking—basically normal stress gone wrong.
8. *Reaction* is the key word here. You cannot control the events or circumstances of your life, but you can control your reactions.

2

Choice and Your Multiple-Perspective Advantage

Main Scripture: Let the peace (soul harmony which comes) from Christ rule (act as umpire continually) in your hearts [deciding and settling with finality all questions that arise in your minds, in that peaceful state] to which as [members of Christ's] one body you were also called [to live]. And be thankful (appreciative), [giving praise to God always]. Colossians 3:15 AMP

Linked Science Concept: Choice is real, and free will exists. You are able to stand outside of yourself, observe your own thinking, consult with God, and change the negative, toxic thought or grow the healthy, positive thought. When you do this, your brain responds with a positive neurochemical rush and structural changes that will improve your intellect, health, and peace. You will experience soul harmony.

These are obvious statements; however, many of us walk through life as though we are victims of the events and circumstances of life and biology and whatever or whomever else we can think of to blame. As a therapist for nearly twenty-two years and having reached millions of people through my seminars, books, and media appearances, the statements I make more than any others are these: "You are not a victim. You can control your reactions. You do have a choice."

Free Will Is Not an Illusion

All of us, including God-fearing Christians, fall prey to media proclamations by neuroscientists and researchers who make the news with such leading questions as, "Is free will an illusion?" The problem, however, is that this point of view cannot be reconciled with what we know about the human brain and what Scripture says about us as humans. In a *New York Times* article, a legal analyst even asked, "Because our brains cause all behavior, could all behavior be potentially excused?"[1]

This is dangerous thinking. They are basically saying that we are not responsible for our actions, which provides an excuse to do whatever we want to do with no consequences.

We must always remember that scientists are not God—though they sometimes act like they are. I am a scientist, and if I can't back up a scientific "fact" with Scripture, I question its validity.

Philosophers and scientists have long debated whether we have free will. Some argue free will is a quaint, old-fashioned idea. Of course, the mere fact that people debate this issue means they are using their free will to formulate their opinions and choose their answers. So they quite literally destroy their own argument.

A typical neuroscientist might argue that free decisions are determined ahead of time by brain activity. This argument says the brain is like a machine that has all these programs running, over which we have no control. This machine produces the mind, and we go through life helplessly at the will and mercy of these programs. Then neuroscientists use brain imaging and fancy terminology to argue that free will is just an illusion.

We Can Choose to Think the Way God Wants Us to Think

As a communication pathologist specializing in the field of cognitive neuroscience, my research is concerned mainly with how humans think and the impact of this thinking on what they say and do, and I have come to a very different conclusion from those who think free will is just an illusion. I'm convinced beyond all doubt that our God-given ability to think and choose means that our free will influences our thinking, which produces our state of mind. This is so important to human behavior and potential that I have dedicated my life to understanding the process of thought and how we can choose to think the way God wants us to think. Far from explaining away free will, the neuroscientific evidence actually explains how free will works.

Molecular biologist Francis Crick, who won a Nobel Prize in 1962 with James Watson for their discovery of DNA in 1953, said free will is "a simple-minded bit of confabulation" and dismissed it as "an exercise in self-delusion."[2] In making this statement, Crick overlooked something important: *He chose with his free will* to formulate that thought and express it.

Proving Free Will

Brain activity can be identified in the prefrontal cortex (just above the eyebrows) and parietal cortex (top side of your

41

head) seven to ten seconds before an actual decision is verbal-
ized or enacted. Many scientists use this fact to argue that
the decision was already encoded.[3] I see it differently, and I
am in good company with scientists like Jeffrey Schwartz,
Norman Doidge, and others.

My argument is that this brain activity is the processing
activity we do unconsciously, on the very real and active
nonconscious level (see chap. 8), which is flavored by the
thoughts—memories—we have implanted into our nonconscious minds over time. In this phase we choose to add our
own unique perception, based on these implanted thoughts
that form our point of view, on our way to verbalization or
action we perform. So in simple terms, what we say and do
is based on what we have already built into our minds. We
evaluate this information and make our choices based on this
information, then we choose to build a new thought, and this
is what drives what we say or do.

This brain activity, seen in brain imaging, is not the result
of machine-like activity; it is simply the build-up to the moment of consciousness. It is the activity of a network of neural
circuits that begin to prepare for an upcoming decision long
before it enters our awareness. It is the intellectualizing that is
happening in the nonconscious mind. In other words, "As he
thinks in his heart, so is he" (Prov. 23:7). We are not driven by
forces beyond our conscious control. We are accountable for
every thought and decision we make.[4] We are highly intelligent
beings with free will, and we are responsible for our choices.

Some forward-thinking researchers have found that when
people doubt free will, they become more dishonest. It is
almost as though denying free will provides the ultimate excuse to behave however people want without accountability
for their actions.[5]

42

Other researchers found that believing in free will guides people's choices toward being more moral and better performers. They go so far as to say that the more researchers investigate free will, the more reasons there are to believe in it, and that to an extent those who believe otherwise delude themselves.

Ecclesiastes 7:29 (NLT) says it like this: "God created people to be virtuous, but they have each turned to follow their own downward path." A standard definition of free will is a "set of capacities for imagining future courses of action, deliberating about one's reason for choosing them, planning one's actions in light of this deliberation and controlling actions in the face of competing desires."[6] This, I believe, is how we choose to follow either God's path or Satan's path.

Science is proving free will right down to the genetic level. Let's take a look at some of the evidence.

Choice Has Mental *Real Estate*

Choice has mental "real estate" around the front of the brain. It includes many circuits that start at the basal forebrain (between your eyebrows) and extend back across the frontal lobe, which is capable of an impressive array of functions and is connected to all other parts of the brain. It is also where connections from all the other parts of the brain converge. Specific circuits go to structures like the insula, corpus callosum, anterior and posterior central gyrus, basal ganglia, precuneus, and subgenuel region of the brain.[7] This arrangement enables the frontal lobe to integrate and manage activities in the other parts of the brain.

We Can Observe Our Own Thoughts

One of the most exciting features of frontal lobes is how they enable us in a sense to stand outside ourselves and observe

Inside the Brain

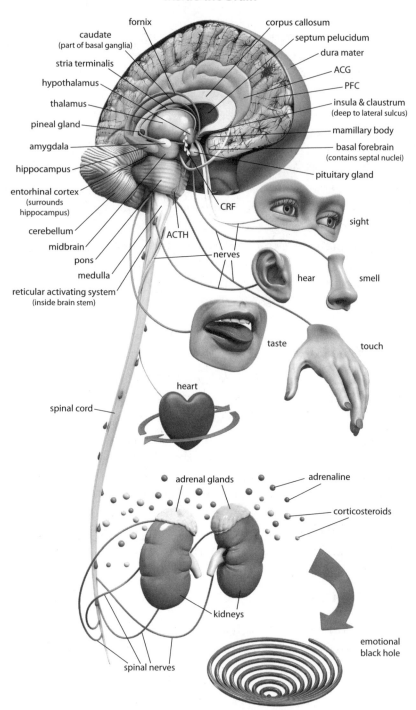

fornix

caudate
(part of basal ganglia)

stria terminalis

hypothalamus

thalamus

pineal gland

amygdala

hippocampus

entorhinal cortex
(surrounds
hippocampus)

cerebellum

midbrain

pons

medulla

reticular activating system
(inside brain stem)

spinal cord

corpus callosum

septum pelucidum

dura mater

ACG

PFC

insula & claustrum
(deep to lateral sulcus)

mamillary body

basal forebrain
(contains septal nuclei)

pituitary gland

CRF

ACTH

nerves

sight

hear

smell

taste

touch

heart

adrenal glands

adrenaline

corticosteroids

kidneys

spinal nerves

emotional
black hole

our own thinking. We can observe our thoughts and actions and make decisions about them. Suddenly, biblical principles such as "bringing all thoughts into captivity," "renewing your mind," "casting all your cares," and "being anxious for nothing" become less difficult when we realize God has given us the equipment to do these things.

When we choose life (Deut. 30:19), the diamond increases its shine; when we choose anything other than life, the diamond loses its shine. This is a simple analogy of what happens in the brain. The wrong choices cause brain damage. The right choices enhance brain function.

Our MPA

We have what I like to call "multiple-perspective advantage"—MPA for short. Our unique, multifaceted nature, made in God's image, allows us to see things from many different angles—like different perspectives. We have the unique opportunity to assess our thoughts and their impact and choose to connect to the vine that is Christ (John 15:1–5)—to restore growth and prune off the branches of toxic thinking.

We are directly responsible for what we choose to think about and dwell on, and we make these decisions in the privacy of our own thinking. As you think, it is important to make a distinction between who you truly are—the real, multifaceted, unique you—and the person you have become through toxic choices. Fortunately, you can see both and choose to reconnect with the vine (John 15) and renew your mind (Rom. 12:2). Your brain will follow the instructions and choices of your mind and change its landscape accordingly. Part 2 of this book will help you do just that.

The Seven Different Types of Thinking

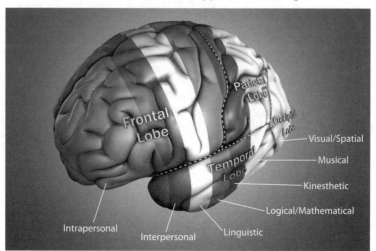

You Are a Thinking Being

Let's go deeper into the brain to see how influential and real your free will and choices are. You are a thinking being; you think all day long, and you are even thinking while you sleep. Daytime thinking is a building process, whereas nighttime thinking is a sorting process. As you think, you are making your way to a decision of some kind, whether it's as simple as what to eat or as complex as choosing one of several different courses of action you face.

All Thinking Activity Is Real

All this thinking activity is real, and it can be seen on various types of brain imaging. When we think, marvelous, wondrously complex, and creative things take place. Even if you don't fully understand what I am saying in the next few paragraphs, be in awe of how intricately God has made us.

46

Just the mind activity from your reading of the next few lines generates electromagnetic, electrochemical, and quantum action in your neurons. It causes

- magnetic fields that can be measured;
- electrical impulses that can be tracked;
- chemical effects that can be seen and measured;
- photons to be activated that can be captured on computer screens;
- energy activity that can be explained using quantum physics; and
- vibrations in the membranes of the neurons that can be picked up by instrumentation.

This combined activity sets up an intricate and organized sequence of actions of neurotransmitters, proteins, and energy that forms a signal. Your thinking has just created a powerful signal that is going to change the landscape of your brain.

You Create Signals

This signal you have just created passes through the membrane of the cell, travels to the cell's nucleus, and enters the chromosome, activating a strand of DNA. The DNA is zipped up, almost as though it is in a cocoon, until activated or unzipped by the signal. When the DNA is zipped up, it is in a dormant or inert state. This cocoon also protects the DNA from the rest of the intracellular environment while in this inert state.

So, the zipped up DNA has to be opened so that the appropriate genetic code needed to build the protein can be read. As it is opened and the code is read, RNA (a type of protein that almost acts like a photocopier) makes a *photocopy* of the code, which serves as a guide or architectural plan to build the proteins within the *machinery* inside the cell. This is called "genetic expression." And these proteins you have caused to be built hold the information you have just read as a thought or a memory. You have created substance.

Molecules are assembled into protein by the genetic instructions in our DNA. These instructions dictate the anatomy and physiology of our bodies, and we control up to 90 percent of this process through our thinking.

While scientists have brilliantly mapped the whole sequence of gene expression and protein assembly, they have given very little attention to the signals that get the whole thing going in the first place.[8]

The Signal That Unzips DNA

Let's take a closer look at these signals.

1. The initiating signals that get the ball rolling come from outside the DNA and are therefore called *epigenetic phenomena*, which means signals that control the genes, so they are *epi*—or over and above—the genes.[9]

2. When there is interference with this signal (for example, thinking a toxic thought or eating unhealthy food), genetic expression does not happen correctly and then proteins do not form like they should. So, on a very simplified level, if you have a toxic thought, the resulting proteins look different and act differently than if you had a healthy thought.

3. These signals are electromagnetic and chemical because there is an electromagnetic and chemical component to every biological process.

4. These signals can come from the environment inside the body—the emotional, biochemical, mental, energy, and spiritual, including from the thought networks inside your brain. Or they can come from the environment outside the body—the food, toxins, social network, and nurturing you receive.[10]

Researchers estimate that about 90 percent of genes in the DNA are working with these signals from these outer and inner environments.[11]

The Switch Gene

One of the many amazing things Kandel discovered was that we have a *switch gene* called the "creb gene," which we *choose* to switch on with our thoughts. So our thoughts are the signal I am talking about in the paragraph above. I wish I could delve further into this fascinating topic, but it is a highly complex process and beyond the purpose of this book, which is not meant to be a scientific tome. However, it is still worth a brief and simple mention because it highlights how God built choice into every sophisticated detail of our being and, once again, gives us the opportunity to admire him.

Here is a simple explanation of this switch gene: As information in the form of electromagnetic and chemical signals moves toward the front part of the brain, it becomes amplified and highly active. This stimulates the release of specialized proteins inside the cell, turning on the creb gene, which acts like a light switch that we choose to switch on or off by our thoughts. This switch creb gene then activates genetic expression (the making of proteins), and we *grow* protein branches that hold our memories, which can also be called our thoughts.[12] So when we choose to switch on the creb gene because of the thoughts we allow to permeate our brain, protein synthesis happens and a new branch grows and makes a connection at a synapse to other branches.

What Does All This Science Mean to You?

All this scientific and biological information is to say two things:

1. Scientific investigation is a way of admiring God. We admire God's grace and greatness when we get a glimpse at how he has made us and constructed the world we live in. This can give us a sense of peace that he is in control.

2. Scientists are discovering precise pathways by which changes in human thinking operate as signals that activate genetic expression, which then produce changes in our brains and bodies. Our genetic makeup fluctuates by the minute based on what we are thinking and choosing. Clearly, then, following the advice of Philippians 4:8 will have a profound healing and regenerative impact on our bodies and minds by affecting our genetic expression: "Finally, brothers and sisters, whatever is true, whatever is noble, whatever is right, whatever is pure, whatever is lovely, whatever is admirable—if anything is excellent or praiseworthy—think about such things" (NIV). Make this truth your life choice.

What Does the Future of Medicine Potentially Hold?

Eric Kandel, the Nobel Prize winner for his research on memory, says the following concerning treating patients in the future: "Social influences will be biologically incorporated into the altered expression of specific genes in specific nerve cells of specific areas of the brain."[13] So a time is coming when medical practitioners will include admonitions like Philippians 4:8 and Romans 12:2 on their prescription pads. Part 2 of this book is designed to help you apply God's prescription.

From the Gene Myth to the Truth

We have been living under a myth called the *gene myth*, which locates the ultimate power over health and mental well-being in the untouchable realm of genes, relegating them to the level of gods. This myth has bound the mental and physical health as well as the peace and happiness of too many people for too long. Almost daily another headline pops up with the highly fashionable concept of a gene for this or a gene for that. You are an alcoholic or depressed or battle with learning disabilities because you have the gene for alcoholism or depression or learning disabilities or whatever. Genes may create an environment within us in which a problem may grow, a predisposition, but they do not produce the problem; we produce it through our choices. Our choices act as the signals that unzip the DNA, which I spoke about earlier in this chapter.

Genes have been made out to be responsible for feelings, spirituality, beliefs—even things like the enjoyment of music—all human behavior, to the extent of determining human affairs, human relationships, and social problems.[14] In fact, genetic predisposition has become entrenched in popular

51

culture to the extent that phrases like "she has good genes" and "he was born that way" are commonplace.

This thinking removes choice and accountability from the equation and is scientifically and spiritually inaccurate. You control your genes; your genes do not control you. Genes may determine physical characteristics but not psychological phenomena. On the contrary, our genes are constantly being remodeled in response to life experiences.[15]

Outstanding research has recently been done by Dr. Gail Ironson, a leading mind-body medicine researcher and professor of psychology and psychiatry at the University of Miami.[16] She found that the most significant factor that made a difference in healing for those with HIV was their choice to believe in a benevolent and loving God, especially if they also chose to have a personal relationship with a benevolent and loving God. Her study ran over four years and her determination of healing was based on the decrease of their viral load, the amount of the AIDS virus in a sample of blood, and the increased concentration of "helper T-cells"— the higher the concentration, the more the body is able to fight disease. She found that those who did not believe God loved them lost helper T-cells three times faster. Their viral load also increased three times faster, and their stress levels were higher, with damaging amounts of cortisol flowing. Dr. Ironson summarizes her research by saying, "If you believe God loves you, it's an enormously protective factor, even more protective than scoring low for depression or high for optimism. A view of a benevolent God is protective, but scoring high on the *personalized* statement 'God loves *me*' is even stronger."[17]

As you can imagine, the implications of this research are enormous, from how we present ourselves to others to how we help others and ourselves manage illness. Our choices have an impact. Our choices become *physiology*, and what we believe as well as what we believe about ourselves alters the facts.

We are not victims of our biology. We are co-creators of our destiny alongside God. God leads, but we have to choose to let God lead. We have been designed to create thoughts, and from these we live out our lives (Prov. 23:7).

Hebrews 11:1 says, "Faith is the substance of things hoped for, the evidence of things not seen." Whatever you believe in and hope for becomes substance on a physical level, and you act upon this. This process can move in either direction—negative or positive.

In the next chapter we look more in depth at the impact of our choices and how to eliminate toxic choices.

Chapter 2 Summary

1. You are not a victim. You can control your reactions. You do have a choice.

2. Free will is not an illusion. Thinking it is an illusion is dangerous thinking, and it basically says that we are not responsible for our actions, thus providing an excuse to do whatever we want to do, with no consequences.

3. Our free will influences our thinking, which produces our state of mind. This is so important to human behavior and potential that I have dedicated my life to understanding the process of thought and how we can choose to think the way God wants us to think. Far from explaining away free will, the neuroscientific evidence actually explains how free will works.

4. What we say and do is based on what we have already built into our minds. We evaluate this information and

make our choices based on this information. Then we choose to build a new thought, and this is what drives what we say and do.

5. Choice has mental *real estate* around the front of the brain. Certain areas light up when we think and choose.

6. One of the most exciting features of frontal lobes is how they enable us in a sense to stand outside ourselves and observe our own thinking.

7. We have what I like to call "multiple-perspective advantage"—MPA for short. Our unique, multifaceted nature, made in God's image, allows us to see things from many different angles or perspectives.

8. All this thinking activity is real, and it can be seen on various types of brain imaging.

9. This *thinking* creates signals that unzip the DNA, which then expresses genes making proteins.

10. We have a switch gene called the "creb gene" that we choose to switch on with our thoughts.

11. Our genetic makeup fluctuates by the minute based on what we are thinking and choosing.

12. A time is coming when medical practitioners will include admonitions like Philippians 4:8 and Romans 12:2 on their prescription pads. Part 2 of this book is designed to help you apply God's prescription.

13. From the gene myth to the truth: We are not victims of our biology; we control our biology.

3

Your Choices
Change Your Brain

Main Scripture: Do not conform to the pattern of this world, but be transformed by the renewing of your mind. Then you will be able to test and approve what God's will is—his good, pleasing and perfect will. Romans 12:2 NIV

Linked Science Concept: Through our thoughts we can be our own micro surgeons as we make choices that will change the circuits in our brains. We are designed to do our own brain surgery and rewire our brains by thinking and by choosing to renew our minds.

Our choices—the natural consequences of our thoughts and imagination—get "under the skin" of our DNA and can turn certain genes on and off, changing the structure of the neurons in our brains. So our thoughts, imagination, and choices can change the structure and function of our brains on every level: molecular, genetic, epigenetic, cellular, structural, neurochemical, electromagnetic, and even subatomic. Through our thoughts, we can be our own brain surgeons as we make choices that change the circuits in our brains. We are designed to do our own brain surgery.

This scientific power of our mind to change the brain is called *epigenetics* and spiritually it is as a man thinks, so is he (Prov. 23:7). The way the brain changes as a result of mental activity is scientifically called *neuroplasticity*. And spiritually, it is the renewing of the mind (Rom. 12:2).

In chapter 2, I introduced you to the science of epigenetics, which is tangible, scientific proof of how important our choices are; they bring life or death, blessing or cursing; and they reach beyond us to influence the next generations (Deut. 30:19). This is because choices become signals that change our brain and body, so these changes are not dictated by our genes. Our thinking and subsequent choices become the signal switches for our genes. What's incredible is that genes are dormant until switched on by a signal; they have potential, but they have to be activated to release that potential. They have to be unzipped. (See chap. 2.)

Epigenetics Is an Ancient Science and Spiritual Truth

Epigenetics is referred to as a new science, but actually it is an ancient science that we find throughout the Bible. At its most basic level, epigenetics is the fact that your thoughts and choices impact your physical brain and body, your mental health, and your spiritual development (Deut. 30:19; Ps. 34:11–16; Prov. 3:7–8). And these choices will impact not only your *own* spirit, soul, and body but also the people with whom you have relationships. In fact, it goes even deeper; your choices might impact the generations that follow: "For the sin of the parents to the third and fourth generation" (Exod. 34:7 NIV; see also Exod. 20:1–6; Num. 14:8; Deut. 5:9).

The decisions you make today become part of the thought networks in your brain. The two copies of the chromosome that you carry in each of your cells contain the entire set of genetic material necessary to make you. An interesting point: A cell in your brain and a cell in your kidney contain the exact same DNA. And while in utero (in the womb), the nascent (emerging, developing) cells differentiate into either a brain cell or a kidney cell *only* when crucial epigenetic processes turn the right genes on or off. So God has designed perfectly timed epigenetic signals to switch on in the womb as the baby is developing. "Before I formed you in the womb I knew you" (Jer. 1:5).

Our Thoughts Can Impact the Next Four Generations

Science has demonstrated how the thought networks pass through the sperm and the ova via DNA to the next four generations.

One of the first studies showing that an epigenetic signal can affect genetic expression was done with mice that had the agouti gene, which caused them to be fat, have a yellow coat, and have an increased incidence of cancer and diabetes. When the agouti gene occurs in humans, it is related to obesity and type 2 diabetes. In the experiment, just before conception, the agouti mother mice were fed a nutritional chemical called a methyl group in the form of a B vitamin. This acts as a methyl donor, which suppresses the gene expression, with the result that the offspring of this group did not get fat or yellow. So an external signal—the nutritional methyl—changed the generational pattern.[1]

This landmark study fostered a host of studies—including some done on humans—that showed that not only does food change generational patterns, but so does thinking.[2] In 2003 the Human Epigenome project was launched, which showed that epigenetics had moved from being a sideshow back in the 1970s to what is now a main show in the biological arena, putting genetics in a more proportional place.[3]

Scientific Mysteries

Epigenetics explains certain scientific mysteries that traditional genetics never could—for example, why one member of a pair of identical twins develops asthma but the other does not. They have the same genome, so they should respond the same way, but their individual perception of the world (what I term the "I-factor") as well as their ability to choose means they think and react differently, which alters their genetic expression. Although their genes are the same, their *patterns of expression can be tweaked* through the signal. And this signal is mainly affected by our reaction to the events and circumstances of life. This is profound and the implications are enormous: the way we react—our thinking and choosing—becomes the signal that activates or deactivates the generational issues in our lives.

The Good, the Bad, and the Ugly

Taken collectively, the studies on epigenetics show us that the good, the bad, and the ugly do come down through the generations, but your mind is the signal—the epigenetic factor—that switches these genes on or off. Therefore, you are not destined to live out the negative patterns of your forebearers—you can instead make a life choice to overcome by tweaking their patterns of expression. Part 2 of this book will show you how.

Taking this further, the Scriptures that tell us the sins of the parents will reach to the third and fourth generation (Exod. 20:5; 34:7; Num. 14:18) seem to imply that we are responsible for the unconfessed sins of our great-great-grandparents. But we can breathe a sigh of relief when we read Deuteronomy 24:16 and Ezekiel 18:19–20, which explain that we are each responsible for our own sins and not those of our ancestors.

I know this seems confusing, because the Scriptures say that, on the one hand, a parent's iniquity will be visited on the children, but, on the other hand, we are only responsible for our own sins. Here is how it works: Epigenetic changes represent a biological response to an environmental signal. That response can be inherited through the generations via the epigenetic marks. But if you remove the signal, the epigenetic marks will fade.

By the same token, if you choose to add a signal—for example, saying something like, "My mother had depression and that's why I have depression, and now my daughter is suffering from depression"—then the epigenetic marks are activated. The thinking and speaking out the problem serve as the signal that makes it a reality. I have seen this over the years in my private practice and in my seminars, and even in my own life and the lives of my family and friends, time and time again. If we don't wake up to these truths, they will catch us when we are not looking, and before you know it you will be living a life you didn't plan on living. If this is you, here is the good news: You *can* change.

Predisposition versus Destiny

Herein lies the key: The sins of parents create a *predisposition*, not a *destiny*. You are not responsible for something you are predisposed to because of ancestral decisions. You are responsible, however, to be aware of predispositions, evaluate them, and choose to eliminate them.

The epigenetic marks in our genes that may predispose us to smoke, eat too much of the wrong foods, be negative, or worry can change. This can cause, for example, the genes for obesity to express too strongly or the genes that control stress reactions to switch off, shortening your life as well as decreasing your quality of life and your peace (soul harmony) and happiness. We also are responsible for our own choices and can apply the work of the cross and confess, repent, and eliminate future sinful choices.

In addition, our choices (the epigenetic signals) alter the expression of genes (the epigenetic markers), which can then be passed on to our children and grandchildren, ready to predispose them before they are even conceived. So our bad choices become their bad predispositions.

The negative alternative is that you can choose to accept the predispositions and live into them, but don't forget that you have to take responsibility for that as well. This very act of accepting the predispositions and living into them becomes the signal that activates you to become *a fat and yellow agouti mouse*. Just the addition of a methyl group signal changes the life of the offspring of the agouti mice. In the same way, the addition of a positive attitude signal or a memorized and meditated-upon Scripture signal can change the expression of the gene.

What your mind creates only your mind can take away.

Scientific Evidence of God's Grace

Another scientific piece of evidence of God's grace can be seen in a structure in the middle of the brain called the *hippocampus*. This seahorse-shaped structure, which processes incoming information, facilitates the conversion of short-term memory to long-term memory, deals with spatial memory, and also helps control our stress response.

Scientists have found that in a loving and nurturing environment, acetyl epigenetic markers increase on the genes in the hippocampus that keep us calm and peaceful. The more acetyl markers, the more these *peace genes* in the hippocampus express and dampen the stress response. A toxic choice produces the opposite effect: The acetyl markers reduce and the methyl markers increase, causing us to have less peace.[4]

So the methyl markers switch off genetic expression and acetyl markers switch on genetic expression. The "switching on or off" is based on the signal, and we can choose to switch. Sometimes we want to switch off—for example switching off the obesity genes in the agouti mice and human research. But we want to switch on good genetic expression—for example the stress control gene in the hippocampus. Whether we switch on happiness, peace, and good health or switch on anxiety, worry, and negativity, we are changing the physical substance of the brain.

The Brain Reorganizes throughout Our Lifetime

In 1930, Santiago Ramón y Cajal[5] wrote that the nerve pathways are fixed and immutable, but now scientists know that the brain has the amazing ability to reorganize throughout life, changing its structure and function through mental experience alone. If the brain can get worse by constantly focusing on the problem, then the brain can get better by understanding how to eliminate and replace the problem.[6]

Inside the Brain

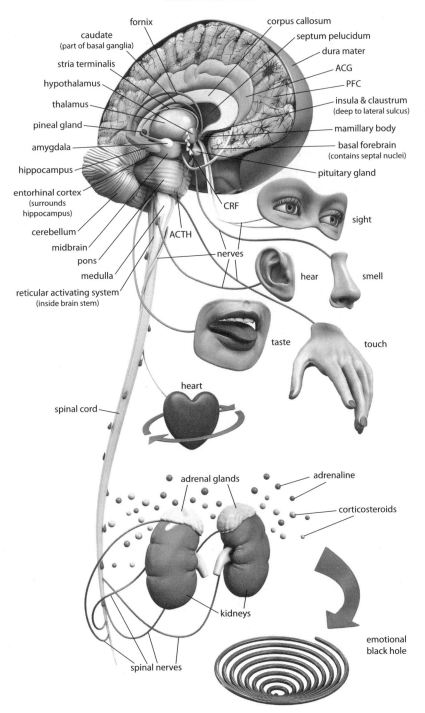

fornix
caudate (part of basal ganglia)
stria terminalis
hypothalamus
thalamus
pineal gland
amygdala
hippocampus
entorhinal cortex (surrounds hippocampus)
cerebellum
midbrain
pons
medulla
reticular activating system (inside brain stem)
spinal cord

corpus callosum
septum peludicum
dura mater
ACG
PFC
insula & claustrum (deep to lateral sulcus)
mamillary body
basal forebrain (contains septal nuclei)
pituitary gland

CRF
ACTH
nerves

sight
hear
smell
taste
touch

heart

adrenal glands
adrenaline
corticosteroids

kidneys

spinal nerves

emotional black hole

The Neuroplasticity Paradox

So neuroplasticity can operate for us as well as against us, because whatever we think about the most will grow—this applies to both the positive and negative ends of the spectrum. For example, in post-traumatic stress disorder (PTSD), neuroplasticity has worked against the person. He or she has experienced a crushing mental event that fundamentally changed the meaning of their life and altered the brain structurally because of the neuroplasticity of the brain. During the trauma, the person's mind was not thinking in soul harmony (Col. 3:15 AMP), so consequently he or she did not choose, process, or react correctly to the event—making the thought that became wired in a jumbled toxic mess. As the person relives the event over and over, it wires itself deeper into the mind, becoming a main filter and disrupting normal function.[7] Flashbacks—reliving the bad memory many times a day—strengthen the circuit, making it worse and more debilitating.

We Can Use Neuroplasticity to Renew Our Minds

How do we fix this? In part 2, I will explain this in depth and supply a simple explanation and a chart of my theory in chapter 8, "The Geodesic Information Processing Theory,"[8] upon which my approach is based. The overriding concept is to apply neuroplasticity in the correct direction by rewiring the event with the positive thinking of Philippians 4:8: "Finally, brothers, whatever is true, whatever is honorable, whatever is just, whatever is pure, whatever is lovely, whatever is commendable, if there is any excellence, if there is anything worthy of praise, think about these things" (ESV).

Thus the person consciously chooses, preferably under the leading of the Holy Spirit, to bring the memory into consciousness where it becomes plastic enough to actually be changed.

This means the physical substrate of the memory becomes weakened, vulnerable, malleable, and able to be manipulated. The person then chooses to replace the crushing mental event with the implanted word of God, which saves the soul (James 1:21). The person, as though an outsider looking in through a window, will observe the toxic, traumatic memory as a weakening and dying experience but, at the same time, observe the new healthy experience that is growing. In practicing this daily, the person wires the healthy new thoughts ever more deeply into the mind.

Neurons that don't get enough signal (the rehearsing of the negative event) will start firing apart, wiring apart, pulling out, and destroying the emotion attached to the trauma. In addition, certain chemicals like oxytocin (bonds and remolds chemicals), dopamine (increases focus and attention), and serotonin (increases feelings of peace and happiness) all start flowing around the traumatic thoughts, weakening them even more. This all helps to disconnect and desynchronize the neurons; if they stop firing together, they will no longer wire together. This leads to wiping out or popping those connections and rebuilding new ones. I explain the practical side of this process in part 2.

More Encouragement from Science

There are even more encouraging pieces of information about neuroplasticity. For example, Universalists believe logic and language are learned at fixed ages, and if you pass that fixed age, you can't learn. Plasticity research proves them wrong.[9] People with learning disabilities can rewire their brains to perceive sound better.[10] My own patients with brain injuries and learning and emotional disabilities, as well as the teachers and students I have worked with in schools, showed significant changes when they did the mental training in my Switch On Your Brain technique.[11]

The media creates incorrect perceptions of scientific discoveries. They may cover a study that sensationalizes that our brain does x, therefore you will do x, as though you cannot think for yourself. This is so wrong. Those who believe you are just your brain believe you have no free will. The active mind changes the brain; the brain is the passive part of existence. As we think, we are making the brain fire in different patterns and combinations, and whenever we make the brain fire differently, we change the brain. Epigenetics research demonstrates that our lifestyles and environment can transform the way our genes are expressed, and evidence from this field shows us we are not being controlled by the structure of our brains.[12]

One brain generates more energy (electrical impulses) in one day than all the cell phones on the planet.[13] So we have the power to make changes; we do not have a spirit of fear, but of love, power, and a sound mind (see 2 Tim. 1:7). Our default mind mode—our soul, which is our intellect, will, and emotions—is powerful, strong, and driven by principles of love. Don't let the media, doctors, or other people in your life convince you otherwise. You have the power in your mind to change the negative, toxic manifestations. Our minds shape the world. This is what neuroplasticity is all about: change. Neuroplasticity is God's design for renewing the mind.

Our Perceptions Count

Our perception of the environment plus how we manage our environment controls our bodies and lives. So if you change your perception, you change your biology. You become the master of your life instead of a victim. But don't do it without Christ; remember, he is the vine from which we grow (John 15:5). The billion-dollar self-help industry does not have sustainability[14] because it misses the basic elements required for success and change: Primarily, it is not connected to the vine. These practitioners try to teach successful living without the originator of successful living: God. Secondly, there is a lot of visualization and verbalizations in their advice, but the intent of the heart is not considered, leaving a disconnect between what is being said and what is really believed and felt deep down. This is called cognitive dissonance. Thirdly, there is often very little real action involved. Action on both a spiritual and scientific level is required for change to take place.

Research also shows that there is a negative side to positive self-statements and affirmations, showing that individuals with low self-esteem felt worse after repeating positive self-statements.[15] Don't become part of that statistic.

The world may tell us that the mind is what the brain does, but God tells us that the brain will do what the mind tells it to do. And when your spirit, under the leading of the Holy Spirit, controls your soul, then the gold standard of thinking is achieved. This is a very different perspective from the traditional view, which tells us we are machines that just need parts changed and chemicals added. Choices are real; you are free to make choices about how you focus your attention, and this affects how the chemicals and wiring of your brain change and function.

Scientists are now proving that the relationship between you and how you understand and perceive your inner thought life, your community, and God has a huge impact on how your brain works.[16] Moment by moment of each day you can choose who you will be in the next moment, and these choices are captured in the resultant thought networks you build. In that process, the precepts of Scripture should be the overarching, undergirding, and foundational framework. They should be so entrenched that our attention is viewed through them and them alone as we form a view of ourselves that God created us to be.

Personally, my spiritual life informs my scientific life. As Joshua 1:8 says, insight, mindfulness, and wisdom come through meditation on God's truth versus rote study of information. I want to shape my world around God's truth because I know as a scientist and a believer, paying attention to my thoughts and purposefully focusing my mind leads to great transformations.

You Have the Power to Change

Your patterns of genetic experience don't determine what you are; you do. How you live, the cultural environment you live in, whatever you immerse yourself in, your beliefs and the beliefs of those around you, how you interact with those people, your faith and how you grow it, what you expose yourself to—all of these lead to differences in the way you focus your attention and have a direct effect on how your proteins are synthesized, how your enzymes act, and how your neurochemicals work together. If you don't believe you have the power to change your thoughts and control your choices, you are not going to do it.

Doing your own brain surgery or neuroplastic intervention of toxic thinking and renewing your mind is based on regular exercising of your brain; change takes place over time through continual persistence. Intervention of the mind changes the brain physically, chemically, structurally, and functionally. Research shows there is no more effective way to produce localized and specific changes in the brain than behavioral or mental intervention. Since psychosocial factors modulate the course of certain diseases—such as cardiovascular disease, diabetes, and asthma—this means the things going on in the environment get into the mind, changing the brain and having an impact on the body. So it is vital for us to pay attention to the precepts laid down in God's Word. Understanding how God designed neuroplasticity to work for and against us will help us move forward.

Chapter 3 Summary

1. Our thoughts, imagination, and choices can change the structure and function of our brains on every level: molecular, genetic, epigenetic, cellular, structural, neurochemical, and electromagnetic, and even subatomic. Through our thoughts, we can be our own brain surgeons as we make choices that change the circuits in our brain. We are designed to do our own brain surgery.

2. Choices become signals that change our brain and body, and these changes are not necessarily dictated by our genes.

3. Epigenetics is referred to as a new science, but actually it is an ancient science that we find throughout the Bible. At its most basic level, epigenetics is the fact that your thoughts and choices impact your physical brain and body, your mental health, and your spiritual development.

4. These choices will affect not only your *own* spirit, soul, and body but also the people with whom you have

68

relationships. In fact, it goes even deeper: Your choices might impact the generations that follow.

5. The landmark study on agouti mice fostered a host of studies—including some done on humans—that show that not only does food change generational patterns, but so does thinking.

6. Taken collectively, these studies show us that the good, the bad, and the ugly do come down through the generations. But your mind is the signal—the epigenetic factor—that switches these genes on or off.

7. Therefore, you are not destined to live out the negative patterns of your forebearers, but you can instead make a life choice to overcome them by tweaking their expression. In part 2 of this book I will show you how.

8. Epigenetic changes represent a biological response to an environmental signal. That response can be inherited through the generations via the epigenetic marks. But if you remove the signal, the epigenetic marks will fade. If you choose to add a signal, then the epigenetic marks are activated.

9. Herein lies the key: The sins of parents can create a *predisposition*, not a *destiny*. You are not responsible for something you are predisposed to because of ancestral decisions. You are responsible, however, to be aware of them, evaluate those predispositions, and choose to eliminate them.

10. When you make a bad choice, genes switch on in the hippocampus that dampen the stress response.

11. Scientists now know that the brain has the amazing ability to reorganize throughout life, changing its structure and function through thinking alone.

12. Neuroplasticity (the ability of the brain to change in response to thinking) can operate for you as well as against you because whatever you think about the most will grow. This applies to both the positive and negative ends of the spectrum.

13. Our perception of the environment plus how we manage our environment controls our bodies and lives. So if you change your perception, you change your biology. You become the master of your life instead of a victim.

4

Catch Those Thoughts

Main Scripture: We destroy arguments and every lofty opinion raised against the knowledge of God, and take every thought captive to obey Christ. 2 Corinthians 10:5 ESV

Linked Science Concept: When you objectively observe your own thinking with the view to capturing rogue thoughts, you in effect direct your attention to stop the negative impact and rewire healthy new circuits into your brain.

The ability to quiet your mind, focus your attention on the present issue, capture your thoughts, and dismiss the distractions that come your way is an excellent and powerful ability that God has placed within you. In the busy age we live in, however, we have trained ourselves out of this natural and necessary skill. *Natural* because it is wired into the design of the brain, allowing the brain to capture and discipline chaotic rogue thoughts; *necessary* because it calms our spirits so we can tune in and listen to God. When we are mindful of catching our thoughts in this way, we change our connection with God from uninvolved and independent to involved and dependent.

Research dating back to the 1970s shows that capturing our thoughts in a disciplined way rather than letting them chaotically run rampant can bring about impressive changes in how we feel and think. This change is evidenced in cognitive, emotional functioning as well as at the neural level.[1] My research shows that controlled focused thinking leads to impressive improvement in cognitive functioning and emotional balance.[2]

Freeing Yourself from Burdens

Getting your thoughts disciplined and under control is one of the first steps in freeing yourself of the burdens of the world and beginning to enjoy life despite the burdens of the world.

When you objectively observe your own thinking with the view to capturing rogue thoughts, you in effect direct your attention to stop the negative impact and rewire healthy new circuits into your brain. Second Corinthians 10:3–5 is so clear in the instructions on this matter: "For though we live in the world, we do not wage war as the world does. The weapons we fight with are not the weapons of the world. On the contrary, they have divine power to demolish strongholds. We demolish arguments and every pretension that sets itself up against the knowledge of God, and we take captive every thought to make it obedient to Christ" (NIV). In Proverbs 4:20–22 the sage advice is to "give attention to my words; incline your ear to my sayings. Do not let them depart from your eyes; keep them in the midst of your heart; for they are life to those who find them, and health to all their flesh."

The primary success of capturing your thoughts will be to focus on God's way first, not the world's ways. And science is showing that meditating on the elements of Jesus's teachings rewires healthy new circuits in the brain.

Science Shows the Benefits of Catching Your Thoughts

When you make a conscious decision to focus and direct your attention correctly, you change physical matter—your brain and your body change in a healthy way. Purposefully catching your thoughts can control the brain's sensory processing, the brain's rewiring, the neurotransmitters, the genetic expression, and cellular activity in a positive or negative direction. You choose.

The benefits are even greater than the scientists back in the '70s and '80s imagined. My patients who were successful in therapy took their first steps to success when they started focusing their attention and capturing their thoughts—for example "I can't do this," "It's too hard," "It's never worked before," and "I am not smart enough." The benefits of catching any negative thoughts like these cannot be emphasized enough. Not catching those thoughts will lead to a potential spiral into confusion and varying levels of mental despair.

Dr. Jekyll and Mr. Hyde

An interesting body of research shows how a certain type of protein, called a "prion protein," operates a bit like a Dr. Jekyll and Mr. Hyde—the story often used as a metaphor of the good man who hides an evil side. When a prion protein folds over itself, it plays a crucial role in neurodegenerative diseases that lead to dreadful syndromes such as the mad cow disease. But scientists have now found that the prion protein abounds in synapses—the contact point where signals are passed from one nerve cell to the next. Prions help create long-term, self-sustaining memories. They are also important in neuroplasticity, which is the change and rewiring that happens in our brain when we think and learn; and finally, they are involved in neurogenesis.[3] The point here is that this protein does amazing things in the brain in response to good signals and goes crazy in response to negative signals. A chaotic mind filled with uncaptured rogue thoughts of anxiety, worry, and any and all manner of fear-related emotions sends out the wrong signal.

Another Example of a Vicious Cycle

Stress is the key to understanding the association between depression and heart disease. Research shows that 40 to 60 percent of heart disease patients suffer clinical depression and 30 to 50 percent of patients who suffer clinical depression are at risk for heart disease.[4]

Not catching and stopping those thoughts leads to negative, toxic thoughts being wired into the brain; this can lead to depressive thoughts, which causes the body to go into stage two of stress. In response, the immune system produces proteins called *cytokines*, including one called *Interleukin-6*, as a positive, inflammatory response to protect the brain and body against stress. If the stress is not controlled, the depression increases and the person moves into stress stage 3; over time the inflammation also increases and can lead to arteriosclerosis (hardening of the arteries) and cardiovascular disease.

All this is from not catching those negative, toxic thoughts. And this is just one disease process; there are a multitude of other manifestations of not stopping this cycle. Recent research has shown that teaching strategies to handle and control stress (the body's reaction to toxic thinking) could make individuals who are vulnerable to schizophrenia and other neuropsychiatric disorders less vulnerable.[5]

It Only Takes Five to Sixteen Minutes a Day

Research has shown that five to sixteen minutes a day of focused, meditative capturing of thoughts shifts frontal brain states that are more likely to engage with the world.[6] Research also showed that those same five to sixteen minutes of intense, deep thinking activity increased the chances of a happier outlook on life.

God has blessed us with powerful and sound minds (2 Tim. 2:17). When we direct our attention by capturing our thoughts, we provide a target for our mental faculties. Then God will give you a project and your balance will be restored. If you don't let God give you a thinking project, the Enemy will surely step in to try to catch your thoughts and destroy your balance.

God has designed the frontal lobe of our brains precisely to do this: handle his thought projects. This perspective is highlighted in the Message version of 2 Corinthians 10:5: "We use our powerful God-tools for smashing warped philosophies, tearing down barriers erected against the truth of God, fitting every loose thought and emotion and impulse into the structure of life shaped by Christ. Our tools are ready at hand for clearing the ground of every obstruction and building lives of obedience into maturity."

Our Normal Is Perfection

Because we are made in God's image (Gen. 1:26) and have the "mind of Christ" (1 Cor. 2:16), our normal state is one of perfection.

Science now is able to demonstrate that we are "wired for love," and fear, which incorporates anything toxic, is therefore not our norm. This means our natural fashioned-after-God inclination is one of optimism and good, healthy thinking. We therefore have a God-given freedom to choose right or wrong—but it comes with conditions attached: "I have set before you life and death, blessing and cursing; therefore choose life, that both you and your descendants may live" (Deut. 30:19). This is clearly evidenced in the brain—when bad choices are made, or those negative thoughts are not captured, the neural wiring becomes distorted, which results in disruption of normal function.

God designed humans to observe our own thoughts, catch those that are bad, and get rid of them. The importance of capturing those thoughts cannot be underestimated because research shows that the vast majority of mental and physical illness comes from our thought life rather than the environment and genes.[7]

An undisciplined mind is filled with a continuous stream of worries, fears, and distorted perceptions that trigger degenerative processes in the mind and body. We cannot afford not to bring all thoughts into captivity to Christ Jesus (2 Cor. 10:5).

Chapter 4 Summary

1. The design of the brain allows us to capture and discipline chaotic thoughts.
2. Catching our thoughts is *necessary* because it calms our spirits so we can tune in and listen to God.
3. When we are mindful of catching our thoughts in this way, we change our connection with God from uninvolved and independent to involved and dependent.

4. Research dating back to the 1970s shows that being introspectively aware of our thoughts in a disciplined way rather than letting them chaotically run rampant can bring about impressive changes in how we feel and think.

5. Purposefully catching your thoughts can control the brain's sensory processing, the brain's rewiring, the neurotransmitters, the genetic expression, and cellular activity in a positive or negative direction. You choose.

6. A chaotic mind filled with uncaptured rogue thoughts of anxiety, worry, and all manner of fear-related emotions sends out the wrong signal right down to the level of the DNA.

7. Research has shown that five to sixteen minutes a day of focused, meditative capturing of thoughts shifts frontal brain states so that they are more likely to engage with the world and increases the chances of a happier outlook on life.

8. We are wired for love and then learn fear.

5

Entering into Directed Rest

Main Scripture: Be still, and know that I am God. Psalm 46:10

Linked Science Concept: When we direct our rest by introspection, self-reflection, and prayer; when we catch our thoughts; when we memorize and quote Scripture; and when we develop our mind intellectually, we enhance the default mode network (DMN) that improves brain function and mental, physical, and spiritual health.

God's order is clearly reflected in the organization of the brain. God has designed the brain to work in a series of coordinated networks. The scientific expression for this is *integrative functional organization*, which basically means that all parts of the brain are connected, work together, and impact each other.

God has also designed the brain in such a way that the intrinsic activity in the nonconscious part of our minds is where most of the *mind-action* takes place, and it is always

dominant, twenty-four hours a day. It is where we are thinking, choosing, building, and sorting thoughts. Simply put, it
is the constant, high-energy activity that is always going on
in the nonconscious mind, even when we are resting. What
we consciously think and what we say and do is all driven by
the information and activity in the nonconscious mind. So
the nonconscious mind has the roots of all our words and actions, and we choose with our minds what these roots will be.

This organizational structure of the brain and body is
described in Ephesians 4:16: "He makes the whole body fit
together perfectly. As each part does its own special work, it
helps the other parts grow, so that the whole body is healthy
and growing and full of love" (NLT).

The constant, high-intrinsic activity in the brain that influences our words and actions can be seen in the Scriptures:
"As he thinks in his heart, so is he" (Prov. 23:7).

What research shows is that when we go into a directed
rest—a focused, introspective state—we enhance and increase
the effectiveness of the activity in the nonconscious. Research
shows that there is a greater increase in gamma waves, which
are involved in attention, memory building, and learning, and
more activity linked to positive emotions like happiness when
we move into this directed rest state. PET scans and EEG
recordings show portions of the brain bulk up that produce
happiness and peace.[1] This is wisdom from Psalm 46:10: "Be
still, and know that I am God."

The Organized Networks in the Brain

Let's take a closer look at these coordinated and organized
networks in our brains that work together in a busy, integrated,

and balanced way, helping our brains maintain a high level of activity 24/7. These networks form the brain's inner life with the default mode network (DMN) dominating and becoming especially active when the mind is introspective and thinking deeply in a directed rest or idling state.

The DMN acts much like the conductor of an orchestra giving timing signals and coordinating activity among the different brain networks and regions and getting the brain ready to react on a conscious level. For example, the DMN coordinates the activity in

- networks that become active during a mental task;
- networks that are active during memory formation and when we pay attention;
- the salience network, which helps determine what we pay attention to; and
- the sensory-motor network, which integrates the brain's control of body movements with sensory feedback.

When your mind is busy with intrinsic activity (which is basically directed rest) such as introspection and thinking things through, letting your mind wander, sleeping, deep thinking, even under anesthetic, there is a constant chatter between the networks of the brain in the nonconscious mind. The energy consumed by this constantly active messaging and thought building in the nonconscious level of our mind is about twenty times more than when we are conscious. When we move into an alert conscious state, the energy consumption in the brain increases by 5 percent. In fact, 60 to 80 percent of all energy used by the brain occurs in circuits inside the brain that are unrelated to any external signal. This is all predominant DMN activity.[2]

Flexibility

An important property of these brain networks is called *anti-correlation*, which means we switch back and forth between the various networks.[3] For example, when we have flexible and creative thinking, we are able to shift between thoughts and capture and control thoughts. This is good and is what we want.

We need this flexibility as we go through life. We cannot control the events and circumstances of life, but we can control our *reactions* to those events and circumstances. Controlling our reactions requires flexibility in our thinking, and God has given us that with our multiple, different networks. God has designed our brain to work for us and not to control us.

Switch Off to Switch On

What I find fascinating is that when we shift into the default mode network (DMN), we don't switch off to rest. Quite the contrary, we *switch off to switch on* to a mode of thinking that gives us perspective and wisdom and the opportunity to connect with God. This is a state of mind in which we switch off to the external and switch on to the internal.

In this deeply intellectual state, involved networks remain active, and the shifting between them remains active, but it is a different kind of activity. It is more focused and introspective. So when our brain enters the rest circuit, we don't actually rest; we move into a highly intelligent, self-reflective, directed state. And the more often we go there, the more we get in touch with the deep, spiritual part of who we are. I believe God has created this state to directly connect us to him and to develop and practice an awareness of his presence. As the Scripture says, "Keep awake (give strict attention, be cautious and active) and watch and pray, that you may not come into temptation. The spirit indeed is willing, but the flesh is weak" (Matt. 26:41 AMP).

The DMN is a primary network that we switch into when we switch off from the outside world and move into a state of focused mindfulness. It activates to even higher levels when a person is daydreaming, introspecting, or letting his or her mind wander in an organized exploratory way through the endless myriad of thoughts within the mind. It's a directed, deeply intellectual focusing inward and tuning out the outside world. It is a cessation from active external, which is like the Sabbath when we switch off from the world and focus on God.

In this directed rest state, you focus inward, you introspect, and you appear to slow down; but actually, your mental resources speed up and your thinking moves onto a higher level. When you think in this way, when you pause your activity and enter into a directed rest, you will emerge far ahead of where you would have been if you just operated within the realms of a shifting, shuffling, limited conscious, cognitive mind. This is the state of being still and knowing that he is God (Ps. 46:10).

The DMN, which used to be thought of as *dark energy* in the brain, is activated into ever-higher states when we engage in self-referential activity. Brain imaging experiments show that there is a persistent level of background activity when a person is in a state of directed rest.[4] This includes recollections, ruminations, imaginations, and self-perceptions; and it involves the ability to focus on a specific memory, thinking through things from different angles while still being solution focused. It is very important in planning future actions.[5]

In fact, miswiring of brain regions involved in the DMN, leading to all kinds of ups and downs in the DMN, may even be part of disorders ranging from Alzheimer's to schizophrenia to other neuropsychiatric disorders. Research is starting to show that, for example, brain areas that atrophy and die in Alzheimer's overlap with major centers of the DMN. Patients with depression show decreased connectivity between certain regions of the DMN and the emotional areas of the brain. And in schizophrenia, many areas of the DMN showed increased activity levels.[6]

Regular meditators—by this I mean those who have adopted a disciplined and focused, reflecting thought life in which they bring all thoughts into captivity—show that their DMN is more active and that there is more switching back and forth between networks.[7] This means the brain is more active, growing more branches and integrating and linking thoughts, which translates as increased intelligence and wisdom and that wonderful feeling of peace. God also throws in some additional benefits such as increased immune and cardiovascular health.

When we pray, when we catch our thoughts, when we memorize and quote Scripture, we move into this deep meditative state. This great state of mind is also activated when we intellectualize deeply about information—perhaps what we are studying or a skill we are developing in our job. We are highly intellectual beings created to have relationship with a highly intellectual God. We should never underestimate how brilliant we are and that we are only limited by how we see ourselves.

In His Great Mercy

In his great mercy, God has wired into the design of our brain these circuits that are spearheaded by the default mode network (DMN) we need to regularly access to keep connected to our spirits and to be able to follow the leading of the Holy Spirit—a time of ceasing from our own activity, ceasing from our own efforts (Heb. 4:9–10). Our minds need time to understand what our spirits already know.

In the busyness of life and the flurry of everyday activity, we expose ourselves to the possibility of developing a chaotic mindset with the net result of neurochemical and electromagnetic chaos in the brain. This feels like endless loops and spirals of thinking that can easily get out of control. When we activate the DMN, however, it is almost like a Sabbath in the brain, which is a cessation from the conscious flurry of work and a withdrawal into the depths of our mind. It is like a mental rebooting process to reconnect with who we are and with our Savior to bring perspective to the issues of life.

The Sabbath in the Brain

In fact, when we don't frequently slow down and enter this rest state, this *Sabbath* in the brain, we disrupt natural functions in the brain. Research shows that when we don't engage in this disciplined and focused self-reflective pattern of thinking that activates the DMN, we may experience negative self-esteem, depression, worry, anxiety, and health issues, and over-focus on generalized and short-term memory issues. We may get stuck, unable to cope, and have a tendency to focus on the problem and not the solution. In fact, as things go wrong in the processing of information in the default mode network, the mishandled data is passed on to other networks in the brain where it creates additional problems.[8] These additional problems can be experienced as memory issues, cloudy and fuzzy thinking, anxiety, depression, and many other manifestations including neuropsychiatric disorders.

The Task Positive Network

In line with the amazing order and balance God created in everything, we find this default mode resting network is balanced by the task positive network (TPN). The TPN supports the active thinking required for making decisions.[9] So as we focus our thinking and activate the DMN, at some point in our thinking process we move into active decision-making. This activates the TPN, and we experience this as action. In my 21-Day Brain Detox Plan (discussed in part 2), I call this action an *active reach*. Brain research—specifically the science of thought[10]—shows that action completes the cycle of building up and breaking down thoughts. We see this in the Scriptures as well: "Faith without works is dead" (James 2:26).

What is very interesting, and sobering, however, is how our DMN and TPN networks, as well as the balance between the two, are thrown off when we choose to be toxic. Toxic negative thinking produces increased activity in the DMN, and activity in the TPN decreases. This results in maladaptive, depressive ruminations and a decrease in the ability to solve problems. This makes us feel foggy, confused, negative, and depressed.

God is a God of order and balance, and he has fashioned our spirit, soul, and body this way. So it is quite simple; when we don't follow his ordinances, there will be consequences. The brain moves into an unbalanced state, producing neurochemical and electromagnetic chaos. "For where you have envy and selfish ambition, there you find disorder and every evil practice" (James 3:16 NIV).

Our Brain Follows Our Mind

Studies using imaging techniques show that the DMN activates abnormally in individuals with depression.[11] Other studies show that in depressed individuals, the front middle part of the brain (anterior medial cortex) has increased activity.[12] This means that although their ruminations increased, this good sign was thrown into disarray by decreased activity in the middle-back part of the brain (the posterior medial cortex). When there is decreased activity in the posterior medial cortex, a pattern of dissociation occurs and there is a tendency to move away from being clear and specific in thinking about memories toward focusing on overly general memories.[13]

What this means is that when rumination turns into unproductive brooding and negative issues are blown out of proportion, it is detrimental to the brain and to good life choices. When this happens, healthy focused introspection activating the DMN turns from a coping-and-solution focus to a passive-and-maladaptive focus, which can result in worrying, anxiety, and depression.

This gives us scientific proof that we need to have the mindset expressed in Philippians 4:8: "Finally, brothers and sisters, whatever is true, whatever is noble, whatever is right, whatever is pure, whatever is lovely, whatever is admirable—if anything is excellent or praiseworthy—think about such things" (NIV). By following this perfect advice from God's Word, you can bring back the balance between the default mode network (DMN) and the task positive network (TPN).

The Seven Different Types of Thinking

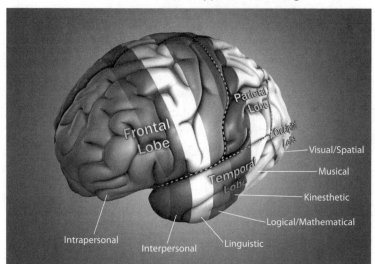

The good news is that this balance can be restored very quickly when you choose to become introspective and ruminate in a positive, directed way.[14] The speed of the change in how you feel and function is not just because of the balance being restored between the DMN and TPN, but also because the brain functions in complex circuits that encompass multiple brain structures and regions, so there is a positive, cascading effect throughout the brain. This is, once again, God's grace in action.

Consequences of Toxic Thinking

Throughout this book, the resounding message is that negative thinking creates atypical responses in the brain, which will result in atypical manifestations. Studies have clearly demonstrated that people with a history of various types of depression exhibit differences in the regions and circuits of the brain associated with knowledge of socially acceptable behavior (anterior temporal lobe) and the awareness of wrong (subgenual region of the brain).[15]

Their thoughts and the choices they have made changed their brain in a negative way so that instead of being convicted of wrong in order to change—which is positive—they felt guilty and condemned, causing the positive to become negative.[16]

Other studies dealing with obsessive compulsive disorders[17] and schizophrenia[18] show definite changes in the brain from the negative to the positive when thinking is brought under control. Some scientists even describe these neuropsychiatric manifestations almost as though negative, toxic thinking opens a gate that allows negative emotions to overwhelm them. And because mind changes matter, this negative thinking changes the brain structure.

Patients with schizophrenia have decreased activity between their thalamus and prefrontal cortex, which affects memory and behavioral flexibility. They also have incorrect activity in their decision-making and emotional areas of the brain. From studies of adolescents starting to show symptoms of schizophrenia, it appears the areas are overactive at first from toxic stress reactions and then become damaged and hypoactive. So if we don't help our children and adolescents manage stress, we are potentially causing brain damage, which in turn leads to more serious problems.[19]

Other research shows that women who have suffered abuse were 60 percent more likely to have a child with autism. The researchers propose that the long-lasting effects of abuse on women's biological systems, such as the immune system and stress-response system, are responsible for increasing their likelihood of having a child with autism.[20] These women were victims of toxic thinking and the stress it causes—and the abuse will therefore impact the next generation as well, and potentially the next three. This is why there are often family histories of autism. I tell you this study to highlight the responsibility we have in not only getting our own minds right but also helping others, especially victims of trauma, get their minds right.

Switch On Your Brain

Choosing to be focused and mindful and to activate your DMN and your TPN in a balanced way by capturing your thoughts will bring you back in alignment with God.

In my 21-Day Brain Detox Plan, I show you how to center your attention on a single element, using my Switch On Your Brain 5-Step Learning Process. When there is a pause in your activity, a quiet state, that is a perfect time to connect to the spiritual part of who you are. In this state your mind can begin to understand what your spirit knows. You can position yourself to let the Holy Spirit deposit truth and direction in your spirit as you "trust in the Lord with all your heart, and lean not on your own understanding; in all your ways acknowledge Him, and He shall direct your paths" (Prov. 3:5–6).

Through modifying our practices of thought toward a more disciplined, focused, and reflective thought life, we can build up healthy neural *real estate* that is better able to bring our thoughts into captivity and deal with the variegated demands of today's modern world. Your mind can powerfully and unexpectedly change your brain in positive ways when you intentionally direct your attention. The most efficient way to improve your brain is a daily step-by-step process— a lifestyle of thinking your brain into better functioning so that it turns into whatever *you* expect it to be: "As he thinks in his heart, so is he" (Prov. 23:7).

Your mind, intellect, will, and emotions are always changing your brain in some way. Directed, disciplined, and focused attention on the correct things is a major key to switching on your brain.

Chapter 5 Summary

1. We have all kinds of coordinated networks in our brains that work together in an organized way, forming a constant, intrinsic *chatter* in the nonconscious part of our mind.

2. Our brains maintain a high level of activity 24/7. This activity forms the brain's inner life, with the default mode network (DMN) dominating and becoming especially active when the mind is introspective and thinking deeply in a directed rest or idle state.

3. As these networks function correctly, we shift into deeply introspective and meditative states that increase our intelligence and health.

4. When we switch back and forth between the various networks—for example, when we have flexible and creative thinking—we are able to shift between thoughts and capture and control them.

5. When we direct our rest by introspection, self-reflection, and prayer; when we catch our thoughts; when we memorize and quote Scripture; when we develop our mind intellectually, we accelerate the default mode network (DMN) and improve brain function as well as mind, body, and spiritual health.

6. The DMN is balanced by the task positive network (TPN), which supports the active thinking required for making decisions. The more balanced we are, the more wisdom we apply in our thinking and decisions. This action step of the TPN is necessary for effective mind and brain change.

7. Miswiring of brain regions involved in the DMN that leads to all kinds of ups and downs in the DMN may even be part of disorders ranging from Alzheimer's to schizophrenia.

8. Toxic thinking produces this miswiring, which causes increased activity in the DMN, resulting in a decrease of activity in the TPN. This causes maladaptive, depressive ruminations and a decrease in the ability to solve problems. This makes us feel foggy, confused, negative, and depressed.

9. Your mind can powerfully and unexpectedly change your brain in positive ways when you intentionally direct your attention.

6

Stop Milkshake-Multitasking

> **Main Scripture:** Dear friend, listen well to my words; tune your ears to my voice. Keep my message in plain view at all times. Concentrate! Learn it by heart! Those who discover these words live, really live; body and soul, they're bursting with health. Keep vigilant watch over your heart; that's where life starts. Proverbs 4:20–23 Message
>
> **Linked Science Concept:** Multitasking is a persistent myth. Paying deep, focused attention to one task at a time is the correct way.

One of the plagues of modern existence is multitasking, which leads to the further plagues of "hurry sickness" and obsessive time management. The truth about multitasking is that it is a persistent myth. What we really do is shift our attention rapidly from task to task, resulting in two bad things: (1) We don't devote as much focused attention as we should to a specific activity, task, or piece of information, and (2) we sacrifice the quality of our attention. I call this "milkshake-multitasking."

Multitasking Is a Persistent Myth

This poor focusing of attention and lack of quality in our thought lives is the complete opposite of how the brain is designed to function and causes a level of brain damage. Every rapid, incomplete, and poor quality shift of thought is like making a milkshake with your brain cells and neuro-chemicals. This milkshake-multitasking, which is the truth behind multitasking, creates patterns of flightiness and lack of concentration that are unfortunately often erroneously labeled ADD and ADHD and that are too often unnecessarily medicated, adding fuel to the fire. And it's a rapid downhill slide from there if we don't get back to our God-design of deep, intellectual attention.

What does deep, focused, intellectual attention look like versus milkshake-multitasking? The answer is modeled in Proverbs 4:20–23: "Dear friend, listen well to my words; tune your ears to my voice. Keep my message in plain view at all times. Concentrate! Learn it by heart! Those who discover these words live, really live; body and soul, they're bursting with health. Keep vigilant watch over your heart; that's where life starts"(Message). It is very interesting that every cell in the body is connected to the heart, and the brain controls the heart and the mind controls the brain. So whatever we are thinking about affects every cell in our body.

We saw in the last chapter that we are deeply intellectual beings and are designed to bring all thoughts into captivity— are you surprised? We are made in God's image, after all. He designed us to think through things one at a time in a focused, quality manner by paying attention, listening intently, keeping our eyes on one thing at a time, and fixing it in our mind.

The 140-Character Tweet

This design described above contrasts undeniably with the general pattern of modern life today in which so much attention is paid to tweeting on Twitter, Instagramming, and Facebooking to the point that we forget all about enjoying the moment. We are told by so-called social media experts that information needs to be in bite-size amounts and in a constant stream of new information before the previous information has even been digested.

This is not stimulation; it is bombardment. We have been reduced to 140 characters and an addiction to looking for the next informational high. Students can't sit quietly and enjoy reading a book, allowing their imagination to take flight.

Before sharing some of the researched consequences of this milkshake-multitasking momentum we are in, I want to assure you that I believe social media plays an important role in society, business, and life. When used correctly and in a balanced way, it is a phenomenal communications tool. I am all for progress. Used incorrectly, however, this good thing becomes a bad thing.

It's All about Balance

It is all about balance. Our brain responds with healthy patterns, circuits, and neurochemicals when we think deeply, but not when we skim only the surface of multiple pieces of information. Colossians 3:15 in the Amplified Bible explains peace as "soul harmony" that comes from Christ and that acts as an umpire who helps us think, choose, decide, and settle with finality all questions that arise in our minds. But milkshake-multitasking switches on confusion in our brain, making soul harmony impossible.

Scientists have found that the amount of time spent milkshake-multitasking among American young people has increased by 120 percent in the last ten years. According to a report in the *Archives of General Psychiatry*, simultaneous exposure to electronic media during the teenage years—such as playing a computer game while watching television—appears to be associated with increased depression and anxiety in young adulthood, especially among men.[1] Considering that teens are exposed to an average of eight and a half hours of multitasking electronic media per day, we need to change something quickly.[2]

Social Media Enthusiast or Addict?

Another concern this raises is whether you are or your teen is a social media enthusiast or simply a social media addict? This is a very real problem—so much so that researchers from Norway developed a new instrument to measure Facebook addiction called the Bergen Facebook Addiction Scale.[3] Social media has become as ubiquitous as television in our everyday lives, and this research shows that multitasking social media can be as addictive as drugs, alcohol, and chemical substance abuse.

A large number of friends on social media networks may appear impressive, but according to a new report, the more social circles a person is linked to, the more likely the social media will be a source of stress.[4] It can also have a detrimental effect on consumer well-being because milkshake-multitasking interferes with clear thinking and decision-making, which lowers self-control and leads to rash, impulsive buying and poor eating decisions. Greater social media use is associated with a higher body mass index, increased binge eating, a lower credit score, and higher levels of credit card debt for consumers with many close friends in their social network— all caused by a lack of self-control.[5]

We Can Become Shallow

Milkshake-multitasking decreases our attention, making us increasingly less able to focus on our thought habits. This opens us up to shallow and weak judgments and decisions and results in passive mindlessness. Deep, intellectual thought, however, results in interactive mindfulness—the "soul harmony" presented in Colossians 3:15 (AMP). This requires engaging passionately with the world. We need to increase our awareness of our thoughts and take the time to understand and reflect on them.

Let's take a look at some studies that show the impact of changing from a milkshake-multitasking mindset to a deep, intellectual mindset.

In 2012 a research group at the University of Washington did an interesting study on the effects of meditation training on multitasking. They found that the subjects of the study had fewer negative emotions, could stay on task longer, had improved concentration, switched between tasks more effectively in a focused and organized way, as opposed to haphazardly dashing back and forth between tasks, and spent their time more efficiently.[6] These results excited me because I found similar results in my own research.[7]

My Research

In my documented research with patients who had traumatic brain injury (TBI) and students and adults who had learning and emotional disabilities, I was astounded at the change in their cognitive and emotional function once they started applying a more deeply intellectual thinking pattern. I abandoned all traditional therapy, trained them in a new technique I had developed, and showed them how to apply it to their daily life. The changes were almost immediate: improved focus, concentration, understanding, shifting efficiency, and overall effectiveness in producing quality work. There were even positive emotional changes, specifically in self-motivation and self-esteem. And it didn't stop there; over time they continued to improve in cognitive and emotional functioning. Once they were set on a healthy thinking path, it continued upward in a cascading fashion.

In the ensuing past twenty years, I have seen these improvements in thousands of patients and clients. This work is the result of God's guidance, because when I started down this path, it was the complete opposite of my academic training. I instinctively began with and continue to use Scripture— specifically the drive and focus that is called for in Proverbs— as guidance and motivation for my research on the science of thought. This research produced my Switch On Your Brain 5-Step Learning Process (discussed in part 2), which teaches people to use disciplined, focused attention to develop the kind of thinking pattern that has huge benefits on attention networks and saves us from the enemy of distraction.

As a communication pathologist in the field of cognitive neuroscience, I saw the benefits of focused thinking and disciplined concentration were and are not just behavioral. Everything you do and say is first a thought in your physical brain.

You think, and then you do, which cycles back to the original thought, changing it and the thoughts connected to it in a dynamic interrelationship. If your thinking is off ("toxic" or "pathological," to be really sciency), then your communication through what you say and do is off, and vice versa. As the Scripture says, "As he thinks in his heart, so is he" (Prov. 23:7).

Scientists See Evidence of the Difference

Scientists are seeing the evidence of deep, intellectual thought versus milkshake-multitasking in the brain.[8] Deep, intellectual thinking activates the prefrontal cortex (just above your eyebrows) in a positive way, producing increased concentration, less distraction, less switching between tasks, more effective switching between tasks, decreased emotional volatility, and overall increase in job completion.

Scientists have also found that deep, intellectual thinking improves connections within and between nerve networks, specifically in the front part of the brain and between the front and middle parts of the brain.[9] Other researchers found that when an individual pays attention to a stimulus, the neurons in the cerebral cortex that represent this object show increased attention.[10] We can also alter these patterns of activity by altering our attention, which remaps the cortex.

Determination Is Key

During the 1990s, when many neuroscientists were reporting on the power of attention, I saw the greatest changes in patients who willfully, determinedly, and persistently chose to focus their attention on improving their skills and restoring function. For example, one of my patients had been in a car accident when she was a junior in high school that had left her with extreme brain damage. Her neurologist and other doctors told her parents not to raise their hopes of her being more than "a vegetable." Even when she got back to a fourth-grade level, the doctors said that was her limit. Fortunately she and her family chose not to pay attention to what they said and instead chose to focus her attention on what she wanted for her life. She was determined not only to correct her disabilities from the traumatic accident but also to catch up with her peer group and finish her senior year with them. Consequently, she built new networks in her mind focused on where she wanted to be and strove to make it happen.

She talked with me about her goals and vision, and we worked together, taking small steps, working consistently toward achieving them. There were times she wanted to give up, but she always picked herself up and carried on. The benefits were evident: Not only did she catch up with her peer group, but she also went on to complete twelfth grade and further her studies after high school. When we applied the various behavioral and neuropsychological tests after her period of therapy and compared them to her functioning before the accident, she had not only restored her original level but had gone way beyond in her functioning.[11]

What I believe happened to this patient is captured in two Scriptures: "Nothing they have imagined they could do would be impossible for them" (Gen. 11:6 AMP), and "Faith is the substance of things hoped for, the evidence of things not seen" (Heb. 11:1). To think positively about our prospects, we must be able to imagine ourselves in the future. Our brains may have stamps from the past, but they are being rewired by our expectation of the future. Imagining a positive future reduces the pain of the past. Faith motivates us to pursue these goals.

Hope leads to expectation, which creates peace, excitement, and health in our minds, thus increasing brain and body health.

Additional Benefits of *Not* Milkshake-Multitasking

An additional benefit from deep thinking is increased *gyrification*, a lovely word that means more folds in the cortex of the brain. These extra folds allow the brain to process information faster, make decisions quicker, and improve memory.[12] Researchers specifically found an increase in folds in the insula, which is an amazing structure that integrates thinking, emotions, and self-regulation.[13] These studies show once again that the more you apply a pattern of deep, intellectual thought in your brain, the more you will improve the physical structure of your brain. Clearly, then, the parts of the brain involved in attention monitoring, working memory (dorsolateral prefrontal cortex), and how well we monitor our own thoughts (insula) and feelings improves dramatically with deep, intellectual thought.[14]

Conclusion

These are just a few of the studies that show us that when we discipline our thoughts, positive, physical brain changes happen. This allows us to become more aligned with God's way of thinking: "Commit your works to the LORD, and your *thoughts* will be established" (Prov. 16:3, emphasis mine). Then we will switch between tasks correctly; monitor our attention, feelings, and thoughts; and function at a higher level. I just love that every instruction God gives us that we actually follow comes with a bonus physically and mentally. You do what God says and peace, happiness, and intelligence will follow.

Chapter 6 Summary

1. The truth about multitasking is that it is a persistent myth.

2. What we really do is shift our attention rapidly and haphazardly from task to task, resulting in two negative things: (1) We don't devote as much focused attention as we should to a specific activity, task, or piece of information, and (2) we sacrifice the quality of our attention. I call this *milkshake-multitasking*.

3. This milkshake-multitasking creates patterns of flightiness and lack of concentration that unfortunately are often erroneously labeled ADD and ADHD. Too often this results in unnecessary medication, which adds fuel to the fire.

4. The general pattern today is that so much attention is paid to tweeting, Instagramming, and Facebooking that we forget all about enjoying the moment.

5. So-called social media experts tell us that information needs to be provided in bite-size amounts and in a constant stream of new information before the previous information has even been digested. This is not stimulation; it is bombardment.

6. Milkshake-multitasking decreases our attention, making us increasingly less able to focus on our thought habits. This opens us up to shallow and weak judgments and decisions, and it results in passive mindlessness.

7. Scientists are seeing the evidence of deep, intellectual thought versus milkshake-multitasking in the brain.

8. I saw the greatest changes in patients who willfully, determinedly, and persistently chose to focus their attention on improving their skills and restoring function.

Thinking, God, and the Quantum Physics Brain

Main Scripture: Today I have given you the choice between life and death, between blessings and curses. Now I call on heaven and earth to witness the choice you make. Oh, that you would choose life, so that you and your descendants might live! Deuteronomy 30:19 NLT

Linked Science Concepts: The process of thinking and choosing is the most powerful thing in the universe after God, and it is a phenomenal gift from God to be treasured and used properly. The basic ingredients of quantum physics are: paying attention, thinking and choosing, and consequence.

As we have explored in previous chapters, our mind activity—the thoughts driven by the power of feelings—are the designers of the landscape of our brains. Thinking and choosing play a central role in who God has made us to be. In linking thought, choice, and science, quantum theory comes up as a star player.

The process of thinking and choosing is the most powerful thing in the universe after God, and it is a phenomenal gift from God to be treasured and used properly.

Three Different Worlds

There is the sensory world of our five senses; there is the world of electromagnetism and the atom; and then there is the subatomic quantum world. This quantum world challenged physicists' perception of linear time, orderly space, and fixed realities and turned on its head the Cartesian Newtonian world that sees humans as machines with exchangeable parts.

This is God's style: Just when humans think they are super smart and know it all, a whole lot of new information enters into the equation and changes everything. In the words of Max Planck, the German theoretical physicist who won the Nobel Prize in 1918 for originating quantum theory, "Science progresses funeral by funeral."[1]

Quantum Physics Is Another Way of Admiring God

Quantum physics is a way of explaining how the things that make up atoms work and makes sense of how the smallest things in nature work. *Quantum* means "energy," and quantum physics tells us how electromagnetic waves—like light waves—and particles work. *Quantum mechanics* is the mathematical framework used to describe this energy and how it works.

Using quantum physics, scientists can describe, predict, and quantify how we choose among a myriad of options. This is a way of *measuring* free will or describing it using a mathematical formula. In essence, quantum physics says that

- your consciousness affects the behaviors of subatomic particles;
- particles move backward and forward in time and appear in all possible places at once; and
- the universe is connected with transfers of information that are faster than light.

Quantum Physics Aligning with Scripture

Quantum theory converts science's conception of humans from being mere cogs in a gigantic, mechanical machine to being freethinking agents whose conscious choices affect the physical world.[2] This is called the *observer effect*: The observer determines the direction in which the possibilities may collapse. In the quantum universe, as we—the observers—affect phenomena, space, and time, we turn possibilities into realities. Mind changes matter.

Here is a simple way of understanding this observer effect. Each day as you go through the events and circumstances of life, you are faced with a multitude of possibilities to choose, from what to wear in the morning to how you are going to react to the email you have just received. There is an endless array of possible choices you can make at any one moment in time, but it is you, with your ability to think, who directs the choice. So you collapse all the probabilities into one choice: "eggs for breakfast," "I will not be upset by the tone of this email," or "I will not say *can't* today." So as you choose, you collapse the probability into an actuality. Satan, the father of lies (John 8:44), will come at you with a thousand negative probabilities, but you always need to remember that a probability has no power. It only becomes powerful when you believe the lie and collapse the probability into an actuality. This is how evil is birthed.

Free Will—A Basic Ingredient of Quantum Physics

Quantum physics has as its basic ingredients free will, directed attention as the result of a choice, and the effects and consequences of these choices. For example, Proverbs 4:20–27 says that if we direct our attention to the Word of God, we will align our thinking and subsequent choices with God, and the outcome will be healing and health.

Thus an intentional act—such as choosing to attend to God's words, listen to them, memorize them—will produce the effect of health to all your flesh. Deuteronomy 30:19 (NIV) can be evaluated in the same way: "I have set before you life and death, blessings and curses"—the options—"Now choose life"—you intentionally evaluate the options and choose your reaction—"so that you and your children may live"—which is the consequence of your intentional choice.

Let's apply the basic ingredients of quantum physics: paying attention, thinking and choosing, and consequence.

1. Information: You get a call from your doctor's office telling you that the results of your blood test are in and asking you to phone them as soon as possible.
2. Thoughts: Multiple thoughts are swirling around in your head. Option one is fear: "They said as soon as possible! Does this mean bad news? What if I have . . ."

And on it goes, down to planning the songs for your funeral. Option two is denial: "This is routine; I'll call when I have time." Option three is trust: "I have faith that this will be good news. I am not moved by any doctor's report."

3. Choice: You choose an option. For instance, if you choose fear, your brain responds by wiring in the thought, "I am sick," and you live into this thought.

4. Consequence: You suddenly feel sick and are sure you are dying.

5. New consequence: You phone the doctor; your results are clear; and suddenly you feel fine (and perhaps a little foolish).

So your brain becomes what you focused on (body carries out the will of the spirit and soul), and what your brain has become produces what you say and do and how you feel physically and mentally.[3]

The Granddaddy of Definitions

Quantum physics has multiple definitions, but the original Copenhagen formulation of quantum theory made by Niehls Bohr of Copenhagen University in 1927 is considered the *granddaddy* of the definitions.[4] It states that the free choices made by human subjects are a subjectively controllable variable, which simply means that you control your choices. Quantum mechanics can be used to prove that thinking and choosing are real and measurable.[5] The way you experience your feelings, the way you interface with your thoughts, and the kind of attention you give them will change how your brain functions.

If you apply this principle, you can free yourself from destructive thoughts and actions and change bad habits for good.

The Quantum Zeno Effect

I love quantum physics, but the quantum physics principle that really caught my attention is called the Quantum Zeno Effect (QZE). QZE is the repeated effort that causes learning to take place. When you go over and over something, reading it, thinking about it, writing it down, and then repeating this process, you deepen your knowledge and understanding, direct your attention, and grow nerve cells. The neurons in your brain line up and fire together because you are firing synapses over and over, which causes genetic expression to happen and makes the synapses and proteins stronger. The changes in your brain caused by this deep, repeated, intellectually targeted focus can be seen with brain imaging techniques.[6]

Basically, the QZE stipulates that your brain becomes *what* you focus on and *how* you focus. So the consequence is structural change in the brain that produces behavior because we operate from what we have built into our brain. Choosing to pay selective attention to and focus on what you are gathering in through your five senses acts on the physical structure of the brain, amplifying activity in particular brain circuits.

In my research and clinical practice I have trained teachers and students how to direct their attention in a systematic, organized, logical way that followed how the brain builds thought. This incorporated gathering the relevant information, reading it over and over, thinking about it over and over, writing it down, checking through it all again for accuracy, teaching it out loud, and applying it. I call this my 5-Step Switch On Your Brain Learning Process. In my PhD research, my control group was the historical academic trend of the school, which used basic study skills intervention and a traditional teaching and learning approach. Once I introduced my Switch On Your Brain Process to a group of students, their academic trend significantly improved. The results showed a 35 to 70 percent improvement in metacognitive and cognitive performance as measured by academic results in four subjects: English, math, history, and science.[7] These students had developed the attitude that persistence and hard work would achieve an end result, and that stretching themselves and challenging their minds is what would make the change. They learned the science behind this in their sessions with me and applied the lessons in their academics—and the results spoke for themselves. This was essentially the Quantum Zeno Effect in action, which I have also seen repeatedly in my other research, the lives of my patients, my children, and even my own life. I have successfully worked with clients as young as three and as old as seventy-eight—a pilot who wanted to change professions and become a CPA.

Part of what I taught these students in their first session was an understanding that intelligence is continually developing, so they could become as intelligent as they wanted to be, based on how much they used their brains. Part of this session also included a basic introduction into how the brain works when we learn and how to build memory, including the concept of neuroplasticity. An important fact I explained was that they were *in control* of the development of their own brains, and that hard work and challenging themselves helped the brain grow more brain cells. Their motivation and enthusiasm for taking responsibility for their own learning was incredible.

Dr. Carol Dweck, a Stanford University research psychologist, found similar results. She found that students who believed that intelligence can grow had increasing math scores. Those that believed that intelligence was fixed experienced a decrease in their math scores. She then compared a group of students who were trained in basic study skills to another group who were told how their brains grow in response to novelty and challenge. At the end of the semester, those who had the "mini neuroscience" approach had significantly better math grades than the other group.[8]

The Law of Entanglement

The *law of entanglement* in quantum physics states that relationship is the defining characteristic of everything in space and time. Because of the pervasive nature of the entanglement of atomic particles, the relationship is independent of distance and requires no physical link. Everything and everyone is linked, and we all affect each other.

The law of entanglement has a biblical correlation: "So we, being many, are one body in Christ, and individually members one of another" (Rom. 12:5). If you are not doing what God put you on this earth to do—your divine sense of purpose (Eccles. 3:11)—then even though you may not know me, you are still affecting my life. We are all part of God, so this interconnectedness is not surprising. Your intentions, your prayers, and your words toward others will have impact because of this law. We see this in the Scriptures: "The effectual fervent prayer of a righteous man availeth much" (James 5:16 KJV). In fact, we are so entangled that our intentions alter not only our own DNA molecules, but the DNA molecules of others as well. An ingenuous experiment set up by the HeartMath Foundation determined that genuine positive emotion, as reflected by a measure called "heart rate variability," directed with intentionality toward someone actually changed the way the double-helix DNA strand coils and uncoils. And this goes for both positive and negative emotions and intentions.[9] Other research shows that even thirty seconds a day of direct heartfelt intention will cumulatively alter not only your own destiny, but impact the lives of others in this generation and the next three at least.[10]

Look at the story of the woman in Matthew 9:20–22 who bled for twelve years. She was so desperate for her healing that when she heard about the man called Jesus who heals, she started directing her intentions with each bit of information she received, cumulatively building a physical thought in her mind of her healing and believing it in her heart—in effect she was applying Genesis 11:6 and Hebrews 11:1. In this way she developed her faith and aligned herself with the healing power of God, and in doing so she built a root thought (Proverbs 23:7) and acted upon it to receive her healing. She collapsed all the probabilities into one, which said, "I will be healed if I just touch the hem of his garment." Furthermore, her entanglement with God (Colossians 1:16) was activated by her choice to believe in her heart and confess with her mouth. There was no cognitive dissonance in her that day, meaning she wasn't thinking one thing and confessing another. Science shows the beauty of what happens when we align with God. Science is a way God shows us that we are part of him, and when we follow his laws we reap the benefit.

I honestly believe that by applying our intelligence, which can be developed and trained, we can become amazingly good at understanding how to practice the presence of God. I have personally reached a point where science has taken my relationship with God to a whole new level. He has become very real and very personal. Through science, you see how much trouble he has gone to in order to show himself to us in every way possible.

We are entangled in each other's lives, and this is reflected in the structure of the brain. We have "mirror neurons" that fire up as we watch someone else laugh or cry or drink a cup of coffee. Giacomo Rizzolatti and his team were the first to discover these mirror neurons in 1995.[11] Through these neurons we literally fire up activity in the brain without actually using our five senses through the normal sensory-cognitive cycle. Empathy is the wonderful God-given ability to identify with, and vicariously understand, the internal experiences of another person, making communication more genuine and valuable.[12] When we empathize, many different regions of the brain collaborate in addition to the tiny, miraculous mirror neurons. We have been hardwired to experience powerful compassion for others, and this compassion crosses all three worlds: sensory, electromagnetic, and quantum.

Particles Behave in a Bizarre Way, Which Is Another Reason Why Prayer Works

Quantum theory calls entanglement "bizarre behavior" for particles—such as two entangled particles behaving as one even when far apart. Physicists call such behavior *nonlocal*, which means that it is physically impossible to know the position and the momentum of a particle at the same time. Another way of saying this is that there is no space-time dimension.

We know God operates outside of the space-time dimension. And we know prayer does too. There are many stories of people praying for each other on different sides of the planet and experiencing the effect of the prayer. In fact, there are many documented studies on the impact of prayer in the world of neuroscience in addition to the millions of testimonies from Christians around the world.

An innovative experiment was done that showed that we are capable of impacting each other's minds and brains even when sensory signals (the five senses), electromagnetic signals, mirror neurons, and insula activity have all been removed. This impact only worked with meditators who had built a relationship with each other, not those in the control group who didn't have a relationship. In the experiment researchers got two people to meditate next to each other in an electronically shielded room, called a "faraday cage." Then they separated them into two separate faraday cages, and as they continued to meditate, researchers shone light in the eye of one of the meditators. The part of the brain that lit up in that person's brain also lit up in the other meditator's brain, even though there was no sensory or electromagnetic connection.[13]

Classical physics says this could only work if there were a prior arrangement—something like, "If this happens, then that will happen." So no space-time dimension seems to violate our sense of cause and effect in space and time. For example, if someone needs heart surgery, then heart surgery is performed and is either successful or not. However, one study showed that those undergoing heart surgery who had spiritual support in the form of prayer and social support showed a mortality rate one seventh of those who did not.[14] Other researchers found that those who attended church regularly and had a stronger faith were less likely to die and had better overall health.[15] There are over *twelve hundred* studies linking intentional prayer and overall health and longevity.[16] Meta-analyses in various medical journals have compiled results that show that intentional prayer significantly affects healing.[17] Dr. David Levy, a practicing neurosurgeon in California, prays for his patients before he operates on them and has amazing results. The majority of his patients want him to pray because it shows them he cares more about their health and about them as a person than a physician who does not discuss spiritual matters with his or her patients.[18]

I love what Dr. Levy says about how he approaches the often life-threatening and frightening brain surgeries that his patients face:

> I have been in this profession for a good number of years and am intimately familiar with most of the new therapies, medical devices, and drugs hitting the market. Many of them are ingenious, and I use them regularly in my practice. I have consulted for several companies to develop better devices and have travelled the world teaching others to use them. I admire and am grateful for modern medical technology. But though technology can prolong a life or reduce pain, it cannot always make life better. My experiences have convinced me that spirituality is a crucial element to the wellbeing of a person as a whole; moreover if we let him, God can do powerful, supernatural things in our everyday lives. That's why I began inviting God into my consultations, exams and surgeries. Many would be surprised that a neurosurgeon—a man of science, logic and human progress—would be such a strong believer in God and divine intervention. Yet the experience has been nothing short of phenomenal.[19]

This experiment highlights how we impact each other through our intentions and prayers. Our prayers impact each other, but so do the negative words we speak over people we are in relationship with. However, we need to remember that "a curse without cause shall not alight" (Prov. 26:2).

Matter Just Keeps Getting Smaller

We have gone from molecules to atoms to quarks, leptons, and bosons; and now physicists are proposing an even smaller concept called *preons* as minuscule particles that make up quarks. They are also proposing a string theory, which says that the ultimate building blocks of matter are tiny, vibrating strings, which are even smaller than preons. One scientist even describes preons as twisted braids of space-time.[20] If preons exist (I think they do), they are unimaginably tiny and would have to fit inside a quark, which is currently the smallest known particle of matter, having a size of zero, and the strings are even smaller.[21]

Thought Moves Faster Than the Speed of Light

Electrons have been observed to jump from one orbit to another without traveling through the intervening space and without time having elapsed.

Scientists say our thought signals also seem to move faster than the speed of light and in ways that classical physics cannot explain. How else do you explain the effect we have on each other, how someone with a negative attitude impacts how you feel?

Remember the mirror neurons in the brain that mirror each other's emotions, facilitating empathy that I spoke about a few paragraphs back? These signals that are passed between us are made up of energy that can be explained—at this time, anyway—in terms of quantum physics.

A Glimpse into the Spiritual World

These observations also give us a glimpse of the spiritual side of the world that is beyond time and space. It could explain how, after Jesus's resurrection, he appeared to two men on the road to Emmaus, then later that evening as soon as they recognized who he was, he suddenly disappeared (Luke 24:31).

A few verses further on in Luke's Gospel, Jesus suddenly appeared among the disciples, and they thought he was a ghost (Luke 24:36–46). Later, Philip suddenly disappears after the Ethiopian's baptism (Acts 8:28–40). These are all mysteries that quantum physics hints at solving, as though God is reeling us in with beautiful and fascinating concepts to try to explain these mysteries.

Unpredictability Is the Norm

Unpredictability is the norm and therefore requires faith and "without faith it is impossible to please God" (Heb. 11:6 NIV). We see this concept in the *Heisenberg uncertainty principle*, which is a radical departure from classical physics in that it replaces dogmatic certainty with ambiguity.

For example, humans are seen as observers outside the system[22] who exert an effect that is unpredictable. And it is not just humans who are unpredictable. The unpredictability reaches down to the level of electrons and photons of light, which cannot have a definite momentum or position at the same time; particles are neither particles nor waves because they are both. And as for quarks, bosons, and now preons and strings, they are simply all over the place.

Quantum Physics Math Predictions
Show Unpredictability

You can try to mathematically predict uncertainty. (Sounds strange, doesn't it?) Quantum physics math prediction is all about mathematically showing this uncertainty, which basically undergirds free will.[23] But you will never be 100 percent accurate in predicting exactly what another person is thinking—even someone you know very well.

This is a God-ordained precept in which it is clear that no human knows another human's thoughts except that person and God. "For what man knows the things of a man except the spirit of the man which is in him? Even so no one knows the things of God except the Spirit of God" (1 Cor. 2:11).

The weather tomorrow, what your friend is going to say, what you will be doing at this time a week from today, in fact all aspects of life in the future—these all follow Heisenberg's uncertainty principle. It gives us two options: faith or fear. I don't know what you are going to choose, but obviously I hope it will be faith. Why worry about tomorrow? Your heavenly Father knows what you need (Matt. 6:25–33).

It's All about Trusting That God Is Who He Says He Is

Heisenberg's uncertainty principle is a nightmare for classical physicists and others who try to explain away God and free will. Einstein, who could never reconcile himself to this random aspect of nature, famously pronounced, "*Der Alte wurfelt nicht*," which is translated, "The old man, that is God, does not play dice." Well, God is not playing dice; he is simply telling us to trust him and stop trying to control everything, which is a full-blown setback for the notion that the future can be accurately forecast. One cannot fathom the intent of God (Ps. 145:3; Eccles. 3:1; Rom. 11:33).

Einstein simply looked at it from the wrong angle. The correct angle is found in Scripture: "Trust in the LORD with all your heart and lean not on your own understanding. In all your ways acknowledge Him, and he will direct your paths" (Prov. 3:5–6), and "Many are the plans in the mind of a man, but it is the purpose of the LORD that will stand" (Prov. 19:21 ESV).

American physicist Don Lincoln, a ground-breaking researcher of particle physics at Fermi National Accelerator Laboratory, captures very succinctly and clearly what I believe God is doing in science:

> We can move easily through air but not through a wall. The sun transmutes one element to another, bathing our planet in warmth and light. Radio waves have carried man's voice to earth from the surface of the moon, whereas gamma rays can inflict fatal damage on our DNA. On the face of it, these disparate phenomena have nothing to do with one another, but physicists have uncovered a handful of principles that fuse into a theory of sublime simplicity to explain all this and much more. This theory is called the standard model of particle physics, and it encapsulates the electromagnetic forces that make a wall feel solid, the nuclear forces that govern the sun's power plant, and the diverse family of light waves that both make modern communications possible and threaten our well-being.[24]

God's Plans

Quantum physics, and neuroscience for that matter, do not provide ultimate answers; they are simply stepping-stones in the development of our understanding of our Almighty God, another way of admiring God. Just as sound waves across the air or big metal planes flying in the sky or nuclear power were inconceivable before the discovery of atomic structure, so would unveiling a new layer of matter or a new, complex brain circuit or a biochemical pathway or a better understanding of genes reveal phenomena we cannot even begin to imagine. God pulls us along in exciting suspense in this enjoyable discovery of his creation. He is trying to show us that "glory belongs to God, whose power is at work in us. By this power he can do infinitely more than we can ask or imagine" (Eph. 3:20 GW).

Let me point out the obvious: God created everything, and that includes science and physics, and he has revealed the laws of this material world we live in over the ages to help us understand him. I am not being a materialist; far from it. I believe God is taking us through the material world into the spiritual world to get to know him more deeply. Why, after all, did he put our soul and spirit in a physical body and place us in a physical world?

Quantum physics is creeping into every field, causing confusion among scientists, dealing a deathblow to the Newtonian dream, all because it points directly back to God, "the old man," who has ultimate control. I love it when his plans come together.

Chapter 7 Summary

1. There is the sensory world of our five senses; there is the world of electromagnetism and the atom; and then there is the deeper quantum world.
2. This quantum world challenges physicists' perception of linear time, orderly space, and fixed realities; and it

turns on its head the Cartesian Newtonian world that sees humans as machines with exchangeable parts.

3. Quantum physics, which is different from classical physics, is a way of explaining how the things that make up atoms work and making sense of how the smallest things in nature work.

4. Quantum means *energy*, so quantum physics also tells us how electromagnetic waves—like light waves—work.

5. Quantum mechanics is the mathematical framework used to describe this energy and how it works.

6. Quantum physics basically says

   • your consciousness affects the behaviors of subatomic particles;

   • particles move backward and forward in time and appear in all possible places at once; and

   • the universe is connected with faster-than-light transfers of information.

7. Five main ideas are presented in quantum theory:

   • Energy is not a continuous stream but comes in small, discrete units.

   • The basic units behave both like particles and like waves.

   • The movement of these particles is random.

   • It is physically impossible to know both the position and the momentum of a particle at the same time.

   • The atomic world is nothing like the world we live in.

8. Quantum theory converts science's conception of humans from being mere cogs in a gigantic, mechanical machine to being freethinking agents whose conscious,

free choices affect the physical world. This is called the *observer effect*.

9. The Copenhagen interpretation of quantum theory says that the particle is what you measure it to be. This means our perceptions determine the outcome; we perceive the world through the thoughts (memories) we have built into our brains.

10. The Quantum Zeno Effect (QZE) is the repeated effort that causes learning to take place.

11. The *law of entanglement* in quantum physics states that relationship is the defining characteristic of everything in space and time. Because of the pervasive nature of the entanglement of atomic particles, relationship is independent of distance and requires no physical link. Everything and everyone is linked, and we all affect each other.

12. Thought signals seem to move faster than the speed of light and in ways that classical physics cannot explain. This means our mind controls matter and is therefore a creative force.

13. Humans are seen as observers outside the system who exert an effect that is *unpredictable*. And it is not just humans who are unpredictable. The unpredictability reaches down to the level of electrons and photons of light, which cannot have a definite momentum or position at the same time; particles are neither particles nor waves because they are both. And as for quarks, bosons, and now preons and strings—they are simply all over the place.

14. The random and unpredictable nature of quantum physics is called the *Heisenberg uncertainty principle*.

This principle is a way God shows us that we do not control the future. He does.

15. Quantum physics math prediction is all about mathematically showing this uncertainty, which basically undergirds free will.

16. I believe God is taking us through the material world into the spiritual world to get to know him more deeply, and the quantum concept is part of this journey.

8

The Science of Thought

Main Scripture: Therefore put away all filthiness and rampant wickedness and receive with meekness the implanted word, which is able to save your souls. James 1:21 ESV

Linked Science Concept: What you wire into your brain through thinking is stored in your nonconscious mind. The nonconscious mind is where 99.9 percent of our mind activity is. It is the root level that stores the thoughts with the emotions and perceptions, and it impacts the conscious mind and what we say and do. Everything is first a thought. The Geodesic Information Processing Theory is a scientific way of understanding this.

The brain is not an input-output machine. You are not an input-output machine. You are not a computer mirroring the outside world. Your brain is designed to respond to your mind. You are intrinsically and brilliantly designed in the sense that your brain carries out the will of the spirit and the soul. Internal activity in your mind is where everything begins, "for as he thinks in his heart, so is he" (Prov. 23:7).

The Power of Your Thought Life

In my research, I spent many years trying to understand science in terms of the truths of Scripture. I researched, developed, and tested a theory that can basically be described as explaining the science of thought—or in simple terms, how we think and the effect of our thoughts on our brain, body, and mind. I applied this in many ways with my patients and in my research over time.[1]

If you look at the image of my theory, "The Geodesic Information Processing Theory" on pages 126–27, it will help you understand this internal activity, the science of thought, a little better.

Before I explain this in a simple way, let me tell you why I am doing this. When you understand the power of your thought life, which has been the emphasis of the first seven chapters in this book, you truly begin to get a glimpse of how important it is to take responsibility for what you are thinking. Thinking is a powerful creative force, both a blessing and a curse, and should not be taken lightly. So, in exposing you to a tested scientific theory, albeit briefly in this chapter, I am giving you some tangible proof (not the only proof) that God was so serious about us capturing our thoughts and renewing our minds that he gave us science as encouragement.

Thomas More explains this so well in his book *Utopia*:

> The scientific investigation of nature is not only a most enjoyable process but also the best possible means of pleasing the Creator. . . . He has the normal reactions of an artist.

Having put the marvelous system of the universe on show for human beings to look at—since no other species is capable of taking it in—He must prefer the type of person who examines it carefully, and really admires his work, to the type that just ignores it and like the lower animals remains quite unimpressed by the whole astonishing spectacle.[2]

You will see there are three levels on the schematic of my theory: (1) Nonconscious metacognitive level; (2) Conscious cognitive level; and (3) Symbolic output level.

Nonconscious Metacognitive Level

The nonconscious metacognitive level is on the far left. It is where 90 to 99 percent of the action in your mind is; your thinking and thought-building happen on this level. This level operates at about four hundred billion actions per second and drives the conscious cognitive level. It operates twenty-four hours a day.

Conscious Cognitive Level

The conscious cognitive level, in the middle, is where up to 10 percent of mind action is. It operates at about two thousand actions per second, so it is much slower and is controlled by the metacognitive level. The cognitive level in turn drives the symbolic output level (end section), which is what you say and do—what the world sees, the output of your thinking. This level operates when we are awake.

Symbolic Action Level

The symbolic output level incorporates the five senses through which you express yourself and experience the world,

THE GEODESIC INFORMATION PROCESSING MODEL

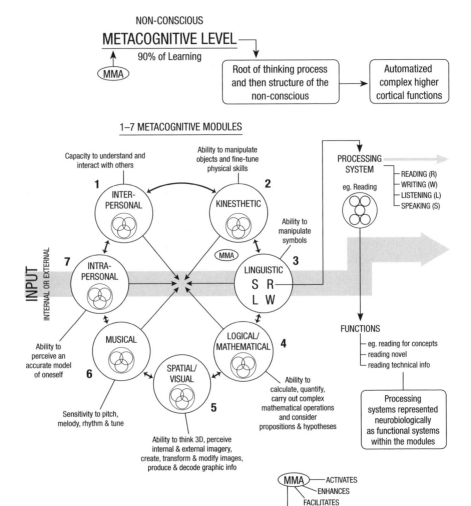

NON-CONSCIOUS

METACOGNITIVE LEVEL

90% of Learning

MMA

| Root of thinking process and then structure of the non-conscious | Automatized complex higher cortical functions |

1–7 METACOGNITIVE MODULES

Capacity to understand and interact with others

Ability to manipulate objects and fine-tune physical skills

1 INTER-PERSONAL

2 KINESTHETIC

Ability to manipulate symbols

PROCESSING SYSTEM
eg. Reading
— READING (R)
— WRITING (W)
— LISTENING (L)
— SPEAKING (S)

7 INTRA-PERSONAL

MMA

3 LINGUISTIC
S R
L W

INPUT
INTERNAL OR EXTERNAL

Ability to perceive an accurate model of oneself

6 MUSICAL

5 SPATIAL/VISUAL

LOGICAL/MATHEMATICAL **4**

FUNCTIONS
— eg. reading for concepts
— reading novel
— reading technical info

Sensitivity to pitch, melody, rhythm & tune

Ability to think 3D, perceive internal & external imagery, create, transform & modify images, produce & decode graphic info

Ability to calculate, quantify, carry out complex mathematical operations and consider propositions & hypotheses

Processing systems represented neurobiologically as functional systems within the modules

MMA — ACTIVATES
— ENHANCES
— FACILITATES
— REPRESENTS

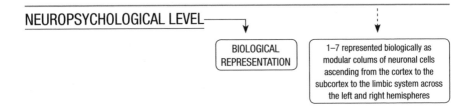

NEUROPSYCHOLOGICAL LEVEL

| BIOLOGICAL REPRESENTATION | 1–7 represented biologically as modular colums of neuronal cells ascending from the cortex to the subcortex to the limbic system across the left and right hemispheres |

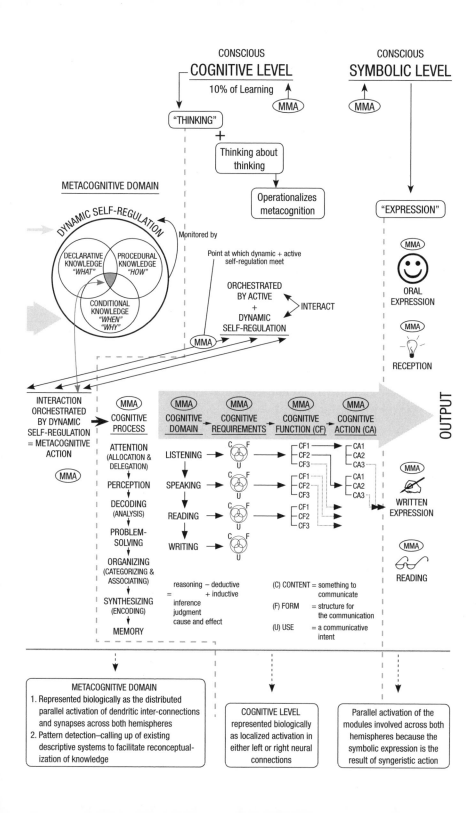

serving as the contact between the external world and the internal world of your mind. Therefore, this model works in reverse as well, forming a perfect circle. So information comes through the five senses, is received consciously by the conscious cognitive level, and then passes into the nonconscious meta-cognitive level where—if you have paid attention and started thinking and choosing—it becomes a physical thought as a result of genetic expression (the making of proteins). This newly built physical thought will, in turn, impact your conscious cognitive and symbolic levels—and so the cycle goes on.

21-Day Brain Detox Plan

Whatever you think about the most will grow, so the more the cycle moves with a particular thought, the stronger it grows. This is in essence the Quantum Zeno Effect (QZE) taking place that I explained in chapter 7. It takes around twenty-one days of this cycling for all the necessary protein changes[3] to happen to create a long-term integrated memory.

This is why my brain detox plan is for twenty-one days. You can't just apply a thought once and think change has happened. It takes repeated work for the QZE to take effect. Each day something is happening to the thought in your non-conscious mind. So if you stop at day 4 or 5, which is often when people do give up, then the consequence will be that the memory denatures—which means it dies and becomes heat energy. Simply put, you forget.

You Feel the Pull

It's important to note that we feel the pull of the sensory information coming in through the symbolic level, but we don't have to go there. These are the events and circumstances from the outside world. The events and circumstances from the outside world also enter into our minds and brains through electromagnetic and the quantum worlds (chap. 7). Remember, we cannot control the events and circumstances of our lives, but we *can control our reactions*. Don't be reactive; take time to slow down and think (see chaps. 4, 5, and 6).

Our five senses activate an emotional response almost immediately, but if we don't take the time to process them, the unprocessed emotion will dominate. This is why all the keys I am describing in part 1 of this book are so important; they help you deal with this pull.

Satan tries to take advantage of the pull of the five senses through this symbolic level, and he would love it if you respond impulsively to them. But you are made in God's image with the mind of Christ, and Jesus told his disciples that all power had been given to him (Matt. 28:18). If all power was given to Jesus, how much power does Satan have? None. When you truly let that sink in, you will realize that you control your reactions, your thinking, and your choices.

What Lies Are You Believing?

It's through the senses that we receive Satan's lies, but—and this is important—we don't have to believe those lies. If we do believe them, we process them into physical realities (through the conscious cognitive to the nonconscious metacognitive) that form the substance of the nerve networks upon which we act. This means that if we listen to and believe the Enemy's lies, we actually choose to process them into physical realities inside our brains. In doing so, we create the evil and act upon it. But we do not have to believe Satan's lies. We as humans create evil when we collapse these probabilities into actualities (chap. 7). So evil does not come from God, obviously, yet people often say that if God created everything, then he created evil as well. God has given us the power to create: this creative force can become good or evil through our choices.

Current neuroscientific and quantum physics research confirms that our thoughts change our brains daily. In fact, neurological literature has coined the term "self-directed neuroplasticity" as a general description of the principle that deep thinking changes brain structure and function.[4] This plastic ability of the brain to change in a positive or negative direction depending on our state of mind is called the *plastic paradox*. Positive plasticity produces positive behavior, and negative plasticity produces negative behaviors.

Distorted Love and Truth Get Wired In

When we distort love and truth, we wire this perversion into our brains and, in a sense, create brain damage. This is not an exaggeration, because our brains are wired for love, not fear, and therefore all the circuits—neurochemical, neurophysiological, neurobiological, electromagnetic, and quantum—are geared up for healthy, not toxic, thinking. If we allow ourselves to learn fear, it creates chaos and havoc in our brains.[5]

For example, one study showed that when patients with OCD remained toxic, obsessing and worrying about an issue, their brains showed damage and incorrect firing.[6] The researcher saw a decrease in activity in the lateral prefrontal cortex (just above your temples) where the circuits would normally have generated and maintained strategy. The medial orbital frontal cortex (behind your eyes) became more imbalanced and busy, which meant their decision-making ability became impaired. In addition, the amygdala (deep inside the middle of your brain running backward from the corner of your eyes) showed less balanced activity, so the patients were not evaluating emotional significance correctly. All this negative brain activity changed positively once the researcher put the patients through a rigid, directed, mental activity program.

If you look back to the chart of my theory again (see pp. 126–27), the bottom part beneath the horizontal line represents the neurological level that I have been describing throughout this book. Essentially the first three levels all describe mind activity, and the bottom level shows that this mind activity signals a change in brain structure. So my theory, the Geodesic Information Processing Theory, falls within the realm of cognitive neuroscience.

I show in my theory that the brain works in neurological pillars and multiple parallel circuits, which means there is a lot of interconnectivity among the neurons.[7] Essentially, the Geodesic Information Processing Theory deals with the science of thought. It is a description of how we think, choose, and build thoughts and the impact of this on our brain and behavior. It is our choices that make something out of nothing. This is basically cognitive neuroscience in action: the mind-brain connection.

My Switch On Your Brain 21-Day Brain Detox Plan, which is based on my theory and research, is designed to help improve your thinking and choices and subsequent happiness and health. It is our choices that create healthy thought universes in our brain, or they turn the powerless lie into a toxic thought universe in our brain. This is the incredible power God has given us: to be able to think and choose and create reality.

Automatization and Riding a Bicycle

After a period of repeated thinking about a choice over two to three cycles of twenty-one days, the new thought moves into the nonconscious metacognitive level, where it becomes part of our internal perception. This process is called *automatization.*

A simple example of automatization is learning to ride a bike. Initially, it was difficult and you wobbled all around. But as you practiced with determination—which means you applied the QZE—and intensely concentrated on the sequence of how to ride a bike, suddenly one day you were riding perfectly. It appeared as though having mastered the skill of bike riding meant you were not thinking about the process of cycling because now you rode the bike automatically. But you were actually thinking very nonconsciously—I know that makes no sense yet, so read on.

All the focused, dedicated, and repeated practice you consciously put into the learning process over time created a very strong thought network. Once the skill was mastered with the repeated and focused practice, it moved from the conscious mind (cognitive level) to the nonconscious mind (metacognitive level). Even though you were not consciously aware of the how-to-ride-a-bicycle thought, it was very much alive, and it was the guiding force behind the cycling. So each time you got on your bike, this memory was still in your metacognitive nonconscious guiding your bicycle riding. And as you ride around on your bike, you bring that thought into your conscious mind and it becomes malleable (plastic and changeable), and a few new branches are added as you cycle over that challenging mountain path or speed-jump over a log trying to keep up with your teenage son. So when you get off that bike, that "cycling thought" has become enriched from the experience you have just gone through.

Automatization Is a Life Principle

Automatization applies to everything in your life, because everything you do and say is first a thought. This means *nothing happens* until you first build the thought, which is like the root of a tree buried under the ground. The thought produces words, actions, behavior, and so on, which can be compared to the tree, branches, leaves, flowers, and fruit you see above the ground. The roots under the ground are like the nonconscious metacognitive mind that nourishes and supports the tree, keeping it alive twenty-four hours a day.[8] The nonconscious metacognitive mind operates and nourishes your conscious cognitive mind twenty-four hours a day.

The nonconscious metacognitive mind is filled with the thoughts you have been building since you were in the womb, and they form the perceptual base from which you see life. Up to 99 percent of the decisions you make are based on what you have built and automatized into your nonconscious metacognitive level.[9] If a person's nonconscious metacognitive mind is filled with negative, toxic trash, then that is what informs his or her decisions on a day-to-day basis, which means that person will speak and act from toxicity. This is metacognitive to cognitive to symbolic—as per my theory.

Obviously the opposite of toxicity is health, and we were originally designed by God for health because we are made in God's image (Gen. 1:26). So we begin with health and then move away through bad choices. Most of the time we are a mix of healthy and toxic—you determine the proportions of these two for yourself.

You cannot sit back and wait to be happy and healthy and have a great thought life; you have to make the choice to make this happen. You have to choose to get rid of the toxic and get back in alignment with God. You can be overwhelmed by every small setback in life, or you can be energized by the possibilities they bring.

Chapter 8 Summary

1. The Geodesic Information Processing Theory deals with the science of thought. It is a description of how we think, choose, and build thoughts and the impact of this on our brain and behavior.

2. I show in my Geodesic Information Processing Theory that the brain works in neurological pillars and multiple parallel circuits, which means there is a lot of interconnectivity among the networks of the brain.

3. It is our choices that make something out of nothing. It's our choices that collapse the probabilities into actualities that define the state of our nonconscious metacognition, which in turn inform our conscious cognition and symbolic actions.

4. My Switch On Your Brain 21-Day Brain Detox Plan, which is based on my theory and research, is designed to help improve your thinking and choices and subsequent happiness and health.

5. It is our choices that either create healthy thought universes in our brain or turn the powerless lie into a toxic thought universe—which is essentially evil. This is the incredible power God has given us: to be able to think and choose and create reality. This reality can be good or evil based on our choices.

6. After a period of repeated thinking about the choice over two to three cycles of twenty-one days, the new thought moves into the nonconscious metacognitive

level where it becomes part of our internal perception. This process is called *automatization*.

7. Everything you do and say is first a thought.

8. The nonconscious metacognitive mind is filled with the thoughts you have been building since you were born, and they form the perceptual base from which you see life.

Now, as you move into part 2 of this book, remember the eight keys from chapters 1 through 8 and refer back to them often to get the most out of the 21-Day Brain Detox:

1. Mind controls matter
2. Choice and your multiple-perspective advantage
3. Your choices change your brain
4. Catch those thoughts
5. Entering into directed rest
6. Stop milkshake-multitasking
7. Thinking, God, and the quantum physics brain
8. The science of thought

Now step into part 2 and switch on your brain!

The 21-Day Brain Detox Plan

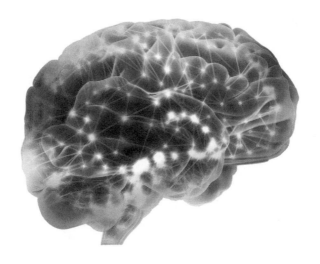

9

What Is the 21-Day Brain Detox Plan?

The hardest part about achieving peak happiness, thinking, and health is remembering that we can choose them. Achieving them is not accomplished by putting on a brave or happy face, nor are they attained by adopting an ostrich mentality and pretending that problems don't exist or that everything will always be great. The way to find this state is by harnessing the neuroplasticity God has designed in our brains and choosing to rewire—or renew—our mind (Rom. 12:2). This is a lifestyle that will bring us ever closer in alignment to our original design of perfection (Matt. 5:48), of being made in God's image (Gen. 1:26).

We can actively choose happiness rather than letting our external and internal world of wired-in and learned thoughts and our biology define happiness for us. We need to wire in positive thought networks that can fill us with the power to get us back on track (2 Tim. 1:7). It is the implanted Word that will save our souls (James 1:21). Who we are is where happiness lies, but this is so often blocked by who we have become.

A Simple Tool That Brings Peace

Even though the 21-Day Brain Detox Plan is based on rigorous science and the Word of God, it is a simple tool to help bring peak happiness, thinking, health, and peace—not only into your life but also into the lives of your loved ones. To detox your thought life, you need to remember *it's your thinking that will actually change your brain.* So you need to do *consciously* what your brain does on a *nonconscious* level to build a thought. You control your brain; your brain does not control you.

A Simple Brain Sequence That Makes Things Happen

In order to make this nonconscious to conscious process happen effectively, what you do each day is my 5-Step Switch On Your Brain Learning Process. This is a "brain sequence" based on my Geodesic Information Processing Theory, which describes the science of thought (see chap. 8). This is a statistically significant and scientifically proven technique that I developed many years ago and have continued to develop and use over the years in my research and clinical experience to help people think and learn for lasting success. It is based on complex science that focuses on the dynamics of the thought process. In this book I will teach you the simple application, but more thorough details can be found in my scientific references if you wish to read further.[1]

The 5-Step Switch On Your Brain Learning Process

The 5-Step Switch On Your Brain Learning Process has at its heart focused, organized, and disciplined deep intellectual thinking to break down toxic thoughts and build up healthy thoughts—and in doing so, change your brain in a positive direction. This will result in peak thinking, happiness, and health. When applied daily within the correct time frames, it becomes a lifestyle of thinking that renews your mind, creates real change and freedom, and brings you ever closer to God.

I am always excited to share this theory and process with people because of the joy it brings to see the positive change it makes in the lives of those who truly apply it.

I demonstrated in my research in the early 1990s that the nonconscious metacognitive mind is much more powerful than the conscious cognitive mind. When you engage the nonconscious mind through deep thinking, you bring memories into the conscious mind in a vulnerable state, which means you can change them—or reconceptualize them. I also found that when the memories go back into the nonconscious mind, they are more complex. You have not simply added information, you have redesigned the memories—and this can go in a positive or negative direction. Scientifically, this is called "creative reconceptualization."[2]

As an individual, you *are* capable of making mental and emotional changes in your life. Through your thinking, you can actively re-create thoughts and, therefore, knowledge in your mind.

God Is Revealing More Each Day

These research results have been reconfirmed recently, specifically related to post traumatic stress disorder (PTSD) trauma. Karim Nader, a professor at McGill University, has done groundbreaking research on memory that scientifically proves that we can renew our minds—more evidence of science catching up with the Bible. He shows that the emotional component of memories can be reconsolidated or changed when recalled into the conscious mind because they become vulnerable. So as a memory moves from the nonconscious mind to the conscious mind, it becomes vulnerable and susceptible to change.[3] This is precisely what I proposed and found in my research.

My Documented Results

Some of my documented results using this deep-thinking, brain-engaging process were very exciting. My patients with closed-head injuries showed between 110 to 140 percent increase in their academic results. This academic increase started within approximately twenty-one days of starting my 5-Step Switch On Your Brain Learning Process. Furthermore, not only did it improve academic function, but intellectual, emotional, and social skills showed dramatic change as well. One patient in particular showed a better intellectual status, as evaluated on neuropsychological testing, after the accident than before. This means she increased her intelligence, according to the neuropsychologist, by up to 20 points post-accident when normally intellectual scores decrease by 20 to 30 points after a traumatic brain injury.

Her memory improvement was almost immediate and continued to improve dramatically over the twelve months of therapy. This improvement continued over time with her going on to further her studies and successfully moving into the work arena. Clinically, this patient became more organized and less confused, and she was perceived by her peers as being no different from them.

This is a major feat because statistical estimates suggest that only one third of patients who suffer traumatic brain injury might return to their previous lifestyle and gainful employment with traditional therapy. In contrast, the 5-Step Switch On Your Brain Learning Process, my nontraditional therapeutic approach, works on metacognitive and cognitive mind issues (see chap. 8), and the improvement in the metacognitive and cognitive mind issues carries over into intellect, emotions, and psychosocial functioning. Probably the most impactful is that the improvement carries over into everyday life and is therefore self-sustaining.

We Can All Get Control of Our Minds

At the same time I was working with traumatic brain injury (TBI) patients, I also worked with students with learning problems as well as students who had no learning problems as such, but who wanted to improve their academic progress. My work also included adults pursuing further education and those in corporate life. In my doctoral research, I showed that significant changes in cognitive, academic, and psychosocial function happened in teachers and students alike when they applied my deep-thinking brain technique. Across the board, I was seeing these same kinds of results. I trained thousands of teachers and therapists in my 5-Step Switch On Your Brain Learning Process, and they have, in turn, reached thousands of students and report great changes.

Put Your Mind to It

I even saw this happening in the most challenging of situations back in my home country of South Africa. For many

143

years I worked with starving children who had literally not eaten for many days. In most cases they didn't have two loving parents at home because at least one if not both had either died of AIDS or had been murdered, and they lived in squalid conditions with more than a 70 percent chance of having been exposed to some form of physical, sexual, or mental abuse—yet they could not get enough of learning how to learn when I ran Switch On Your Brain courses in their schools.

Even though I was working through the medium of academics in these schools, the sessions became like church services when those brave children recognized that they could use their minds to rise above their circumstances, and that they could change their life with this incredible mind and brain God had given them. They saw learning as an exciting opportunity and wanted to be at school, despite the fact that there were often a hundred hungry, dirty, traumatized children squeezed into a classroom where we would have only one textbook to work from and one old-fashioned chalkboard. They were desperate to learn and sat for hours listening raptly and hardly moving, as though trying to absorb everything I was teaching into every fiber of their being. It was a privilege to be there with those magnificent minds dressed in rags, and this was where I learned some of my greatest lessons about the power of choice and deep, intellectual thought to change the mind.

It's Not a Heavy Burden

Some researchers who visited Soweto, South Africa, where I worked for years, have compared these amazing children in Soweto to Harvard students, though you could not have two more different worlds.[4] Their results showed that 95 percent of the Soweto children said they loved schoolwork and learning; in comparison, about 80 percent (4 out of 5) of the Harvard students suffered from depression so debilitating they could not function.[5] This is shocking considering that Harvard has some of the brightest minds, magnificent facilities, and is mentioned often as the gold standard of education.

When you see choosing to change your mind and to learn as a heavy burden, you miss out on the opportunities in front of you. When you see choosing to change your mind and to learn as a wonderful privilege, suddenly you see the opportunities.

What I saw in the people I have worked with over the years, some of whom are described in the studies in earlier chapters and above, was a mindset that chose to change and excel. They chose not to allow their difficult life experience to block them. They *chose to change*. They chose not to succumb to the pressure nor to get stuck in a neutral position and settle for the status quo.

Do you want to choose to change? Choosing life is the mindset that brings renewal and revival. This is what I hope my 21-Day Brain Detox Plan will help you achieve.

Chapter 9 Summary

1. You have to *choose* to have a controlled thought life and to be happy and healthy. Everyone can learn how to improve their thinking, learning, and intelligence.

2. We need to wire in positive thought networks that can fill us with the power to get us back on track (2 Tim. 1:7).

3. Even though the 5 Steps of the Switch on Your Brain Learning Process that are used daily in the 21-Day Brain Detox are based on rigorous science and the Word of

God, they are a simple tool to help bring peak happiness, thinking, and health not only into your life but also the lives of your loved ones.

4. To detox your thought life, you need to remember *it's your thinking that will actually change your brain.*

5. Science is catching up with the Bible daily.

6. If you put your mind to it, you can achieve what God says you can achieve.

7. You control your brain; your brain does not control you.

10

How and Why the 21-Day
Brain Detox Plan Works

The Switch On Your Brain 21-Day Brain Detox Plan technique is a rigorous, disciplined, daily routine that becomes a lifestyle of renewing your mind. It is a lifestyle of neuroplastically rewiring your nerve networks. It is driven by you, but led by the Holy Spirit. It gets you into a state of deep, intellectual, introspective self-reflection, activating all eight keys I described in part 1.

Your Daily Routine

Once you have worked through this book and mastered the concepts (and take your time with this; it's worth not rushing through), your daily routine will take *seven to ten* minutes minimum, although some like to go longer. During this time you will be doing 5 steps, daily, for 21 days. These 5 steps are based on my research on the science of thought and the brain (see chapter 8) and are called the 5-Step Switch On Your Brain Learning Process.

You can do up to *seventeen* 21-Day Brain Detox Plan cycles per year.[1] Research shows that deep-thinking exercises repeated daily over a period of twenty-one days help create long-lasting change.

Your year can start whenever you want it to, so if you have picked up this book in September, for example, then you simply work through the book during September and then begin your year in October.

Who needs this? Everyone. As you have seen from the eight keys discussed in part 1, no one is exempt from mind issues. From the moment God created us with free will, we entered a realm of creative responsibility for our choices.

It is obviously a highly complex process, but I have simplified the Switch On Your Brain technique sequence into five steps:

1. Gather
2. Focused Reflection
3. Write
4. Revisit
5. Active Reach

You Are Doing Your Own Brain Surgery

Each of these steps activates phenomenal and complex neurophysiology and neurobiology. So in essence, what you will be doing with the 5 steps is bringing the toxic thought into consciousness and then proceeding, over 21 days, to destroy it (see chap. 8). Mind controls matter, as we learned in part 1.

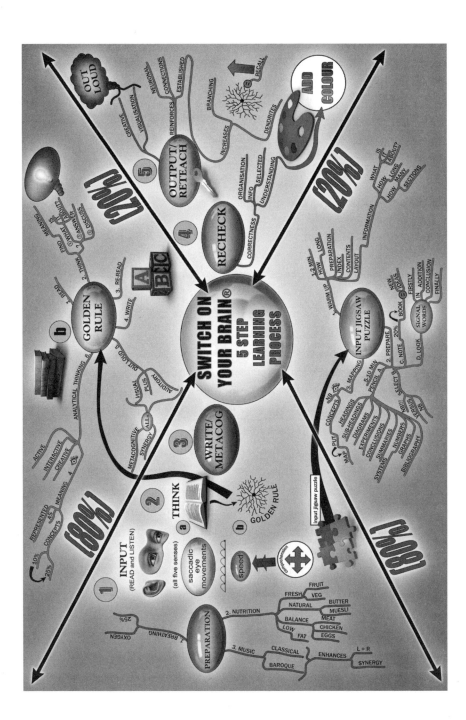

At the same time, you will be growing a healthy new thought to replace the toxic one, so you will be consciously and simultaneously building up healthy thoughts and tearing down toxic thoughts. You work on only *one* thought network each 21-day cycle, breaking down the toxic and simultaneously building up the healthy.

You Can Repeat the Cycle

You may repeat a cycle if you feel you haven't fully dealt with the issue. Many times we start working through something only to discover the root issue a few days in. That's fine; just focus in on the root issue for the rest of the 21 days and then redo the cycle. Twenty-one days is just the minimum time needed to build the neural network.[2]

What this means is that it takes repeated updating or rethinking through information in a sequenced way for it to take root and form a stable memory. If this reinforcement does not take place over the 21 days, then the newly found neural network will decay in less than a month. If you don't use the memory, the proteins it is made from will denature and the memory will disassemble. Wherever there is more thinking activity, there will be more wiring. Whatever you think about the most will grow, because thinking stimulates the genetic expression required to make proteins. Every hour the connections are doubling.[3]

You may also just feel at the end of the cycle that the toxic thought was so dominant or strong that it warrants working on it another 21 days. Sometimes there is a lot of guilt and condemnation or "I can't" mindsets that can keep you from progressing. These mindsets alone require a 21-day brain detox before the next issue can be tackled.

Pay More Attention to the New, Healthy Memory

This is why it is so important to build up the new healthy memory and pay more attention to it rather than to the toxic memory you are breaking down: Repeated replaying is central to the process of creating durable, long-term memories. And remember, this works in both the negative and positive direction.

As you move through the five steps and into deep, focused reflection, your brain will have moments of insight that are accompanied by bursts of high frequency gamma waves in the brain.[4] These create an ideal mindset for learning and integration across the brain. Neurons have their own rhythmic activity, almost like an internal chatter, and changes in these fluctuations underlie how we perceive things.[5] It is our choice to pay attention that influences this internal chatter in a positive or negative direction. You want as much of this happening over the 21 days as possible because it will enhance your effectiveness. We need to be almost obsessive in our desire to change, to "Be perfect, therefore, as your heavenly Father is perfect" (Matt. 5:48 NIV).

So Many Good Things Are Happening

The brain is always learning how to learn, always changing. As you use the 5-Step Switch On Your Brain Learning Process through the 21 days you are influencing so many good things to happen. Here are just a few. When you think deeply and are learning, BDNF (brain derived neurotrophic factor) is released to consolidate the connections between neurons to enhance recall in the future. This BDNF also promotes increase in the fatty substance called myelin, which insulates the nerves. This is a good thing, because increased myelination means faster thinking and better memory. As you start paying attention and focusing your thinking, BDNF is released, and this in turn increases attention by activating the nucleus basalis. And when the nucleus basalis is turned on, the brain becomes extremely plastic and ready to change, build, and rewire—and therefore, renew.[6]

The Work Doesn't End at 21 Days

At the end of the 21-day cycle, the toxic thought is gone and the new healthy thought is like a "tiny new plant" that will need nurturing to grow. Our *thinking* is that nurturing. This means that if you don't practice using it, it will not be properly automatized (see chap. 8), and it is very possible that your mind will shift back to regrowing that toxic thought.

To avoid this you make a conscious effort to practice using the new thought as much as you can until you reach automatization. Automatization means that particular way of thinking or reacting embedded in the new thought tree has become an automatic part of you; you do it driven by the nonconscious mind, not the conscious mind. So, to make sure that you have automatized the new healthy memory, research shows you will need to consciously practice using it daily for at least two more 21-day cycles, or 63 days total.[7] Please continue to consciously keep practicing using the new habit until you feel comfortable—which can even sometimes take between 84–154 days of consciously using the new healthy thought. The point is that the duration or automatization of the habit formation is likely to differ based on what you are trying to do and, of course, the uniqueness of who you are as a person. As long as you continue *doing*—which I call an "active reach," the fifth step that you do each day—consistently in a given situation, the healthy new way of thinking, the healthy "habit," will form.

Bumps, Lollipops, and Mushrooms

In the brain, automatization physically looks like lots more tree branches that are thick and well established, with many branches interconnecting with other thought networks. And if you could zoom in closely to the connections the branches grow from, you would see little things called *spines*. These spines change shape, from a bump at around 7 days, to a lollipop shape at around 14 days, to a mushroom shape at around 21 days as the thought becomes stronger. This is because the proteins change progressively by day 21, with peak changes being at 7 and 14 days, to become self-sustaining proteins, which are like a long-term memory. This applies in both the negative and positive direction—this is the concept of the plastic paradox I spoke of earlier. And even a long-term memory can be broken down. If, after wiring out a toxic thought, you have stopped using the healthy new thought and revert back to the toxic thought, you reverse the process you went through in the first place, breaking down the healthy thought and rebuilding the toxic thought. This is why we need to make a choice to be alert, practicing the presence of God by sharpening our conscience and listening to our intuition. This is what creates a lifestyle of renewing the mind.

So at the end of the 21 days, you integrate the new healthy thought into your lifestyle, into your repertoire of reactions to life so that you keep strengthening that reaction. It can take anywhere from three to four 21-day cycles to automatize

A Neuron with Dendrites, Showing Bumps, Lollipops, and Umbrellas

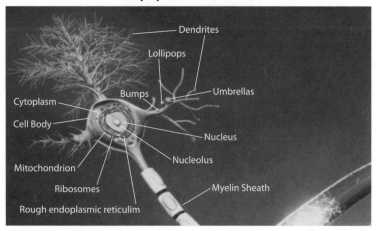

the new healthy thought pattern and to make sure the toxic thought doesn't grow back.[8] A lot also depends on the individual, the thought pattern you are detoxing, and the healthy replacement pattern you are building. So for some thoughts it might take one 21-day cycle, and for other thoughts it might take more, as I explained earlier.

The 21-Day Brain Detox Plan Is a Deliberate Practice

The best way to change, learn, and build memory meaningfully is through deliberate and disciplined practice. This is not mindless repetition. The five steps of the Switch On Your Brain technique in the 21-Day Brain Detox Plan include deliberate, conscious setting of goals, obtaining immediate feedback, and concentrating as much on the process as on the outcome. The 21-Day Brain Detox Plan will work best when you set the challenge just beyond the edge of your comfort zone; a challenge is good for you.[9] We are designed as deeply intelligent beings and our minds and brains respond to and rise up to challenge. In fact, they get better.

You are made from God's perfectness, but it is up to you to create your expertise in life. God gives us the blueprint, but we need to choose to make it happen.

The point is that you are playing to win and you don't give up. "I press on toward the goal to win the prize for which God has called me heavenward in Christ Jesus" (Phil. 3:14 NIV). As you go through this process, you will be fulfilling what God calls us to do in Romans 12:2, "renewing" the mind, and in Matthew 5:48, "Be perfect, just as your Father in heaven is perfect." In the next five chapters I will explain each of the five steps of my Switch On Your Brain technique. It is necessary to get a deep understanding of each of these steps so you use them properly on a daily basis. If you skip a step or only sort of use the step, the changes you create will also be "sort of" and not effective.

You will see questions interspersed in the text—please stop to take a moment to answer the questions because they will help you experience and understand the Switch On Your Brain process much more deeply, and it will make it easier to apply the 21-Day Brain Detox Plan. The questions help you start understanding how to get into the mindset that will increase your chance of success.

Chapter 10 Summary

1. The 21-Day Brain Detox Plan is a deliberate, disciplined, and rigorous renewing of the mind lifestyle, not a one-time activity.
2. Your daily routine will take seven to ten minutes minimum, although some like to go longer.

3. You will be doing approximately seventeen 21-Day Brain Detox Plan cycles per year.

4. Each day you do my 5-Step Switch On Your Brain Learning Process for the seven to ten minutes.

5. Over the 21 days, you are breaking down the toxic thought and building up the healthy replacement memory.

6. It takes 21 days for certain protein changes to happen in the brain for the new memory to become self-sustaining and for the old memory to be broken down.

7. By approximately day 7 the protein connection holding the memory in place is a bump shape; by approximately day 14 it is a lollipop shape; and by approximately day 21 it is a mushroom shape.

8. You need to repeat the 21-day cycle for up to three more times for it to become automatized.

9. *Automatization* means it is in your nonconscious controlling the conscious thinking that precedes what you do.

11

Gather

Step 1

You have to develop disciplined thought lives, and part of that is increasing your awareness of what you are allowing into your mind. The *gather* step is, therefore, all about becoming aware of all the signals that are coming into your mind from the external environment through the five senses and understanding the internal environment of your mind. So as you answer the questions in this section, you are focusing on developing *awareness*, which means you are starting the process of bringing those rogue thoughts into captivity.

The Signals Come from Two Sources

These signals come from two sources: (1) the external environment that comes in through the five senses, electromagnetic and quantum signals, and (2) the thoughts deep in the nonconscious metacognitive part of your mind (your memories).

Let me explain what I mean. Perhaps, as you read this, you have some of your favorite music playing in the background. You might be sitting in a comfortable chair, smelling a scented candle while savoring a piece of fruit. If you are in this idyllic setting, all five of your senses—sight, sound, smell, touch, and taste—will be your link between the external world and the internal world of your mind.

QUESTION: What are you experiencing through your five senses as you are reading this? Try to describe this in as much detail as possible. This is a simple exercise just to help you become aware of what is coming into your mind. This simple awareness can be developed to the point where you learn not to let any thought go through your mind unchecked.

As we move on with this section, there is a lot of brain information. Take your time and just enjoy how intricately God has made you. And please remember, you are brilliant and intelligent and totally capable of understanding because you are made in his image (Gen. 1:26).

The Signals Enter the Brain

This incoming information then travels through some astonishing brain structures (some of which include the thalamus, insula, and basal ganglia) that flavor, enrich, and distribute the information all along the way. You think with groups of brain areas (circuits and columns), not with single brain areas. So once the information enters the brain, it is a signal that creates major cascading, intrinsic (inside your brain) activity. The circuits and columns around the basal ganglia (deep down inside the middle of the brain), for example, get

158

Inside the Brain

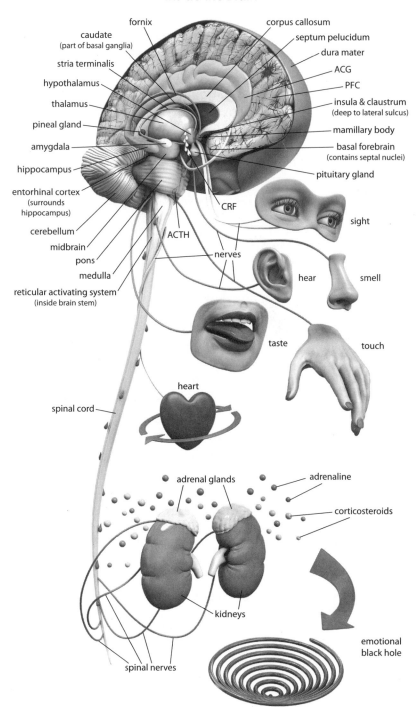

fornix
corpus callosum
caudate (part of basal ganglia)
septum pelucidum
stria terminalis
dura mater
hypothalamus
ACG
thalamus
PFC
pineal gland
insula & claustrum (deep to lateral sulcus)
amygdala
mamillary body
hippocampus
basal forebrain (contains septal nuclei)
entorhinal cortex (surrounds hippocampus)
pituitary gland
cerebellum
CRF
midbrain
ACTH
pons
nerves
medulla
sight
reticular activating system (inside brain stem)
hear
smell
taste
touch
heart
spinal cord
adrenal glands
adrenaline
corticosteroids
kidneys
spinal nerves
emotional black hole

the brain into a state of expectation as preparation to build the new, incoming information. Part of this activity is the movement of thoughts (existing memories), linked in some way to the incoming information, moving from the nonconscious metacognitive level to the conscious cognitive level (see chap. 8 to remind yourself of these concepts).

"Magic Trees of the Mind" Golgi Stain

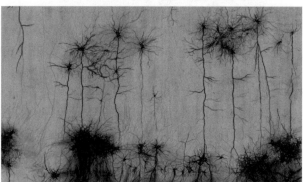

These thoughts in your brain look like trees in a forest. And as the signals sweep through these trees like a wind, research shows they will activate around four to seven[1] thought trees (memories) that will then move into the conscious, and you will become aware of them (see chap. 8). I call this the "breeze through the trees."

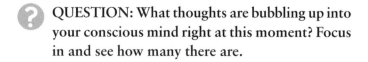 QUESTION: What thoughts are bubbling up into your conscious mind right at this moment? Focus in and see how many there are.

Thoughts Have an Emotional Component

When you think, you *also feel*. This is because thoughts have an emotional component in addition to the information, or what the actual memory is about. This means that when you bring a thought into consciousness, you also bring up the attached emotion. When the thought along with its emotions bubble up into the conscious mind, you *feel* the emotions.

So there is a difference between emotions and feelings; every thought has *emotions* as part of its structure, and they are stored in the nonconscious mind. When the thoughts move into the conscious mind, we *feel* the emotions of the thoughts.

Attitude

Attitude is a *state of mind*—a thought plus its attached emotions—and it influences what you say and do.

If the attitude that is activated is negative, then the emotional response will naturally be a negative or stressful feeling. If the attitude is positive, the feeling will be peaceful. The truth is that your attitude will be revealed no matter how much you try to hide it.

 QUESTION: Can you determine the attitude of the thoughts that are currently moving through your conscious mind? Try to focus in on the feelings they are generating and describe them in as much detail as possible. How does your mind feel? How does your body feel?

Thoughts Can't Be Hidden; Attitudes Aren't Harmless

Your attitudes—positive or negative—not only can't be hidden from others, but they also have a profound impact on your own brain and body. You can refer back to chapter 7 for a reminder of how this works.

When a thought, plus its emotions (attitudes), moves into the conscious mind, it produces a signal. The hypothalamus (see image), which does many amazing things—one of which is to respond to our emotional state of mind or our attitude—responds to this signal.

The Hypothalamus Responds

Part of what the hypothalamus does is alert the rest of the brain to release chemicals like serotonin and glutamate to help with the process of building a new memory. The endocrine system is a collection of glands and organs that mostly produce and regulate your hormones. And the hypothalamus is often referred to as the "brain" of the endocrine system, controlling things like thirst, hunger, body temperature, and the body's response to your emotional life. The hypothalamus is also like a pulsating heart responding to your emotions and thought life, greatly impacting how you function emotionally and intellectually.

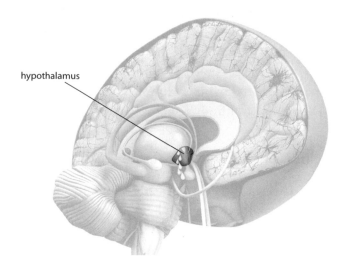

hypothalamus

This means that if you are anxious or worried about something, the hypothalamus will respond by releasing more chemicals than it should. This in turn causes the pituitary to release too many chemicals, and the result is neurochemical chaos. So instead of being focused in our thinking, we have chaotic and foggy thinking.

The endocrine system secretes the hormones responsible for organizing the trillions of cells in your body to deal with focus and learning. Negative, toxic thoughts have the opposite effect, shifting your body's focus to protection and survival, thus reducing your ability to process and think with wisdom or grow healthy thoughts.

However, if you change your attitude and determine to apply God's excellent advice not to worry, the hypothalamus will cause the secretion of chemicals that facilitate the feeling of peace, and the rest of the brain will respond by secreting the correct formula of neurotransmitters—chemicals that transmit electrical impulses—for thought-building and clear thinking.

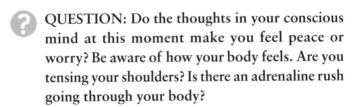 **QUESTION: Do the thoughts in your conscious mind at this moment make you feel peace or worry? Be aware of how your body feels. Are you tensing your shoulders? Is there an adrenaline rush going through your body?**

Although you may not be able to control your environment all of the time, you can control how it affects your brain.

You Can Control How the Signals Affect Your Brain

How? The incoming information is still in a temporary state. It has not yet lodged itself into your memory, or become a part of your spirit, which defines who you are. You can choose to reject the presently activated thoughts and the incoming information, or you can let the information make its way into your mind, soul, and your spirit, eventually subsiding in your nonconscious and becoming automatized, dominating who you are. Even though you can't always control your circumstances, you can make fundamental choices that will help you control your reaction to your circumstances and keep toxic input out of your brain.

QUESTION: Do you feel like a victim of or a victor over what is swarming through your mind at the moment from the external and internal signals?

Brain Structures and Circuits That Help You Make Good Choices

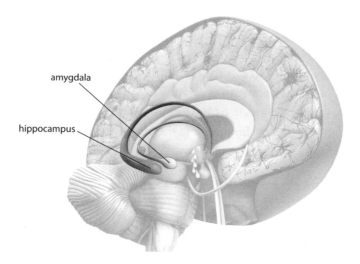

The amygdala and hippocampus, and their connected circuits, can help you make good choices. The amygdala deals with the passionate, perceptual emotions attached to incoming thoughts and all the thoughts already in your head. The hippocampus deals with memory and motivation.

This is where you consciously step up to center stage; you need to choose, and decide whether or not these incoming thoughts will become part of who you are. Let's look more closely at how you control this decision to accept or reject information.

 QUESTION: Did you know you are able to accept or reject the thoughts flowing through your mind?

The Amygdala: Perceptual Library

The amygdala, a double almond–shaped structure located in your brain, is designed to keep you emotionally alert. When you become toxic in your thinking, it steps up to protect you from any threat to your body and mind—such as danger or stress. It puts the passion behind the punch of memory formation by influencing another structure that is very important to memory formation, the hippocampus, enabling you to give more focused attention to your existing memories. The amygdala is basically designed to deal with positive love-based emotions like joy and happiness, but it doesn't work as well when you are in a negative state of mind.

The Thalamus Acts Like a Transmitter Station

The thalamus (deep in the middle of the brain) functions like a transmitter station, alerting the amygdala of any incoming information from the five senses. How does it do this?

The amygdala functions like a library, storing the emotional perceptions that occur each time a thought is built. In other words, every time you build a memory, you activate emotions. The endocrine system in the brain has to release the correct

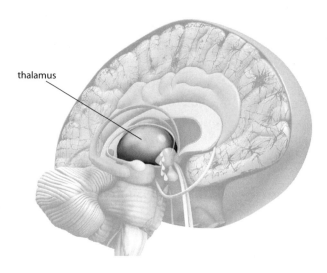

thalamus

chemicals—the molecules of emotion and information— necessary to build healthy or toxic memories. Because the amygdala is in constant communication with the hypothalamus, which secretes chemicals in response to your thought life, you are able to feel your body's reaction to your thoughts. These physical reactions—rapid heartbeat and adrenaline rushes—force you to decide whether to accept or reject the information, basing your decision on how you feel physically.

To help you even more, the amygdala has lines of communication connected to the frontal lobe, which controls reasoning, decision-making, analyzing, and strategizing—all executive-level functions. This connection enables you to balance the emotions you physically experience in your body and allows you to react reasonably. Here is the exciting part: At this moment you can choose *not* to think about this issue anymore, and those temporary thoughts will disappear.

 QUESTION: You do not have to be dominated by your perceptual library—in other words your emotions. Do you feel dominated by your feelings that have arisen out of the thoughts active in your mind?

The Hippocampus: Memory Converter

If you don't manage to stop thinking about the issue, however, all the information, including the awakened toxic or nontoxic attitude, will flow into a sea horse–shaped structure called the hippocampus.

The hippocampus is a sort of clearinghouse for thoughts. It classifies incoming information as having either short- or long-term importance and files it accordingly, converting temporary thoughts into permanent thoughts that become part of who you are (a lot of this happens at night while you are sleeping). To do this, the hippocampus has to work with the central hub of the brain—a group of structures with circuits that integrate all the activated memories and work with the hippocampus to convert information into your permanent memory storage.

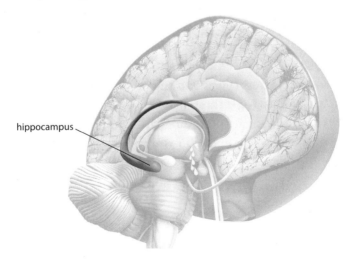

hippocampus

This is where you begin some serious reflection in order to make some life-changing decisions.

 QUESTION: Ask yourself, "Do I want this information to be a part of me?"

Stress

A good point to remember is that toxic memories create the negative stage two and negative stage three of stress. Stage one of stress is good and keeps you alert and focused. Stage two and three are normal stress gone wrong.

The hippocampus is extremely vulnerable to stress because it is rich in stress hormone receptors that are normally used to reinforce memories. These receptors are like tiny doorways on cells that receive chemical information. For these brain cells, excessive stress is almost like an explosion, causing the hippocampus to lose cells and shrink. This affects the communication between the hippocampus and the central circuits of the brain, keeping it from building new good thoughts (memories) as well as causing memory loss. This is seen a lot in depression, Alzheimer's, dementias, and other neuropsychiatric disorders.

 QUESTION: Toxic thoughts are the result of bad choices. Stress stages two and three are your body's reaction to toxic thoughts. Can you feel the stress reaction—heart pounding, adrenaline pumping, or muscles tensing up in your body?

Chapter 11 Summary

1. Sensory information flows into the brain through the five senses.

2. Existing memories in the nonconscious are activated.

3. This activates memories to move from nonconscious to the conscious mind and attitudes are invoked.

4. The hypothalamus responds to the attitude by releasing chemicals necessary for memory building and emotions.

5. This activates the amygdala to recall linked emotional perceptions and to start building in new emotional perceptions.

6. All this information enters the hippocampus, which is involved in converting short-term memory to long-term memory.

7. All this electromagnetic, chemical, and quantum physics activity moves to the front of the brain.

Let's move to the reflection stage and see how the hippocampus works with the central hub circuits of the brain in building thoughts.

12

Focused Reflection

Step 2

It is always fun to see science catching up with the Bible, as we discussed in part 1. Focused reflection is an example of this. It is an ancient biblical principle most of us know. But it is also the current rage in neuroscience, and there are hundreds of studies with headlines like

"Mindfulness Meditation May Relieve Chronic Inflammation"[1]

"Evidence Supports Health Benefits of 'Mindfulness-Based Practices'"[2]

"Breast Cancer Survivors Benefit from Practicing Mindfulness-Based Stress Reduction"[3]

"Don't Worry, Be Happy: Understanding Mindfulness Meditation"[4]

"Mindfulness Meditation Training Changes Brain Structure in Eight Weeks"[5]

You get the idea.

It Always Boils Down to One Thing

Although a lot of these studies talk about Eastern meditation techniques, what it boils down to every time is deep,
intellectual, disciplined thinking with attention regulation,
thinking, body awareness, emotion regulation, and a sense of
self that changes the brain positively. Consequently, people
gain health, happiness—and peace—exactly the instruction
and consequence of Philippians 4:8: "Finally, brothers and
sisters, whatever is true, whatever is noble, whatever is right,
whatever is pure, whatever is lovely, whatever is admirable—
if anything is excellent or praiseworthy—think about such
things" (NIV). In fact, throughout the book of Proverbs we
are instructed to gain wisdom and meditate on knowledge
until we understand.

Getting Out of a Toxic-Thinking Block

If you are going to get out of any toxic-thinking block, you
need to think, understand, and apply the wisdom you gain.[6]

Thankfully, you have all the structures and physiological
processes at your disposal to do this. Neuroplasticity (key 3)
and quantum physics (key 7) are for your benefit and can help
you enjoy every day. Don't forget that, as a neuroplastician,
you can do your own brain surgery. This means no thought
should ever be allowed to control you (see chaps. 1 and 2).

So once you have gone through the whole gathering awareness step above—which disciplines you to be careful of what's
going into your brain as well as what is coming out from
inside—then you need to go deep and focus your reflection.
As you apply keys 4 and 5 in this step (catch your thoughts
and enter into directed rest), an incredible change happens

in your brain. Let's look at some of the technical side interspersed with some focused questions to help you digest the science.

Just a quick reminder here: Each of these 5 steps that you do daily for 21 days are simple, yet there are profound parallel and simultaneous neurophysiological things going on in your brain that are so marvelous you cannot help but be one who "admires God's work," as Thomas More put it. So don't let yourself get overwhelmed by the science; instead, look at it with fascination and admiration of our gracious God. Science is pure evidence of grace.

The Rush to the Front of the Brain

After the gathering stage, the electromagnetic signals—your thinking and those existing memories that have been brought into consciousness—speed through the hippocampus, moving toward the front of the brain—the basal forebrain and orbitofrontal cortex, which are behind the inside corners of

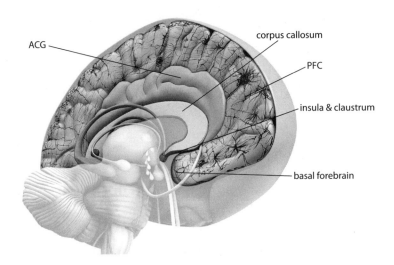

ACG

corpus callosum

PFC

insula & claustrum

basal forebrain

your eyes and above your eyebrows respectively. The information flows through in the hippocampus for twenty-four to forty-eight hours, constantly being amplified each time it cycles to the front.

Free Will

The amplification sets in motion a delightful string of events so magnificent that it can only reflect the work of your Creator. This string of events is your free will and decision-making ability, a true gift. (Before you go on, please look back at the summaries of keys 1, 2, 3, and 7.)

The Thought Becomes Vulnerable to Change

This amplification means the thought is conscious and becomes "labile," which means it is unstable and changeable. In fact, it must change (see chap. 3). The science of thought demands that change must occur either by reinforcing the thought as it is or by changing some or all of it.

The memory cannot sink back as part of your attitude into your nonconscious mind without being changed in some way. This is marvelous news for you, but it also emphasizes the responsibility you need to take for your thought life. No thought is harmless, nor does it stay the same—it constantly changes. As I said in part 1, you are constantly changing the landscape of your brain moment by moment. You are a thinking, creative being—quite brilliant.

 QUESTION: Now that you are aware that thoughts are unstable and changeable when they are in your conscious cognitive mind, can you focus on one in particular and experimenting with changing it?

When You Think, You Change

This constant change means that the deeper you think, the more change you can make. This change is real and happens via electromagnetic and quantum forces as well as neurotransmitters activating genetic expression and protein synthesis (see chaps. 2 and 3).

As a reminder, proteins are made and used to grow new branches to hold your thoughts. So if you don't get rid of the thought, you reinforce it. This is phenomenal because science confirms that you can choose with your free will to interfere with genetic expression, which is protein synthesis (chap. 2). If you say you can't or won't, this decision will actually cause protein synthesis and change in your brain into "I can't" or "I won't." Remember: mind controls matter (chap. 1). Now "bringing into captivity every thought" (2 Cor. 10:5 KJV) becomes a lot more important. Thoughts are constantly remodeled by the "renewing of your mind" (Rom. 12:2 NIV).

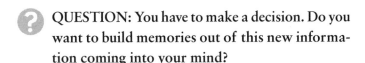

QUESTION: You have to make a decision. Do you want to build memories out of this new information coming into your mind?

When you do this, as you saw in chapters 2 and 3, you actually change the physical structure—neuroplasticity—of your brain. This is because thinking causes important neurotransmitters—chemicals in the brain that carry electrical impulses—to flow. These neurotransmitters plus electromagnetic and quantum activity cause changes deep inside the cell, affecting genetic expression and protein synthesis, as I have described earlier.

Imagining Builds Physical Thoughts

Research has shown that mental practice—imagination, visualization, deep thought, and reflection—produces the same physical changes in the brain as would physically carrying out the same imagined processes. We see this principle in the Bible: "Nothing they have imagined they can do will be impossible for them" (Gen. 11:6 AMP). Brain scans show that the parts of the brain activated by action are the same parts of the brain activated by simply thinking about an action. This sheds new depths of understanding for the Scripture, "Faith is the substance of things hoped for, the evidence of things not seen" (Heb. 11:1).

Rehearsing things mentally is a great everyday example of how you can think and more deeply reflect on daily actions, because each time you do this, you change the memory. For example, if a surgeon is about to perform an operation, he first mentally rehearses each precise step, as would an athlete before a game or a student about to take an exam. As you mentally rehearse it, the newly built memory becomes increasingly stronger and begins to grow more connections to neighboring nerve cells, integrating that thought into other thought patterns. This leads to automatization, which I spoke about in chapter 8.

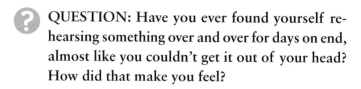 **QUESTION: Have you ever found yourself rehearsing something over and over for days on end, almost like you couldn't get it out of your head? How did that make you feel?**

A healthy thought and a toxic thought can both be built with mental rehearsal. But you can tear toxic strongholds down by choosing to bring the thought into conscious awareness for analysis and then changing it through repentance and forgiveness—which causes protein synthesis—and replacing it with the correct information, using Philippians 4:8 or a similar Scripture guideline.

 QUESTION: How do you tear down the toxic stronghold?

The Contribution of the Heart

When talking about thinking, free will, and understanding, you need to also consider the exciting contribution the heart makes to thinking and decision-making. Your heart is not just a pump; it helps with decision-making and choices, acting like a checking station for all the emotions generated by the flow of chemicals from thoughts. In fact, every single cell is connected to your heart and, because your heart responds to and is controlled by your brain, every single cell in your body is affected by your thoughts.

Your heart is in constant communication with your brain and the rest of your body, checking the accuracy and integrity of your thought life. As you are about to make a decision, your heart pops in a quiet word of advice. It is well worth listening to this advice, because when you listen to your heart, it secretes the ANF (atrial natriuretic factor)—a hormone produced by the heart that regulates blood pressure and can give you a feeling of peace.

 QUESTION: What role does the heart play in focused reflection?

Expertise

When you think deeply to understand, you go beyond just storing facts and answers to storing key concepts and strategies

Inside the Brain

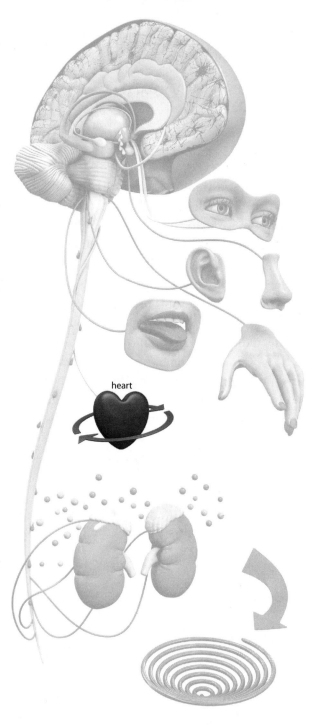

heart

that can help you come up with your own answers. These thoughts have been consolidated and stabilized sufficiently so that you have immediate access to them. When this happens, you have achieved a level of expertise. But this can happen in a negative or positive direction, with all the contributing effects.

You should be aiming for that which you were naturally designed—deep, intellectual, nontoxic thought (Matthew 5:48). Focused reflection helps with this process, but for protein synthesis to consolidate, stabilize, and become part of you, repetition and rehearsal in frequent, spaced intervals is necessary. The next three stages in thought formation—writing, revisit, and active reach—show you how to take advantage of this to stabilize your protein synthesis or bring your memory back up again to retranscribe or change it.

Chapter 12 Summary

1. Focused thinking is specifically focusing on one thought with its interconnections.
2. It is a directed and deep, intellectual process.
3. It is a disciplined way of thinking that has the elements of attention regulation, controlling raging, and preventing chaotic thoughts from moving through the mind.
4. It includes body awareness, emotion regulation, and sense of self that changes the brain positively.
5. Keys 1 through 8 really kick in at this point.
6. Huge activity in the center and front of the brain happens when we focus our thinking.
7. Neuroplasticity is dominant because, as you focus your thinking, you are starting to redesign your brain.

13
Write
Step 3

Your brain writes through genetic expression, so when you write things down on paper or type into your computer or iPad or whatever gadget you use, you are mirroring this process. Writing down your thoughts is important in the Switch On Your Brain technique because the actual process of writing consolidates the memory and adds clarity to what you have been thinking about. It helps you better see the area that needs to be detoxed by allowing you to see your nonconscious and conscious thoughts in a visual way. It is almost like putting your brain on paper.

QUESTION: What does writing do to help your detoxing?

The basal ganglia, the cerebellum, and the motor cortex are involved in this process. Let's talk about the basal ganglia first.

The Industrious Basal Ganglia

Nestling between the cerebral cortex (on the outside of the brain) and the midbrain (in both the left and right hemispheres)

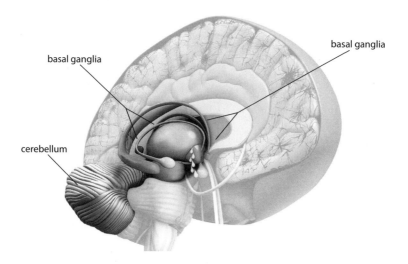

are intricate bundles of neurological networks that are interconnected with the cerebral cortex. These bundles are the basal ganglia. The basal ganglia also put their imprint on the process of thinking and learning by helping the hippocampus, frontal lobe, and corpus callosum turn thought and emotion into immediate action.

Remember, all the parts of the brain work together in harmony; the process never involves just one structure alone. The basal ganglia do this by helping to ensure the memory gets built into the trees of the cerebral cortex. They also smooth out fine motor actions and set the idle rate for anxiety. Together with the motor cortex of the brain, the cerebellum helps you write down the information you have just understood. The cerebellum also helps with cognitive fluency, which is the ability to flow through a thought process smoothly as you evaluate the options.

Obviously, all your brain structures become very involved in the writing process because writing is a complex cognitive and metacognitive process requiring deep thinking. For example, the structures in the frontal lobe become highly active in the thinking and decision-making part of writing; the temporal lobe and hippocampus become involved in calling up existing memories; the emotional parts of every activated thought generate feelings; and the structures in the middle of the brain dealing with emotional perceptions work harder, just to mention a few things. The complexity God has designed is beautiful.

 QUESTION: What do the basal ganglia help with?

How to Write Your Thoughts

How you write down your thoughts is very important because there are ways of writing down information that work more effectively with your brain processes than traditional linear and one-color note taking. My workbook and DVD series called *Switch On Your Brain*[1] provides ideas on how to be brain-compatible when you are writing.

I always encourage anyone who keeps a thought journal to be creative with their notes. I also encourage anyone moving through the process of detoxifying thoughts to be playful with their thought journal. Don't limit yourself to just writing in straight lines. If there are word associations or groupings that seem natural as you focus on information, group those on a page. Draw a picture or diagram to go along with that thought expression. Add color or texture. Pour out the impressions in your mind onto the page.

The Metacog

When I am helping students develop their learning and retention skills, I teach them a method I've developed called *Metacog*. The name might seem a little odd, but the process is fascinating.

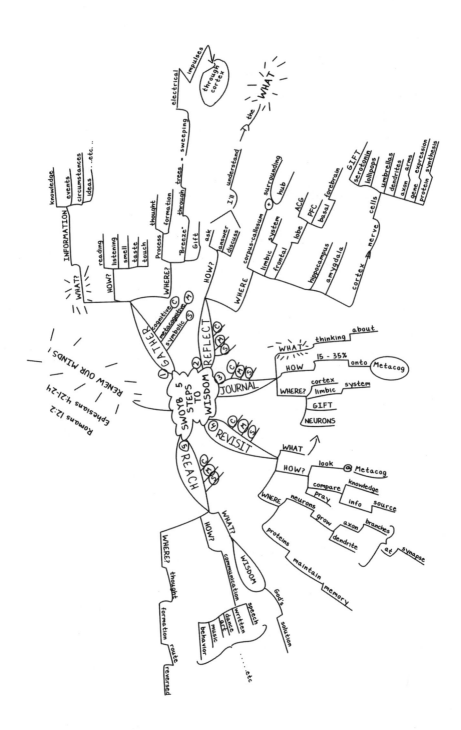

It is simple: Group patterns that radiate from a central point. Each pattern linked to the central point creates a branch. Then continue to develop each of the branches by linking more detailed patterns. The process can continue until you have explored every nuance of your thought.

This method of pouring out your thoughts encourages both sides of the brain to work together to integrate the two perspectives of thought—the left side of the brain looks at information from the detail to the big picture and the right side of the brain from the big picture to the detail.

For full understanding to take place—which will result in the conversion of short-term memory to long-term memory—both perspectives of thought need to come together. So a Metacog is a way of seeing your thoughts on paper and evaluating the way you think and what you are thinking about. It is a great way of following your thought patterns so you can detox your thought life.

Chapter 13 Summary

1. The actual process of writing consolidates thoughts (memory).
2. Writing adds clarity to what you have been thinking about.
3. Writing helps you better see the area that needs to be detoxed by allowing you to see your nonconscious and conscious thoughts in a visual way.
4. Keep a thought journal.
5. Pour your thoughts out and only sort them in the next step—the revisit.

14
Revisit

Step 4

evisiting what you have written will be a revealing
process. This is exciting as well because it is a pro-
gressive "moving-forward" step; you revisit where
you are and look at how to make change happen.

After you have gathered awareness and done your focused
reflection and writing, you will have stimulated major neuroplastic activity, putting your brain in a highly active and
dynamic state for marvelous and positive change. This is the
perfect state to be in to rewire.

This step is all about you wiring in what changes you want.
You get to design your new healthy thought to replace the
toxic thought you want to get rid of. It's all about redesigning, reorganizing, and re-creating the specific thought you
are working on.

Thoughts Become Plastic Enough to Be Redesigned

Earlier I explained that when thoughts are activated and
pushed into the conscious mind, they enter a labile state—
meaning they can be altered. When a memory is in this plastic

Healthy Memory: Adapted Graphic Sketch

Toxic Memory: Adapted Graphic Sketch

state, it can be modified, toned down, or retranscribed and reconceptualized by interfering with protein synthesis—an important molecular process in thought building. This is where you do some serious brain surgery (see chap. 3).

This is exciting, because once the thought is in the conscious mind after the gather, focused reflection, and writing you can redesign the thought and change it or keep it the same but make it stronger. You choose. Obviously, if you are doing the 21-Day Brain Detox Plan, you have chosen to change the negative, toxic thoughts.

God builds into the science of thought this amazing ability to renew our minds, which in turn rewires the brain. This means that each time a thought dominates your conscious mind, you can do something with it. You are not a victim of your biology; you can control your reactions to events and circumstances. You can choose to keep your thinking the same or change it. Either way, protein synthesis happens. The toxic memory will either be changed or be strengthened. This process is the major role of the revisit stage.

 QUESTION: How can thoughts be redesigned?

How to Redesign Thoughts

In the revisit, you evaluate what you have written down and work out what the healthy new thought you want to build is going to be. You work out the way forward, a little at a time. Remember, you have twenty-one days to do this, so don't try to do it all in one day. Visualize what you want the end result to be, but get there in 21 days.

Not only do you have the opportunity to examine your thoughts on paper, but you have the opportunity to rethink through your reaction to the information—evaluating how toxic the thought is and then retranscribing it to be a healthy and strong part of your memory library.

By consciously becoming aware of your thought life you are retranscribing and changing your underlying neuronal networks. You need to uncover the toxic thoughts that create such powerful internal conflicts in your mind and that are capable of causing such radical electrochemical imbalances that, when taken to the extreme, cause parts of yourself to be cut off from the rest of you. While gather, focused reflection, and writing are hugely instrumental in this retranscribing and rewiring process, revisiting is a self-reflective process (see chap. 5) that has the purpose of getting free from the internal conflicts with positive planning of the way out. It is a constructive step that takes you through the problem, and it is cumulative. This means you need to think deeply and apply all the keys, which takes twenty-one days for the kind of depth in thinking that results in change. So you don't have to solve everything on day one—in fact, that would not be wise.

QUESTION: What is the main purpose of this self-reflection?

In revisiting, you are not only looking at how you go about dealing with your circumstances, but you are also thinking through your reactions again, evaluating the toxicity levels, and retranscribing them. This is a positive, looking-for-the-solution step. It feels safe because you are working out the way forward.

This is where the Bible is so perfect as a guide, because it lays out all the correct management principles for toxicity. At this revisit stage, if you discover you are a worrier, the Scripture in Matthew 6:25, which instructs us to not worry about tomorrow, is a good verse for you to apply.

So, if you line up your revisit with the principles outlined in God's Word instead of worldly psychology, you have a foolproof method for doing the right thing.

Chapter 14 Summary

1. The revisit step is a moving-forward step during which you are working out solutions and ways to overcome.
2. This is when you evaluate where you have come from and where you are going.
3. You also have the opportunity to think through your reactions again, evaluating the toxicity levels, and re-organizing, redesigning, and retranscribing.

15

Active Reach

Step 5

Active reaches are the challenging but fun part of this plan because they are actions and exercises you say and/or do during the course of the day and evening. You in essence practice using the new healthy thought until it becomes automatized like a good habit (see chap. 8). You decide what these active reaches will be in steps 4 and 5 each day and then you monitor, evaluate, and change them each subsequent day of the 21-Day Brain Detox Plan.

The Doing Gets the Results

It is the *doing* nature of the active reaches that results in *ungluing* the branches from your thought trees. Steps 1–4 have loosened and weakened the branches, but step 5 literally destroys the branches. Here is how this works, and why the active reaches are so important.

Inside the Brain

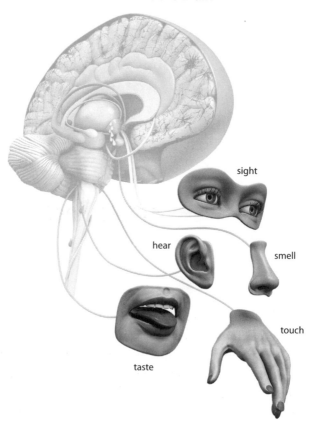

The branches with all the memories and emotions are attached to a cell body with a type of protein that is like glue—like branches attached to a tree trunk. There is more glue on the branches that are used the most, so when you shift your attention from the negative, toxic thought to the positive, healthy, new replacement thought, three things happen.

1. The electromagnetic and quantum signals from your decision to change attack the branches of the toxic

thoughts, weakening them because the signals are more powerful than the negative thoughts.

2. This causes neurochemicals to flow like oxytocin, which remolds; dopamine, which increases motivation and focus; and serotonin, which makes you feel good. These chemicals also weaken the toxic branches.

3. The "glue" starts moving away from the toxic tree to the healthy tree.

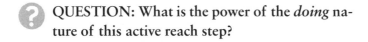 QUESTION: What is the power of the *doing* nature of this active reach step?

Your Faith Manifests

The active reach is the stage in which you reach out beyond toxic thinking by applying the principle, "Faith without works is dead" (James 2:20). This is where your faith manifests and you actually do something with the detoxing that has been going on until now—you reach further. It is the final step to switching on the brain and detoxing. But you can't reach with success without the foundation created in the previous steps. Only when you have been through all of those steps and completed the process can you move forward, changed in a positive direction.

An active reach is not just the decision to forgive; it is the actual forgiving. It is not just the decision to believe that God heals; it is the actual believing. It is not just the decision to stop worrying about your children and trust they will make the right decisions because God is watching over them; it is actually stopping the worrying. It is not just confessing God will meet your needs; it is the actual believing. It is not just the decision to lose weight; it is the actual lifestyle change to lose the weight. It is not just the decision to stop dwelling on the past; it is the actual stopping the dwelling on the past. It is not just the decision not to talk negatively; it is the actual not talking negatively no matter how tempting it is to do so. This is when you reach beyond where you are.

Moving through the Sequence

When you have moved through the 5-Step sequence—gather, reflect, write, revisit, active reach—to detox your thoughts and simultaneously build the healthy thought, you will have built a secure foundation for change, health, and wholeness. It will not work, however, if you just mouth a positive confession without a solid foundation. This creates what science calls "cognitive dissonance."

Building a structure for change on a faulty foundation will never create persistent patterns in your brain to bring you peace. Instead, it will fall down when the proverbial wolf (trouble) blows down your house of sticks (confessions without foundation).

Integrity in the Brain

In the brain, building a foundation is called having integrity, which means you are using your words and actions to line up the thought with its beliefs and feelings. Neuroscientifically, the progression goes like this:

- the amygdala provides input to the mind about the emotions—*gather*;

- the thalamus and hypothalamus provide input on motivation; *and* the memory networks provide information on the *existing memories—reflect*;
- the central hub in the brain mixes and integrates this all together—*write*; and
- the heart acts as the checking station, and you make the decision—*revisit*.

You can be presented with all the reason, logic, scientific evidence, and just plain common sense in the world, but you won't believe something is true unless your brain's limbic system—the central location of your emotions—allows you to feel that it is true. So you can't imagine and feel—change your brain structurally—one way and speak something different, because if you do, there will be a lack of integrity operating in your brain, which will leave an overwhelming feeling of being out of control.

Active Reaching Helps You Feel Truth

The active reach helps you feel whether or not something is true. It helps you line up the thought (imagination) with the confession (words coming out of your mouth) and action. Clearly, then, "Confess with your mouth the Lord Jesus *and* believe in your heart" (Rom. 10:9, emphasis mine) becomes the principle operating here.

Here is an example of active reach: You are working on the toxic thought of saying—out loud or in your mind—a lot of could-have, would-have, should-have, if-only statements. Your active reach step is saying, "I will not say this, I am putting the past behind me"; or visualizing the situation, event, or issue disappearing in a puff of smoke; or quoting a verse that's applicable; or doing something fun like smiling, yawning, or tapping your foot.

A second example: If the toxic thought is that you keep trying to change the past by playing movies in your mind, thinking that if you did *that* then *this* would have happened, and then *this* should have happened, and then you wouldn't have . . . active reach is to say, "I choose to stop playing this movie" or "I am switching that movie off," quoting a Bible verse that applies, or praying a prayer you have created for that situation.

A third example: The toxic thought is that you find it hard to accept that something is over, done, and in the past, and you won't let it go. The active reach is to visualize the walls of Jericho falling down and see those walls as this past experience; telling yourself "I can't" is a decision, but so is "I can"—choose "I can" or quote a Scripture.

You can't trick yourself, and you can't trick God. After all, you are made in his image and are, therefore, exceptionally intelligent. Now using your exceptional intelligence, look at the simple summary below of how to do the 21-Day Brain Detox Plan and start renewing your mind and rewiring your brain.

Summary for the 21-Day Brain Detox Plan

1. You do the 5 steps of the Switch On Your Brain technique daily for 21 days on one specific toxic thought.

2. It takes you seven to ten minutes to work through the 5 steps, and then you do your selected active reach at least seven times throughout the day. So the active reach, step 5, has an action component that you *do* throughout the day. You have worked out what your active reach would be through using the insight you gained from steps 1–4.

3. One brain detox cycle is 21 days.

4. You can do as many 21-day cycles as you need on the same toxic thought to rewire it, but most times one cycle will do.

5. You are simultaneously breaking down a toxic thought and building up a healthy thought.

6. You need to practice automatizing the new healthy tree by consciously practicing using it for at least two more 21-day cycles.

Below is a guide to help you master the 21-Day Brain Detox.

Learning to Break Down the Toxic Thought

1. Gather (1–2 minutes)
   - Purpose: bring thought into consciousness
   - Example: worrying about money
   - Don't forget, it is the Holy Spirit who "will guide you into all the truth" (John 16:13 NIV), so let him—and not yourself or someone else—make the decision about what you need to renew.
   - Activity: go to chapter 11 for all the step 1 gather questions to guide you.

2. Focused Reflection (1–2 minutes)
   - Purpose: loosen up branches
   - Activity: review chapter 12

3. Writing (1–2 minutes)
   - Purpose: start shaking the branches to loosen the glue
   - Activity: review chapter 13

4. Revisit (1–2 minutes)
- Purpose: shift the glue to the new healthy thought
- Activity: review chapter 14

5. Active Reach (1–2 minutes)
- Purpose: start melting down the branches
- Activity: review chapter 15

Learning to Build Up the Healthy Thought

Now let's look at the parallel building-up process, which you do at exactly the same time as you do the breaking-down process to balance the negative with the positive. You don't want to get stuck in the negative—toxicity—so you immediately bring balance to the situation.

1. **Gather**
   - As you identify the toxic thought in the breaking-down process, you immediately, prayerfully, consciously think of the replacement thought. For example: "My God will supply every need of yours according to his riches in glory in Christ Jesus" (Phil. 4:19 ESV). (See chap. 11.)

2. **Focused Reflection**
   - Grow and integrate healthy branches by reflecting on the positive and not just dwelling on the negative. (See chap. 12.)

3. **Write**
   - Add more information and links with other branches by writing the positive alongside the negative. (See chap. 13.)

4. **Revisit**
   - You are doing the same thing in the breaking-down and building-up processes here. The steps cross over

because you are planning the solution to replace the problem. This starts stabilizing the branches to firm up the "glue" bonds. (See chap. 14.)

5. **Active Reach**

- This is the same step as in the breaking-down process, but here you actually *do* the active reaches. This strengthens the new thought branches. (See chap. 15.)

Repeating steps 1 through 5 daily for about seven minutes eventually eliminates the toxic tree and stabilizes the healthy tree. Like the Scripture says in Mark 11:22–23, "You can say to this mountain, 'May you be lifted up and thrown into the sea,' and it will happen" (NLT).

Afterword

As I sat down to write this, I wondered why it is that certain things stick in your brain. Then I thought, *Why is it that the guy writing an afterword for a book about how the brain works is asking questions about how the brain works? Why don't I just read the book and get my answers?* Caroline certainly answers my enigma in these pages.

Let me digress. For me, some of the "stuck" memories are events, locations, smells, feelings, visions, and dreams. Some are good; some are not as good. Diesel exhaust is a real bummer of a memory for me; it can almost immediately make me nauseated. (I went to Israel numerous times as a teenager, and traveled the length and breadth of the Holy Land by diesel-belching buses.) When I feel extreme cold, I think of football. (I opened the door of a hotel one time in Detroit for Lions' great Hall of Famer Barry Sanders.)

The geometry definition "two lines cut by a transversal so that alternate interior angles are congruent and the lines are parallel" is burnt into my brain. (I was rudely awakened

203

from an awesome daydream and then traumatized by a math teacher summoning me to the blackboard to solve a math equation from another planet in front of my entire class.)

When Laurie, my wife of almost thirty years now, tilts her head at a certain angle to look up at me, I feel a "slap a ring on that girl's finger and run down the aisle and get married" kind of LOVE. I am taken back to the fall of 1984, standing in Pastor Don Price's church embracing her, instantly in love, holding her longer, tighter, and wondering how many people were like, *Um . . . What's up with the major PDA in church!* We were hardly ever apart after that fateful evening and married a few months later.

When I am introduced to a person named Tom and/or sometimes just hear the name Tom, I want to giggle, seriously! My brain can replay a movie of Laurie looking at but past me, eyes going wide like she was seeing a ghost over my shoulder! (We were at a friend's home in Los Angeles for a dinner party, and unbeknownst to me two-time Academy award–winning actor Tom Hanks was standing behind me, waiting to say hello to our host, but I was mid-story and rambling on and on, and Laurie was desperately trying to tell me to shut up and turn around with her "Lucy Ricardo" eye gestures! I finally did, and Tom said, "Hi, I'm Tom." I said, "Yes, I know.")

When I see an advertisement for a certain global technology company that manufactures telephone systems, tears can well up in my eyes. I answered a phone call in 1991 to the sounds of sobbing on the other end of the line. (Laurie choked out the news to me that she had miscarried our second child.) I can remember where I was when I heard about President Reagan being shot; the Challenger disaster; September 11, 2001; the birth of my boys, Caylan and Cody, their first steps, birthday cake being smashed into faces, etc.

Hopefully you are tracking with me here. I pray you are able to conjure up your own random memories, good and not so good, and are asking the same questions I am. Why do these events become us, become the very persona of who we are? Why *those* memories? What makes them "stick" in our brains?

This book is the owner's manual for how our brain works. Refer to it regularly. Caroline Leaf's first appearance on TBN's *Praise The Lord* program with Laurie and me is one of the "stuck" memories in my brain too. I remember thinking that I was not listening to a doctor's opinion regarding how God created our brains but was actually hearing a revelation that was divinely inspired. I vividly recall saying, "Let me repeat what I think you just said. Our thoughts are actually 'proteins' forming the way our brains will actually think about matters in the future? So the Scripture that says, 'as a man thinks, so is he' actually means that 'as a man thinks, so is he'? Wow! Science is actually catching up with the Bible!"

That was Caroline's first program with us. She has taught us more and more truth over the years, and is now in production on an entire TV series that will air on TBN for years!

These pages are not information—they are revelation. And Caroline's revelation will change the way you think.

Literally!

Matthew Crouch,
Trinity Broadcasting Family of Networks

Notes

Chapter 1 Mind Controls Matter

1. Eric R. Kandel, *In Search of Memory: The Emergence of a New Science of Mind* (New York: Norton, 2006).

2. Sigmund Freud, quoted in D. Church, *The Genie in Your Genes* (Fulton, CA: Energy Psychology Press, 2008).

3. Norman Doidge, *The Brain That Changes Itself: Stories of Personal Triumph from the Frontiers of Brain Science* (New York: Penguin Books, 2007); Joe Dispenza, *Evolve Your Brain: The Science of Changing Your Brain* (Deerfield Beach, FL: Health Communications, 2007); Henry Markram, director of the Brain and Mind Institute of the *Ecole Polytechnique Fédérale de Lausanne* that founded the Blue Brain Project, which accurately predicts connections between neurons, *Science Daily*, September 17, 2012, www.sciencedaily.com /releases/2012/09/120917152043.htm?utm_source=feedburner&utm_medium=email&utm_campaign=Feed%3A+sciencedaily%2Fmind_brain%2Fneuroscience+%28ScienceDaily%3A+Mind+%26+Brain+News+—+Neuroscience%29; and Allan Jones, http://www.ted.com/speakers/allan_jones.html.

4. 98 percent of mental and physical illnesses come from our thought life: www.stress.org/americas.htm; www.naturalwellnesscare.com/stress-statistics.html; Harvard Medical School's Mind-Body Institute, www.massgeneral.org/bhi/research/; Church, *Genie in Your Genes*. The Institute of HeartMath discusses an experiment titled "Local and Nonlocal Effects of Coherent Heart Frequencies on Conformational Changes of DNA." http://appreciativeinquiry.case.edu/practice/organizationDetail.cfm?coid=852&sector=21. A study by the American Medical Association found that stress is a factor in 75 percent of all illnesses and diseases that people suffer from today. The association between stress and disease is a colossal 85 percent, Brian Luke Seaward, www.brianlukeseaward.net/articles/SuperStress-WELCOA-Seaward.pdf.

"Cancer Statistics and Views of Causes," *Science News* 115, no. 2 (January 13, 1979): 23; H. F. Nijhout "Metaphors and the Role of Genes and Development," *BioEssays* 12 (1990): 444–46; W. C. Willett, "Balancing Lifestyle and Genomics Research for Disease

Prevention," *Science* 296 (2002): 695–98; C. B. Pert, *Molecules of Emotion: Why You Feel the Way You Feel* (New York: Simon and Schuster, 1997); B. Lipton, *The Biology of Belief: Unleashing the Power of Consciousness, Matter and Miracles* (Santa Cruz, CA: Mountain of Love Productions, 2008).

5. C. M. Leaf, *The Gift in You: Discover New Life through Gifts Hidden in Your Mind* (Nashville: Thomas Nelson, 2009).

6. Church, *Genie in Your Genes.*

7. Herbert Benson MD, president of Harvard Medical School's Mind-Body Institute, www.massgeneral.org/bhi/research.

8. Glen Rein and Rollin McCraty, "Local and Nonlocal Effects of Coherent Heart Frequencies on Conformational Changes of DNA," Proceedings of the Joint USPA/IAPR Psychotronics Conference, Milwaukee, Wisconsin, 1993, http://www.heartmath.org/ templates/ihm/e-newsletter/publication/2012/winter/emotions-can-change-your-dna. php; Rollin McCraty et al., "Modulation of DNA Conformation By Heart-focused Intention." HeartMath Research Center, Institute of HeartMath, publications no. 03–08, Boulder Creek, CA, 2003.

9. "Stress," Your Dictionary, http://www.yourdictionary.com/stress. Emphasis mine.

10. Sheldon Cohen et al., "Psychological Stress and Disease," *JAMA* 14 (2007): 1685, http://www.bbc.com/future/story/20120619-how-stress-could-cause-illness; http://www. stress.org/stress-and-heart-disease/.

11. Brian Luke Seaward, *Managing Stress: Principles and Strategies for Health and Wellbeing* (London: Jones and Bartlett Learning, 2006).

12. "Cancer Statistics and Views of Causes," *Science News* 115, no. 2 (January 13, 1979): 23.

13. Lipton, *The Biology of Belief.*

14. Nijhout, "Metaphors and the Role of Genes and Development."

15. Willett, "Balancing Lifestyle and Genomics Research for Disease Prevention."

16. "Stress and Heart Disease," http://www.stress.org/stress-and-heart-disease/.

Chapter 2 Choice and Your Multiple-Perspective Advantage

1. Jeffery Rosen, "The Brain on the Stand," *New York Times*, March 11, 2007, www.nytimes.com/2007/03/11/magazine/11Neurolaw.t.html.

2. Francis Crick, quoted in John Tierney, "Do You Have Free Will? Yes, It's the Only Choice," *New York Times*, March 21, 2011, www.nytimes.com/2011/03/22/ science/22tier.html?pagewanted=all&_r=0.

3. Benjamin Libet, "Unconscious Cerebral Initiative and the Role of Conscious Will in Voluntary Action," *Behavioral and Brain Sciences* 8 (1985): 529–66; John Dylan-Haynes et al., "Unconscious Determinants of Free Decisions in the Human Brain," *Nature Neuroscience* 11 (2008): 543–45.

4. Hagop Sarkissian et al., "Is Belief in Free Will a Cultural Universal?" *Mind and Language* 25 (2010): 346–58.

5. Kathleen D. Vohs and Jonathan W. Schooler, "The Value of Believing in Free Will: Encouraging a Belief in Determinism Increases Cheating," www.csom.umn.edu/ assets/91974.pdf.

6. Articles in *Science* and *NewScientist* have recently discussed x-phi work on free will from authors including Eddy Nahmias and Dylan Murray, "Experimental Philosophy on Free Will: An Error Theory for Incompatibilist Intuitions," in *New Waves in Philosophy of Action*, ed. Jess Aguilar, Andrei Buckareff, and Keith Frankish (Basingstoke,

Hampshire, UK: Palgrave-Macmillan, 2011); and Eddy Nahmias, Stephen G. Morris, Thomas Nadelhoffer, and Jason Turner "Is Incompatibilism Intuitive?" *Philosophy and Phenomenological Research* 73, no. 1 (2006): 28–53.

7. H. S. Mayberg, "Defining the Neural Circuitry of Depression: Toward a New Nosology with Therapeutic Implications," *Biological Psychiatry* 61, no. 6 (March 2007): 729–30.

8. Church, *Genie in Your Genes*; "Epigenetics: A Web Tour," *Science*, www.sciencemag.org/feature/plus/sfg/resources/res_epigenetics.dtl.; Ethan Watters, "DNA Is Not Destiny: The New Science of Epigenetics Rewrites the Rules of Disease, Heredity, and Identity," *Discover*, November 2006, http://discovermagazine.com/2006/nov/cover.

9. Elizabeth Pennisi, "Behind the Scenes of Gene Expression," *Science* 293, no. 553 (2001): 1064–67.

10. Ibid.

11. Ken Richardson, *The Making of Intelligence* (New York: Columbia University Press, 2000).

12. Eric R. Kandel, James H. Schwartz, and Thomas M. Jessell, eds. *Essentials of Neural Science and Behavior* (New York: Appleton and Lange, 1995); Eric R. Kandel, "Molecular Biology of Memory: A Dialogue between Genes and Synapses," http://www.nobelprize.org/mediaplayer/index.php?id=1447; Eric. R. Kandel, "A New Intellectual Framework for Psychiatry," *American Journal of Psychiatry* 155, no. 4 (1998): 457–69.

13. Ibid.

14. Dorothy Nelkin, *The DNA Mystique* (New York: Norton, 1995), 15.

15. Lipton, *Biology of Belief*. B. Lipton, K. G. Bensch, and M. A. Karasek, "Microvessel Endothelial Cell Transdifferentiation: Phenotypic Characterization," *Differentiation* 46 (1991): 117–33.

16. Gail Ironson et al., "An Increase in Religiousness/Spirituality Occurs after HIV Diagnosis and Predicts Slower Disease Progression over Four Years in People with HIV," *Journal of General Internal Medicine* 21 (2006): 62–68.

17. As quoted in Church, *Genie in Your Genes*, 65.

Chapter 3 Your Choices Change Your Brain

1. Watters, "DNA Is Not Destiny."

2. John Cloud, "Why Your DNA Isn't Your Destiny," *Time*, www.time.com/time/magazine/article/0,9171,1952313-2,00.html.

3. Robert Weinhold, "Epigenetics: The Science of Change," *Environmental Health Perspectives* 114, no. 3 (March 2006).

4. "Learning Without Learning," *The Economist*, September 21, 2006, 89.

5. www.cajal.csic.es/ingles/index.html.

6. In part 2, I will explain how this can be done.

7. Jeffrey M. Schwartz and Sharon Begley, *The Mind and the Brain* (New York: Harper Perennial, 2002); Jeffrey M. Schwartz and Rebecca Gladding, *You Are Not Your Brain* (New York: Avery, 2012).

8. Caroline M. Leaf, "The Mind Mapping Approach: A Model and Framework for Geodesic Learning" (unpublished doctoral dissertation, University of Pretoria, Pretoria, South Africa, 1997); Caroline M. Leaf, Brenda Louw, and Isabel Uys, "The Development of a Model for Geodesic Learning: The Geodesic Information Processing Model," *The South African Journal of Communication Disorders* 44 (1997): 53–70; Leaf, "The Move from Institution Based Rehabilitation (IBR) to Community Based

Rehabilitation (CBR): A Paradigm Shift," *Therapy Africa* 1, no. 1 (August 1997): 4; Leaf, "An Altered Perception of Learning: Geodesic Learning," *Therapy Africa* 1, no. 2 (October 1997): 7.

9. Doidge, *Brain That Changes Itself.*

10. Barbara Arrowsmith and Norman Doidge, *The Woman Who Changed Her Brain: And Other Inspiring Stories of Pioneering Brain Transformation* (New York: Free Press, 2012).

11. Caroline M. Leaf, *The Switch On Your Brain 5-Step Learning Process* (Dallas: Switch On Your Brain, 2008).

12. Arrowsmith and Doidge, *Woman Who Changed Her Brain*; Church, *Genie in Your Genes*; Doidge, *Brain That Changes Itself*; Dispenza, *Evolve Your Brain*; Leaf, "Mind Mapping Approach"; Leaf, *Switch On Your Brain 5-Step Learning Process*; Caroline M. Leaf, *Who Switched Off My Brain? Controlling Toxic Thoughts and Emotions* (Dallas: Switch on Your Brain, 2007) and DVD series (Johannesburg, South Africa: Switch on Your Brain, 2007); C. M. Leaf, M. Copeland, and J. Maccaro, "Your Body His Temple: God's Plan for Achieving Emotional Wholeness," DVD series (Dallas: Life Outreach International, 2007).

13. Joe Dispenza, *Breaking the Habit of Being Yourself* (New York: Hay House, 2012).

14. Richard Wiseman, "Self Help: Forget Positive Thinking, Try Positive Action," *The Observer*, June 30, 2012, http://www.guardian.co.uk/science/2012/jun/30/self-help-positive-thinking; Jim Taylor, "Is the Self-help Industry a Fraud?" April 18, 2011, http://blog.ctnews.com/taylor/2011/04/18/is-the-self-help-industry-a-fraud/#.UVedEdRXVA4. email; Michael Shermer, "SHAM Scam: The Self-Help and Actualization Movement Has Become an $8.5-Billion-a-Year Business. Does It Work?" April 23, 2006, http://www.scientificamerican.com/article.cfm?id=sham-scam.

15. "The Problem with Self-Help Books: Study Shows the Negative Side to Positive Self-Statements," *e! Science News*, July 2, 2009, http://esciencenews.com/articles/2009/07/02/the.problem.with.self.help.books.study.shows.negative.side.positive.self.statements.

16. Schwartz and Begley, *Mind and the Brain*; Schwartz and Gladding, *You Are Not Your Brain.*

Chapter 4 Catch Those Thoughts

1. Ellen Langer and Mihnea Moldoveanu, "The Construct of Mindfulness," *Journal of Social Issues* 56, no. 1 (2000): 1–9; Leaf, *Who Switched Off My Brain?*; Leaf, *The Gift in You.*

2. Caroline M. Leaf, Isabel C. Uys, and Brenda Louw, "An Alternative Non-Traditional Approach to Learning: The Metacognitive-Mapping Approach." *The South African Journal of Communication Disorders* 45 (1998): 87–102.

3. Sissa Medialab, "The Good Side of the Prion: A Molecule That Is Not Only Dangerous, but Can Help the Brain Grow," *Science Daily*, February 14, 2013, www.sciencedaily.com/releases/2013/02/130214075437.htm?utm_source=feedburner&utm_medium=email&utm_campaign=Feed%3A+sciencedaily%2Fmind_brain+%28Science Daily%3A+Mind+%26+Brain+News%29.

4. Loyola University Health System, "New Evidence for Link between Depression and Heart Disease," *Science Daily*, February 18, 2013.

5. "Brain Signs of Schizophrenia Found in Babies," *Science Daily*, June 9, 2010, http://www.sciencedaily.com/releases/2010/06/100621111240.htm; "Alterations in Brain

Activity in Children at Risk of Schizophrenia Predate Onset of Symptoms," *Science Daily*, March 22, 2013, http://www.sciencedaily.com/releases/2013/03/130322174343.htm.

6. Leaf, *Who Switched Off My Brain?*; Maria Konnikova, *Mastermind: How to Think Like Sherlock Holmes* (New York: Viking Penguin, 2013); Maria Konnikova, "The Power of Concentration," *New York Times Sunday Review*, December 15, 2012, http://www.nytimes.com/2012/12/16/opinion/sunday/the-power-of-concentration.html?pagewanted=1&_r=2&ref=general&src=me&.

7. Schwartz and Begley, *Mind and the Brain*; Schwartz and Gladding, *You Are Not Your Brain*; Dispenza, *Evolve Your Brain*; Dispenza, *Breaking the Habit of Being Yourself*; Allan Jones, www.ted.com/speakers/allan_jones.html.

Chapter 5 Entering into Directed Rest

1. Richard J. Davidson et al., "Alterations in Brain and Immune Function Produced by Mindfulness Meditation," *Psychosomatic Medicine* 65 (2003): 564–70.

2. Marcus E. Raichle et al., "A Default Mode of Brain Function: A Brief History of an Evolving Idea," *Neuroimage* 37 (2007): 1083–90.

3. Matthew R. Brier et al., "Loss of Intranetwork and Internetwork Resting State Functional Connections with Alzheimer's Disease Progression," *Journal of Neuroscience* 32, no. 26 (2012): 8890–99; Christian F. Beckmann et al., "Investigations into Resting-State Connectivity Using Independent Component Analysis," *Philos Trans R Soc Lond, B, Biol Sci* 360 (2005):1001–13.

4. Marcus E. Raichle, "The Brain's Dark Energy," *Scientific American*, March 20, 2012, 44–49, www.hboorcca.com/pdf/brain/The%20Brain's%20Dark%20Energy%20Scientific%20American%20March%202010.pdf; Raichle et al., "A Default Mode of Brain Function," 1083–90.

5. Yvette I. Sheline et al., "The Default Mode Network and Self-Referential Processes in Depression," *Proceedings of the National Academy of Sciences USA* 106, no. 6 (January 26, 2009): 1942–47; Washington University School of Medicine research cited in "Alzheimer's Breaks Brain Networks' Coordination," *Science Daily*, September 17, 2012, www.sciencedaily.com/releases/2012/09/120918090812.htm.

6. Raichle, "The Brain's Dark Energy"; Raichle et al., "A Default Mode of Brain Function."

7. Konnikova, "The Power of Concentration."

8. Brier et al., "Loss of Intranetwork and Internetwork Resting State Functional Connections with Alzheimer's Disease Progression."

9. J. Paul Hamilton et al., "Default Mode and Task Positive Network Activity in Major Depressive Disorder: Implications for Adaptive and Maladaptive Rumination," *Biological Psychiatry* 70, no. 4 (2011): 327–33.

10. Caroline M. Leaf, "Mind Mapping: A Therapeutic Technique for Closed Head Injury," unpublished master's dissertation (University of Pretoria, Pretoria, South Africa), 1990.

11. "Activity in Brain Networks Related to Features of Depression," *Science Daily*, April 3, 2012, www.sciencedaily.com/releases/2012/04/120403111954.htm#.T4HbzAjE61c.mailto.

12. Xueling Zhu et al., "Evidence of a Dissociation Pattern in Resting-State Default Mode Network Connectivity in First-Episode, Treatment-Naive Major Depression Patients," *Biological Psychiatry* 71, no. 7 (2012): 611.

13. Norman A. S. Farb et al., "Mood-Linked Responses in Medial Prefrontal Cortex Predict Relapse in Patients with Recurrent Unipolar Depression," *Biological Psychiatry* 70, no. 4 (August 15, 2011): 366–72.

14. Leaf, "The Mind Mapping Approach"; Hamilton et al., "Default Mode and Task Positive Network Activity in Major Depressive Disorder."

15. Sophie Green et al., "Guilt-Selective Functional Disconnection of Anterior Temporal and Subgenual Cortices in Major Depressive Disorder," *Archives of General Psychiatry* 69, no. 10 (2012): 1014–21, http://archpsyc.jamanetwork.com/article.aspx?articleID=1171078.

16. Ibid.

17. Schwartz and Begley, *Mind and the Brain*; Schwartz and Gladding, *You Are Not Your Brain*.

18. Michael M. Merzenich et al., "Prophylactic Reduction and Remediation of Schizophrenic Impairments through Interactive Behavioral Training," 2001, http://www.google.com/patents?hl=en&lr=&vid=USPAT6231344&id=3BQIAAAAEBAJ&oi=fnd&dq=Merzenich+schizophrenia+research&printsec=abstract#v=onepage&q=Merzenich%20schizophrenia%20research&f=false; Melissa Fisher et al., "Neuroplasticity-Based Cognitive Training in Schizophrenia: An Interim Report on the Effects 6 Months Later," *Schizophrenia Bulletin*, March 5, 2009, http://schizophreniabulletin.oxfordjournals.org/content/36/4/869; "Thread: New Therapy Available Now for Cognitive problems in Schizophrenia," http://www.schizophrenia.com:8080/jiveforums/thread.jspa?threadID=16719; Sophia Vinogradov, "What's New in Schizophrenia Research," November 28, 2007, http://www.thomastthomas.com/Schizophrenia%20Research,Vinogradov,112807.pdf.

19. Sarah J. Hart et al., "Altered fronto-limbic activity in children and adolescents with familial high risk for schizophrenia," *Psychiatry Research* 212, no. 1 (2013): 19; Sebastien Parnaudeau et al., "Inhibition of Mediodorsal Thalamus Disrupts Thalamofrontal Connectivity and Cognition," *Neuron* 77, no. 6 (2013): 1151.

20. "Women Abused as Children More Likely to Have Children With Autism," *Science Daily*, March 20, 2013, http://www.sciencedaily.com/releases/2013/03/130320212818.htm#.UVCuOUPuaJE.email.

Chapter 6 Stop Milkshake-Multitasking

1. Brian A. Primack et al., "Association Between Media Use in Adolescence and Depression in Young Adulthood," *Archives of General Psychiatry* 66, no. 2 (2009): 181–88, http://archpsyc.jamanetwork.com/article.aspx?articleid=210196.

2. Mark W. Becker, Reem Alzahabi, and Christopher J. Hopwood, "Media Multitasking Is Associated with Symptoms of Depression and Social Anxiety," *Cyberpsychology, Behavior, and Social Networking* 16, no. 2 (2012): 132–35.

3. "Are You a Facebook Addict?" *Science Daily*, May 7, 2012, www.sciencedaily.com/releases/2012/05/120507102054.htm.

4. Report from the University of Edinburgh Business School, "More Facebook Friends Means More Stress, Says Report," *Science Daily*, November 26, 2012, www.sciencedaily.com/releases/2012/11/121126131218.htm.

5. Keith Wilcox and Andrew T. Stephen, "Are Close Friends the Enemy? Online Social Networks, Self-Esteem, and Self-Control," *Social Science Research Network*, September 22, 2012, http://ssrn.com/abstract=2155864.

6. David M. Levy et al., "The Effects of Mindfulness Meditation Training on Multi-tasking in a High-Stress Information Environment," *Proceedings of Graphics Interface*, May 2012; University of Washington research referenced in "Mindful Multitasking: Meditation First Can Calm Stress, Aid Concentration," *Science Daily*, June 13, 2012, www.sciencedaily.com/releases/2012/06/120614094118.htm.

7. Leaf, "Mind Mapping: A Therapeutic Technique for Closed Head Injury"; Leaf, "The Mind Mapping Approach."

8. University of Washington study cited in Konnikova, "The Power of Concentration."

9. University of Washington and Emory University studies referenced in Konnikova, "The Power of Concentration"; Michael Merzenich, cited in Schwartz and Begley, *Mind and the Brain*; Gaëlle Desbordes et al., "Effects of Mindful-Attention and Compassion Meditation Training on Amygdala Response to Emotional Stimuli in an Ordinary, Non-Meditative State," *Frontiers in Human Neuroscience*, November 1, 2012, www.frontiersin. org/human_neuroscience/10.3389/fnhum.2012.00292/abstract.

10. Michael Merzenich cited in Schwartz and Begley, *Mind and the Brain*. Desbordes et al., "Effects of Mindful-Attention and Compassion Meditation Training on Amygdala Response to Emotional Stimuli in an Ordinary, Non-Meditative State"; Massachusetts General Hospital, Boston University, "Meditation Appears to Produce Enduring Changes in Emotional Processing in the Brain," *Science Daily*, www.science daily.com/releases/2012/11/121112150339.htm.

11. Leaf, "Mind Mapping: A Therapeutic Technique for Closed Head Injury."

12. Eileen Luders et al., "The Unique Brain Anatomy of Meditation Practitioners: Alterations in Cortical Gyrification," *Frontiers in Human Neuroscience*, February 29, 2012, www.frontiersin.org/Human_Neuroscience/10.3389/fnhum.2012.00034/abstract.

13. Eileen Luders et al., "Enhanced Brain Connectivity in Long-Term Meditation Practitioners," *NeuroImage* 4 (August 15, 2011): 1308–16.

14. University of California, Los Angeles research cited in "Meditation May Increase Gray Matter," *Science Daily*, May 13, 2009, www.sciencedaily.com/releases/2009/05 /090512134655.htm.

Chapter 7 Thinking, God, and the Quantum Physics Brain

1. "Max Planck Quotes," www.goodreads.com/author/quotes/107032.Max_Planck.

2. Schwartz and Begley, *Mind and the Brain*; Schwartz and Gladding, *You Are Not Your Brain*; Jeffrey Schwartz, Henry Stapp, and Mario Beauregard, "Quantum Physics in Neuroscience and Psychology: A Neurophysical Model of Mind/Brain Interaction," www.physics.lbl.gov/~stapp/PTB6.pdf.

3. This intentional mental act and its unpredictability can be represented mathemati-cally by an equation that is one of the key components of quantum theory. It is beyond the scope of this book to explore the equation more deeply, but if you are interested, you can begin exploring further by reading, "Quantum Physics in Neuroscience and Psychology: A Neurophysical Model of Mind/Brain Interaction," by Jeffrey M. Schwartz, Henry P. Stapp, and Mario Beauregard, http://www.scribd.com/doc/94124369/Quantum-Physics -in-Neuroscience-by-Jeffrey-M-Schwartz-Henry-P-Stapp-Mario-Beuregard.

4. James Higgo, "A Lazy Layman's Guide to Quantum Physics," 1999, www.higgo. com/quantum/laymans.htm.

5. Schwartz, Stapp, and Beauregard, "Quantum Physics in Neuroscience and Psychology."

6. Schwartz and Begley, *Mind and the Brain*; Schwartz and Gladding, *You Are Not Your Brain*; Schwartz, Stapp, and Beauregard, "Quantum Physics in Neuroscience and Psychology."

7. Caroline Leaf, "The Mind Mapping Approach: A Model and Framework for Geodesic Learning," unpublished DPhil dissertation, University of Pretoria, South Africa, 1997; Caroline Leaf, "The Mind Mapping Approach: A Technique for Closed Head Injury," unpublished master's dissertation, University of Pretoria, South Africa, 1990.

8. Carol Dweck, "Implicit Theories of Intelligence Predict Achievement Across Adolescent Transition: A Longitudinal Study and an Intervention," *Child Development* 78 (2007): 246–63.

9. McCraty, "Modulation of DNA Conformation by Heart-Focused Intention," 4.

10. Church, *Genie in Your Genes*.

11. Giacomo Rizzolatti and L. Craighero, "The Mirror-Neuron System," *Annual Review of Neuroscience* 27 (2004): 169–92.

12. Caroline Leaf, *Who Switched Off Your Brain? Solving the Mystery of He Said/She Said* (Nashville: Thomas Nelson, 2011).

13. Dean Radin, "Testing Nonlocal Observation as a Source of Intuitive Knowledge," *Explore* 4, no. 1 (2008): 25.

14. Thomas E. Oxman et al., "Lack of Social Participation or Religious Strength and Comfort as Risk Factors for Death after Cardiac Surgery in the Elderly," *Psychosomatic Medicine* 57 (1995): 5.

15. Linda H. Powell et al., "Religion and Spirituality: Linkages to Physical Health," *American Psychologist* 58, no. 1 (2003): 36.

16. Larry Dossey, *Prayer Is Good Medicine* (San Francisco: HarperOne, 1997).

17. John A. Astin et al., "The Efficacy of 'Distant Healing': A Systematic Review of Randomized Trials," *Annals of Internal Medicine* 12 (2000): 903; Wayne B. Jonas, "The Middle Way: Realistic Randomized Controlled Trials for the Evaluation of Spiritual Healing," *The Journal of Alternative and Complementary Medicine* 7, no. 1 (2001): 5–7.

18. David Levy and Joel Kilpatrick, *Gray Matter: A Neurosurgeon Discovers the Power of Prayer . . . One Patient at a Time* (Wheaton, IL: Tyndale, 2012); Matt Donnelly, "Faith Boosts Cognitive Management of HIV and Cancer," *Science & Theology News* (2006): 16.

19. Levy and Kilpatrick, *Gray Matter*, 19.

20. Sundance Bilson-Thompson, Fotini Markopoulou, and Lee Smolin, "Quantum Gravity and the Standard Model," *Classical and Quantum Gravity* 24, no. 16 (2007): 3975–93.

21. Don Lincoln, "The Universe Is a Complex and Intricate Place," *Scientific American*, November 2012, 38–43.

22. This is the terminology of the Heisenberg principle—quantum physics is known for its weird wording and almost ambiguous statements.

23. Henry Stapp, "Philosophy of Mind and the Problem of Free Will in the Light of Quantum Mechanics," www-physics.lbl.gov/~stapp/Philosophy.pdf; Henry Stapp, *Mindful Universe: Quantum Mechanics and the Participating Observer* (London: Springer, 2007).

24. Don Lincoln, "The Inner Life of Quarks," *Scientific American*, November 2012, 38.

Chapter 8 The Science of Thought

1. Leaf, "Mind Mapping"; Leaf, "Mind Mapping Approach"; Leaf, Louw, and Uys, "Development of a Model for Geodesic Learning," 44, 53–70.

2. Thomas More, *Utopia*, updated edition (London: Penguin Classics, 2003), 81.

3. Leaf, *Switch On Your Brain 5-Step Learning Process*; Leaf, *Who Switched Off My Brain?*; Caroline M. Leaf, "Who Switched Off My Brain? Controlling Toxic Thoughts and Emotions," DVD series (Johannesburg, South Africa: Switch On Your Brain, 2007).

4. Schwartz and Begley, *Mind and the Brain*.

5. Andrew Newberg, Eugene D'Aquili, and Vince Rause, *Why God Won't Go Away: Brain Science and the Biology of Belief* (New York: Ballantine, 2001).

6. Schwartz and Begley, *Mind and the Brain*; Schwartz and Gladding, *You Are Not Your Brain*; Schwartz, Stapp, and Beauregard, "Quantum Physics in Neuroscience and Psychology."

7. Leaf, "Mind Mapping"; Leaf, "The Mind Mapping Approach"; Leaf, Louw, and Uys, "Development of a Model for Geodesic Learning," 44, 53–70.

8. Ibid.

9. "Blue Brain Project Accurately Predicts Connections between Neurons," *Science Daily*, September 17, 2012, www.sciencedaily.com/releases/2012/09/120917152043.htm.

Chapter 9 What Is the 21-Day Brain Detox Plan?

1. Leaf, "Mind Mapping"; Leaf, "The Mind Mapping Approach"; Leaf, Louw, and Uys, "Development of a Model for Geodesic Learning," 44, 53–70.

2. Leaf, "Mind Mapping Approach: Technique for Closed Head Injury."

3. Karim Nader, http://blogs.mcgill.ca/science/2009/04/30/karim-nader-on-memory -reconsolidation; Karim Nader, Glenn E. Schafe, and Joseph E. Le Doux, "Fear Memories Require Protein Synthesis in the Amygdala for Reconsolidation after Retrieval," *Nature* 406, no. 6797 (2000): 722–26; A. H. Maslow, *Motivation and Personality* (New York: Harper & Row, 1970).

4. Shawn Achor, *The Happiness Advantage* (New York: Crown Business, 2010).

5. *Harvard Crimson* poll, 2004, cited in ibid.

Chapter 10 How and Why the 21-Day Brain Detox Plan Works

1. This is 365 days in a year divided by 21 days in a cycle, which gives you 17 cycles per year.

2. Kandel, *In Search of Memory*.

3. Church, *Genie in Your Genes*.

4. Ibid.

5. Rodolfo Llinas, "Rodolfo Llinas's Fearless Approach to Neurophysiology Has Redefined Our Thinking about Individual Neurons and How They Create Movement and Consciousness," U. S. Columbian Medical Association, http://uscma.org/2010/09/12/ rodolfo-llinas's-fearless-approach-to-neurophysiology-has-redefined-our-thinking-about-individual-neurons-and-how-they-create-movement-and-consciousness; Rodolfo Llinas, *I of the Vortex* (Cambridge, MA: MIT Press, 2002).

6. Michael Merzenich as cited in Doidge, *Brain That Changes Itself*.

7. Phillippa Lally et al., "How Are Habits Formed: Modelling Habit Formation in the Real World," *European Journal of Social Psychology* 40, no. 6 (2010): 998–1009.

8. Ibid.

9. See K. Anders Ericsson, Michael J. Prietula, and Edward T. Cokely, "The Making of an Expert," *Harvard Business Review*, July 2007, http://hbr.org/2007/07/the -making-of-an-expert/ar/1.

Chapter 11 Gather

1. Jennifer Wiley and Andrew F. Jarosz, "Working Memory Capacity, Attentional Focus, and Problem Solving," *Current Directions in Psychological Science* 21, no. 4 (2012): 258. See also, "Greater Working Memory Benefits Analytic, Not Creative, Problem-Solving," *Science Daily*, August 7, 2012, www.sciencedaily.com/releases/2012/08/120807132209.htm.

Chapter 12 Focused Reflection

1. "Mindfulness Meditation May Relieve Chronic Inflammation," *Science Daily*, January 16, 2013, http://www.sciencedaily.com/releases/2013/01/130116163536.htm.

2. "Evidence Supports Health Benefits of 'Mindfulness-Based Practices,'" *Science Daily*, July 11, 2012, http://www.sciencedaily.com/releases/2012/07/120711104811.htm.

3. "Breast Cancer Survivors Benefit from Practicing Mindfulness-Based Stress Reduction," *Science Daily*, December 29, 2011, http://www.sciencedaily.com/releases/2011/12/111229203000.htm.

4. "Don't Worry, Be Happy: Understanding Mindfulness Meditation," *Science Daily*, November 1, 2011, http://www.sciencedaily.com/releases/2011/10/111031154134.htm.

5. "Mindfulness Meditation Training Changes Brain Structure in Eight Weeks," *Science Daily*, January 21, 2011, http://www.sciencedaily.com/releases/2011/01/110121144007.htm.

6. I explain this in depth in chapter 5 (key 5) and chapter 6 (key 6). It's worth taking the time to look back at these chapters at this point.

Chapter 13 Write

1. Caroline Leaf, *The Switch On Your Brain 5-Step Learning Process DVD/Workbook* (Dallas: Switch On Your Brain, 2009).

Recommended Reading

The concepts I teach in this book cover a wide spectrum, including years of reading, research, and working with clients in private practice as well as in schools and business corporations. If I had to provide all the citations to document the origin of each fact for complete scientific scholarship that I have used, there would be almost as many citations as words. So I have used a little more flexibility to write this book in a more popular style that communicates my message as effectively as possible. There are only a few citations in the actual text that are more general, and the book list that follows is a list of recommended reading of some of the great books and scientific articles I have used in my research.

Achor, S. *The Happiness Advantage*. New York: Crown Business, 2010.

Adams, H. B., and B. Wallace. "A Model for Curriculum Development: TASC." *Gifted Education International* 7 (1991): 194–213.

"Aging Brains Lose Less than Thought." *Harvard University Gazette*. www.news.harvard.edu/gazette/1996/10.03/AgingBrainsLose.html.

Alavi, A., and L. J. Hirsch. "Studies of Central Nervous System Disorders with Single Photon Emission Computed Tomography and Positron Emission

Tomography: Evolution Over the Past 2 Decades." *Seminars in Nuclear Medicine* 21, no. 1 (January 1991): 51–58.

Alesandrini, K. L. "Imagery: Eliciting Strategies and Meaningful Learning." In *Journal of Educational Psychology* 62 (1982): 526–30.

Allen D., and P. Amua-Quarshie et al. "Mental Health at Work" (White Paper). Pecan Ltd., Peckham, London, UK. 2004.

Allport, D. A. "Patterns and Actions: Cognitive Mechanisms and Content Specific." In *Cognitive Psychology: New Directions*. Edited by G. L. Claxton. London: Routledge and Kegan Paul, 1980.

Amen, D. G. *Change Your Brain, Change Your Life*. New York: Three Rivers Press, 1998.

———. *Magnificent Mind at Any Age*. New York: Harmony Books, 2008.

Amend, A. E. "Defining and Demystifying Baroque, Classic and Romantic Music." In *Journal of the Society for Accelerative Learning and Teaching* 14, no. 2 (1989): 91–112.

Amua-Quarshie, P. "Basalo-Cortical Interactions: The Role of the Basal Forebrain in Attention and Alzheimer's Disease." Unpublished master's thesis. Rutgers University, 2008.

Anastasi, M. W., and A. B. Newberg. "A Preliminary Study of the Acute Effects of Religious Ritual on Anxiety." *The Journal of Liberal and Complementary Medicine* 14, no. 2 (March 2008). www.liebertonline.com/doi/abs/10.1089/acm.2007.0675.

Anderson, J. R. *Cognitive Psychology and Its Complications*. 2nd ed. New York: Freeman, 1985.

Arnheim, R. "Visual Thinking in Education." *The Potential of Fantasy and Imagination*. Edited by A. Sheikll and J. Shaffer. New York: Brandon House, 1979, 215–25.

Arrowsmith, B., N. Doidge. *The Woman Who Changed Her Brain: And Other Inspiring Stories of Pioneering Brain Transformation*. New York: Free Press, 2012.

Atkins, R. C. *Dr. Atkins' Health Revolution*. Boston: Houghton Mifflin, 1990.

———. *Dr. Atkins' New Diet Revolution*. London: Ebury Press, 2003.

"Babies Born to Stressed Mothers More Likely to Be Bullied at School." *Science Daily*. November 14, 2012. http://www.sciencedaily.com/releases/2012/11/12 1114083821.htm?utm_source=feedburner&utm_medium=email&utm _campaign=Feed%3A+sciencedaily%2Fmind_brain+%28ScienceDaily%3A+ Mind+%26+Brain+News%29.

Bach-y-Rita, P., C. C. Collins, F. Saunders, B. White, and B. Scadden. "Vision Substitution by Tactile Image Projection." *Nature* 221, no. 5184 (1969): 963–64.

Barker, J. A. *Discovering the Future: A Question of Paradigms*. Johannesburg, South Africa: Charterhouse Productions, South African Breweries, 1987.

Bartlett, F. C. *Remembering: A Study in Experimental and Social Psychology*. Cambridge, UK: Cambridge University Press, 1932.

"Basic and Translational Neuroscience. 30th Annual Postgraduate Review Course, Topics and Speakers." December 1, 2007–March 8, 2008. http://cumc.columbia.edu/dept/cme/neuroscience/neuro/speakers.html.

Baxter, R., S. B. Cohen, and M. Ylvisaker. "Comprehensive Cognitive Assessment." *Head Injury Rehabilitation: Children and Adolescents*. Edited by M. Ylvisaker. San Diego: College-Hill Press, 1984, 247–75.

Beauregard, M., and D. O'Leary. *The Spiritual Brain*. New York: Harper Collins, 2007.

Bereiter, L. "Toward a Solution of the Learning Paradox." *Review of Educational Research* 55 (1985): 201–25.

Berninger, V., A. Chen, and R. Abbot. "A Test of the Multiple Connections Model of Reading Acquisition." *International Journal of Neuroscience* 42 (1988): 283–95.

Bishop, J. H. "Why the Apathy in American High Schools?" *Educational Researcher* 18, no. 1 (1989): 6–10.

Block, N., and G. Dworkin. *The I.Q. Controversy*. New York: Pantheon, 1976.

Bloom, B. S. "The Z Sigma Problem: The Search for Methods of Group Instruction as Effective as One-to-One Tutoring." *Educational Researcher* 13, no. 6 (1984): 4–16.

Bloom, F. E., M. F. Beal, and D. J. Kupfer, eds. *The Dana Guide to Brain Health: A Practical Family Guide from Medical Experts*. New York: Dana Press, 2003.

Boller, K., and C. Rovee-Collier. "Contextual Coding and Recording of Infants' Memories." *Journal of Experimental Child Psychology* 53, no. 1 (1992): 1–23.

Borkowski, J. G., W. Schneider, and M. Pressley. "The Challenges of Teaching Good Information Processing to the Learning Disabled Student." *International Journal of Disability, Development and Education* 3, no. 3 (1989): 169–85.

Botha, L. "SALT in Practice: A Report on Progress." *Journal of the Society for Accelerative Learning and Teaching* 10, no. 3 (1985): 197–99.

Botkin, J. W., M. Elmandjra, and M. Malitza. *No Limits to Learning: Bridging the Human Gap: A Report of the Club of Rome*. Oxford: Pergammon Press, 1979.

Boyle, P. "Having a Higher Purpose in Life Reduces Risk of Death among Older Adults." *Science Daily*, June 18, 2009. http://www.sciencedaily.com/releases/2009/06/090615144207.htm.

Brain and Mind Symposium. Columbia University. May 13–14, 2004. http://c250.columbia.edu/c250_events/symposia/brain_mind/brain_mind_vid_archive.html.

Bransford, J. D. *Human Cognition*. Belmont, CA: Wadsworth, 1979.

Braten, I. "Vygotsky as Precursor to Metacognitive Theory, II: Vygotsky as Metacognitivist." *Scandinavian Journal of Educational Research* 35, no. 4 (1991): 305–20.

Briggs, M. H. "Team Talk: Communication Skills for Early Intervention Teams." *Journal of Childhood Communication Disorders* 15, no. 1 (1993): 33–40.

Broadbent, D. E. *Perception and Communication*. London: Pergammon Press, 1958.

Brown, A. L. "Knowing When, Where and How to Remember: A Problem of Meta-Cognition." In *Advances in Instructional Psychology*. Edited by R. Glaser. Hillsdale, NJ: Melbourne, 1978.

Bunker, V. J., W. M. McBurnett, and D. L. Fenimore. "Integrating Language Intervention throughout the School Community." *Journal of Childhood Communication Disorders* 11, no. 1 (1987): 185–92.

Buzan, T. *Head First*. London: Thorsons, 2000.

———. *Use Both Sides of Your Brain*. New York: Plume, 1991.

Buzan, T., and R. Keene. *The Age Heresy*. London: Ebury Press, 1996.

Bynum, J. *Matters of the Heart*. Lake Mary, FL: Charisma House, 2002.

Byron, R. *Behaviour in Organisations: Understanding and Managing the Human Side of Work*. 2nd ed. Boston: Allyn and Bacon, 1986.

Byron, R., and D. Byrne. *Social Psychology: Understanding Human Interaction*. 4th ed. Boston: Allyn and Bacon, 1984.

Calvin, W., and G. Ojemann. *Conversations with Neil's Brain*. Reading, MA: Addison-Wesley, 1994.

Campbell, B., L. Campbell, and D. Dickinson. *Teaching and Learning through Multiple Intelligences*. Seattle: New Horizons for Learning, 1992.

Campione, J. C., A. L. Brown, and N. R. Bryant. "Individual Differences in Learning and Memory." In *Human Abilities: An Information Processing Approach*. Edited by R. J. Sternberg. New York: West Freeman, 1984, 103–26.

Cantor, C. "Rutgers-Newark Program Aims to Combat Alzheimer's Disease in Black Communities." *Rutgers Focus*. March 26, 2008. http://news.rutgers.edu/focus/issue.2008-03-26.6300207636/article.2008-03-26.8293146433.

Capra, F. "The Turning Point: A New Vision of Reality." *The Futurist* 16 no. 6 (1982): 19–24.

Caskey, O. "Accelerating Concept Formation." *Journal of the Society for Accelerative Learning and Teaching* 11, no. 3 (1986): 137–45.

Chi, M. "Interactive Roles of Knowledge and Strategies in the Development of Organized Sorting and Recall." In *Thinking and Learning Skills*, vol. 2. Edited by S. F. Chipman, J. W. Segal, and R. Glaser. Hillsdale, NJ: Lawrence Erlbaum, 1985.

Childre, D., and H. Martin. *The Heartmath Solution*. San Francisco: HarperCollins, 1999.

Church, D. *The Genie in Your Genes*. Fulton, CA: Energy Psychology Press, 2008.

Clancey, W. "Why Today's Computers Don't Learn the Way People Do." Paper presented at the Annual Meeting of the American Educational Research Association, Boston, 1990.

Clark, A. J. "Forgiveness: A Neurological Model." *Medical Hypotheses* 65 (2005): 649–54.

Colbert, D. *The Bible Cure for Memory Loss*. Lake Mary, FL: Siloam Press, 2001.

———. *Deadly Emotions: Understand the Mind-Body-Spirit Connection That Can Heal or Destroy You*. Nashville: Thomas Nelson, 2003.

Cook, N. D. "Collosal Inhibition: The Key to the Brain Code." *Behavioral Science* 29 (1984): 98–110.

Costa, A. L. "Mediating the Metacognitive." *Educational Leadership* 42, no. 3 (1984): 57–62.

Cousins, N. *Anatomy of an Illness as Perceived by the Patient.* New York: Bantam, 1981.

———. "Anatomy of an Illness as Perceived by the Patient." *New England Journal of Medicine* 295 (1976): 1458–63.

Crick, F. *The Astonishing Hypothesis: The Scientific Search for the Soul.* New York: Scribner, 1995.

———. "Thinking about the Brain." *Scientific American* 241, no. 3 (1981): 228.

Cromie, W. J. "Childhood Abuse Hurts the Brain." *Harvard University Gazette.* http://news.harvard.edu/gazette/2003/05.22/01-brain.html.

———. "Research Links Sleep, Dreams, and Learning." *Harvard University Gazette.* www.news.harvard.edu/gazette/1996/02.08/ResearchLinksSl.html.

Damasio, A. R. *The Feeling of What Happens: Body and Motion in the Making of Consciousness.* New York: Harcourt, Brace, 1999.

Damico, J. S. "Addressing Language Concerns in the Schools: The SLP as Consultant." *Journal of Childhood Communication Disorders* 11, no. 1 (1987): 17–40.

Dartigues, J. F. "Use It or Lose It." *Omni*, February 1994, 34.

De Andrade, L. M. "Intelligence's Secret: The Limbic System and How to Mobilize It through Suggestopedy." *Journal of the Society for Accelerative Learning and Teaching* 11, no. 2 (1986): 103–13.

De Capdevielle, B. "An Overview of Project Intelligence." *Per Linguam* 2, no. 2 (1986): 31–38.

Decety, J., and J. Grezes. "Neural Mechanisms Subserving the Perception of Human Actions." *Trends in Cognitive Sciences* 3, no. 5 (May 1999): 172–78. http://condor.depaul.edu/dallbrit/extra/psy588/Decety-Grezes.pdf.

———. "The Power of Simulation: Imagining One's Own and Other's Behavior." *Brain Research* 1079 (2006): 4–14.

Decety, J., and P. L. Jackson. "A Social Neuroscience Perspective of Empathy." *Current Directions in Psychological Science* 15 (2006): 54–58.

Derry, S. J. "Remediating Academic Difficulties through Strategy Training: The Acquisition of Useful Knowledge." *Remedial and Special Education* 11, no. 6 (1990): 19–31.

Dhority, L. *The ACT Approach: The Artful Use of Suggestion for Integrative Learning.* Bremen, West Germany: PLS Verlag, An derWeide, 1991.

Diamond, M. *Enriching Heredity: The Impact of the Environment on the Brain.* New York: Free Press, 1988.

Diamond, M., and J. Hopson. *Magic Trees of the Mind: How to Nurture Your Child's Intelligence, Creativity, and Healthy Emotions from Birth through Adolescence.* New York: Penguin, 1999.

Diamond, S., and J. Beaumont, eds. *Hemisphere Function of the Human Brain.* London: Elek, 1974, 264–78.

Dienstbier, R. "Periodic Adrenalin Arousal Boosts Health Coping." *Brain-Mind Bulletin* 14, no. 9a (1989).

Dispenza, J. *Breaking the Habit of Being Yourself*. New York: Hay House, 2012.

———. *Evolve Your Brain: The Science of Changing Your Brain*. Deerfield Beach, FL: Health Communications, 2007.

Dixon, T., and T. Buzan. *The Evolving Brain*. Exetar, UK: Wheaten, 1976.

Dobson, J. *The New Hide or Seek: Self-Confidence in Your Child*. Grand Rapids: Revell, 1999.

Doidge, N. *The Brain That Changes Itself: Stories of Personal Triumph from the Frontiers of Brain Science*. New York: Penguin Books, 2007.

Dukas, H., and B. Hoffman. *Albert Einstein, the Human Side: New Glimpses from His Archives*. Princeton, NJ: Princeton University Press, 1979.

"Dwelling On Stressful Events Can Create Inflammation in the Body, Study Finds." *Science Daily*. March 13, 2013. http://www.sciencedaily.com/releases/2013/03/130313182255.htm?utm_source=feedburner&utm_medium=email&utm_campaign=Feed%3A+sciencedaily+%28ScienceDaily%3A+Latest+Science+News%29.

Edelman, G. M., and V. B. Mountcastle, eds. *The Mindful Brain*. Cambridge, MA: MIT Press, 1982.

Edelman, G. M., and G. Tononi. *A Universe of Consciousness: How Matter Becomes Imagination*. New York: Basic Books, 2000.

Edwards, B. *Drawing on the Right Side of the Brain*. Los Angeles: J. P. Torcher, 1979.

Ende, R. N. *Rene A. Spitz: Dialogues from Infancy*. Madison, CT: International Universities Press, 1984.

Entwistle, N. "Motivational Factors in Students' Approaches in Learning." In *Learning Strategies and Learning Styles*. Edited by R. R. Schmeck. New York: Plenum, 1988, 21–51.

Entwistle, N. J., and P. Ramsdon. *Understanding Student Learning*. London: Croom Helm, 1983.

"Epigenetics: http://www.docstoc.com/docs/129237704/Introduction-to-Epigenetics.

Eriksen, C. W., and J. Botella. "Filtering versus Parallel Processing in RSVP Tasks." *Perception and Psychophysics* 51, no. 4 (1992): 334–43.

Erskine, R. "A Suggestopedic Math Project Using Non-Learning Disabled Students." *Journal of the Society for Accelerative Learning and Teaching* 11, no. 4 (1986): 225–47.

Farah, M. J., F. Peronnet, L. L. Weisberg, and M. Monheit. "Brain Activity Underlying Visual Imagery: Event Related Potentials During Mental Image Generation." *Journal of Cognitive Neuroscience* 1 (1990): 302–16.

Faure, C. *Learning to Be: The World of Education Today and Tomorrow*. Paris: UNESCO, 1972.

Feldman, D. *Beyond Universals in Cognitive Development*. Norwood, NJ: Ablex, 1980.

Feuerstein, R. *Instrumental Enrichment: An Intervention Programme for Cognitive Modifiability*. Baltimore: University Park Press, 1980.

Feuerstein, R., M. Jensen, S. Roniel, and N. Shachor. "Learning Potential Assessment." *Assessment of Exceptional Children*. Haworth Press, 1986.

"Five for 2005: Five Reasons to Forgive." *Harvard Health Publications Newsletter* 2, no. 5 (January 15, 2005). http://harvardhealth.staywell.com/viewNewsletter.aspx?NLID=30&INC=yes.

Flavell, J. H. "Metacognitive Development." In *Structural/Process Theories of Complete Human Behaviour*. Edited by J. M. Scandura and C. J. Brainerd. Alphen aan den Rijn, The Netherlands: Sijthoff and Noordoff, 1978.

Flavell, P. *The Developmental Psychology of Jean Piaget*. New York: Basic Books, 1963.

Fodor, J. *The Modularity of Mind*. Cambridge, MA: MIT/Bradford, 1983.

Fountain, D. *God, Medicine, and Miracles: The Spiritual Factors in Healing*. New York: Random House, 2000.

Frassinelli, L., K. Superior, and J. Meyers. "A Consultation Model for Speech and Language Intervention." *ASHA* 25 no. 4 (1983): 25–30.

Freeman, W. J. *Societies of Brains: A Study in the Neuroscience of Love and Hate*. Hillsdale, NJ: Lawrence Erlbaum Associates, 1995.

"Free Tools to Help You Cope with Stress." *Harvard Health Publications*. Harvard Medical School. www.health.harvard.edu/topic/stress.

Galton, F. *Inquiries into Human Faculty and Its Development*. London: L. M. Dent, 1907.

Gardner, H. *Frames of Mind*. New York: Basic Books, 1985.

———. *The Quest for Mind: Piaget, Levi-Strauss, and the Structuralist Movement*. Chicago: University of Chicago Press, 1981.

Gardner, H., and D.P. Wolfe. "Waves and Streams of Symbolization." In *The Acquisition of Symbolic Skills*. Edited by D. Rogers and J. A. Slabada. London: Plenum Press, 1983.

Gazzaniga, M. S. *Handbook of Neuropsychology*. New York: Plenum, 1977.

———, ed. *The New Cognitive Neurosciences*. Cambridge, MA: MIT/Bradford, 2004.

Gelb, M. *Present Yourself*. Los Angeles: Jalmar Press, 1988.

Gerber, A. "Collaboration between SLP's and Educators: A Continuity Education Process." *Journal of Childhood Communication Disorders* 11, no. 1–2 (1987): 107–25.

"Ghost in Your Genes." PBS NOVA. www.pbs.org/wgbh/nova/genes.

Glaser, R. *Adaptive Education: Individual Diversity and Learning*. New York: Holt, Rhinehart and Winston, 1977.

Glasser, M. D. *Control Theory in the Classroom*. New York: Harper & Row, 1986.

Goldberg, E., and L. D. Costa. "Hemisphere Differences in the Acquisition and Use of Descriptive Systems." *Brain and Language* 14 (1981):144–73.

Golden, F. "Albert Einstein: Person of the Century." *Time*, December 31, 1999.

Gould, S. "Commission on Nontraditional Study." *Diversity by Design*. San Francisco: Jossey-Bass, 1973.

———. *The Mismeasure of Man*. New York: Norton, 1981.

Griffiths, D. E. "Behavioural Science and Educational Administration." In *63rd Yearbook of the National Society for the Study of Education*. Chicago: NSSE, 1964.

Gungor, E. *There Is More to the Secret*. Nashville: Thomas Nelson, 2007.

Guse, J. "How the Marx Brothers Brought Norman Cousins Back to Life." *The Healing Power of Laughter*. http://thehealingpoweroflaughter.blogspot.com/2007/07/how-marx-brothers-brought-norman.html.

Guyton, A. C., and J. E. Halle. *Textbook of Medical Physiology*. 9th ed. Philadelphia: W. D. Saunders, 1996.

Haber, R. N. "The Power of Visual Perceiving." *Journal of Mental Imagery* 5 (1981): 1–40.

Halpern, S., and L. Savary. *Sound Health: The Music and Sounds That Make Us Whole*. San Francisco: Harper & Row, 1985.

Hamilton, P. J., D. J. Furman, C. Chang, M. E. Thomason, E. Dennis, and I. H. Gotlib. "Default-Mode and Task-Positive Network Activity in Major Depressive Disorder: Implications for Adaptive and Maladaptive Rumination." *Biological Psychiatry* 70, no. 4 (2011): 327–33.

Hand, J. D. "The Brain and Accelerative Learning." *Per Linguam* 2, no. 2 (1986): 2–14.

Hand, J. D., and B. L. Stein. "The Brain and Accelerative Learning, Part II: The Brain and Its Functions." *Journal of the Society for Accelerative Learning and Teaching* 11, no. 3 (1986): 149–63.

Harlow, H. Databank Entry in "People and Discoveries: Harry Harlow." *PBS: A Science Odyssey*. www.pbs.org/wgbh/aso/databank/entries/bhharl.html.

Harrell, K. D. *Attitude Is Everything: A Tune-Up to Enhance Your Life*. Dubuque, IA: Kendall Hunt, 1995.

Harrison, C. J. "Metacognition and Motivation." *Reading Improvement* 28, no. 1 (1993): 35–39.

Hart, L. *Human Brain and Human Learning*. New York: Longman, 1983.

Hatfied, R. W. "Touch and Human Sexuality." In *Human Sexuality: An Encyclopedia*. Edited by V. Bullough, B. Bullough, and A. Stein. New York: Garland, 1994.

Hatton, G. I. "Function-Related Plasticity in the Hypothalamus." *Annual Review of Neuroscience* 20 (1997): 375–97.

Hawkins, D. B. *When Life Makes You Nervous: New and Effective Treatments for Anxiety*. Colorado Springs: Cook, 2001.

Hayman, J. L. "Systems Theory and Human Organization." In *A Systems Approach to Learning Environments*. Edited by S. D. Zalatimo and P. J. Steeman. Roselle, NJ: MEDED Projects, 1975.

"The Health Benefits of Laughter." http://heyugly.org/LaughterOneSheet2.php.

Healy, J. "Why Kids Can't Think: Bottom Line." *Personal* 13, no. 8 (1993): 1–3.

Hinton, G .E., and J. A. Anderson. *Parallel Models of Associative Memory*. Hillsdale, NJ: Erlbaum, 1981.

Hochberg, L. R., M. D. Serruya, G. M. Friehs, J. A. Mukand, M. Saleh, A. H. Caplan, A. Branner, D. Chen, R. D. Penn, and J .P. Donoghue. "Neuronal Ensemble Control of Prosthetic Devices by a Human with Tetraplegia." *Nature* 442, no. 7099 (July 18, 2006): 164–71.

Holden, C. "Child Development: Small Refugees Suffer the Effects of Early Neglect." *Science* 305 (1996):1076–77.

Holford, P. *How Children Fail*. New York: Pitman, 1964.

———. *The Optimum Nutrition Bible*. London: Piatkus, 1997.

———. *Optimum Nutrition for the Mind*. London: Piatkus, 2003.

———. *The 30-Day Fat Burner Diet*. London: Piatkus, 1999.

Hubel, D. H. "The Brain." *Scientific American* 24, no. 13 (1979): 45–53.

Hunter, C., F. Hunter, and F. Contreras. *Laugh Yourself Healthy—Keep the Doctor Away with a Giggle a Day*. Lake Mary, FL: Christian Life, 2008.

Hyden, H. "The Differentiation of Brain Cell Protein, Learning, and Memory." *Biosystems* 8, no. 4 (1977): 22–30.

Hyman, S. E. "Addiction: A Disease of Learning and Memory." *American Journal of Psychiatry* 162 (2005): 1414–22.

Iaccino, J. *Left Brain–Right Brain Differences: Inquiries, Evidence, and New Approaches*. Hillsdale, NJ: Erlbaum, 1993.

Institute of HeartMath. www.heartmath.org/research/science-of-the-heart.html.

Iran-Nejad, A. "Active and Dynamic Self-Regulation of Learning Processes." *Review of Educational Research* 60, no. 4 (1990): 573–602.

———. "Associative and Nonassociative Schema Theories of Learning." *Bulletin of the Psychonomic Society* 27 (1989): 1–4.

———. "The Schema: A Long-Term Memory Structure or a Transient Functional Pattern." In *Understanding Reader's Understanding*. Edited by R. J. Teireny, P. L. Anders, and J. N. Mitchell. Hillsdale, NJ: Erlbaum, 1987, 109–28.

Iran-Nejad, A., and B. Chissom. "Active and Dynamic Sources of Self-Regulation." Paper presented at the Annual Meeting of the American Psychological Association, Atlanta, Georgia, 1988.

Iran-Nejad, A., and A. Ortony. "A Biofunctional Model of Distributed Mental Content, Mental Structures, Awareness and Attention." *Journal of Mind and Behavior* 5 (1984): 171–210.

Iran-Nejad, A., A. Ortony, and R. K. Rittenhouse. "The Comprehension of Metaphonical Uses of English by Deaf Children." *American Speech-Language-Association* 24 (1989): 551–56.

Jacobs, B., M. Schall, and A. B. Scheibel. "A Quantitative Dendritic Analysis of Wernickes Area in Humans: Gender, Hemispheric and Environmental Factors. *Journal of Comparative Neurology* 327, no. 1 (1993): 97–111.

Jensen, A. *Bias in Mental Testing*. New York: Free Press, 1980.

Jensen, E. *Brain-Based Learning and Teaching*. Johannesburg, South Africa: Process Graphix, 1995.

Johnson, D. W., R. T. Johnson, and E. Holubec. *Circles of Learning: Cooperation in the Classroom*. Edina, MN: Interaction Books, 1986.

Johnson, J. M. "A Case History of Professional Evolution from SLP to Communication Instructor." *Journal of Childhood Communication Disorders* 11, no. 4 (1987): 225–34.

Jorgensen, C. C., and W. Kintsch. "The Role of Imagery in the Evaluation of Sentences." *Cognitive Psychology* 4 (1973): 110–16.

Kagan, A, and M. M. Saling. *An Introduction to Luria's Aphasiology Theory and Application*. Johannesburg, South Africa: Witwatersrand University Press, 1988.

Kalivas, P. W., and N. Volkow. "The Neural Basis of Addiction: A Pathology of Motivation and Choice." *American Journal of Psychiatry* 162 (2005): 1403–13.

Kandel, E. R. *In Search of Memory: The Emergence of a New Science of Mind*. New York: W. W. Norton, 2006.

———. "The Molecular Biology of Memory Storage: A Dialog between Genes and Synapses." Nobel Lecture. December 8, 2000. www.nobelprize.org/nobel_prizes/medicine/laureates/2000/kandel-lecture.pdf.

———. "A New Intellectual Framework for Psychiatry." *American Journal of Psychiatry* 155, no. 4 (1998): 457–69.

Kandel, E. R, J. H. Schwartz, and T. M. Jessell, eds. *Essentials of Neural Science and Behavior*. New York: Appleton and Lange, 1995.

———, eds. *Principles of Neural Science*. 4th ed. New York: McGraw-Hill, 2000.

Kaniels, S., and R. Feuerstein. "Special Needs of Children with Learning Difficulties." *Oxford Review of Education* 15, no. 2 (1989): 165–79.

Kaplan-Solms, K., and M. Sloms. *Clinical Studies in Neuro-Psychoanalysis*. New York: Karnac, 2002.

Kazdin, A. E. "Covert Modelling, Imagery Assessment and Assertive Behaviour." *Journal of Consulting and Clinical Psychology* 43 (1975): 716–24.

Kimara, D. "The Assymmetry of the Human Brain." *Scientific American* 228, no. 3 (1973): 70–80.

———. "Sex Differences in the Brain." *Scientific American* 267, no. 3 (September 1992): 119–25.

King, D. F., and K. S. Goodman. "Whole Language Learning, Cherishing Learners and their Language." *Language, Speech and Hearing Sciences in Schools*, 21 (1990): 221–29.

Kintsch, W. "Learning from Text, Levels of Comprehension, or: Why Anyone Would Read a Story Anyway?" *Poetics* 9, 1980, 87–98.

Kline, P. *Everyday Genius*. Arlington, VA: Great Ocean Publishers, 1990.

Kluger, J. "The Biology of Belief." *Time*, February 12, 2009. www.time.com/time/health/article/0,8599,1879016,00.html.

Knowles, M. *The Adult Learner: A Neglected Species*. Houston: Gulf Publishing, 1990.

Konnikova, M. *Mastermind*. New York: Viking, 2013.

———. "The Power of Concentration." *New York Times Sunday Review*. December 15, 2012. www.nytimes.com/2012/12/16/opinion/sunday/the-power-of-concentration.html?pagewanted=1&_r=2&ref=general&src=me&.

Kopp, M. S., and J. Rethelyi. "Where Psychology Meets Physiology: Chronic Stress and Premature Mortality: The Central–Eastern European Health Paradox." *Brain Research Bulletin* 62 (2004): 351–67.

Kosslyn, S. M., and O. Koenig. *Wet Mind: The New Cognitive Neuroscience*. New York: Free Press, 1995.

Kubzansky, L. D., I. Kawachi, A. Spiro III, S. T. Weiss, P. S. Vokonas, and D. Sparrow. "Is Worrying Bad for Your Heart? A Prospective Study of Worry and Coronary Heart Disease in the Normative Aging Study." *Circulation* 94, no. 4. (1997): 818–24.

Lahaye, T., and D. Noebel. *Mind Siege: The Battle for Truth in the New Millennium*. Nashville: Word, 2000.

Lally, P., C. H. M. van Jaarsveld, H. W. W. Potts, and J. Wardle. "How Are Habits Formed: Modelling Habit Formation in the Real World." *European Journal of Social Psychology* 40, no. 6 (2009): 998–1009.

Langer, E., and M. Moldoveanu. "The Construct of Mindfulness." *Journal of Social Issue* 56, no. 1 (2000): 1–9.

Larsson, G., and B. Starrin. "Effect of Relaxation Training on Verbal Ability, Sequential Thinking and Spatial Ability." *Journal of the Society of Accelerative Learning and Teaching* 13, no. 2 (1988): 147–59.

Lazar, C. "A Review and Appraisal of Current Information on Speech/Language Alternative Service Delivery Models in Schools." *Communiphon* 308 (1994): 8–11.

Lazar, S. W., and C. E. Kerr. "Meditation Experience Is Associated with Increased Cortical Thickness." *NeuroReport* 16, no. 17 (2005): 189–97.

Lea, L. *Wisdom: Don't Live Life without It*. Guilford, Surrey, UK: Highland Books, 1980.

Leaf, C. M. "An Altered Perception of Learning: Geodesic Learning." *Therapy Africa* 1, no. 2 (October 1997): 7.

———. "An Altered Perception of Learning: Geodesic Learning: Part 2." *Therapy Africa* 2, no. 1 (January/February 1998): 4.

———. "The Development of a Model for Geodesic Learning: The Geodesic Information Processing Model." *The South African Journal of Communication Disorders* 44, (1997): 53–70.

———. "Evaluation and Remediation of High School Children's Problems Using the Mind Mapping Therapeutic Approach." *Remedial Teaching* 7/8, University of South Africa (September 1992).

———. "The Mind Mapping Approach: A Model and Framework for Geodesic Learning." Unpublished DPhil. dissertation, University of Pretoria, South Africa, 1997.

———. "The Mind Mapping Approach (MMA): Open the Door to Your Brain Power: Learn How to Learn." *Transvaal Association of Educators Journal* (December 1992).

———. "The Mind Mapping Approach: A Technique for Closed Head Injury." Unpublished master's dissertation, University of Pretoria, South Africa.

———. "Mind Mapping as a Therapeutic Intervention Technique." Unpublished workshop manual, 1985.

———. "Mind Mapping as a Therapeutic Technique." *Communiphon* 296 (1989): 11–15. A publication of the South African Speech-Language-Hearing Association.

———. "The Move from Institution Based Rehabilitation (IBR) to Community Based Rehabilitation (CBR): A Paradigm Shift." *Therapy Africa* 1, no. 1 (August 1997): 4.

———. *Switch On Your Brain 5-Step Learning Process.* Dallas: Switch on Your Brain, 2008.

———. *Switch On Your Brain: Understand Your Unique Intelligence Profile and Maximize Your Potential.* Cape Town, South Africa: Tafelberg, 2005.

———. *Switch On Your Brain with the Metacognitive-Mapping Approach.* Elkhart, IN: Truth Publishing, 2002.

———. "Teaching Children to Make the Most of Their Minds: Mind Mapping." *Journal for Technical and Vocational Education in South Africa* 121 (1990): 11–13.

———. *Who Switched Off My Brain? Controlling Toxic Thoughts and Emotions.* Dallas: Switch on Your Brain, 2007.

———. "Who Switched Off My Brain? Controlling Toxic Thoughts and Emotions." DVD series. Johannesburg, South Africa: Switch On Your Brain, 2007.

Leaf, C. M., M. Copeland, and J. Maccaro. "Your Body His Temple: God's Plan for Achieving Emotional Wholeness." DVD series. Dallas: Life Outreach International, 2007.

Leaf, C. M., I. C. Uys, and B. Louw. "An Alternative Non-Traditional Approach to Learning: The Metacognitive-Mapping Approach." *The South African Journal of Communication Disorders* 45 (1998): 87–102.

———. "The Development of a Model for Geodesic Learning: The Geodesic Information Processing Model." *The South African Journal for Communication Disorders* 44 (1997).

———. "The Mind Mapping Approach (MMA): A Culture and Language-Free Technique." *The South African Journal of Communication Disorders* 40 (1992): 35–43.

LeDoux, J. *Synaptic Self: How Our Brains Become Who We Are.* New York: Penguin, 2002.

Leedy, P. D. *Practical Research: Planning and Design.* New York: Macmillan, 1989.

Lehmann, E. L. *Non-Parametric: Statistical Methods Based on Ranks.* San Francisco: Holden-Day, 1975.

Leuchter, A. F., I. A. Cook, E. A. Witte, M. Morgan, and M. Abrams. "Changes in Brain Function of Depressed Subjects During Treatment with Placebo." *American Journal of Psychiatry* 159, no. 1 (2002): 122–29.

Levy, J. "Interview." *Omni* 7, no. 4 (1985).

———. "Research Synthesis on Right and Left Hemispheres: We Think with Both Sides of the Brain." *Educational Leadership* 40, no. 4 (1983): 66–71.

Lewis, R. "Report Back on the Workshop: Speech/Language/Hearing Therapy in Transition." *Communiphon* 308 (1994): 6–7.

Liebertz, C. "Want Clear Thinking: Relax." *Scientific American* (September 21, 2005). www.scientificamerican.com/article.cfm?id=want-clear-thinking-relax.

Lipton, B. *The Biology of Belief: Unleashing the Power of Consciousness, Matter and Miracles*. Santa Cruz, CA: Mountain of Love Productions, 2008.

Lipton, B. H., K. G. Bensch, and M. A. Karasek. "Microvessel Endothelial Cell Transdifferentiation: Phenotypic Characterization." *Differentiation* 46, no. 2 (1991): 117–33.

Llinas, R. *I of the Vortex*. Cambridge, MA: MIT Press, 2002.

Lozanov, G. *Suggestology and Outlines of Suggestopedy*. New York: Gordon and Breach Science Publishers, 1978.

Lozanov, G., and G. Gateva. *The Foreign Language Educator's Suggestopaedic Manual*. New York: Gordon and Breach Science Publishers, 1989.

L. T. F. A. "Brain-Based Learning." Unpublished lecture series. Johannesburg, South Africa: Lead the Field Africa, 1995.

Luria, A .R. *Higher Cortical Functions in Man*. 2nd ed. New York: Basic Books, 1980.

Lutz, K. A., and J. W. Rigney. *The Memory Book*. New York: Skin and Day, 1977.

MacLean, P. "A Mind of Three Minds: Educating the Triuine Brain." *77th Yearbook of the National Society for the Study of Education*. Chicago: University of Chicago Press, 1978, 308–42.

Margulies, N. *Mapping Inner-Space*. Tucson, AZ: Zephyr Press, 1991.

Markram, H. "'Blue Brain' Project Accurately Predicts Connections between Neurons." *ScienceDaily* (September 17, 2012). Reprinted from materials provided by Ecole Polytechnique Fédérale de Lausanne. www.sciencedaily.com/releases/2012/09/120917152043.htm.

Marvin, C. A. "Consultation Services: Changing Roles for the SLP's." *Journal of Childhood Communication Disorders* 11, no. 1 (1987): 1–15.

Maslow, A. H. *Motivation and Personality*. New York: Harper & Row, 1970.

Mastropieri, M. A., and J. P. Bakken. "Applications of Metacognition." *Remedial and Special Education* 11, no. 6 (1990): 32–35.

Matheny, K. B., and J. McCarthy. *Prescription for Stress*. Oakland, CA: New Harbinger Publications, 2000.

McAllister, A. K. "Cellular and Molecular Mechanisms of Dendritic Growth." *Cerebral Cortex* 10, no. 10 (2000): 963–73.

229

McEwan, B. S. "Stress and Hippocampal Plasticity." *Annual Review of Neuroscience* 22 (1999): 105–22.

McEwan, B. S., and E. N. Lasley. *The End of Stress as We Know It.* Washington, DC: National Academies Press, 2002.

McEwan, B. S., and T. Seeman. "Protective and Damaging Effects of Mediators of Stress: Elaborating and Testing the Concepts of Allostasis and Allostatic Load." *Annals of the New York Academy of Science* 896 (1999): 30–47.

McGaugh, J. L., and I. B. Intrioni-Collision. "Involvement of the Amygdaloidal Complex in Neuromodulatory Influences on Memory Storage." *Neuroscience and Behavioural Reviews* 14, no. 4 (1990): 425–31.

"Meditation's Positive Residual Effects: Imaging Finds Different Forms of Meditation May Affect Brain Structure." *Harvard Gazette.* http://news.harvard.edu/gazette/story/2012/11/meditations-positive-residual-effects.

Merzenich, M. M. "Cortical Plasticity Contributing to Childhood Development." In *Mechanisms of Cognitive Development: Behavioral and Neural Perspectives.* Edited by J. L. McClelland and R. S. Siegler. Mahwah, NJ: Lawrence Erlbaum, 2001.

———. "Promising Results in Controlling Tinnitus with Brain Training." http://merzenich.positscience.com.

Meyer, J. *The Battlefield of the Mind: Winning the Battle in Your Mind.* New York: Faith Words, 1995.

———. *Life without Strife: How God Can Heal and Restore Troubled Relationships.* Lake Mary, FL: Charisma House, 2000.

Miller, G. A. "The Magical Number Seven, Plus or Minus Two: Some Limits on Our Capacity for Processing Information." *Psychological Review* 63 (1956): 81–97.

Miller, T., and D. Sabatino. "An Evaluation of the Educator Consultant Model as an Approach to Main Streaming." *Exceptional Children* 45 (1978).

"Mind/Body Connection: How Emotions Affect Your Health." FamilyDoctor. org. http://familydoctor.org/online/famdocen/home/healthy/mental/782.html.

Mogilner, A., J. A. Grossman, U. Ribary, M. Joliot, J. Volkmann, D. Rapaport, R. W. Beasley, and R. R. Llinas. "Somatosensory Cortical Plasticity in Adult Humans Revealed by Magnetoencephalography." *Proceedings of the National Academy of Sciences* 90, no. 8 (1993): 3593–97.

Montessori, M. *The Absorbent Mind.* Amsterdam: Clio Press, 1989.

Mountcastle, V. "An Organizing Principle for Cerebral Function: The Unit Module and the Distributed System." In *The Mindful Brain.* Edited by G. M. Edelman and V. Mountcastle. Cambridge, MA: MIT Press, 1978.

Nader, K. "Manipulating Memory." *MIT Technology Review.* www.technologyreview.com/video/413181/manipulating-memory.

Nader, K., G. E. Schafe, and J. E. Le Doux. "Fear Memories Require Protein Synthesis in the Amygdala for Reconsolidation after Retrieval." *Nature* 406, no. 6797 (2000): 722–26.

National Institute of Mental Health statistics. www.nimh.nih.gov/statistics/index.shtml.

Nelson, A. "Imagery's Physiological Base: The Limbic System: A Review Paper." *Journal of the Society for Accelerative Learning and Teaching* 13, no. 4 (1988): 363–71.

Nelson, R., ed. *Metacognition Core Readings*. Boston: Allyn and Bacon, 1992.

Newberg, A., E. D'Aquili, and V. Rause. *Why God Won't Go Away: Brain Science and the Biology of Belief*. New York: Ballantine, 2001.

Novak, J. D., B. Gowin, and J. B. Kahle. *Learning How to Learn*. Cambridge, UK: Cambridge University Press, 1984.

Nummela, R. M., and T. M. Rosengren. "Orchestration of Internal Processing." *Journal for the Society of Accelerated Learning and Teaching* 10, no. 2 (1985): 89–97.

Odendaal, M. S. "Needs Analysis of Higher Primary Educators in KwaZulu." *Per Linguam*, special issue no. 1 (1985): 5–99.

Okebukola, P. A. "Attitudes of Educators Towards Concept Mapping and Vee-Diagramming as Metalearning Tools in Science and Mathematics." *Educational Research* 34, no. 3 (1992): 201–12.

O'Keefe, J., and L. Nadel. *The Hippocampus as a Cognitive Map*. New York: Oxford University Press, 1978.

Olivier, C. *Let's Educate, Train and Learn Outcomes-Based: A 3D Experience in Creativity*. Pretoria, South Africa: Benedic, 1999.

Olsen, K. E. *Outcomes Based Education: An Experiment in Social Engineering*. Kranskop, South Africa: Christians for Truth. 1997.

O'Mathuna, D., and W. Larimore. *Alternative Medicine: The Christian Handbook*. Updated and expanded. Grand Rapids: Zondervan, 2007.

Ornstein, R. E. *The Psychology of Consciousness*. New York: Penguin Books, 1975.

Ornstein, R. *The Right Mind: Making Sense of the Hemispheres*. Orlando, FL: Harcourt, Brace, 1997.

Palincsar, A. S., and A. L. Brown. "Reciprocal Teaching of Comprehension Fostering and Monitoring Activities." *Cognition and Instruction* 1 (1984): 117–75.

Palmer, L. L., M. Alexander, and N. Ellis. "Elementary School Achievement Results Following In-Service Training of an Entire School Staff in Accelerative Learning and Teaching: An Interim Report." *Journal of the Society for Accelerative Learning and Teaching* 14, no. 1 (1989): 55–79.

Paris, S. G., and P. Winograd. "Promoting Metacognition and Motivation of Exceptional Children." *Remedial and Special Education* 11, no. 6 (1990): 7–15.

Pascuale-Leone, A., and R. Hamilton. "The Metamodal Organization of the Brain." In *Progress in Brain Research*. Edited by C. Casanova and M. Ptito (2001), 134.

Paul-Brown, D. "Professional Practices Perspective on Alternative Service Delivery Models." *ASHA Bulletin* 12 (1992).

Perlemutter, D., and C. Coleman. *The Better Brain Book*. New York: Penguin, 2004.

Pert, C. B. *Molecules of Emotion: Why You Feel the Way You Feel*. London: Simon and Schuster, 2004; New York: Simon and Schuster, 1999.

Pert, C., G. Pasternak, and S. H. Snyder. "Opiate Agonists and Antagonists Discriminated by Receptor Binding in the Brain." *Science* 182 (1973): 1359–61.

Peters, T. *Playing God? Genetic Determinism and Human Freedom*. 2nd ed. New York: Routledge, 2003.

Planck, M. "Max Planck Quotes." www.goodreads.com/author/quotes/107032. Max_Planck.

"The Pleasure Centres Affected by Drugs." *Canadian Institutes of Health Research*. http://thebrain.mcgill.ca/flash/i/i_03/i_03_cr/i_03_cr_par/i_03_cr_par.html.

Plotsky, P. M., and M.J. Meaney. "Early Postnatal Experience Alters Hypothalamic Corticotropin-Releasing Factor (CRF) mRNA, Median Eminence CRF Content and Stress-Induced Release in Adult Rats." *Molecular Brain Research* 18, no. 3 (1993): 195–200.

"Positive Psychology: Harnessing the Power of Happiness, Mindfulness, and Personal Strength." *Harvard Health Publications*. Harvard Medical School. www.health. harvard.edu/special_health_reports/positive-psychology-harnessing-the-power -of-happiness-personal-strength-and-mindfulness.

"Power of Forgiveness—Forgive Others." *Harvard Health Publications*. Harvard Medical School. December 2004. www.health.harvard.edu/press_releases/ power_of_forgiveness.

"The Prevalence of Mental Illness Today." *Harvard Health Publications*. Harvard Medical School. www.health.harvard.edu/newsweek/Prevalence-and-treatment-of-mental-illness-today.htm.

Pribram, K. H. *Languages of the Brain*. Monterey, CA: Brooks/Cole, 1971.

Pulvermuller, F. *The Neuroscience of Language: On Brain Circuits of Words and Serial Order*. Cambridge, UK: Cambridge University Press, 2002.

Raichle, M. E., A. M. MacLeod, A. Z. Snyder, W. J. Powers, D. A. Gusnard, and G. L. Shulman. "A Default Mode of Brain Function: A Brief History of an Evolving Idea." *Neuroimage* 37 (2007): 1083–90.

Rajechi, D. W. *Attitudes: Themes and Advances*. Sunderland, MA: Sinauer, 1982.

Ramachandran, V. S., and S. Blakeslee. *Phantoms in the Brain*. New York: William Morrow, 1998.

Redding, R. E. "Metacognitive Instruction: Trainers Teaching Thinking Skills." *Performance Improvement Quarterly* 3, no. 1 (1990): 27–41.

Restak, K. *The Brain: The Last Frontier*. New York: Doubleday, 1979.

Restak, R. *Mysteries of the Mind*. Washington, DC: National Geographic, 2000.

———. *Think Smart: A Neuroscientist's Prescription for Improving Your Brain Performance*. New York: Riverhead Books, 2009.

"Revised National Curriculum Statement Grades R-9." Policy document. Pretoria, South Africa: Department of Education, 2002.

Rizzolotti, G., and M. F. Destro. "Mirror Neurons." *Scholarpedia* 3, no. 1 (2008): 2055. http://www.scholarpedia.org/article/Mirror_neurons.

Rogers, C. R. *Freedom to Learn*. Columbus, OH: Merrill, 1969.

Rosenfield, I. *The Invention of Memory*. New York: Basic Books, 1988.

Rosenzweig, E. S., C. A. Barnes, and B. L. McNaughton. "Making Room for New Memories." *Nature Neuroscience 5*, no. 1 (2002): 6–8.

Rosenzweig, M. R., and E. L. Bennet. *Neuronal Mechanisms of Learning and Memory*. Cambridge, MA: MIT Press, 1976.

Rozin, P. "The Evolution of Intelligence and Access to the Cognitive Unconscious." *Progress in Psychobiology and Physiological Psychology* 6 (1975): 245–80.

Russell, P. *The Brain Book*. London: Routledge and Kegan Paul, 1986.

Rutherford, R., and K. Neethling. *Am I Clever or Am I Stupid?* Van-derbijlpark, South Africa: Carpe Diem Books, 2001.

Sagan, C. *The Dragons of Eden*. New York: Random House, 1977.

Saloman, G. *Interaction of Media, Cognition and Learning*. San Francisco: Jossey-Bass, 1979.

Samples, R. E. "Learning with the Whole Brain." *Human Behaviour* 4 (1975): 16–23.

Sapolsky, R. M. "Why Stress Is Bad for Your Brain." *Science* 273, no. 5276 (1996): 749–50.

Sarno, J. *The Mind-Body Prescription: Healing the Body, Healing the Pain*. New York: Werner Books, 1999.

Schallert, D. L. "The Significance of Knowledge: A Synthesis of Research Related to Schema Theory." In *Reading Expository Material*. Edited by W. Otto and S. White. New York: Academic, 1982, 13–48.

Schneider, W., and R. M. Shiffrin. "Controlled and Automatic Information Processing: I. Detection, Search and Attention." *Psychological Review* 88, no. 1 (1977): 1–66.

Schon, D. A. *Beyond the Stable State*. San Francisco: Jossey-Bass, 1971.

Schory, M. E. "Whole Language and the Speech Language Pathologists." *Language, Speech, and Hearing Services in Schools* 21 (1990): 206–11.

Schuster, D. H. "A Critical Review of American Foreign Language Studies Using Suggestopaedia." Paper delivered at the Aimav Linguistic Conference at the University of Nijmegen, the Netherlands, 1985.

Schwartz, J. M., and S. Begley. *The Mind and the Brain: Neuroplasticity and the Power of Mental Force*. New York: Regan Books/Harper Collins, 2002.

Schwartz, J. M., and R. Gladding. *You Are Not Your Brain*. New York: Avery, 2012.

Schwartz, J., H. Stapp, M. Beauregard. "Quantum Physics in Neuroscience and Psychology: A Neurophysical Model of Mind-Brain Interaction." *Philosophical Transactions of the Royal Society*. www.physics.lbl.gov/~stapp/PTB6.pdf.

Scruggs, E., and J. Brigham. "The Challenges of Metacognitive Instruction." *RASE* 11, no. 6 (1987): 16–18.

Seaward B. L. "Stress in America Today: Are Your Wellness Programs Prepared for the Super Stress Superstorm?" *Wellness Council of America News and Views*, 1996. www.brianlukeseaward.net/articles/SuperStress-WELCOA-Seaward.pdf.

Segerstrom, S. C., and G. E. Miller. "Psychological Stress and the Human Immune System: A Meta-Analytic Study of 30 Years of Inquiry." *Psychological Bulletin* 130, no. 4 (2004): 601–30.

Shapiro, R. B., V. G. Champagne, and D. De Costa "The Speech-Language Pathologist: Consultant to the Classroom Educator." *Reading Improvement* 25, no. 1 (1988): 2–9.

Shepard, B. "The Plastic Brain: Part 2." *UAB Magazine*. University of Alabama, Birmingham. www.uab.edu/uabmagazine/2009/may/plasticbrain2.

Sheth, B. R., D. Janvelyan, and M. Kahn. "Practice Makes Imperfect: Restorative Effects of Sleep on Motor Learning." *PLoS One* 3, no. 9 (2008): 3190.

Simon, C. S. "Out of the Broom Closet and into the Classroom: The Emerging SLP." *Journal of Childhood Communication Disorders* 11, no. 1–2 (1987): 81–90.

Singer, T., cited in Daniel Kane. "How Your Brain Handles Love and Pain." *NBC News: Science Mysteries*. www.msnbc.msn.com/id/4313263.

Sizer, T. R. *Horacel's Compromise: The Dilemma of the American High School*. Boston: Houghton Mifflin, 1984.

Slabbert, J. "Metalearning as the Most Essential Aim in Education for All." Paper presented at University of Pretoria, Faculty of Education, 1989.

Slife, B. D., J. Weiss, and T. Bell. "Separability of Metacognition and Cognition: Problem Solving in Learning Disabled and Regular Students." *Journal of Educational Psychology* 77, no. 4 (1985): 437–45.

Smith, A. *Accelerated Learning in Practice*. Stafford, UK: Network Educational Press, 1999.

Solms, M. "Forebrain Mechanisms of Dreaming Are Activated from a Variety of Sources." *Behavioral and Brain Sciences* 23, no. 6 (2000): 1035–40; 1083–1121.

Sperry, R. "Hemisphere Disconnection and Unity in Conscious Awareness." *American Psychologist* 23 (1968).

Springer, S. P., and G. Deutsch. *Left Brain, Right Brain*. New York: Freeman, 1998.

Sprouse, E. "5 Notable Discoveries in Epigenetics Research." http://dsc.discovery.com/tv-shows/curiosity/topics/5-discoveries-epigenetics-research.htm.

Stephan, K. M., G. R. Fink, R. E. Passingham, D. Silbersweig, A. O. Ceballos-Baumann, C. D. Firth, and R. S. J. Frackowiak. "Functional Anatomy of Mental Representation of Upper Extremity Movements in Healthy Subjects." *Journal of Neurophysiology* 73, no. 1 (1995): 373–86.

Sternberg, R. "The Nature of Mental Abilities." *American Psychologist* 34 (1979): 214–30.

Stickgold, R., J. A. Hobson, R. Fosse, and M. Fosse. "Sleep, Learning, and Dreams: Off-Line Memory Reprocessing." *Science* 294, no. 5554 (2001): 1052–57.

Stickgold, R., and P. Wehrwein. "Sleep Now, Remember Later." *Newsweek*, April 17, 2009. www.newsweek.com/id/194650.

Sylwester, R. "Research on Memory: Major Discoveries, Major Educational Challenges." *Educational Leadership* 42, no. 7 (1985): 69–75.

Tattershall, S. "Mission Impossible: Learning How a Classroom Works Before It's Too Late!" *Journal of Childhood Communication Disorders* 11, no. 1 (1987): 181–84.

Taub, E., G. Uswatte, M. Bowman, A. Delgado, C. Bryson, D. Morris, and V. W. Mark. "Use of CI Therapy for Plegic Hands after Chronic Stroke." Presentation at the Society for Neuroscience, Washington DC, November 16, 2005.

Taubes, G. *Good Calories, Bad Calories: Fats, Carbs and the Controversial Science of Diet and Health.* New York: Anchor Books, 2008.

Thembela, A. "Education for Blacks in South Africa: Issues, Problems and Perspectives." *Journal of the Society for Accelerative Learning and Teaching* 15, no. 1–2 (1990): 45–57.

Thurman, S. K., and A. H. Widerstrom. *Infants and Young Children with Special Needs: A Developmental and Ecological Approach.* 2nd ed. Baltimore: Paul H. Brookes, 1990.

Tunajek, S. "The Attitude Factor." Wellness Milestones. *AANA NewsBulletin,* April 2006. www.aana.com/resources2/health-wellness/Documents/nb_milestone_0406.pdf.

Uys, I. C. "Single Case Experimental Designs: An Essential Service in Communicatively Disabled Care." *South African Journal of Communication Disorders* 36 (1989): 53–59.

Van der Vyver, D. W. "SALT in South Africa: Needs and Parameters." *Journal of the Society for Accelerative Learning and Teaching* 10, no. 3 (1985): 187–200.

Van der Vyver, D. W., and B. de Capdeville. "Towards the Mountain: Characteristics and Implications of the South African UPPTRAIL Pilot Project." *Journal of the Society for Accelerative Learning and Teaching* 15, no. 1–2 (1990): 59–74.

Van Praag, H., A. F. Schinder, B. R. Christie, N. Toni, T. D. Palmer, and F. H. Gage. "Functional Neurogenesis in the Adult Hippocampus." *Nature* 415, no. 6875 (2002): 1030–34.

Van Praag, H., B. L. Jacobs, and F. Gage. "Depression and the Birth and Death of Brain Cells." *American Scientist* 88, no. 4 (2000): 340–46.

Vaughan, S. C. *The Talking Cure: The Science Behind Psychotherapy.* New York: Grosset/Putnam, 1997.

Vaynman S., and E. Gomez-Pinilla. "License to Run: Exercise Impacts Functional Plasticity in the Intact and Injured Central Nervous System by Using Neurotrophins." *Neurorehabilitation and Neural Repair* 19, no. 4 (2005): 283–95.

Von Bertalanaffy, L. *General Systems Theory.* New York: Braziller, 1968.

Vythilingam, M., and C. Heim. "Childhood Trauma Associated with Smaller Hippocampal Volume in Women with Major Depression." *American Journal of Psychiatry* 159, no. 12 (2002): 2072–80.

Walker, M. P., and R. Stickgold. "Sleep, Memory and Plasticity." *Annual Review of Psychology* 57 (2006): 139–66.

Wark, D. M. "Using Imagery to Teach Study Skills." *Journal of the Society for Accelerative Learning and Teaching* 11, no. 3 (1986): 203–20.

Waterland, R. A., and R. L. Jirtle. "Transposable Elements: Targets for Early Nutritional Effects on Epigenetic Gene Regulation." *Molecular and Cellular Biology* 23, no. 15 (2003): 5293–300.

Watters, Ethan. "DNA Is Not Destiny: The New Science of Epigenetics Rewrites the Rules of Disease, Heredity, and Identity." *Discover: The Magazine of Science, Technology, and the Future*, November 2006. http://discovermagazine.com/2006/nov/cover.

Wenger, W. "An Example of Limbic Learning." *Journal of the Society for Accelerative Learning and Teaching* 10, no. 1 (1985): 51–68.

Wertsch, J. V. *Culture, Communication and Cognitions.* Cambridge, MA: Cambridge University Press, 1985.

Whitelson, S. "The Brain Connection: The Corpus Callosum Is Larger in Left-Handers." *Science* 229, no. 4714 (1985): 665–68.

Widener, C. *The Angel Inside: Michelangelo's Secrets for Following Your Passion and Finding the Work You Love.* New York: Crown Publishing, 2004.

Wiley, J., and A. F. Jarosz. "Working Memory Capacity, Attentional Focus, and Problem Solving." *Current Directions in Psychological Science* 21, no. 4 (2012): 258.

Wilson, R. S., C. F. Mendes De Leon, L. L. Barnes, J. A. Schneider, J. L. Bienias, D. A. Evans, and D. A. Bennett. "Participation in Cognitively Stimulating Activities and Risk of Incident Alzheimer Disease." *JAMA* 287, no. 6 (2002): 742–48.

Wright, N. H. *Finding Freedom from Your Fears.* Grand Rapids: Revell, 2005.

Wurtman, J. *Managing Your Mind and Mood through Food.* New York: HarperCollins, 1986.

Young, L. J. "Being Human: Love: Neuroscience Reveals All." *Nature* 457, no. 148 (February 2009). www.nature.com/nature/journal/v457/n7226/full/457148a.html.

Zaidel, E. "Roger Sperry: An Appreciation." In *The Dual Brain.* Edited by D. F. Benson and E. Zaidel. New York: Guilford, 1985.

Zakaluk, B. L., and M. Klassen. "Enhancing the Performance of a High School Student Labelled Learning Disabled." *Journal of Reading* 36, no. 1 (1992).

Zdenek, M. *The Right Brain Experience.* Maidenhead, Berkshire, UK: McGraw-Hill, 1983.

Zimmerman, B. J., and D. H. Schunk. *Self-Regulated Learning and Academic Achievement: Theory, Research and Practice.* New York: Springer-Verby, 1989.

Since 1985, **Dr. Caroline Leaf**, a communication pathologist and audiologist, has worked in the area of cognitive neuroscience. She has specialized in traumatic brain injury (TBI) and learning disabilities, focusing specifically on the science of thought as it pertains to thinking and learning. She developed The Geodesic Information Processing Theory and did some of the initial research in neuroplasticity back in the 1990s, showing how the mind can change the brain. A large part of her research in recent years has been to link scientific principles with Scripture, showing how science is catching up with the Bible.

She applied the findings of her research in clinical practice for nearly twenty years and now lectures and preaches around the world on these topics. She is a prolific author of many books, articles, and scientific articles. She has been a featured guest of *Enjoying Everyday Life* with Joyce Meyer; *LIFE Today* with James and Betty Robison; Marilyn Hickey; Sid Roth; and TBN's *Doctor to Doctor*, among many others. She now hosts her own show on TBN called *Switch On Your Brain*.

Leaf's passion is to help people see the link between science and Scripture as a tangible way of controlling their thoughts and emotions, so they can learn how to think, learn, and find their sense of purpose in life.

Caroline and her husband, Mac, live in Dallas, Texas, with their four children.

For more information, visit her website at www.drleaf.com.

New *from*
DR. CAROLINE LEAF